Building Open Source Hardware

Building Open Source Hardware

DIY Manufacturing for Hackers and Makers

Alicia Gibb

with

Steven Abadie

Ed Baafi

Matt Bolton

Kipp Bradford

Gabriella Levine

David A. Mellis

Catarina Mota

Joshua Pearce

Becky Stern

Tiffany Tseng

Addie Wagenknecht

Michael Weinberg

Amanda Wozniak

Lars Zimmerman

✦✦Addison-Wesley

Upper Saddle River, NJ • Boston • Indianapolis • San Francisco
New York • Toronto • Montreal • London • Munich • Paris • Madrid
Capetown • Sydney • Tokyo • Singapore • Mexico City

For information about buying this title in bulk quantities, or for special sales opportunities (which may include electronic versions; custom cover designs; and content particular to your business, training goals, marketing focus, or branding interests), please contact our corporate sales department at corpsales@pearsoned.com or (800) 382-3419.

For government sales inquiries, please contact governmentsales@pearsoned.com.

For questions about sales outside the U.S., please contact international@pearsoned.com.

Visit us on the Web: informit.com/aw

Library of Congress Control Number: 2014952506

ISBN-13: 978-0-321-90604-5
ISBN-10: 0-321-90604-7

Text printed in the United States on recycled paper at RR Donnelley in Crawfordsville, Indiana.
First printing, December 2014

❖

Dedicated to Aaron Swartz, a friend, a mentor,
and the greatest teacher of open source.

❖

Contents

Introduction xiii

Acknowledgments xxiii

About the Authors xxv

Part I: Open Source Hardware Theory 1

1 History of the Open Hardware Movement 3

The First Programs, Organizations, and Definitions 4

TAPR OHL 6

OHANDA 6

OSHW Definition, Summit, and Logo 7

CERN OHL 8

Forking of Open Hardware and Open Source Hardware 9

Creation of OSHWA 9

References 11

2 OSHW Definition and Best Practices 13

Open Source Hardware Definition 13

Best Practices 16

Summary 30

3 Licensing Open Source Hardware 31

Licensing 31

Open Licenses in the Context of OSHW 32

Copyright, Patent, and Trademark: Rights That You Might Be Able to License 33

Actually Licensing a Copyright, Patent, or Trademark 36

What to Do Now 39

Summary 40

Resources 41

4 Standardization of Open Source Hardware 43

Firming up the Soft Parts: Making Software Firmer 44

Softening up the Hard Parts: Making Hardware More Flexible 47

Other Standardization and Regulation 49

Summary 51

Part II: Hands On! 53

5 The Design Process: How to Get from Nothing to Something 55

The Phase of Projects 56

Iterative Design and Concept Refinement 58

Setting up Your Workflow 60

Managing Constant Iteration 61

Every Master Plan Has an Exit Strategy 61

Preparing for Manufacturing 62

Summary 63

Resources 63

6 Making a Derivative 65

Derivatives and Open Source Hardware 65

Blinky Buildings Project 69

Summary 81

7 Modifying the Shape of an Arduino 83

Shapes of an Arduino Derivative 83

Before You Begin 84

Determining Your Board Outline 87

Lay Out Your Arduino Derivative in Eagle 89

Manufacturing Your Board 91

Summary 93

Resources 94

8 Remix a 3D Print(er) 95

Dawn of the Desktop 3D Printer 95

Open Hardware Design for 3D Printing 98

Next Steps 107

Summary 108

Resources 109

9 Wearables 111

History of Wearables 111

Conductive Textiles 117

Sewable Microcontrollers and Components 118

EL Wire/Tape/Panel 119

Tools and Techniques 120

Managing Expectations **125**

Future of Wearables **126**

Summary **127**

Resources **127**

10 Physical Materials **129**

Centralized Online Hub for Information Sharing **129**

Benefits for the Designers and Customers **130**

Flexing the Open Source Hardware Definition to Fit Other Physical Objects and Products That Require Multiple Types of Manufacturing **130**

A Range of Products and Industries **134**

Summary **150**

Part III: Production Bits 151

11 Personal Manufacturing in the Digital Age **153**

Personal Fabrication, Processes, Parts, and Materials **154**

Case Studies **157**

Questions for the Future **165**

Summary **166**

12 Accelerate from Making to Manufacturing **167**

Manufacturing Partner Decision **168**

How SparkFun Electronics Grew to Scale **170**

Kitting **174**

Design for Manufacturability **174**

Equipment Selection and Implementation **177**

Supply Chain/Purchasing **182**

Resource Planning and Scheduling **184**

Testing and Quality Control **185**

Future of Open Source, Small-Scale Manufacturing **189**

Summary **194**

13 Troubleshooting from Your Design to Your Manufacturer **197**

Manufacturable Designs **198**

Selecting Manufacturers **205**

The Manufacturing Handoff **206**

What Could Really Go Wrong? **209**

x   Contents

Quality Control **212**

Creative Fixes **213**

Summary **216**

14 Taxonomy of Hardware Documentation **219**

README.txt **220**

Product Webpage **221**

Hardware Source Files **223**

Making the Pieces Visible: Bill of Materials **225**

Tutorials **226**

Creating Community **229**

Summary **230**

Resources **231**

15 Business **233**

A Natural Business Model **233**

The Brand **234**

The Open Source Hardware and Open Design Business Model Matrix **235**

Summary **251**

16 Building Open Source Hardware in Academia **253**

Life in the Ivory Tower: An Overview **254**

Benefits of OSHW for the Academic **255**

Increased Visibility, Citations, and Public Relations **263**

Increased Funding Opportunities and Student Recruitment **264**

Virtuous Cycle **265**

OSHW Teaching and Service **268**

Summary **275**

References **275**

Conclusion 279

Changing Incentives **279**

Maturity of the Open Source Hardware Movement **280**

Looking to the Future **281**

A Open Source Hardware Checklist **283**

OSHW Musts and Mays **284**

B Open Source Hardware Security Do's and
Don'ts **285**
Resources **286**

C Design Process Checklist **289**
Concept Refinement **289**
Managing Iteration **289**
Preparing to Manufacture **290**

D Design for Manufacture Checklists **291**
Finding the Right Contract Manufacturer **291**
SparkFun's Core Design for Manufacturability Standards **292**
SparkFun's Ancillary Design for Manufacturability Standards **293**
Troubleshooting **294**

E Mach 30's Documentation Ground Rules **297**

F Blinky Buildings Source Files **301**
README **301**
About This Kit **301**
Materials and Tools **301**
Attribution **302**
Licensing **302**
Source Files **302**

Glossary 311

Index 317

Introduction

Building Open Source Hardware is an anthology written to get users and makers of open source hardware to the next step of developing for the masses and manufacturing. This book involves a hands-on approach, providing guides for developing and manufacturing open source hardware. Although many books have been published on specific pieces of open source hardware, to date there has not been a book published on the community or the steps to work all the way through designing and manufacturing a piece of open source hardware. There has been a burst of activity around making and do-it-yourself (DIY) projects, but the DIY and maker movements are growing to a new stage, wanting to produce on larger scales and move projects to products. If you have been hacking on some hardware in your basement and want to start building multiples of it and selling them on your website as open source, this book is for you.

This book covers both the theoretical side of open source hardware and the practices and methods necessary to create a piece of open source hardware. It is intended to be a holistic experience, moving from developing to manufacturing of open source hardware, while explaining the benefits, standards, and incentives found at the various stages of this process. This book includes beginner- to intermediate-level technical concepts and is coupled with an open source hardware kit that can be purchased separately to foster experimentation.

The intended audience of this book includes people from a multitude of fields, all of whom are interested in creating open source hardware and would like a guide for the theory, standards, and hands-on advice. Individuals and companies, large and small, that are already interested in the DIY and maker movement, but still need some help on how to create, document, and think about licensing, manufacturing, and selling open source hardware will also benefit from this book.

I chose not to self-publish for a number of reasons. The major one, however, was that without a publisher inviting me to write a book on this topic, the thought would have never occurred to me. My publisher is also well known in the open source software community for publishing portions of books with open source licenses, so this book is partially open source, too! The chapters written under a Creative Commons license are listed on the copyright page.

What Is Open Source Hardware?

Open source hardware—sometimes abbreviated OSH or OSHW—is hardware whose source files are publicly available for anyone to use, remanufacture, redesign, and resell. The open source hardware movement, similar to the DIY and maker movement, is not a new concept, but rather is a revitalization of historical methods that were displaced as modern manufacturing came to the fore. Modern manufacturing produces hardware cheaply and efficiently (albeit stifled with legal boundaries) and, as a result, has created a consumer culture, rather than a DIY culture. In the past 10 years, the pendulum has begun to swing back in favor of creating and fixing things rather than buying them.

Open source hardware values sharing, transparency, and accepting predecessors and successors to your work, both in the form of a company that might build something off your hardware and a project that might copy part or all of your hardware design. Transparency in hardware is becoming increasingly important as technologies become more opaque as their size dwindles, making it more difficult to discover with the naked eye how they work. As more complexities are added, the design also gets harder to discern. Open source hardware, in contrast, offers freedom of information in a physical format. Freedom of information for hardware means that the source files are accessible and easily available to rebuild the object. Source files may include schematics, diagrams, code, and assembly instructions, to name a few options.

Open source hardware does have some restrictions; in that sense, it differs from the total freedom found in the public domain. As Wendy Seltzer, a renowned legal professional, reminded the community when writing the definition of open source hardware, any limitations that we add to hardware make the hardware more closed than it already is, as hardware is actually open until it is patented. The basic open source hardware limitations are fairly simple: Anyone has the freedom to remix, remanufacture, and resell an item, provided that the hardware remains open source and attribution is given.

Maturity of the Open Source Hardware Movement

It would be irresponsible to write this book as though every aspect of open source hardware has been figured out and that there is a manual to follow to a "T." The definition of open source hardware created by the community even upholds "the spirit" of open source hardware as a consideration for labeling your hardware as open source. This open-ended sentiment shows the underdeveloped nature of the movement, and accepts the likelihood that future formats and defining characteristics will change.

For example, much of the gray area within open source hardware arises from the fact that openness does not yet extend to all layers of hardware. The process of getting raw materials out of the ground is not considered open, since most of us have no idea where the copper comes from that we use in our boards. Moreover, several software programs used to build hardware are not open. Even integral pieces of hardware, such as the chip, are often closed. I'm excited to say, however, that while this book was being written, Parallax announced its launch of an open source silicon.[1] This is a giant step forward for open source hardware. As you can see from the preceding examples, the community suspends

---

1. www.parallax.com/microcontrollers/propeller-1-open-source

the reality of fully open sourced hardware, and considers the existing limitations to be acceptable. Open source hardware is a malleable movement, subject to change when more openness comes along. The authors in this book represent a slice in time of the state of open source as it pertains to current hardware availabilities and challenges.

The Open Source Hardware Community

The open source hardware community includes people from many backgrounds and several different industries. In a recent OSHWA survey in this area, people identified with more than 45 different job titles, ranging from engineer to journalist. Although the open source hardware community first became popular in the electronics industry, several other industries are now making open source hardware.

Arduino was the first large-scale success in open source hardware. It was produced by a team at Ivrea Institute and was derivative of Wiring in its hardware and Processing in its integrated development environment (IDE). The community grew around Arduino and it quickly became a permanent feature within the open source hardware community. We first saw component-level modification based on Arduino and lots of break-out boards and electronic kits, but we're now seeing advancements in open source tools—for example, laser cutters, jigsaws, and 3D printers. In 3D printing, the success of Makerbot (formerly open source) was due to it being open source hardware and building off the RepRap community, which had operated in the open source hardware space for the past decade. Other industries like ecology, DIY bio (creating things like open polymerase chain reaction [PCR] devices), automotive design, and disaster relief have all joined the open source hardware community. For a longer list of industries opening up physical things and materials, see Chapter 10. Given the growing number of successful companies selling open source hardware, the movement is quickly taking shape.

During this time period there was also a growth of hackerspaces in the United States. Hackerspaces (sometimes called makerspaces) are collectives of people who experiment with art, technology, and science and who generally use nontraditional methods for innovation. Hackerspaces focus on a shared space, shared tools, and shared knowledge. Many hackerspaces teach classes and have open hack nights for the public to come learn some tricks of many different trades. During the past 10 years, the DIY movement also picked up its pace, with a resurgence of people focusing on building their own projects, reusing items, and fixing things themselves. These trends combined promote growth of the open source hardware community.

The open source hardware community is also a global community. According to 2012 and 2013 survey data from the OSHWA surveys, open source hardware projects are under way in 79 countries. This number is most likely an underestimate due to the survey being conducted only in English. Having such a widespread global movement is challenging in that the laws governing open source projects are likely to be different in each country. In addition, at a cultural level, we may not always have the best understanding of one another. An unfortunate example of this is the xenophobia that Americans display when they talk about Chinese-made items being copies and rip-offs. Some of this language has drifted into the open source hardware community, with people forgetting that open source hardware by definition can be directly copied. It may help to point out that China wrote its patent laws in 1984, so perhaps the country just has a norm of sharing and copying rather than rebuilding the wheel. The more than 200-year-old patent system embedded within the United States and some European cultures obfuscates our view, causing us to forget that there is nothing natural about a patent system. Intellectual property exists because of human-made governing structures. The open source hardware community aims to be welcoming to all types of people, no matter what their culture, gender, race, and skill level (e.g., beginner or master manufacturer). Thus it is inappropriate for the open source hardware community to be xenophobic regarding other countries' practices vis-à-vis sharing.

In further effort to be a welcoming community, every year the Open Hardware Summit establishes an anti-harassment policy[2] for the conference, which is derived from the Ada Initiative's[3] policy. The 2012 survey reported that only 4% of the open source hardware community identified as female. The anti-harassment policy, along with offers of travel grants to women, is a direct response intended to boost the number of women in the open source hardware community.

Open Source Software

Some history of open source hardware has followed in the footsteps of the history of open source software. The open source software movement is well established as a household name, enjoying popularity with developers and being a well-known concept to the masses. Open source software has been around 20 to 30 years longer than the hardware movement has. Thus, as the open source hardware movement builds in popularity, it can glean many lessons from the open source software movement. Open source hardware looks to the history of open source software for forms of governance within nonprofit and company structures, and the different options regarding implementation that open source offers.

As open source software licenses are ported to hardware, the differences in dealing with hardware versus software are becoming apparent. While the spirit behind open source software and hardware is relatively similar, some key differences emerge when working with atoms rather than bits. The main differences between open source hardware and open source software are the legal aspects regarding patent versus copyright, physical resources, creating copies, and distribution. There are other differences as well. Hardware and software are viewed by the law differently, with hardware being protected by patents and software by copyright. In the software world, resources tend to be humans and servers, but buying and selling hardware can broaden to include dependencies on specific materials, such as copper, silicon, and ABS plastics. For hardware, copying and creating a physical good often takes specialized machines, which can come with a high price point

---

2. http://2014.oshwa.org/policies/
3. http://adainitiative.org/

that has not yet become low enough to permit purchase by the average user. This difference is comparable to software's early days when owning a computer (or a computer with enough space and speed) was not always feasible for the average user. Distributing hardware means shipping, which adds another extra cost to hardware-based ventures (open source or not). In contrast, open source software is typically easy and cheap to copy and distribute via the Internet, typically through a repository.

What Is the Open Source Hardware Association?

In 2012, a newly formed 501(c)3 nonprofit association for open source hardware took on the challenge of advocating, educating, and uniting stewardship of the open source hardware movement. The Open Source Hardware Association (OSHWA; pronounced ä-sh-wa) aims to be the voice of the open source hardware community, ensuring that technological knowledge of open source is accessible to everyone, and encouraging the collaborative development of technology that serves education, environmental sustainability, and human welfare. OSHWA was created largely to fill the need for an umbrella organization that would encompass many communal efforts, including channeling the funds needed to support the Open Hardware Summit. The need for an organization to handle expenditures and act as a uniform resource unaffiliated with a company became apparent. The leadership of this movement involves and celebrates many individuals. The history of OSHWA is written in Chapter 1.

Since its inception, OSHWA has functioned to support the open source hardware community. We expect that these functions may change as the community develops. The next years for OSHWA will be crucial to program development that reflects these purposes. The organization runs on donations and memberships. Because this book was written with the help of so many community members in support of open source hardware, proceeds from the book's sales will go to OSHWA.

How This Book Is Organized

I have many years of involvement in the open source hardware community, chairing the Open Hardware Summit, running OSHWA, and serving as a sounding board for much of the community in those two roles. As a reflection of my experiences, this book is laid out to give useful advice to the most often asked questions and concerns. The community as a whole is moving from building things for individual purposes, to building things en masse and starting businesses, which are two very different problem sets. Building things for yourself is covered in many other formats, both in print and online. Indeed, there are a great many examples in the form of guides, tutorials, blogs, and articles. This book is meant to cover the entire process of building things on an open source basis, for which there are not yet as many resources. It is meant to be a practical resource organized in three parts.

The first part, Open Source Hardware Theory, covers the "what" and "why" of open source hardware. What does open source hardware entail, and why was it determined that way? What do the license structures mean, and why and when should you use licenses? Which types of standards do we need to be looking for in the future and why are they important? All of these questions are addressed in Part I.

The second and third sections are the "how" of open source hardware. Part II is called Hands On! Each chapter in this part walks through a different aspect of how to do something with open source hardware, be it working through a design process, making various derivatives, 3D printing, creating wearables, or figuring out source files for different types of materials. Part III, Production Bits, takes you through the production processes step by step. It covers how to manufacture products at several different scales using different methods. Production covers many different aspects, not just manufacturing, so this section also includes documenting, setting up your business, and producing open lab equipment in the research and academic field.

This book is not necessarily meant to be read from cover to cover. You may find it useful to skip to the sections or chapters that best fit your current needs. If you're researching the theory of open source hardware, you'll probably want to start at the beginning, with Part I including the theoretical chapters. Chapter 1, History of the Open Hardware Movement, is closely tied to how and why Chapter 2, OSHW Definition and Best Practices, came to be. To jump straight to the hands-on section, go to Part II. That is where you'll find ways to start building and modifying open source hardware and the acceptable ways of doing so. Part II is for people who want to dip their toes in and see the practical nature of how open sourcing hardware works. Chapter 6 provides step-by-step instructions for how to make a derivative, which you can do with existing open source hardware, and others can do with your open source hardware. Chapter 7 teaches board shape modification, and picks up where Chapter 6 leaves off. Chapters 8 and 9 delve into two open source fields, 3D printing and wearables, respectively. Chapter 10 exemplifies a number of projects that consider different types of materials and source files. If you already have your open source hardware product prototyped and you're looking for advice about going through the manufacturing process, flip to Part III. There are chapters on DIY fabrication (Chapter 11), manufacturing (Chapter 12), and troubleshooting manufacturing problems (Chapter 13). If you have already started your manufacturing process and need help ensuring your documentation is written to the standards of the open source hardware community, skip to Chapter 14. If you're most interested in benefits of starting an open source hardware business, go to Chapter 15. If you work in academia and are interested in producing open source lab equipment, flip to Chapter 16. During the course of this book, while the focus will be on open source hardware, general building and manufacturing are also covered because certain methods are not specific to open or closed source development.

Given that the open source hardware community has many contributors, it seems only right that this book should also reflect the communal voice of the movement. You will notice that different chapters have different authors. Due to the multiple authors, the voice may differ from chapter to chapter.

This authors and arrangement of the book are as follows:

Part I: Open Source Hardware Theory

1. History of the Open Hardware Movement by Catarina Mota

   The history of the open source hardware community is mirrored in this chapter from the oshwa.org website. This chapter describes when and how decisions on open source hardware were made. Catarina Mota has been instrumental in the open source hardware community: researching hackerspaces, leading the open source hardware community surveys, and having been a previous OSHWA board member and chair of the Open Hardware Summit.

2. OSHW Definition and Best Practices by Alicia Gibb

   In 2010, a definition of open source hardware was widely adopted by the open source hardware community. In 2013, the community came out with best practices, both are recorded in this chapter with some historical references.

3. Licensing Open Source Hardware by Michael Weinberg

   The appropriate times when one should use trademarks, copyrights, and patents can be confusing to the average hardware builder. This chapter was written by a legal professional to help educate the open source hardware community about the forms of intellectual property (IP) on which open source alternatives are dependent. Michael Weinberg has been very active from the start of the open source hardware community; he continues to write about open source hardware at Public Knowledge, and organizes relevant events in Washington, D.C.

4. Standardization of Open Source Hardware by Ed Baafi

   Standardization refers to making open source hardware parts more open, focusing on the interfaces between hardware and software, and standards that make open source easiest to understand. Ed Baafi has been promoting these types of standards for the past few years within the open source hardware community. He is the founder of Modkit, and an advocate for open source hardware in education.

Part II: Hands On!

Part II of the book teaches you to use open source hardware in different ways.

5. The Design Process: How to Get from Nothing to Something by Amanda Wozniak

   The design process is the first chapter you should read to dig into the hands-on portion of this book. Amanda Wozniak has spoken at multiple Open Hardware Summits on this topic and is well known in the open source hardware community for her knowledge of engineering, systems, and the design process with regard to open source.

6. Making a Derivative by Alicia Gibb

This chapter walks through an example of how to make a derivative. An open source hardware kit, sold separately, accompanies this chapter, which you are free to use, remake, remix, and resell. I wrote this chapter so that I would have the ability to open the hardware and use it as an example of how derivatives work.

7. Modifying the Shape of an Arduino by Tiffany Tseng

Tiffany Tseng has reformed her own Arduino derivative as part of her research at MIT. She wrote this chapter based on her experience with form from a design perspective, and her engineering know-how of walking through all the steps it takes to create an Arduino derivative based on the form factor of the board.

8. Remix a 3D Print(er) by Steven Abadie

This chapter gives you resources for using open source hardware 3D printers, and walks through the steps to remix a 3D printable object. Steven Abadie is the chief operating officer of Aleph Objects, which produces the Lulzbot, an open source hardware line of 3D printers. The Lulzbot printers are regarded as the most innovative line of 3D printers in the open source hardware community, and were derived from RepRap.

9. Wearables by Becky Stern

As the concept of wearables becomes more widely known, this chapter reminds us how to make wearables open source. Becky Stern, a talented technologist and seamstress, is a well-known individual in open source hardware circles, working first at *Craft*, then writing for *Make,* and now serving as the Wearables Director at Adafruit.

10. Physical Materials by Gabriella Levine

Gabriella Levine, who serves as president of the OSHWA, has highlighted different industries and different types of source files that are employed in each industry. Because new industries are coming into the open source hardware fold, this important chapter establishes examples of source files that may not come from traditional electronics sources.

Part III: Production Bits

11. Personal Manufacturing in the Digital Age by David Mellis

Personal manufacturing is a concept in which David A. Mellis is considered an expert. He is part of the Arduino team, and studied personal fabrication for his PhD. His chapter looks at case studies of hardware and tools used to make things yourself, also called personal manufacturing.

12. Accelerate from Making to Manufacturing by Matt Bolton

Matt Bolton is the Director of Production at SparkFun Electronics. His role at SparkFun is integral to what it means for a hardware hacker, DIYer, or maker to manufacture a product. This chapter explains the manufacturing process at a beginner level, for those looking to take their open source hardware to a larger scale.

13. Troubleshooting from Your Design to Your Manufacturer by Kipp Bradford

    This chapter should be read alongside the various manufacturing chapters within the book for further advice on what to do when you need to troubleshoot your hardware. This chapter should make troubleshooting easier, if you follow Kipp Bradford's advice. Kipp has worked in manufacturing in multiple fields, from toys to military-grade equipment, and has played a part at every Open Hardware Summit to date.

14. Taxonomy of Hardware Documentation by Addie Wagenknecht

    Addie Wagenknecht, founder of Lasersaur, knows all about documentation because of the unique way Lasersaur has initiated its bill of materials (BOM) as a parts list that can be purchased at any hardware store around the world, rather than focusing on collecting and shipping materials. Addie covers the integral documentation needed for hardware source files and other useful documents to help your users. Addie is also chair of the Open Hardware Summit and interfaces with the open source hardware community on a regular basis.

15. Business by Lars Zimmerman

    This chapter explores the possibilities and options that open source hardware businesses can leverage and benefit from. It was important this chapter was written by a third party rather than any single open source hardware business to show the entire landscape of open source hardware business models. Lars is the co-founder of the Open It Agency, which helps businesses learn about and implement open source hardware.

16. Building Open Source Hardware in Academia by Joshua Pearce

    Dr. Joshua Pearce is a professor at Michigan Tech University and has written the book *Open-Source Lab*. He has created open source lab equipment to take the place of closed source equipment, a topic that is highlighted in his chapter. This chapter also discusses the crucial nature of marrying open source and education together, so that students may learn without boundaries.

Special Elements

Within the chapters in this book, readers will also find a few special elements. Community members wrote anecdotes giving small snippets of their experiences with open source hardware. These can be found throughout the chapters of the book in gray boxes identified by word "Anecdote." The authors for the anecdotes further the perspectives and examples of each chapter.

This book can be accompanied with a hardware kit that was built for Chapter 6, but also used in several places as an example throughout this book. The kit can be thought of as an add-on for hands-on learning and is sold separately. You can purchase at bit.ly/blinkybuildings or at SparkFun.com.

Acknowledgments

This book would have never been written if Debra Williams-Cauley had not invited me to write it. I thank Debra and her team for being absolutely awesome editors to work with—and for having the idea in the first place.

Of course, a huge "thank you" to the authors who undertook writing each chapter. Your thoughts, time, and willingness to give the royalties to OSHWA is so appreciated! Thank you to the community members who wrote anecdotes to add perspectives to the chapters, and to Davy Uittenbogerd and Geoff Steele for sharing open source files for me to base the Blinky Buildings project from! Thank you to Stephen Murphey and Adrianna Danaila for letting me modify their icons on the cover of this book.

Thank you to my readers for taking their time to make this book better: Max Whitney, who did an outstanding job of catching both technical errors and improving my critical thinking skills, along with Nathan Seidle, Bryan Smith, and Jeffrey Osier-Mixon.

Thank you to my loving husband, Nathan. Nathan has made this book possible in so many ways, from fixing me three square meals a day to being one of my readers and discussing my thoughts anytime day or night. It definitely helps to have a partner in the same industry and educated about the subject matter when writing a book!

And finally, thanks to Mom and Daggles for continuously asking me, "What is it you do again?" Their questions honed my ability to define and explain the reasons why open source hardware is important.

About the Authors

Alicia Gibb is an advocate for open hardware, a researcher, and a hardware hacker. Alicia has worked within the open source hardware community since 2008. She is the founder and Executive Director of the Open Source Hardware Association (OSHWA), an organization to educate and promote building and using open source hardware. She directs the BTU Lab at Colorado University at Boulder, where she teaches in the areas of physical computing and information technologies. Previous to serving OSHWA, Alicia was a researcher and prototyper at Bug Labs, where she ran the academic research program and the Test Kitchen, an open R&D lab. She was awarded a National Science Foundation SBIR grant for her sensor-based data collection module while at Bug Labs. She is a member of NYC Resistor, where she has curated two international art shows; cofounded and co-chaired two Open Hardware Summits; and sits on the board of the Ada Initiative. Her electronics work has appeared in *Wired* magazine, *IEEE Spectrum, Hackaday,* and the *New York Times.* When Alicia is not researching at the crossroads of open technology and innovation, she is prototyping work that twitches, blinks, and might even be tasty to eat.

Steven Abadie is an MFA graduate from the University of Georgia. His research as a sculptor included work with open hardware 3D printing. This experience in 3D printing evolved into his current position as the COO of Aleph Objects, a company with a fierce commitment to open hardware and free software.

Ed Baafi is an educator and entrepreneur focused on making tools for technology innovation accessible to all. As an educator, Ed helped shape Boston's Learn 2 Teach, Teach 2 Learn youth technology program, along with the Boston Fab Lab. As an entrepreneur, Ed founded Modkit (http://modkit.com) to develop accessible programming tools for controlling the physical world. He is also a co-founder of Made by Cafe (http://madebycafe.com), which aims to bring an innovative cafe-like environment to designers and makers.

Matt Bolton is the Director of Production at SparkFun Electronics, where he leads the manufacturing team in building more than 500 unique DIY electronics circuit boards and kits for the makers, inventors, and hackers of the world. He is on a mission to make manufacturing sexy once again in the United States, with a vision for a new generation of manufacturing that contradicts the "dirty, dumb, and dangerous" stereotype that manufacturing held only a few decades ago. Matt is also the emcee every year at SparkFun's annual Autonomous Vehicle Competition. In his spare time, he loves to take part in just about every "quintessentially Colorado" activity possible: hiking, bouldering, snowboarding, cycling, sipping on a mug of hot black coffee, strumming his guitar, and posting pictures of his amazing dog, Olive, to Instagram.

Kipp Bradford is an entrepreneur, technology consultant, and educator with a passion for making things. He is the founder or co-founder of start-ups in the fields of transportation, consumer products, HVAC, and medical devices, and holds numerous patents for his inventions. Some of his more interesting projects have been turned into kippkitts. Kipp is the author of Distributed Network Data (hardware hacking for data scientists, with Alasdair Allan) and is one of the co-founders of the Data Sensing Lab. He is an advisor to Highway1, the leading hardware start-up accelerator, and founded the Innovation Institute, a National Science Foundation–funded project that teaches innovation to underserved youth in New York City. Kipp also co-founded Revolution by Design, a nonprofit education and research organization dedicated to empowerment through technology. He founded and co-organizes Rhode Island's Mini Maker Faire and the Washington, D.C., Mini Maker Faire. He is one of the USA Science and Engineering Festival's "Nifty Fifty." Kipp was the Demo Chair of the 2013 Open Hardware Summit, was on the program committee and a keynote speaker for the O'Reilly Solid conference, and has been recognized as a leading innovator at Frost & Sullivan's GIL 2013. As the former Senior Design Engineer and Lecturer at the Brown University School of Engineering, Kipp taught several engineering design and entrepreneurship courses. He serves on the boards of the Maker Education Initiative, the Rhode Island Museum of Science and Art, and the Providence Athenaeum. He is also on the technical advisory board of *Make* magazine, is a Fellow at the College of Design, Engineering and Commerce at Philadelphia University, and is an Adjunct Critic at the Rhode Island School of Design.

Gabriella Levine is an artist with a background in hardware design and biology. She holds a master's degree in design and technology from ITP Tisch School of the Arts, New York University. She has created robotics start-ups including Protei, open hardware shape-shifting sailing robots to sense and protect the oceans, which are being used for sensing radioactivity, mapping plastic trash in the Pacific Ocean, and collecting oil near sites of oil spills; and Sneel, bio-inspired swimming robotic snakes that can sense environmental data in the water. Gabriella serves as President of the Open Source Hardware Association (OSHWA.org), promoting open source accessible technologies worldwide. Gabriella has exhibited work internationally, including at Ars Electronica, Eyebeam (NYC), the Science Gallery (Dublin), Interactive Art Fair Miami Art Basel, and Fountain Art Fair New York Armory Show. She received the 2012 Prix Ars Electronica Hybrid Arts Award, Gulfstream Navigator Ocean Exchange Grant, and Awesome Foundation Grant, and was a fellow of Unreasonable at Sea, a radical experiment circumnavigating the world by boat. She teaches at ITP and CIID, and her work has been written up in *Wired,* the *New York Times, Creator's Project, Vice, Scientific American,* and *Hyperallergic.* Gabriella is currently an engineer on the Rapid Evaluation team at Google and a part-time artist-in-residence at Autodesk's Instructables.

David A. Mellis is a PhD student at the MIT Media Lab. He has a master's degree in interaction design from the Interaction Design Institute Ivrea (Italy) and taught at the Copenhagen Institute of Interaction Design (Denmark). David is one of the creators of Arduino, an open source hardware and software platform for electronic prototyping, and a member of the board of directors for the Open Source Hardware Association.

Catarina Mota is co-founder of Open Materials (do-it-yourself smart materials), Everywhere Tech (open source technology transfer), and AltLab (Lisbon's hackerspace). She has taught numerous hands-on workshops on high-tech materials and simple circuitry with the goal of encouraging people with little to no science background to take a proactive interest in science, technology, and knowledge sharing. Catarina is wrapping up her PhD dissertation on the social impact of open and collaborative practices for the development of physical goods and technologies. She is currently a visiting scholar at ITP-NYU, Research Chair at the Open Source Hardware Association, TED Fellow, and member of NYC Resistor. Previously, she co-chaired the Open Hardware Summit 2012, served on the board of directors of the Open Source Hardware Association, taught as an adjunct faculty member at ITP-NYU, and was a fellow of the National Science and Technology Foundation of Portugal.

Joshua M. Pearce received his PhD in materials engineering from the Pennsylvania State University. He then developed the first sustainability program in the Pennsylvania State System of Higher Education as an assistant professor of physics at Clarion University and helped develop the applied sustainability graduate engineering program while at Queen's University, Canada. He currently is an Associate Professor cross-appointed in the Department of Materials Science & Engineering and in the Department of Electrical & Computer Engineering at Michigan Technological University, where he runs the Open Sustainability Technology Research Group. His research concentrates on the use of open source appropriate technology to find collaborative solutions to problems in sustainability and poverty reduction. His research spans areas of electronic device physics and materials engineering of solar photovoltaic cells, and RepRap 3D printing, but also includes applied sustainability and energy policy. He is the author of *The Open-Source Lab: How to Build Your Own Hardware and Reduce Research Costs.*

Becky Stern is the Director of Wearable Electronics at Adafruit. Each week she publishes a new do-it-yourself craft+tech project tutorial and video and also hosts the YouTube Live show called "Wearable Electronics with Becky Stern." Becky has been combining textiles with electronics since 2005, and has helped develop the Adafruit FLORA wearable Arduino-compatible product line. She has been shooting video since age 5 and sewing since age 8. Becky studied at Parsons The New School for Design and Arizona State University; she now teaches at the School of Visual Arts' Products of Design graduate program. She is a member of the Brooklyn art combine Madagascar Institute and the Internet-based group Free Art & Technology (FAT).

Tiffany Tseng is a mechanical engineer and designer who is researching new ways to help makers document and share what they design. She is currently a PhD student at the MIT Media Lab in the Lifelong Kindergarten Group and is developing Build in Progress, a platform for people to share the story of their design process. Prior to joining the Media Lab, Tiffany received an MS in mechanical engineering from Stanford University and a BS in mechanical engineering from MIT. Along the way, she has worked at a variety of design companies, including IDEO and Fisher-Price, with a special interest in designing products for children. She is also a college radio DJ and a reviewer of tasty snacks.

Addie Wagenknecht is an American artist based in Austria, whose work explores the tension between expression and technology. She seeks to blend conceptual work with traditional forms of hacking and sculpture. Wagenknecht's work employs a peculiar blend of hacking and visual aesthetics drenched with conceptualism. Her past exhibitions include MuseumsQuartier Wien, Vienna, Austria; La Gaîté Lyrique, Paris, France; the Istanbul Modern; and MU, Eindhoven, Netherlands; and Phillips Auction House, New York City. Addie is a member of the Free Art & Technology (FAT) Lab and chairs the Open Hardware Summit. She also co-produced the open source laser cutter Lasersaur. Her work has been featured in numerous academic papers, books, and magazines, such as *Time, Wall Street Journal, Vanity Fair,* the *Economist,* and the *New York Times.* She holds a master's degree from the Interactive Telecommunications Program at New York University, and has previously held fellowships at Eyebeam Art + Technology Center in New York City, Culture Lab UK, Institute HyperWerk for Postindustrial Design Basel (CH), the Frank-Ratchye Studio for Creative Inquiry at Carnegie Mellon University, and, most recently, the Warhol Foundation. She is represented by bitforms gallery in New York City.

Michael Weinberg is a Vice President at Public Knowledge, a nonprofit digital advocacy group in Washington, D.C. As part of its advocacy mission, Public Knowledge has pushed to introduce the concept of open source hardware to policymakers and members of Congress. Michael oversees PK Thinks, Public Knowledge's in-house think-tank, and is involved in a wide range of issues focusing primarily on copyright issues before the Federal Communications Commission (FCC) and emerging technologies such as 3D printing and open source hardware.

Amanda "w0z" Wozniak is a professional engineer with a passion for open source hardware. She holds SB and MEng degrees from MIT in electrical engineering and computer science with a minor in biomedical engineering. She has worked as an Applications Engineer for Analog Devices, as a Staff Engineer at the Wyss Institute for Biologically Inspired Engineering, and most recently as a Principal Engineer at NxStage Medical. Her freelance projects have included the Ninja Networks electronic badges for DEFCON 17 and 18, along with presenting industry best practices to the maker community at three Open Hardware Summits. She has a strong interest in learning, understanding the failure modes of complex systems, building useful things, and enabling others to do the same. She lives in Boston.

Lars Zimmermann (Berlin, 1980) is a Berlin-based artist interested in economy. In 2009, he started a project on open source for regenerative design and production called the OWi project (http://owiowi.org). Zero waste and resource life management with open source dynamics. This was his way into the field and the discourse on open source. Now he works as an open source economist trying to develop and push the field in many different ways. Everything is still tied to his initial interest in making openness work for a zero waste economy. In 2014, Lars co-founded the Open It Agency (http://openitagency.eu), an agency that helps companies, projects, and communities discover, develop, and use open source strategies. He is researching better tools for hardware documentation and communication and blogs a lot these days on open source hardware and freedom, business models, material cycles, education, and more. Visit his blog and website (http://bloglz.de).

Open Source Hardware Theory

1 History of the Open Hardware Movement

2 OSHW Definition and Best Practices

3 Licensing Open Source Hardware

4 Standardization of Open Source Hardware

1

History of the Open Hardware Movement

Catarina Mota

"Above all things physical, it is more important to be beautiful on the inside—to have a big heart and an open mind and a spectacular spleen."

—Ellen DeGeneres

The history of open source hardware has been written by the Open Source Hardware Association's Research Chair, Catarina Mota. Included in her history is an overview of the movement and the community. Catarina is a well-respected scholar in open hardware who wrote her PhD dissertation on the social impact of open and collaborative practices for the development of physical goods and technologies. The history of the movement, as it is written here, and any future updates can be found on the research branch of the OSHWA website: www.oshwa.org/research. The following text was written by Catarina Mota.

Open source hardware was preceded, influenced, and shaped by several prominent cases in which important technologies were developed collaboratively and out in the open. Its historical antecedents include the open source and free software movements, from which it derived its principles; the Homebrew Computer Club and hacking traditions, which flourished when early computers were sold in kits or shipped with schematic diagrams; and the ham radio community, from which it inherited a long tradition of amateur engineering and knowledge-sharing practices.

Despite the deep roots of these legacies, open source hardware became known as such only in the 2000s. This was mostly due to the rise of the Internet, which made sharing hardware designs possible; the commercial success of open source software, which gave it public visibility; and the decrease in costs of production tools, which made it feasible. This chapter describes the emergence and evolution of a series of organizations and initiatives that, in conjunction with a growing number of projects and businesses, have helped solidify open source hardware.

The First Programs, Organizations, and Definitions

In 1997, Bruce Perens (creator of the Open Source Definition, co-founder of the Open Source Initiative, and a ham radio operator) launched the Open Hardware Certification Program (Perens 1997). The goal of this program was to allow hardware manufacturers to self-certify their products as open. This implied making a set of promises about the availability of documentation for programming the device-driver interface of a specific hardware device. The program was free, and vendors of certified equipment had the right to apply the program's open hardware logo to their packaging and to state in advertising that their devices were certified. In turn, those purchasers who bought certified equipment were assured that a change in operating system or even the demise of the manufacturer would not make it impossible to have new software written for their devices. The Open Hardware Certification Program was one of the first attempts at extending software's open source practices to hardware and, as part of this effort, Perens trademarked "open hardware" and the domain openhardware.org, which he committed to the certification program. Openhardware.org can be viewed through the Internet Archive as of January 2014: http://web.archive.org/web/20140715000000*/http://openhardware.org.

In 1998, shortly after the launch of the Open Hardware Certification Program, David Freeman announced the Open Hardware Specification Project (OHSpec), another attempt at licensing hardware components whose interfaces are available publicly and creating an entirely new computing platform as an alternative to proprietary computing systems (Freeman 1998). Also in 1998, Troy Benjegerdes made public his intention of starting an entrepreneurial venture to apply the principles of open source software to the design and development of hardware (Benjegerdes 1998). In the same year, Reinoud Lamberts launched Open Design Circuits, a website dedicated to collaboratively designing low-cost and open design circuits (Lamberts 1998). Between 1998 and 1999, Graham Seaman made several attempts at defining open source hardware (Seaman n.d.).

Despite the initial burst of activity around the nascent concept of open source hardware, most of these initiatives faded out within a year or two. Only in the mid-2000s did open source hardware again become a hub of activity. This was mostly due to the emergence of several major open source hardware projects, such as OpenCores, RepRap, Arduino, and companies such as Adafruit and SparkFun. Thus, in 2007, Perens reactivated the openhardware.org website with the following statement:

> *Surprise! After a long dark period of being used to divert traffic to a bling vendor, OpenHardware.org is back in the control of its founder. The domain was created by me (Bruce Perens) to operate an Open Hardware certification program, while I was associated with SPI (Software in the Public Interest).[1] At the time, Linux was not yet commercially accepted, and thus there*

---

1. SPI is a nonprofit organization created to help other organizations develop and distribute open hardware and software. It encourages programmers to use any license that allows for the free modification, redistribution, and use of software, and hardware developers to distribute documentation that will allow device drivers to be written for their product. See http://spi-inc.org/.

wasn't tremendous demand for such a program. I think only Cyclades registered while I was connected with the program. I passed management of the program to Vincent Renardias to operate as part of SPI. I think Vincent may have allowed the domain to go inactive after that, or passed it to someone else who allowed that to happen. Somehow SPI managed to let the domain expire—I assume not deliberately, but SPI was asleep at the switch for long enough that the domain was on registrar hold for some time and then was allowed to expire. The domain was then picked up by some sort of search engine optimizer/domain squatter and used to provide ersatz traffic (that is traffic intending to get the previous site) to HipHopCapital. com, a bling vendor, for several years.

I used a domain capture service, a little money, and several years of patience to pick up the domain again. It was transferred to the ownership of Perens LLC on September 2, 2007 (US-Pacific time). I feel that I have to take responsibility for making OpenHardware work this time rather than leaving it for others to drop the ball.

The domain will be operated by techp.org (a not-for-profit organization that I operate for Open-Source-related activities) and used to operate an Open Hardware certification program again according to my original goals. I trust it will have more demand now. (Perens 2007)

Four years later, openhardware.org would house an organization by the same name. But the first Open Hardware Foundation came out of the Open Graphics Project (an effort to design, implement, and manufacture a free and open 3D graphics chip set and reference graphics card). Realizing that the initial run of Open Graphics chips would cost approximately $2 million to manufacture, Timothy Miller, founder of the Open Graphics Project, decided to create an offshoot company called Traversal Technology. One of Miller's concerns was how the company would interact with the project's community and suggested the creation of an organization to safeguard the interests of the Open Graphics Project community (McNamara 2007a). Thus, Patrick McNamara founded the Open Hardware Foundation (OHF) in 2007, in partnership with Traversal Technology, with the goal of facilitating the design, development, and production of free and open hardware. Another goal of the OHF was to help fund the production of open graphics products by providing Traversal Technology with a known number of sales. Traversal Technology benefited by having less financial risk associated with producing the graphics chip, and the open source community benefited by having hardware available at reduced or no cost for developers who could contribute further to the project (McNamara 2007a). In 2009, McNamara announced that to better support the Open Graphics Project, the OHF's funds (the product of donations) were being applied toward the Linux Fund[2] (McNamara 2009).

---

2. The Linux Fund is an organization that has been raising funds and making donations to free and open source software projects since 1999.

TAPR OHL

Also in 2007, TAPR created the first open hardware license. The Tucson Amateur Packet Radio Corporation (TAPR), founded in 1982, is a nonprofit organization of amateur radio operators with the goals of supporting R&D efforts in the area of amateur digital communications, disseminating information on packet and digital communications, providing affordable and useful kits for experimenters and hobbyists, pursuing and helping advance the amateur art of communications, and supporting publications, meetings, and standards in the area of amateur digital communications. As part of its role in supporting groups of amateurs working on digital communications projects, TAPR offers help in turning concepts into reproducible designs and making them available as kits or finished products to others. In 2005, TAPR began working with one such group, which was developing high-performance software-defined radio products and wanted to contribute their free time and expertise to the ham radio community (Ackermann 2009). The group feared that their efforts might be co-opted by commercial entities and, therefore, asked for TAPR's assistance in developing a license to achieve their goals (Ackermann 2009). The result was the TAPR Open Hardware license, the first hardware-specific open source license.

OHANDA

In July 2009, at the Grounding Open Source Hardware summit held at the Banff Center, a group of participants created the Open Hardware Design Alliance (OHANDA). One of the project's first goals was to launch a service for open hardware design based on a certification and registration model (OHANDA 2011). OHANDA thus created a label, in the sense of trademark, which stands for the Four Freedoms derived from the Free Software movement and adapted to hardware: (1) the freedom to use the device for any purpose; (2) the freedom to study how the device works and change it (access to the complete design is precondition to this); (3) the freedom to redistribute the device and/or design (remanufacture); and (4) the freedom to improve the device and/or design, and release improvements (and modified versions in general) to the public, so that the whole community benefits.

Designers who wish to apply the OHANDA label to their projects begin by registering with the organization. When they do so, they accept OHANDA's terms and conditions; that is, they grant their products' users the four freedoms the organization stands for. Creators can then register their designs and receive a unique product ID, the OKEY. The OHANDA label and the OKEY are subsequently printed/engraved on each copy of the device. This way the link to the documentation and to the contributors travels with the physical device itself and makes it a visible piece of open source hardware. Through the OHANDA registration key on the product, the user is linked back to the designer, the product description, design artifacts, and the public domain or copyleft license through OHANDA's web-based service. Through this process OHANDA seeks to make public sufficient information to test/reproduce the device; collect information on new innovation; ensure openness; make the description/documentation publicly accessible; protect common knowledge; make the standard generic, universal, and simple; and create a venue for time-stamping, quality control, and trust (Neumann and Powell 2011).

OSHW Definition, Summit, and Logo

In early 2010, Ayah Bdeir, then a Creative Commons fellow, was trying to turn her project littleBits (a system of open source hardware modules) into a company. She consulted with her Creative Commons advisor, John Wilbanks, with whom she had several discussions about how to launch, run, and protect open source hardware enterprises. Together they decided to hold a workshop to share the questions and possible solutions they had been debating with other open-hardware developers. The Opening Hardware workshop, which took place at Eyebeam in New York City in March 2010 (Eyebeam 2010), coincided with a major Arduino meeting that had brought several stakeholders to the city. Among those present were Alicia Gibb (R&D director at Bug Labs), Andrew "bunnie" Huang (founder of Chumby), Chris Anderson (editor-in-chief of *Wired* magazine, author of *The Long Tail,* and founder of DIY Drones), David A. Mellis, Gianluca Martino, Massimo Banzi, Tom Igoe (four of the five members of the Arduino Team), Nathan Seidle (founder of Spark-Fun), Zach Smith (co-founder of MakerBot), Limor Fried (founder of Adafruit), Phillip Torrone (creative director of Adafruit), Becky Stern (then editor at *Make* magazine), Benjamin Mako Hill (MIT), Jonathan Kuniholm (Open Prosthetics Project/Shared Design Alliance), Ken Gilmer (Bug Labs), and Ken Gracey (Parallax).

During the workshop, Thinh Nguyen (legal counsel at Creative Commons) and Wilbanks talked extensively about legal protections and recourse for open source hardware, and advised attendees to determine the practice's norms instead of opting for a probably long and painful legal recourse. Based on this, Bdeir, Mellis, and Windell Oskay (EMSL) orchestrated a series of posterior communications among the workshop's participants that culminated in the open source hardware definition 0.1 (OSHW Definition) (Freedom Defined n.d.).

Also in early 2010, Peter Semmelhack, founder of Bug Labs (a company that produced an open source modular system for building devices), approached Alicia Gibb and asked her if it would make sense to hold a meeting about open source hardware:

> Peter asked if I thought a bunch of people would want to come together and hear all the issues and complications of manufacturing open source hardware and doing business as an open hardware company. He was thinking 20 people and I told him we could get 300, it would be an entire conference. And so I started planning the Summit—but it was only on the sides of manufacturing and business. When Ayah and I later joined forces, she brought the legal side to the Summit. On January 18, 2010, in an email to Gibb, Peter came up with the name "Open Hardware Summit." Then Peter and I sat down with Dale Dougherty and the decision was made to have it happen in conjunction with Maker Faire. (Gibb, personal communication)

These two parallel efforts converged in June 2010 when Bdeir and Gibb joined forces to organize the first Open Hardware Summit (OHS). The Summit took place in New York City on September 23, 2010. Approximately 320 people attended, with their numbers being limited simply because the venue could not hold more. Thereafter, the Summit became an annual event. The second edition of the Open Hardware Summit, chaired by Gibb and Bdeir, had 350 attendees and 22 speakers plus breakout sessions and demonstrations. As the open source hardware practice and community continued to grow, so did the event. Its 2012 edition, chaired by Catarina Mota and Dustyn Roberts, saw close to 500 attendees and 42 speakers. Topics covered at the conference ranged from electronics, 3D printers, and airplanes to biomedical devices, neuroscience, and fashion.

In the meantime, a group of stakeholders had continued to iterate the open source hardware definition, with large contributions from David Mellis and Windell Oskay, and made version 0.3 public on July 13, 2010 (Freedom Defined n.d.). Through feedback and contributions from the public, and over a period of several months, the definition continued to be discussed and refined.

In December 2010, Nathan Seidle sent an email to the Summit's mailing list proposing the adoption of an open source hardware logo created by SparkFun's designer. Seidle wanted to somehow indicate on SparkFun's products that they were open source; a logo/stamp was needed for this purpose. Bdeir suggested that the logo created for the Open Hardware Summit be used instead, and Jonathan Kuniholm proposed that the OHANDA logo be adopted. A long discussion ensued not just on the topic of the logo, but also on the status of the definition and the need for greater cohesion among open source hardware stakeholders. Eventually, the OSHW Definition 1.0 was released on February 10, 2011 (Bdeir 2011a) and endorsed by the majority of those involved. It was also decided to hold a design competition for the logo. The competition received 129 submissions, from which 10 were selected, by a group of stakeholders invited by Bdeir, and put up for public vote. On April 7, 2011, the group announced that the design "Golden Orb" by Macklin Chaffee had received the most votes (Bdeir 2011b) and was consequently selected as the symbol of agreement with and abidance by the OSHW Definition. The first open source hardware developer to apply this community mark on a product was Parallax. It has since been used on an increasing number of projects and products.

CERN OHL

In July 2011, CERN (the renowned European Organization for Nuclear Research) issued a press release declaring that it had created an open source hardware license (CERN OHL). In this announcement, Javier Serrano, an engineer at CERN's Beams Department and the founder of the Open Hardware Repository,[3] explained the decision as follows: "By sharing designs openly, CERN expects to improve the quality of designs through peer review and to guarantee their users, including commercial companies, the freedom to study, modify and manufacture them, leading to better hardware and less duplication of efforts" (CERN 2011). The license was initially drafted to address CERN-specific concerns,

---

3. An online framework for collaboration among research institutes and beyond, with the goal of making available designs and documentation for modification/redistribution by all: http://web .archive.org/web/20110719151842/http://www.ohwr.org/projects/ohr-support/wiki/Manifesto.

such as tracing the impact of the organization's research, but in its current form it can be used by anyone developing open source hardware (Ayass 2011).

When these licenses, trademarks, and definitions are under consideration, the nuances and protections of each should be discussed with a legal professional for advisement on use.

Forking of Open Hardware and Open Source Hardware

Only a few days after the 2011 Open Hardware Summit, and in the midst of several heated debates[4] on licenses and what constitutes open source hardware, Bruce Perens abandoned the concerted efforts of those involved in the summit and the OSHW Definition. Perens's justification for this course of action was a concern that the selected logo could not be trademarked[5] and that the new licenses could not be legally enforced (Perens 2011b). The counter-arguments, voiced mostly—although not exclusively—by Phillip Torrone, maintained that the logo had been selected by public vote and therefore should not be abandoned; that the existing system, albeit informal, had worked so far; and that most open source hardware developers couldn't handle the expense of litigation even with legally enforceable licenses to protect their work (Jones 2011; Torrone 2011a).

As a result, and despite several attempts at reconciling these differences, the community forked into two parallel efforts: one under the banner "open hardware" ("open hardware" had been trademarked several years earlier by Perens) and another under the banner "open source hardware" (OSHW). Thus, openhardware.org, now viewable through the Internet archive, housed an organization by the same name, led by Bruce Perens, whose main goal was to identify and promote practices that meet all the combined requirements of the Open Source Hardware Definition, the Open Source Definition, and the Four Freedoms of the Free Software Foundation (Perens 2011a). Meanwhile, oshwa.org became the home of the Open Source Hardware Association (OSHWA), with founding efforts by Alicia Gibb, her board (Catarina Mota, Danese Cooper, Wendy Seltzer, Windell Oskay, and Nathan Seidle), legal counsel Aaron Williamson, and the first members of the organization. OSHWA seeks to become a hub of open source hardware activity of all genres, while cooperating with other entities such as TAPR, CERN, and OSI.

Creation of OSHWA

As the 2011 Summit came to a close, it became apparent that an organization was needed to house the Summit websites, financials, and general business. Gibb held a meeting at the Brooklyn-based hackerspace NYC Resistor and brought in several open source hardware companies to determine whether a business league or an educational nonprofit

---

4. This debate took place through both private email exchanges and on the Summit's mailing list. Even though several people chimed in, the most vocal participants on the discussion were Phillip Torrone and Bruce Perens.
5. A company was (unsuccessfully) attempting to trademark the label "Open Source Hardware," and the current OSHW logo had been based on the one adopted by the Open Source Initiative.

organization would be more appropriate. Together, the group chose to implement a 501(c)3 educational nonprofit organization. In the interest of the community, the role of OSHWA was expanded to take on other activities in open source hardware, such as housing the definition in multiple languages, providing information about standards, assisting the setup of international branches, educating the general public on what open source hardware is, collecting and publishing metrics on the movement, and encouraging projects to be open for the areas of education and economic development. The organization is intended to be built for the community, by the community, with a rotation of board members and leaders every two years.

The first task of OSHWA, aside from setting up the infrastructure of the organization, was defending the open source hardware community mark (also known as the OSHW or gear logo) that had previously been selected by community vote. An email from the president of the OSI was sent to Gibb informing her of infringement of the OSI logo and asking for immediate removal of the logo. OSHWA worked with the community to reach an agreement with OSI stating that the logos are used in different fields and, therefore, are different enough to avoid confusion between the two and infringement of OSI's trademark. OSHWA further chose not to trademark the open source hardware community mark because it's available for use to anyone whose products have followed the definition and existed in that format for three years.

OSHWA has identified five purposes to serve the community:

1. Organize conferences and community events.

2. Educate the general public about open source hardware and its socially beneficial uses.

3. Organize the open source hardware movement around shared values and principles.

4. Facilitate STEM education through the use of open source hardware conferences and other events focused on open source hardware.

5. Collect, compile, and publish data on the open source hardware movement.

Since the incorporation of OSHWA, the definition, its translations, and variations of the open source hardware logo are now housed on the OSHWA website. OSHWA created a community-based Best Practices document and an OSHW Quick Reference Guide included in Appendix A (or downloadable from www.oshwa.org/open source-quick-reference-guide/), as well as a poster of what "must" versus "may" be allowed to call hardware open source. In addition, the Summit is held annually. OSHWA has held other events as well. For example, it gathered key lawyers in the field of open source hardware for a legal day to discuss IP practices and open source hardware. OSHWA hosted a symposium with Congressman Jared Polis, and wrote up instructions for the community to host similar symposiums. OSHWA hopes to continue adding to resources and events about open source hardware in the future.

References

Ackermann, J. 2009. "Toward Open Source Hardware." *University of Dayton Law Review* 34 (2): 183–222. http://www.tapr.org/Ackermann_Open_Source_Hardware_Article_2009.pdf.

Ayass, M. 2011. "CERN's Open Hardware License." http://www.openhardwaresummit.org/wp-content/uploads/2011/09/The-CERN-OHL_OSHW-Summit.pdf.

Bdeir, A. 2011a. "Open Hardware Definition 1.0 RELEASED!" Open Hardware Summit. http://www.openhardwaresummit.org/2011/02/10/open-hardware-definition-1-0-released/.

———. 2011b. "OSHW Logo Selected!" Open Hardware Summit. http://www.openhardwaresummit.org/2011/04/07/oshw-logo-selected/.

Benjegerdes, T. 1998. "Open Source Hardware Page." http://web.archive.org/web/19981202022558/http://web.dodds.net/%7Ehozer/opensource.html.

CERN. 2011. "CERN Launches Open Hardware Initiative." http://public.web.cern.ch/press/pressreleases/Releases2011/PR08.11E.html.

Eyebeam. 2010. "Opening Hardware: A Workshop on Legal Tools."

Freedom Defined. 2011. "Open Source Hardware Definition." http://freedomdefined.org/OSHW.

———. n.d. "OSHW Older Drafts." http://freedomdefined.org/OSHW_older_drafts.

Freeman, D. 1998. "OHSpec: The Open Hardware Specification Project." http://web.archive.org/web/19990220025612/http://www.wpi.edu/~free779/main.html.

Jones, D. 2011. "Promoting Open Hardware." http://lists.openhardwaresummit.org/pipermail/updates-openhardwaresummit.org/2011-September/000566.html.

Lamberts, R. 1998. "Open Design Circuits." http://web.archive.org/web/19981207075641/http://circu.its.tudelft.nl/.

McNamara, P. September 2007a. "Open Hardware." Open Source Business Resource (Defining Open Source). http://www.osbr.ca/ojs/index.php/osbr/article/view/379/340.

———. 2007b. "Why Open Hardware?" P2P Foundation. http://p2pfoundation.net/Why_Open_Hardware%3F.

———. 2009. "Goodbye." Open Hardware Foundation. http://web.archive.org/web/20091129210640/http://www.openhardwarefoundation.org/.

Neumann, J. and Powell, A. "Developing an Open Hardware Standard." http://www.openhardwaresummit.org/wp-content/uploads/2011/09/OSH-Summit-presentation.pdf.

OHANDA. 2011. "Open Source Hardware and Design Alliance." http://www.ohanda.org/.

Perens, B. 1997. "Announcing: The Open Hardware Certification Program." Debian Announce List. http://lists.debian.org/debian-announce/1997/msg00026.html.

———. 2007. "OpenHardware.org." Open Hardware. http://web.archive.org/web/20071228050204/http://www.openhardware.org/.

———. 2011a. "Open Hardware: Constitution." Open Hardware. http://wiki.openhardware .org/Project:Constitution.

———. 2011b. "Promoting Open Hardware." http://lists.openhardwaresummit.org /pipermail/updates-openhardwaresummit.org/2011-September/000565.html.

Seaman, G. n.d. "What Is 'Open Source Hardware'?" Open Collector. http://www .opencollector.org/Whyfree/.

TAPR. n.d. "Organization." http://www.tapr.org/organization.html.

Torrone, P. 2007. "Open Source Hardware, What Is It? Here's a Start." *Make.* http://blog .makezine.com/archive/2007/04/open-source-hardware-what.html.

———. December 2009. "Open Source Hardware 2009." *Make.* http://blog.makezine .com/archive/2009/12/open-source-hardware-2009-the-def.html.

———. 2011a. "Promoting Open Hardware." http://lists.openhardwaresummit.org /pipermail/updates-openhardwaresummit.org/2011-September/000567.html.

———. 2011b. "Trademark, skdb—and breaking news, the osi logo was *actually* designed by phil torrone in 2001—5 years before it was trademarked by OSI." http://lists.openhardwaresummit.org/pipermail/updates-openhardwaresummit.org /2011-September/000527.html.

2

OSHW Definition and Best Practices

Alicia Gibb

"Yes, the universe continues to evolve."

—Neil deGrasse Tyson

Open Source Hardware Definition

The Open Source Hardware (OSHW) Definition serves as a set of agreed-upon standards for the main characteristics that open source hardware must have to be defined as open source hardware. Although open source software licenses and Creative Commons licenses existed prior to this definition, the open hardware community recognized that while these worked for documentation and source files, they did not fit the needs of physical formats. The major issue with these existing licenses is that hardware is not protected by copyright, which the Creative Commons licenses, GNU General Public License (GPL), and copyleft licenses all depend on. Instead, hardware is protected by patent law. A patent is not granted upon creation like copyright is, but rather has to be applied for.

The OSHW Definition, although uses the term "license" many times to describe what a license may or may not include, is not a license itself. The reason it is not a license is that it does not hold rights to anything that a license could be granted to give away. (See Chapter 3, Licensing Open Source Hardware, for further explanation of the legal and intellectual property implications of hardware.) The OSHW Definition is a social contract that the open hardware community has agreed to uphold. It allows the community to have agreement on decisions such as whether open source hardware can be created with a noncommercial clause attached (it cannot) and whether the source files must be free of charge and accessible via a website (they must).

Once the definition was created, issues arose regarding specific methods and processes of open hardware. In turn, a Best Practices document was created to notify the community of practices such as the following: no delaying the release of files if the product is being advertised as open source hardware, labeling which parts are open and which are closed if the hardware is a hybrid, and respecting other inventors' trademarks.

The following is the direct language of the OSHW Definition. It is an open-source hardware statement of principles, developed by members of the open source hardware community. However, much of the writing is attributed to Windell Oskay and David Mellis, and the conversation about starting a definition is attributed to Ayah Bdeir. These documents were originally edited on the wiki at freedomdefined.org/OSHW, which hosts all the individual endorsements of the definition and add your name to the list. To show that your hardware follows the definition, place the open source hardware logo[1] on your hardware, which signifies to the community that your hardware abides by the definition and creates a social contract with the community. Numerous translations of the definition are hosted at http://www.oshwa.org/definition/.

The following text was taken from http://www.oshwa.org/definition/.

Open Source Hardware (OSHW) Statement of Principles 1.0

Open source hardware is hardware whose design is made publicly available so that anyone can study, modify, distribute, make, and sell the design or hardware based on that design. The hardware's source, the design from which it is made, is available in the preferred format for making modifications to it. Ideally, open source hardware uses readily-available components and materials, standard processes, open infrastructure, unrestricted content, and open-source design tools to maximize the ability of individuals to make and use hardware. Open source hardware gives people the freedom to control their technology while sharing knowledge and encouraging commerce through the open exchange of designs.

Open Source Hardware (OSHW) Definition 1.0

The Open Source Hardware (OSHW) Definition 1.0 is based on the Open Source Definition for Open Source Software. That definition was created by Bruce Perens and the Debian developers as the Debian Free Software Guidelines.

Introduction

Open Source Hardware (OSHW) is a term for tangible artifacts—machines, devices, or other physical things—whose design has been released to the public in such a way that anyone can make, modify, distribute, and use those things. This definition is intended to help provide guidelines for the development and evaluation of licenses for Open Source Hardware.

Hardware is different from software in that physical resources must always be committed for the creation of physical goods. Accordingly, persons or companies producing items ("products") under an OSHW license have an obligation to make it clear that such products are not manufactured, sold, covered under

---

1. http://www.oshwa.org/open-source-hardware-logo/

warranty, or otherwise sanctioned by the original designer and also not to make use of any trademarks owned by the original designer.

The distribution terms of Open Source Hardware must comply with the following criteria:

- **Documentation:** The hardware must be released with documentation including design files, and must allow modification and distribution of the design files. Where documentation is not furnished with the physical product, there must be a well-publicized means of obtaining this documentation for no more than a reasonable reproduction cost, preferably downloading via the Internet without charge. The documentation must include design files in the preferred format for making changes, for example the native file format of a CAD program. Deliberately obfuscated design files are not allowed. Intermediate forms analogous to compiled computer code—such as printer-ready copper artwork from a CAD program—are not allowed as substitutes. The license may require that the design files are provided in fully-documented, open format(s).

- **Scope:** The documentation for the hardware must clearly specify what portion of the design, if not all, is being released under the license.

- **Necessary Software:** If the licensed design requires software, embedded or otherwise, to operate properly and fulfill its essential functions, then the license may require that one of the following conditions are met: (a) The interfaces are sufficiently documented such that it could reasonably be considered straightforward to write open source software that allows the device to operate properly and fulfill its essential functions. For example, this may include the use of detailed signal timing diagrams or pseudocode to clearly illustrate the interface in operation. (b) The necessary software is released under an OSI-approved open source license.

- **Derived Works:** The license shall allow modifications and derived works, and shall allow them to be distributed under the same terms as the license of the original work. The license shall allow for the manufacture, sale, distribution, and use of products created from the design files, the design files themselves, and derivatives thereof.

- **Free Redistribution:** The license shall not restrict any party from selling or giving away the project documentation. The license shall not require a royalty or other fee for such sale. The license shall not require any royalty or fee related to the sale of derived works.

- **Attribution:** The license may require derived documents, and copyright notices associated with devices, to provide attribution to the licensors when distributing design files, manufactured products, and/or derivatives thereof. The license may require that this information be accessible to the end-user using the device normally, but shall not specify a specific format of display. The license may require derived works to carry a different name or version number from the original design.

- **No Discrimination Against Persons or Groups:** The license must not discriminate against any person or group of persons.
- **No Discrimination Against Fields of Endeavor:** The license must not restrict anyone from making use of the work (including manufactured hardware) in a specific field of endeavor. For example, it must not restrict the hardware from being used in a business, or from being used in nuclear research.
- **Distribution of License:** The rights granted by the license must apply to all to whom the work is redistributed without the need for execution of an additional license by those parties.
- **License Must Not Be Specific to a Product:** The rights granted by the license must not depend on the licensed work being part of a particular product. If a portion is extracted from a work and used or distributed within the terms of the license, all parties to whom that work is redistributed should have the same rights as those that are granted for the original work.
- **License Must Not Restrict Other Hardware or Software:** The license must not place restrictions on other items that are aggregated with the licensed work but not derivative of it. For example, the license must not insist that all other hardware sold with the licensed item be open source, nor that only open source software be used external to the device.
- **License Must Be Technology-Neutral:** No provision of the license may be predicated on any individual technology, specific part or component, material, or style of interface or use thereof.

Afterword

The signatories of this Open Source Hardware definition recognize that the open source movement represents only one way of sharing information. We encourage and support all forms of openness and collaboration, whether or not they fit this definition.

Best Practices

After the OSHW Definition was put to the test over the course of a few years, best practices came about to clarify parts of the definition. Together, Nathan Seidle and David Mellis collected feedback from the community via a Google document to reflect the community's feelings about and best practices related to the definition. The best practices tell people how to document their hardware in the best light of the definition. Skipping or not following *some* of the best practices in no way detracts from the validity of your source being open; however, skipping or not following *some* of the other best practices, such as no noncommercial (NC) clauses, could leave you in violation of the definition. Because the best practices include both suggestions and strict rules of the definition, it is advised that you read the Open Source Hardware Definition and Best Practices documents together. Following the best practices as a secondary set of guidelines helps strengthen the community.

Many of the best practices were directed at resolving ambiguities within the definition. Confusion occurred within the community where certain aspects of the definition were not being followed as intended. For example, some companies were releasing their hardware as open source, but delaying the public release of the source files. To combat this problem, the Best Practices document states it is not appropriate to claim a project is open source before the release of the source files: "Don't refer to hardware as open-source until the design files are available. If you plan on open-sourcing the product in the future, say that instead." One reason this best practice exists is exemplified by the evolution of the Kickstarter category "Open hardware," nested in the "Technology" category, which for a while was the only category one could choose at Kickstarter for funding hardware. Creators chose this category even though they never intended to create open hardware or release their products as open hardware once they made money from their first shipment. Because the category pigeon-holed several projects as "open source," the OSHW community saw a growth in the number of projects delaying the release of their source files. Kickstarter now has a "Hardware" category that allows developers to avoid using the "open source" label when that is not the intended outcome. The education around this best practice was quite successful, and delaying the release of files has become largely a non-issue as of the writing of this book.

Several members of the community wanted further guidance as to which file formats were acceptable, since the definition does not identify specific formats. For example, Eagle, the program that many people use for circuit layout, is a closed source product. Nevertheless, the community determined that Eagle files were acceptable as well as PDFs, due to the ease with which both types of files can be accessed. When the definition was written, the community recognized that file formats might change; consequently, they didn't want to pigeon-hole specific formats as correct, given that those formats might later become obsolete or no longer represent the best possible solution.

For clarity, in the Best Practices document, acceptable file formats have been listed for many different types of hardware. You can find listings of file formats under the headings "Original Design Files" and "Auxiliary Design Files." A review of open source hardware projects reveals that the most comprehensive library of varying file formats is Open Source Ecology.[2] Open Source Ecology also includes great examples of open documentation and would be an excellent resource from which to learn best practices. Its hardware spans the complex grid of documenting machinery to build as a global construction kit. Chapter 10, Physical Materials, goes into more detail about file formats for various types of hardware.

---

2. http://opensourceecology.org/

The author notes in the next section designated by the heading "Note" are not part of the community-written Best Practices. The following text was taken from http://www .oshwa.org/sharing-best-practices/.

Best Practices for Open Source Hardware 1.0

As described in the open-source hardware definition and statement principles, the essence of open-source hardware (OSHW) is sharing the design files for a piece of hardware for others to modify or make hardware from (including for commercial purposes). There are, in addition, many other things you can do to encourage the development of a vibrant community of people who use and improve your open-source hardware project. This document discusses these best practices.

Elements of an Open-Source Hardware Project

Here are some files that you should consider sharing when publishing your open source hardware project. You are not required to post them all, but the more you share the more the community benefits and the higher the likelihood the community will pick up your project.

Overview/Introduction

Your open-source hardware project should include a general description of the hardware's identity and purpose, written as much as possible for a general audience. That is, explain what the project is and what it's for before you get into the technical details. A good photo or rendering can help a lot here.

Original Design Files

These are the original source files that you would use to make modifications to the hardware's design. The act of sharing these files is the core practice of open-source hardware.

Ideally, your open-source hardware project would be designed using a free and open-source software application, to maximize the ability of others to view and edit it. For better or worse however, hardware design files are often created in proprietary programs and stored in proprietary formats. It is still essential to share these original design files; they constitute the original "source code" for the hardware. They are the very files that someone will need in order to contribute changes to a given design.

Try to make your design files easy for someone else to understand. Organize them in a logical way; comment complex aspects; note any unusual manufacturing procedures; etc.

Examples of original design files include:

- 2D drawings or computer-aided design (CAD) files, such as those used to describe two-dimensional laser cut, vinyl cut, or water-jet cut part, in their original format. Example formats: Native 2D design files saved by Corel Draw (.cdr), Inkscape (.svg), Adobe Illustrator (.ai), AutoCAD, etc.

- 3D designs that can be 3D printed, forged, injection molded, extruded, machined, etc. Example formats: Native files saved by SolidWorks (.sldprt, .sldasm), Rhino, etc.

- Circuit board CAD files such as capture files (schematics) and printed-circuit board (layout) design files. Example formats: Native files saved by Eagle, Altium, KiCad, gEDA, etc.

- Component libraries (symbol, footprint, fastener, etc.) necessary for native modification of CAD files.

- Additional technical drawings in their original design formats, if required for fabrication of the device.

- Additional artwork that may be used on the device and is included as part of the OSHW release, such as an emblem, or cosmetic overlay in the original design format.

In the event that a design was originally created in an alternative format, even one that might normally be considered as an auxiliary design file (as discussed in the following section), that original design in the original format could be considered the "original design files".

Examples of alternative formats that could constitute original design files under special circumstances include:

- Hand-coded G-code for a machined part. (G-code)

- Scans of hand-drawn blueprints. (JPEG)

- Detailed 3D scans of a hand-carved resin-casting mold. (STL)

- Mask pattern for etching a single-side circuit board, as drawn in MS Paint. (PNG)

Auxiliary Design Files

Beyond the original design files, it is often helpful to share your design in additional, more accessible formats. For example, best practice open-sourcing a CAD design is to share the design not just in its native file format, but also in a range of interchange and export formats that can be opened or imported by other CAD programs.

It is also helpful to provide ready-to-view outputs that can easily be viewed by end users who wish to understand (but not necessarily modify) the design—for example, a PDF of a circuit board schematic, or an STL of a 3D design. These auxiliary design files allow people to study the design of the hardware, and sometimes even fabricate it, even without access to particular proprietary software packages. However, note that auxiliary design files are never allowed as substitutes for original design files.

Examples of auxiliary design files include:

- 2D drawings or CAD files, in a 2D export or interchange format. Example formats: DXF, SVG.

- 2D drawings or CAD files, in an easily viewable 2D export format. Example formats: PDF, JPEG, PNG, etc. (Where possible, vector formats are preferred over bitmap formats.)

- 3D designs or CAD files, in a 3D export or interchange format. Example formats: STEP, IGES.
- 2D or 3D designs in manufacturing-ready export formats. Example formats: G-code, STEP-NC, STL, AMF.
- Circuit board design files in export or interchange formats. Example formats: EDIF, Open JSON.
- Circuit board designs in manufacturing-ready formats. Example formats: Gerber
  RS-274X, Excellon.
- Additional technical drawings in their original formats, if required for fabrication of the device, in a commonly-readable format such as PDF.
- Additional artwork, for example different colored skins for an instrument panel.

Bill of Materials

While it might be possible to infer from the design files which parts make up a piece of hardware, it is important to provide a separate bill of materials. This can be a spreadsheet (e.g., CSV, XLS, Google Doc) or simply a text file with one part per line. If your CAD package has integrated or add-on BOM management tools, those are also a good option. (Examples include the built-in tools in Solid-Works and bom-ex for Eagle.) Useful things to include in the bill of materials are part numbers, suppliers, costs, and a short description of each part. Make it easy to tell which item in the bill of materials corresponds to which component in your design files: use matching reference designators in both places, provide a diagram indicating which part goes where, or otherwise explain the correspondence.

Software and Firmware

You should share any code or firmware required to operate your hardware. This will allow others to use it with their hardware or modify it along with their modifications to your hardware. Document the process required to build your software, including links to any dependencies (e.g., third-party libraries or tools). In addition, it's helpful to provide an overview of the state of the software (e.g., "stable" or "beta" or "barely-working hack").

Photos

Photos help people understand what your project is and how to put it together. It's good to publish photographs from multiple viewpoints and at various stages of assembly. If you don't have photos, posting 3D renderings of your design is a good alternative. Either way, it's good to provide captions or text that explain what's shown in each image and why's it's useful.

Instructions and Other Explanations

In addition to the design files themselves, there are a variety of explanations that are invaluable in helping others to make or modify your hardware:

- **Making the hardware.** To help others make and modify your hardware design, you should provide instructions for going from your design files to the working physical hardware. As part of the instructions, it's helpful to link to datasheets for the components/parts of your hardware and to list the tools required to assemble it. If the design requires specialized tools, tell people where to get them.

- **Using the hardware.** Once someone has made the hardware, they need to know how to use it. Provide instructions that explain what it does, how to set it up, and how to interact with it.

- **Design rationale.** If someone wants to modify your design, they'll want to know why it is the way it is. Explain the overall plan of the hardware's design and why you made the specific choices you did.

Keep in mind that these instructions may be read by someone whose expertise or training is different from yours. As much as possible, try to write to a general audience, and check your instructions for industry jargon, be explicit about what you assume the user knows, etc.

The instructions could be in a variety of formats, like a wiki, text file, Google Doc, or PDF. Remember, though, that others might want to modify your instructions as they modify your hardware design, so it's good to provide the original editable files for your documentation, not just output formats like PDF.

Open Source Hardware Processes and Practices

Note

The processes and practices section designates further instructions for sharing your tools, materials and source. The first section gives practical advice about making it easy to obtain the hardware and files you've used. The second section covers where source files can be stored. The third section discusses labeling your open hardware project and how others might process a derivative, also known as licensing, and the forth section covers distribution. Finally, the last section is a set of rules to follow for creating derivatives when building on other people's open source hardware.

Designing Your Hardware

If you're planning to open-source a particular piece of hardware, following certain best practices in its design will make it easier for others to make and modify the hardware:

Use free and open-source software design (CAD) tools where possible. If that's not feasible, try to use low-cost and/or widely-used software packages.

Use standard and widely-available components, materials, and production processes. Try to avoid parts that aren't available to individual customers or processes that require expensive setup costs.

Hosting Your Design Files

A basic way of sharing your files is with a zip file on your website. While this is a great start, it makes it difficult for others to follow your progress or to contribute improvements.

We recommend using an online source-code repository (like GitHub, Gitorious, or Google Code) to store your open-source hardware projects. All files (design, bill of materials, assembly instructions, code, etc.) should be version controlled where possible. If you want to develop your hardware publicly, online repositories make it easy to publish changes to your files as you make them. Or, you might publish updates in conjunction with releases of the hardware.

Most online repositories also include issue trackers, which are a good way to keep track of the bugs in and future enhancements planned for your software in a way that others can view and comment on. Some include wikis, which can be good places to document your project.

As an alternative to an online repository, you might develop your project in an online CAD tool (like Upverter). Or, you could share your files on a site like Thingiverse.

Licensing Your Designs

Note

In no way should this section be considered legal advice. Due to the complexities of hardware licenses and the governing law for hardware being patent law, if you are thinking of using a hardware license, the safest way to understand your protections would be talking to a lawyer. There is more information about licensing in Chapter 3 of this book.

While licensing is a complex subject, use of licenses is an important way of signaling how others can and should use your work. By explicitly applying an open-source license to your hardware design files and other documentation, you make it clear that others can copy and modify them. When licensing your project, keep in mind that someone who makes a derivative of your hardware will probably also want to build on your software, instructions, and other documentation; you should license not just the hardware design files but also these other elements of your project.

Note that copyright (on which most licenses are based) doesn't apply to hardware itself, only to the design files for it—and, then, only to the elements which constitute "original works of authorship" (in U.S. law) and not the underlying functionality or ideas. Therefore, it's not entirely clear exactly which legal protections are or aren't afforded by the use of a copyright-based license for hardware design files—but they're still important as a way of making clear the ways in which you want others to use your designs.

There are two main classes of open-source or free-software licenses: copyleft (or viral) licenses, which require that derivatives be licensed under the same terms; and permissive licenses, which allow others to make modifications without releasing them as open-source hardware. Note that the definition of open-source hardware specifies that you must allow modification and commercial re-use of your design, so do not use licenses with a no-derivatives or non-commercial clause.

Popular copyleft licenses include

- Creative Commons Attribution, Share-Alike (BY-SA)
- GNU General Public License (GPL)
- Hardware-specific licenses: TAPR OHL, CERN OHL

Permissive licenses include:

- FreeBSD license
- MIT license
- Creative Commons Attribution (BY)

It is good practice to include a copy of the license in the version control repository, and a statement in every file or at least the README specifying the author(s) and year(s) of non-trivial modifications, and the license.

Distributing Open Source Hardware

- Provide links to the source (original design files) for your hardware on the product itself, its packaging, or its documentation.
- Make it easy to find the source (original design files) from the website for a product.
- Label the hardware with a version number or release date so that people can match the physical object with the corresponding version of its design files.
- Use the open-source hardware logo on your hardware. Do so in a way that makes it clear which parts of the hardware the logo applies to (i.e., which parts are open-source).
- In general, clearly indicate which parts of a product are open-source (and which aren't).
- Don't refer to hardware as open-source until the design files are available. If you plan on open-sourcing the product in the future, say that instead.

DEV-11113 RoHS✓ ♯ 3D

Figure 2.1   The amenities of a particular piece of hardware which
discerns it from the closed source hardware.
(Source: www.sparkfun.com/products/11113)

Note

As stated in the beginning, some of the best practices came from a lack of
foresight when writing the original definition—a problem that can't be avoided
in community-driven guidelines. The points that follow were created due to
issues that arose once the OSHW Definition had been signed by more than
130 open source hardware advocates and inventors, but still needed clarity.
The original conversation around the definition did not include the possibility
that some projects would have both open source and closed aspects, such
as a trade secret or a patent on one component of the overall project and an
open source component on another part. Another example of both open and
closed hardware is hardware for which some versions (usually early versions)
are open, but others (more contemporary versions) are closed. Projects such
as these are considered to have both open and closed aspects, and their
existence caused the OSHW community to recognize a gap in the guidelines for
labeling.

Another example is a hardware provider selling multiple projects, some open
source and some not. It is best to label those that are open source appropriately.
In most places the open source hardware logo is used as an easy graphical way to
tell users your hardware follows the OSHW definition. After a review of open source
hardware resellers, SparkFun Electronics has the best examples of how to tell
users which products are open source. It has an "Open Hardware" tab listed in its
right-side navigation webpage that brings up all open hardware products if a user
only wants to browse those. An innovative approach has been taken to show icons
of the amenities for each product on their product page. In an example in Figure 2.1, the user can see, at a glance, three pieces of information after the product number: RoHS compliance information, the open source hardware logo, and a
logo denoting that there is a 3D enclosure file. The two tactics of having an Open
Hardware category in the navigation and the open hardware logo on the product
website mean a user does not have to dig through product pictures or source files
to know that a product is open source. To delve more into the topic of documenting and sharing files for open source hardware, see Chapter 14, Taxonomy of Hardware Documentation.

Finally, it is not in keeping with the spirit of open source hardware to obfuscate
your source files or information pertaining to how the open source hardware project was built. Obfuscation can come in many forms—from posting files at a reso-
lution that is too small to see, to forcing users to email you and ask for the files
rather than posting them publicly.

Building on Open Source Hardware

- Respect the trademarks of others.
- While direct commercial use of existing open source hardware designs is explicitly allowed, it is better—when possible—to make useful improvements to the design and to release that improved version as open source hardware.
- Share your changes and improvements with the creator of the original hardware.
- Be emotionally prepared to allow your project to be copied (unless your trademark is violated, then act according to trademark law).

Note

Since building derivatives is such an integral aspect to open source hardware, this section speaks to derivatives specifically. Currently, two issues for which the Open Source Hardware Association (OSHWA) is committed to providing education are as follows: (1) trademarks need to be respected and (2) noncommercial licenses are not open source. People may fall into routines and not necessarily mean to infringe on a trademark or apply a NC license. It's all too easy to forget that not all Creative Commons licenses are open source. Likewise, in some situations, people don't realize the Arduino name is trademarked, but instead view it as a generic term. In this case, OSHWA wants to ensure that trademarks and NC licenses are not used accidentally, and that people are cognizant of these two areas.

Last updated: April 18, 2013 by the OSHWA mailing list, coordinated by David A. Mellis.
Initial version: November 21, 2012 by Nathan Seidle and the OSHWA mailing list.

As the definition grows and the best practices get put to the test, other groups, such as Mach 30, have begun to write their own guides. These guides can be somewhat specific to particular industries, but overlap with the general advice that is useful to the open source hardware community.

Anecdote: The OSHW Prime Directive

J. Simmons

In 2013, I was fortunate enough to attend the Open Source Hardware Documentation Jam. One of the central themes to come out of that work was the need to improve documentation tools if we wanted people to document their projects. At the time I completely agreed, and I am still in favor of developing improved tools and processes for documenting open source hardware. Since the Doc Jam, though, I have been thinking what we really need to do is remind ourselves of just how important documentation is. We need to remember that documenting our hardware designs is our mission as open source hardware developers.

(continues)

Why? Because nothing motivates one to do the hard work like the siren's song of a mission one cares about.

If you haven't done so lately, I encourage you to read the Definition of Open Source Hardware (http://www.oshwa.org/definition/). Allow me to direct your attention to the "Statement of Principles 1.0":

> Open source hardware is hardware whose design is made publicly available so that anyone can study, modify, distribute, make, and sell the design or hardware based on that design. The hardware's source, the design from which it is made, is available in the preferred format for making modifications to it. Ideally, open source hardware uses readily-available components and materials, standard processes, open infrastructure, unrestricted content, and open-source design tools to maximize the ability of individuals to make and use hardware. Open source hardware gives people the freedom to control their technology while sharing knowledge and encouraging commerce through the open exchange of designs.

Stop and consider this statement for a moment. For a piece of hardware to be open source, anyone must be able to study and modify the design; and they must be able to make their own copies of the hardware for any purpose including distribution with or without profit (more on this last part later). In other words, hardware can only be open source, and we can only achieve our great and mighty mission, when the hardware has sufficient documentation to support studying, modifying, and making the hardware.

This, dare I say, requirement begs the question: How do we as open source hardware developers know when we have sufficiently documented our projects so they meet the values expressed in the "Statement of Principles"? At Mach 30, we have come up with a rather simple (and admittedly obvious) test: Have someone replicate the project from its design documentation (no, not a kit, the actual documentation including bill of materials, assembly instructions, operating manual, safety manual... you get the idea). This test has become such a key to our work that we consider it a turning point in the development of a project, worthy of celebration just as much as the first successful test of a prototype or the first sale of a kit. When the Coca-Cola Space Science Center (CCSSC) built the first copy of the Shepard Test Stand (https://opendesignengine.net/projects/shepard-ts), a small rocket test stand built for use in education and training programs, Mach 30 shared it on our social media channels, in video conferences, and on our blog (http://mach30 .org/2013/07/29/achievements-unlocked/).

At Mach 30, we go further than just sharing our designs, because I personally believe the values expressed in the "Statement of Principles" should apply to all aspects of open source hardware. So, we share the final design and everything leading up to it, including design decisions, tests of the project's function, proposed modifications, and operating instructions. Guided by this belief and the Definition of Open Source Hardware, I propose the following Prime Directive of Open Source Hardware:

> If someone else cannot reproduce your project, your test, your modification, or any other aspect of your work, go back and improve the documentation until they can.

Like Starfleet's Prime Directive, the Open Source Hardware Prime Directive gives concrete direction on how to carry out our mission. If one's work (e.g., a design, a test, user instructions) doesn't pass the test embodied by the Prime Directive, the work is at best incomplete. At worst, a lack of sufficient and accessible documentation is a sign of a potentially non-open source project masquerading as open source. Even the whiff of such a project will inevitably raise the ire of one or more members of the open source hardware community (myself included; http://mach30.org/2011/06/09/an-open-source-flashlight-well-not-exactly/).

All of this discussion about replication inevitably brings up the subject of cloners. I realize cloners can be, shall we say, a touchy subject in the open source hardware community. But I also think they are an integral and important part of the open source economy, albeit with one important caveat. Cloners are, simply put, proof of a project's success. When someone decides to clone an open source hardware project, they are demonstrating two important aspects of that project. First, the project abides by the Prime Directive. If someone can clone the project, that certainly counts as replication. Second, the project has developed enough demand to warrant financial investment from third parties. Even where there is no need to spend money on research and development, setting up a production line for a cloned project is still an investment, and one the cloners feel is financially viable, indicating a fairly significant level of demand and popularity.

Now, a word about the caveat I mentioned. While I believe cloners are an integral part of the open source economy, I cannot abide freeloaders. Clearly, I do not believe all cloners are freeloaders. If one goes to the trouble of developing one's own brand, of creating and running one's own support system, and if one builds high-quality products, then I don't think that person is a freeloader. But, if one fails to live up to those standards, then the person is unfairly profiting off of the hard work of the original project. That is decidedly uncool, and is more akin to theft than being an integral part of the open source economy.

So, let us all boldly go and document projects that have not been documented before, but not because someone made us or because we finally have that silver bullet that makes it easy. Instead, let us document our projects because it is what we were called to do. It is the very reason we are open source hardware developers, and it is the reason we should be proud of our work.

Mach 30's OSHW Ground Rules

Unlike many open source hardware projects which come out of a single lab/shop/company/makerspace, at Mach 30 we have had to learn how to develop hardware in a distributed environment from day one. Mach 30 does not have a shop of its own. Instead, volunteers from across the United States develop hardware in their homes, garages, and local makerspaces and share the results on Open Design Engine, the free open source hardware project portal run by Mach 30. As you can imagine, working with people in different locations, often in different time zones, adds a whole new level of complexity to project management.

But it also makes our projects more open. The same steps we take to ensure distributed project teams are up to speed on current design discussions and decisions ensure visitors to our projects can get up to speed quickly and easily. And getting visitors up to speed quickly and easily promotes contributions (bug fixes, design ideas, documentation assistance), replication (building or buying their own copy of a project), and forking/remixing (taking parts of a project and integrating them into a new project)—three of the best indicators of a project's success.

(continues)

We have captured these steps as a series of ground rules for open source hardware at Mach 30. Think of these rules as being more like rules in a board game than a royal decree. It is important to follow them, but only so everyone is working together in the same way toward the same goal: creating amazing open source hardware that can change the world.

Remember the Prime Directive of Open Source Hardware: If someone else cannot reproduce your project, your test, your modification, or any other aspect of your work, go back and improve the documentation until they can.

If your work doesn't pass this test, it is at best incomplete and at worst just a vanity project. Yes, documentation is hard, and it isn't always as fun as making something, but it is the whole point of the project from an open source perspective. When in doubt, get a buddy or fellow maker to try and replicate your work. Any questions that person has are items to address in the documentation.

Have a process and follow it (enough). When working on a project, be sure to follow the steps of your chosen (or assigned) design process. Do the requirements analysis before designing the hardware. Calculate predicted performance before testing, when there are specific performance numbers available. Do your design review, even if you are the only one on the project and you just take 20 minutes to review your design to ensure it meets the requirements before moving on. Of course, not every project needs to cover every step of every process, so there are certainly times when you will need to intentionally skip a step. When that happens, just be sure it is intentional and then document that decision. Don't just jump straight to a build because that's where the personal payoff is. Doing so will simply force you to go back and work harder to capture the design later (and you will invariably lose details along the way). Following the process also makes it easier for other team members to follow along with your work and to know when their contributions are expected.

Use forums instead of email to communicate (except where matters of privacy and confidentiality are in play). Are you about to send an email out to half of the project team? STOP! Unless that email contains private or confidential information (e.g., people's email addresses, order numbers, physical addresses, unreleasable technical documents from vendors/partners), that message should in all likelihood be posted to a publicly available forum. Most project portals specifically include project-level forums so that they can maintain a public record of design and support discussions. Use them! Information that is exchanged over email ultimately has to be copied over to project documentation. This rarely happens, and when it does, the information that is copied over is usually incomplete.

This rule also goes for social media. Do not hold design discussions over Facebook, Google+, or Twitter. Discussions scattered randomly across the Internet are difficult to track down and place in context, and are often not publicly visible. All of these factors make using them as references for design decisions challenging at best, and nearly useless at worst.

Do use social media to connect to people outside your project. Social media platforms are great for reaching a larger audience. Use them to share resources from your project's site (e.g., news announcements, forum posts with awesome videos), but avoid having technical discussions over social media. Do you want to reach out to a social network for help? Try one of these two options:

- Start the discussion on project forums, post a link to the forum on social media, and lock comments on the social media post.

- If you feel you simply must have a technical discussion in a social media context, post the question on the social media site, ensuring when possible the post and comments are visible to users who don't have an account on the social media site. Then post the best suggestions (with link back to post/comments on social media site) on your project's wiki or forums. This is a risky move, as you must remember to actually capture the results of the technical discussion in your project's documentation.

Use a balance of synchronous and asynchronous discussions. Project teams need to balance synchronous discussions (e.g., meetings, video conferences, live chats) and asynchronous discussions (e.g., forum posts, blog posts with comments). Each style serves a different function. Meetings and other synchronous discussions allow for direct and complex interactions in real time. These interactions are especially good for finalizing decisions and working through complex issues that do not have obvious answers. Forums and other asynchronous discussions allow team members to do time-consuming work (such as analysis or drafting) on their own, then present their work and receive feedback. The slower pace gives everyone involved more time to process the material being discussed and to do further work as required without holding everyone up in a meeting.

Test early and test often. So, how do you know if a new design idea is a good one or if it even works? For very large projects or very risky ones, analysis is the order of the day. However, most open source hardware projects are at a small-enough scale that it is far more efficient to put a prototype together and test it. This approach of testing designs early and often is recommended owing to the success of famous makers like the crew at Armadillo Aerospace, who designed winning rocket-powered landers by iteratively testing their vehicles, often to the point of failure. The lessons learned from actual tests, especially those involving failure of the system under testing conditions, proved to be invaluable to the Armadillo Aerospace team. The same is true for smaller projects. Recently, a co-developer of the Holoseat (https://opendesignengine.net/projects/holoseat) suggested we could replace a linear potentiometer used to adjust the difficulty setting with a desktop application in the system tray. He worked up a prototype in a couple of hours and we tested it. The desktop application worked so well that it not only proved the point that we didn't need the potentiometer, but also led to a number of new features for the project that we could not implement without the desktop application in the design (such as activity tracking with badges and social media integration and per-user configurations).

Share your failures along with your successes. I realize this recommendation may be difficult to swallow. After all, we live in a world that worships success and shies away from failure. But, consider this: Would you rather make the same mistake everyone does when trying to build the first open source car/boat/plane/tractor, or would you rather learn from everyone else working on this same goal and be able to make new mistakes (or maybe even find a working design)? The answer is simple: We would all rather spend our time advancing the project than repeating the same mistakes everyone makes. Simply put, it is a waste of time and effort to have to rediscover what doesn't work, just as much as—and possibly even more so—it is wasteful to have to rediscover what does work. So, if we want to leverage the full benefit of the open source method when it comes to hardware, we must open source our failures along with our successes, so those who come behind us can build on our complete experience and not just the times when we have found things that work. In other words, we must change our culture to one that asks, "What do you mean you didn't share your failure?!?"

Summary

Although many individuals and companies have endorsed both the OSHW Definition and Best Practices, the open source hardware movement is still young, and the documents continue to be malleable. Moreover, as we've seen with Mach 30's OSHW Ground Rules, the documents have room for growth. For this reason, the wiki[3]—where the OSHW Definition was originally written—is still available for edits, as is the Best Practices doc.[4] The definition has also served as a jumping-off point for several open source hardware licenses. For further explanation of the legal and intellectual property implications of hardware, see Chapter 3. For the history of how the movement has grown, see Chapter 1.

The OSHW Definition and Best Practices are lengthy, in-depth documents. To help disseminate key points, see the open source hardware checklist and the "must" and "may" bulleted lists in Appendix A in this book. Since the definition and best practices lie at the heart of the open source hardware movement, you may be interested in other aspects of open source development. If you have read this chapter to ensure your hardware is open source and are currently building your hardware, you may want to flip to Chapter 12, Accelerate from Making to Manufacturing. If you are looking for resources on documentation, read Chapter 14, Taxonomy of Hardware Documentation. If you're just getting started, you may want some advice from Chapter 5, The Design Process: How to Get from Nothing to Something.

---

3. http://freedomdefined.org/OSHW
4. http://bit.ly/oshwbestpractices

Licensing Open Source Hardware

Michael Weinberg

> "Gu's shoulders slumped, and Juan got a closer look at
> the component boxes. Every one had physical signage: NO
> USER-SERVICEABLE PARTS WITHIN."
>
> —Vernor Vinge, *Rainbows End*

For many people, a key component of open source is the license that is attached to the project. But what is a license, and what role does licensing play in open source hardware? This chapter covers the different types of intellectual property (IP) and the basics of IP licensing with respect to open source hardware. The good news is that most hardware is born open. Unless it is explicitly covered by a patent, most hardware is available to be copied, improved, and built upon by default. This chapter is written from the perspective of U.S. law. Of course, this chapter is merely an introduction to the topic of licensing and should not serve as a substitute for legal advice. It's always a good idea to talk to a lawyer before making specific licensing decisions.

Licensing

A *license* is permission to do something. Usually, that permission is conditioned on some sort of behavior or action. For example, a movie theater owner obtains a license from a studio to show a new movie. In return for permission to show the movie, the theater owner promises to pay the studio a percentage of the revenue generated by ticket sales. Because the movie studio owns the copyright in the movie, if the movie theater owner decided to show a movie without a license from the studio, the studio could sue the theater owner for copyright infringement.

Critically, if you do not need permission to do something, you do not need a license. In the movie theater example, the theater owner needed permission from the studio to show the movie because the right to show a movie is one of the rights that flows from owning a copyright in a work. However, the theater owner does not need permission—a license—from the studio owner to discuss the movie with her friend. That is because copyright law does not prevent people from discussing movies, so having such a conversation without a license does not open the theater owner up to an infringement lawsuit.

There is one additional twist on needing and giving licenses. A license is only worth something from someone with the power to grant it. The theater owner does not just need permission to show the movie—she needs permission to show the movie *from the studio that owns the movie.* Getting permission from some random person on the street will not be much of a defense when the studio decides to sue the theater owner for copyright infringement.

Finally, although many people think of licenses in terms of intellectual property, they are actually much broader than that. A driver's license is permission to drive on roads, conditioned on passing a driving test and maintaining a reasonably safe driving record. A concert ticket can be thought of as a license to enter a venue and attend a show, conditioned on paying money.

In the context of open source hardware (OSHW), most of the licenses involved will relate to intellectual property rights. By and large, these licenses will grant permission to do things like copy, incorporate, and build upon existing projects.

Open Licenses in the Context of OSHW

It is probably safe to say that the GPL and Creative Commons (CC) licenses are the best-known existing licenses among people interested in open source hardware. That renown is well deserved. These licenses and their brethren (which can loosely be thought of as "open licenses") have helped to build a massive common pool of writing, photography, films, software, and countless other types of creative expression. At the same time, they have helped to raise awareness about copyright more generally. Because of this success, they are worth considering specifically in the context of open source hardware.

The real genius of open licenses is that they take something that was viewed as a barrier to sharing and turn it into an asset. As will be discussed in more detail later, one of the unique aspects of copyright is that it protects automatically. If you create a type of thing that fits within the scope of copyright (like a movie or a piece of code), it is protected as soon as it is created. This copyright protection happens regardless of the creator's interest in protecting his or her work under copyright. That is why a license is so important, even for works that no one really wanted to protect with copyright in the first place. Without an explicit license, anyone trying to build upon that work is potentially infringing upon the creator's copyright. Remember, if you didn't include an open license for your files in GitHub (or wherever you store your files), they are automatically protected by copyright to the fullest extent possible. Merely making the files public is not enough to make them open.

Instead of seeing this automatic protection as a barrier to sharing, open licenses view it as an opportunity to promote and encourage sharing. Using an open license is an affirmative declaration in support of building a commons.

An open license can also be used to force others to share. Remember, open licenses are built upon a legal right: copyright. That foundation allows creators to sue anyone who does not comply with the conditions of the license for copyright infringement. Including a "share alike" provision in a CC license is not a polite request that anyone who builds upon the work contribute back to the commons; rather, it creates a legal requirement. This legal requirement helps bring people and companies that do not care about building a commons into the world of sharing. If they want to benefit from the commons by copying, building upon, or integrating the commons into their own work, the open license can legally compel them to add to it as well.

Adding hardware to the mix makes things a bit more complicated. The legal requirement that forms the foundation for GPL and CC licenses is copyright. For things that fit easily within the scope of copyright—music, movies, photographs, and so on—this does not pose a problem. But for things that do not fit neatly within the scope of copyright—hardware being the most important example in this book—that copyright basis for traditional open licenses can complicate things.

The fact that hardware is not protected by copyright does not mean that it is impossible to license. It just means that the process is not as straightforward as adding an open license to the design. In thinking about licensing open source hardware, it is critical to understand what you are actually licensing—and what you do not have any power to license.

Copyright, Patent, and Trademark: Rights That You Might Be Able to License

Before considering the parts of a given project that could be licensed in an open source hardware way, you must first understand a little bit about the different types of intellectual property. Being able to identify the contours of each will help you to understand which rights you might actually have and how you might want to license them.

Copyrights and patents are designed as inducements to create. The theory is that, in return for spending the time and energy creating something and sharing it with the world, the creator receives a limited monopoly on that thing from the government. Although they are often lumped together, copyright, patent, and trademark are actually complementary sets of rights.

Copyright

Copyright is a type of intellectual property that most people encounter on a daily basis (Table 3.1). In large part, this daily interaction flows from the types of things that copyright protects and how a work qualifies for protection.

Copyright is intended to protect "creative" works. Generally speaking, creative works are the types of things that you would expect an artist to produce. However, in the context of copyright, creative works are defined fairly broadly. The category goes well beyond things like sculptures, paintings, and songs. Copyright essentially protects any slightly

Table 3.1 **Copyright Tip Sheet**

Types of Things Protected	Relevant Features
Painting	Automatic protection
Books	Protection lasts for life of author, plus 70 years after death
Movies	
Photographs	
Artistic sculptures	
Code	

creative thing that is written down—notes to yourself, doodles on a pad, the finger paint-ing of a child. It also protects software code as a "literary work" in the same way that it protects a novel.

As the name implies, copyright is primarily concerned with copying of the works that it protects. While plenty of other actions are regulated by copyright (for example, publicly performing a protected work, even if it does not create a copy, can violate the copyright), as a general matter copyright violations occur when a protected work is copied without the permission of the person who owns the rights to it. This copying can take the form of literal copying (e.g., duplicating a movie file) or nonliteral copying (e.g., turning a novel into a movie).

Getting a copyright is easy. Copyright automatically protects the types of works that fall within its purview. While there are many reasons to register your copyright, a covered work is protected from the moment it exists ("fixed in a tangible medium" is the technical term). That means that everyone is the owner of thousands, and possibly tens of thousands of copyrights—whether they want them or not.

How long does that protection last? For quite a while. For most works, protection lasts for the entire lifetime of the author plus 70 years after his or her death. The reason so many of us feel surrounded by copyrights is because they are so easy to get and last for so long.

Patent

Whereas copyright focuses on artistic works, *patents* focus on "useful articles," which are things that do stuff[1] (Table 3.2). You can think of these as the things that engineers pro-duce. For most potential open source hardware projects, "things that do stuff" will form the heart of the project. For that reason, it is likely that most of the important parts of the project fall within the scope of patent law, not copyright law.

Unlike with copyright, just because something is protectable by patent does not mean that it will ever actually be protected by patent. To obtain a patent you need to apply for

---

1. In addition to traditional "utility" patents, you can get design patents, which are something of a middle ground between a copyright and a patent. They protect nonfunctional parts of objects, but only for 14 years.

Table 3.2 **Patent Tip Sheet**

Types of Things Protected	Relevant Features
Microchips	Need to apply to protection
Mechanical tools	Protection lasts for 20 years
Processes	Must be truly novel for protection

it—a process that costs both time and money. In addition to filling out paperwork, you will need to prove that the thing that you are trying to patent is novel, meaning it is actually new in the world.

If and when you make it through the patent application process and are granted a patent, that patent will last for 20 years. While 20 years is a long time, it is significantly shorter than a copyright's protection (the creator's lifetime plus 70 years).

Finally, patent law and copyright law are mutually exclusive. In other words, something either fits within the scope of patent law *or* it fits within the scope of copyright law. In cases where an object seems to combine both creative and functional parts, the law does its best to separate the two elements out. The goal of this process is to avoid giving copyright protection to functional items outside of its traditional scope.

Trademark

In contrast to copyrights and patents, *trademarks* are all about identifying goods in the market and giving consumers' confidence in what they are buying (Table 3.3). If you have a headache and run to the pharmacy in search of some painkillers, you want to be sure that the bottle marked "Tylenol" actually came from the Tylenol people. Perhaps just as important, if you buy the Tylenol bottle and something goes wrong, it is important to know that you could sue the Tylenol people for harming you. What is critical about trademark is that it is a way for a manufacturer to identify itself in the marketplace.

Trademark is also limited in important ways. At their core, copyrights and patents are about copying or reproducing. Trademark law does not really care about copying for the sake of copying. Rather, trademark law cares about using marks in commerce and confusing consumers.

That means that not every use of a trademark qualifies as trademark infringement. Using someone else's trademark in an attempt to pass off your product as theirs is trademark

Table 3.3 **Trademark Tip Sheet**

Types of Things Protected	Relevant Features
Company/product names	Need to apply for protection
Company/product logos	No explicit term limit
Nonfunctional elements of appearance that help identify product	Does not prevent unauthorized use for comparison/compatibility purposes

infringement. But using someone else's trademark in a comparison or as a descriptor is not trademark infringement.

For example, using the "Arduino" trademark on a microprocessor that I create myself will be trademark infringement: A consumer might (wrongly) think that Arduino was behind my microprocessor as well. In contrast, describing my microprocessor as "Arduino-compatible" may not be trademark infringement. In this second example, I am using Arduino's trademark to explain a feature of my own board, not to suggest that Arduino made it. It would be pretty hard to tell a potential customer that my microprocessor is compatible with Arduino without using the word "Arduino," and the law recognizes that fact. Similarly, I can use the Arduino trademark for comparison—"My microprocessor is five times slower and ten times harder to use than Arduino"—without running into trademark trouble.

Finally, the process of getting a trademark is something like an easier version of getting a patent. You still need to apply for the trademark and fill out forms, but the process will probably be easier and faster than a patent application. You may still need to hire a lawyer to help you with this process, but the bill should be significantly lower than the bill for a patent application.

Actually Licensing a Copyright, Patent, or Trademark

The previous discussion of the general types of intellectual property is all well and good, but if you are reading this book, you are probably a bit more interested in their application.

Licensing a Copyright

As mentioned earlier in this chapter, copyrights are the type of intellectual property that most people think of first. Copyrights are easy to get, so almost everyone has some. Also, because software is protected by copyright, copyright forms the core of the open source software movement. It is only natural to try and draw parallels when thinking about open source hardware.

But hardware is different, and not just because it is tangible. Because the core of most open source hardware projects is some sort of functionality—which is excluded from the world of copyright—copyright may not actually protect very much of an open source hardware product.

Of course, this does not mean that nothing in an open source hardware project will be protectable by copyright. Obviously, any software you include in your project is protectable by copyright and should be licensed accordingly. Many (but not necessarily all) design files will be protectable by copyright as well. Also, in most cases, nonfunctional, decorative flourishes are exactly the type of thing that is protectable by copyright.

For example, the Evil Mad Scientist Diavolino development board has a cool design screened onto its backside (http://shop.evilmadscientist.com/productsmenu /tinykitlist/180-diavolino). That design does not contribute to the actual working of the board; it would work fine without it. But it is a nice artistic flourish—exactly the type of nonfunctional flourish that is protectable by copyright. In contrast, the mostly functional designs on the front of the board that identify the pins and various components are much less likely to be protected by copyright.

Thus the nonfunctional design elements of your project may very well be protected by copyright and, therefore, licensable under existing open licenses, such as Creative Commons. That protection will not extend to the functional parts of the project, however.

If you are looking for a good rule of thumb about which parts of your project might be protectable by copyright, ask yourself what would happen if the part in question disappeared. If the project still works as expected, the part is probably protected by copyright (or totally unnecessary and should be removed, but that's an entirely different discussion). If the project stops working, or stops working as well, then the part may be the kind of functional element that is protectable by patent.

Licensing a Patent

At first glance, patents seem to be at the core of open source hardware. After all, patents protect things that do things—that's hardware! And if patents are to hardware as copyrights are to software, then the key to licensing open source hardware is to find a way to license the patents.

While reasonable on its face, this impulse breaks down in practice. First, as discussed earlier, just because something is the type of useful object that falls within the scope of patent does not mean that it is actually patentable. To get a patent, you need to prove that the thing itself is novel. For many projects, that simply will not be possible. While it might be a new open source hardware project, there may be plenty of earlier examples that would prevent it from actually being patentable.

Perhaps more importantly, even if your project could qualify for a patent, getting a patent is expensive in terms of both time and money. Obviously, this is a barrier to open source hardware projects that are bootstrapping or that do not have easy access to patent attorneys. Of course, these descriptions apply to many hardware start-ups.

There is also another barrier to obtaining a patent that is unique to open source hardware. One of the things that makes open licenses like those maintained by Creative Commons so popular is that they allow people to give away rights that they acquired for free. Everything that you can license with a CC license is protected by copyright, whether you like it or not. For many people, the fact that they made no effort to secure the copyright protection makes it that much easier to release it to the larger community.

Patent fundamentally shifts that calculus. You need to take affirmative, expensive steps to get that patent. Obtaining a patent with the specific purpose of broadly licensing it to the community can make the financial commitment a hard one to justify. This is especially true when other ways to share with the community—namely, not patenting your hardware at all and doing a good job of documenting the project—are so much easier. For many projects, obtaining a patent will be like building an expensive cage to trap a wild animal just so that you can turn around and set the animal free again. It is probably easier for everyone to just keep the animal—and the invention—free from IP restrictions in the first place.

In many ways, this lack of automatic protection is a great strength of open source hardware. Open licenses were originally designed to circumvent a defect in the law—namely, the problem that copyright was automatically locking up creativity for the life of the author plus 70 years. In many cases, that defect does not exist for hardware. Most hardware is born free, and anyone is free to copy it unless the creator goes out of his or her way to protect it.

Unfortunately, this freedom inherent in hardware—in so many ways a positive thing—also comes at a cost: virality. Because there is an existing right (copyright) that requires permission for copying, that permission can be given conditionally. You are allowed to copy a copyrighted work under an open source license as long as you allow people to copy your work on the same terms. This factor has helped the idea of sharing spread beyond communities that care about sharing for its own sake and into communities that just need to access the stuff. Without an underlying patent, however, it will be harder to pull that second community—the one that doesn't care about sharing but wants access to the stuff—into the world of open source hardware.

Ultimately, only two types of open source hardware projects are likely to be interested in getting patents. The first are projects attached to institutions that have a process in place to patent everything as a matter of course. In those cases, because the patents already exist, it makes sense to find a way to openly license them. The second are projects backed by individuals or companies with lots of money who feel truly passionately about open source hardware. In those cases, the value of having a viral license that can spread the ethos of open source hardware will balance out the costs of actually obtaining the patent. If you choose to license your patent, you should talk to a patent attorney, because each case is different.

Licensing a Trademark

In the context of open source hardware, a trademark may become the most important type of intellectual property. This is because of the trademark's ability to identify the source of a product in the marketplace. The source is not only who conceived of it, but who actually assembled it and stands behind its quality. Even if you cannot control how people copy or incorporate your project into their own, you can control how they identify it.

Let's turn again to the world of open source software to see how this works. Mozilla owns the trademark for the Firefox web browser. Because Firefox is an open source browser, anyone can take the code and adapt it to their own purposes (e.g., Ice Weasel is a version of Firefox for the Debian operating system). However, while anyone is free to take the code, they cannot take the name along with the code. Only Mozilla's version of Firefox can use the Firefox trademark.

The result of this is that if you, as a user, find a Firefox installer online, you can be confident that it will install the Mozilla version of Firefox. It does not really matter where you find the installer—on Mozilla's own website or on some third-party site. As long as it is branded as "Firefox,"[2] you know that Mozilla stands behind the browser.

---

2. And the person who put the installer there is not a trademark infringer peddling counterfeit versions of Firefox.

The same is true, but potentially even more so, in the world of hardware. Someone who is getting ready to buy a piece of open source hardware wants to know who designed the product, just as someone who is getting ready to download some open source software wants to know who designed the software. But that open source hardware customer also cares about who actually assembled the product. While anyone can compile a software package with essentially the same result, two different people can assemble an identical piece of hardware with very different results.

For this reason, controlling the trademark of your open source hardware project can be very important. Although you will have to come to terms with people creating poorly made versions of your product (it will happen), passing those poorly made versions off as coming from you should be a different matter. Registering your trademark helps you to build a reputation for quality and reliability by giving you the ability to make sure that only products that are up to your standards get to use the name.

This does not mean that you cannot license your trademark to others. In theory, you could license your trademark under the same types of terms that you license copyrights or patents. You could allow other parties to use your trademark as long as they complied with conditions that forced them to share their derivative in the same way, or to not use the mark on commercial products.

In practice, it probably makes more sense to hold your mark a bit closer to the chest. Remember, a trademark is your project's identity in the marketplace. People will rightly assume that anything identified with the mark came from you and is up to your standards. If they find that not to be the case, it may undermine their confidence in everything that you do. If you choose to license your trademark, you should talk to a trademark attorney, because each case is different.

What to Do Now

By this point in the chapter, you may have concluded that the licensing issues surrounding open source hardware are a bit more complicated than those surrounding open source software. If you haven't, you haven't been reading that closely. Unlike software, which is automatically and completely protected by copyright from the moment it is typed out, hardware is a mix of possibly copyright-protected elements, patent-protected elements, and entirely unprotected elements. As a consequence, it is unlikely that we will see an easy-to-understand, widely applicable, commonly agreed-upon license for open source hardware soon.

Fortunately, this does not mean that all hope is lost. Remember, the core of open source hardware is about sharing. Regardless of the license you do or do not use, sharing means documenting and engaging with the community. The truth of the matter is that your time may be better spent documenting your project than trying to figure out how to license each and every part of it.

That being said, licensing is important. It can make your intentions clear and give people confidence that they can build upon your project without creating a legal trap for themselves. The easiest part of licensing your hardware will probably be finding an open copyright license that has terms with which you are comfortable. To the extent that there are copyrightable parts of your project (including software), using the license you find will give people permission to use those parts of the project with legal clarity. This is a good first step, but you need to be realistic about what the copyright license does and does not cover.

No copyright license can cover the functional parts of your project. That means coming to terms with the fact that people may copy or build upon the functional parts of your project without complying with your copyright license. If they do, it is your responsibility to respond in a way that accurately represents your actual ability to control the use of your project. If someone is copying functional parts of your project in a way you do not approve of and all you have are a bunch of copyrights, don't threaten them with a copyright lawsuit. That's a threat that you can't back up—and it is an obnoxious one to make. Don't be that person.

Once you have your copyright house in order, you will need to think long and hard about patents. In most cases, patenting something just so you can license it openly will not make financial sense. But if you decide to go that route, make sure you choose an open license that is written specifically for patents. Simply adding a copyright license to a patent will just create confusion.

Finally, consider obtaining a trademark. In many ways, your trademark will become your identity in the marketplace. It will allow you to control how others perceive your project, and possibly whether people develop confidence in it. It takes some money and effort to apply for a trademark, but in many cases it is well worth it.

Summary

Where does this leave us? The good news is that most hardware is born open. Unless it is explicitly covered by a patent, all hardware is available to be copied, improved, and built upon. That puts hardware well ahead of software. The less good news is that licensing hardware is more complicated than licensing software. It may be a long time before there is something as simple and all-encompassing for hardware as a Creative Commons or GPL license, because the basis for licensing software is so much more straightforward than the basis for licensing hardware.

Where does that leave you? First, take the time to document your project. Regardless of whether the hardware is protected by intellectual property regulations, documentation is a big part of what separates open source hardware from hardware that merely lacks intellectual property protections (and go read Chapter 14, Taxonomy of Hardware Documentation). Second, if your project has parts that are protected by copyright, pick a permissive license. This makes it easy for people to use your project, and it gives them guidance on how you would prefer they use it. Third, a trademark may end up being the most important type of protection for open source hardware projects looking to scale up. Being able to show the world that your hardware comes from you can go a long way in building your reputation and an enthusiastic community for your work.

Resources

Here are resources from which to learn more about the topics discussed in this chapter.

General IP News Sources

Public Knowledge: www.publicknowledge.org

Peer to Patent: www.peertopatent.org

Article One: www.articleonepartners.com

Ask Patents: www.patents.stackexchange.com

EFF Chair to Eliminate Stupid Patents: www.eff.org/about/staff/daniel-nazer

Resources from the Copyright Office

Copyright Office circular: www.copyright.gov/circs/circ01.pdf

Resources from the U.S. Patent and Trademark Office about Trademarks

Trademark Basics: http://www.uspto.gov/trademarks/basics/index.jsp

Trademark Process: http://www.uspto.gov/trademarks/process/TMIN.jsp

4

Standardization of Open Source Hardware

Ed Baafi

"Our heritage and ideals, our code and standards—the things we live
by and teach our children—are preserved or diminished by how freely
we exchange ideas and feelings."

—Walt Disney

This chapter defines further standards from which open source hardware can benefit,
beyond the Open Source Hardware Definition and Best Practices. This ironic quote from
Walt Disney, given how the copyright world has locked down cultural exchange on be-
half of Disney movies, is actually quite valid when it comes to open exchange within the
open source community. This chapter focuses the goals of making open even more open
through standardization and walks through several instances of module design principles as
a method of further opening your hardware.

At their core, standards are a way for people to work together. Think of all the standards we take for granted each hour in every day of our lives. Your alarm starts to buzz
at 6:45 A.M. You quickly shower and get dressed to be ready for an early 8:30 meeting.
When you get in the car, you glance at the gas gauge and notice it's almost empty. After
stopping to get gas and getting caught at a few stop lights, you walk into the office with
just a few minutes to spare. You say a hurried "Good morning" to a coworker as you make
your way to the conference room.

If you're already thinking about standards, you might have noticed all the standards at
play as you make your way through your day. But if you're like most of us, you take all of
these standards for granted and just assume that's how things are. Without standard definitions of time, how would we plan times to meet others? Without standard electrical
outlets, how would we plug in our alarm clock (or phone with an alarm app)? Without
standards, would we even have a phone at all? With no standard sizes, how would you buy
clothes without first trying them on? And without the communication standards commonly called language, how would we communicate with others at all?

Unless you live in the woods, isolated from civilization, you most assuredly rely on many different standards in every aspect of your life. Some standards are fuzzy, like clothes sizes (which can run smaller or larger than the norm) or the gas gauge that dips below empty (yet you still have enough gas to make it to the station). Some are firm, like standard scientific measurements and the meaning of a red traffic light. And just like standards in general, hardware standards are a way for people, companies, and devices to work together. Think about the USB flash drive you may use to transfer files between computers and other devices. When companies realize they would benefit by not isolating themselves and their products from other companies, competition is put aside and standards like USB are born and given a chance to grow.

When open source hardware needs to communicate with other hardware products, whether open or proprietary, mainstream standards including USB, Bluetooth, and Wi-Fi are obvious choices. But there are other forms of communication and collaboration that open source hardware makers are concerned with beyond interfacing with products, including making their hardware easier to modify or reproduce. These are the areas where new standards specific to open source hardware will emerge out of necessity.

Firming up the Soft Parts: Making Software Firmer

Software, by definition, is modifiable and reproducible. This is so inherent to the concept of software that the word "soft" in its name refers to this almost clay-like property. Like clay, software can take almost any form, being molded into one thing one moment and into something completely different the next. Because software is stored like any other file on computers and devices, reproducing it is as simple as copying a file. Of course, depending on the programming language, software "code" is often compiled into a machine-readable (but not human-readable) form called binary code. Because binary code is not human readable, it is very difficult to modify it, similar to clay that has been baked in a kiln. One of the requirements of open source, however, is that code is available in the original and most human-readable form, which aims to ensure that all open source software is modifiable. In fact, it is software's almost clay-like property that often makes it so difficult to modify. Open source developers say, "The source is open—go modify it," forgetting that there are so many ways to do so that the modifications may be difficult, or that once the software is modified it will never be practical that those changes get pulled back into the original open source project. Some of these considerations need to be explored before expecting others to modify or extend your work, and software's clay-like property needs to be "firmed up" to clarify how best to do so.

The process of firming up software is not to be confused with the term "firmware." **Firmware** consists of software that runs on hardware other than general-purpose computing platforms such as personal computers, tablets, or phones. This is a double entendre referring to the mixture of software running on hardware (i.e., soft + hard = firm). Updating the software running on these single-purpose computing platforms is often reserved for manufacturers, so the actual practice of updating this software once a product is shipped is actually quite rare. But for all intents and purposes, software and firmware are synonymous. Firming up software to enable modification is the same for traditional software as it is for firmware: It involves software running on hardware or, in this case, open source hardware.

Software Interfaces

One way to make software more "firm" so as to promote its modification is to use the concept of software interfaces. Such interfaces define how you talk to a piece of software without defining how it actually accomplishes this task. This modular technique allows different implementations of the same interface to be swapped out, allowing for much greater code reuse when only the code "hidden" behind the interface needs to be changed.

Take, for example, a communication interface that defines two methods: send and receive messages. Imagine that the system designer initially used only two implementations of this interface: one over USB and another over Bluetooth radio. By decoupling the interface definition from the implementation, the original designer makes it easy to add other communication channels that can replace these original implementations. This makes it possible for later developers to add a Twitter module that sends messages as Tweets and receives messages as Twitter mentions on a particular Twitter account.

When applying this concept to open source hardware, we can go one step further by using software interfaces to abstract whole classes of hardware and specify how we communicate with them. For instance, a system could consist of a button as input and an LED as output. Imagine we define the hardware interface with modular design as follows: The button exposes the "pressed" method, which returns whether it is currently being pressed, and the light exposes the "turn(on/off)" method, which allows the programmer to turn it on or off. Now imagine that the original hardware design had just a single LED and a small button that are mounted on a small device. By utilizing interfaces, we would enable future designers to modify the design to work with a large floor pad (that a user can step on) and control all the lights in a building instead of a single LED. Applying software interfaces to open source hardware is a powerful way to enable future modifications to the hardware that the original designers could never foresee.

Extensions: Plugins and Configurations versus Forks

While software interfaces are a great way to enable future modifications, they are typically used to modify the whole system for a new use or domain and rely on developers rather than end users to make these changes. In the open source world, this often results in multiple forks of a project for different use cases. A **fork** is created when a developer or set of developers starts working with a copy of the code and goes off in a new direction. Unless these changes are "merged" back into the original codebase quickly, it often becomes difficult to merge the code later to allow the developers to work together. In many cases, the original developers are not concerned with the problem domain addressed by the fork and cannot justify the overhead associated with maintaining the new code. Multiple forks for minor changes often result in wasted developer resources, including duplicated mainte- nance efforts that can be avoided with a bit of forethought.

If developers can anticipate which parts of a system people may want to customize, unnecessary forks can be avoided. One way to accomplish this is by providing a number of ways that the system can be configured. For instance, imagine a hardware system that contains a piezo vibration sensor. To encourage customization of the hardware, the origi- nal developer can allow the end user or other developers to configure the amplification (gain) to allow different piezo sensors to be chosen while not affecting the rest of the system. Configuration options are a great way to enable modifications without writing any new code!

Plugins are another way to enable customization by end users and developers alike. For developers, a well-crafted plugin system allows one to add to a system without forking the original code. Browser plugins are a great example. While only a handful of popular browsers are used by the majority of Internet users, thousands of plugins and extensions are available for each of these browsers, enabling browsing experiences to be as diverse as the Internet's user base.

Programming Environments, Libraries, and Compliers

As we continue to discuss software standards for open source hardware, it is important to note that it is only possible to write software for a hardware system if that hardware contains some kind of microcontroller or other processor to run it. Thus, one of the most powerful ways to modify and extend open source hardware is to replace the processor with a different, possibly cheaper or more capable one. Of course, if doing so means devel- opers have to learn new programming tools or write whole chunks of library code to run on the new processor, then swapping out processors will not be practical. Open source hardware can benefit greatly with standard programming environments and libraries.

We have seen some of these benefits with the Wiring language and integrated devel- opment environment (IDE), which were created by Hernando Barragan and extended by the Arduino project. To date, Wiring has been ported to more than a dozen different microcontroller architectures, along with many IDEs for the different microcontroller families. As a consequence, people can move between microcontrollers with greater ease and products that are programmable with Wiring are ripe for porting to different micro- controllers. This work is still quite fragmented, as there are many individual forks of the Wiring project, but these efforts hint at the demand for unified programming environ- ments and libraries that work across multiple microcontrollers.

Behind the scenes, standard compilers have played a big role in unifying programming environments and libraries. Microcontrollers often require special language extensions to support programming languages like C/C++, and each microcontroller architecture requires changes to existing compilers in the form of a new "backend." Without standard open source compilers, such as GCC and LLVM, it would not be possible to truly write once and deploy anywhere.

Bootloaders and Programming Tools: Making Traditional Firmware Softer

As mentioned earlier, the term "firmware" is a double entendre pointing to software that runs on hardware (i.e., soft + hard = firm), and highlighting the fact that it is usually harder to update than general-purpose software once a product is deployed to end users. Of course, open source hardware is all about letting users modify the products they use. Thus getting new software onto your open source hardware device should be made as easy as possible.

While many electronic products may be programmable during production, or possibly in the field with expensive specialty equipment, it is important that microcontroller-based open source hardware should be easily programmable with common tools. By employing a USB-based bootloader, a microcontroller can be programmed in-system by simply plugging in a standard USB cable and connecting to a computer. If you really want to enable your end users, care should be taken to simplify the setup of the host computer, including drivers or software to run there.

Softening up the Hard Parts: Making Hardware More Flexible

Whereas software has a clay-like nature, hardware is by definition fixed in stone, or at least fixed in whatever circuit board reaches an end user. While experienced electrical engineers or motivated tinkerers can repurpose any piece of hardware to add new functionalities or simply for fun, the average piece of hardware goes unchanged during its life from factory floor to dump site. But this does not have to be the case. Just like with software, our goal is to make hardware practically modifiable by many people rather than by just a small set of dedicated enthusiasts. With a little forethought and effort, hardware can be made almost as flexible as software. Just imagine how much electronic waste could be avoided if all of our outdated electronics could simply be repurposed for a new and important function!

Standard Electronic Components and Mechanical Hardware

Personal fabrication tools and online services make it possible for almost any motivated hardware developer to get a new circuit board, mechanical system, and enclosure in his or her hands in a matter of a few hours to just a few days. 3D printed plastics and metals as well as chemically etched copper circuit boards are like clay that can be sculpted into just about any form. Just like a software compiler can take a high-level software program and compile it into machine code to run on your personal computer or tablet, computer-aided manufacturing (CAM) software can take high-level computer-aided design (CAD) descriptions of your mechanism, enclosures, and circuit boards and produce them in physical form right before your eyes.

Hardware is just like software, you say? Not quite—or at least not yet. While some materials and processes are as easily moldable as clay, other components and hardware still have to be ordered online or sourced locally. For example, a given widget might require hundreds of electrical components, a few off-the-shelf motors, and a dozen or so fasteners (e.g., screws, bolts) before other developers can begin to make additions to your design. Having a circuit board, mechanisms, and enclosure in your hand in hours means nothing if you have to wait days or weeks for the last of the required components to arrive. The situation becomes even worse if you have to search for the requirements and order them from dozens of different vendors. Hardware becomes truly accessible when it relies only on standard and readily available components and hardware. When designing your open source hardware, take care to do research into the availability of the components you are evaluating not just online, but everywhere you expect your product to reach.

Physical Communication

How your open source hardware communicates is just as important as what it's made of. There are many standards—for example, USB, I2C, RS-232, UART, 1-Wire, Ethernet, Bluetooth, Zigbee, and RS-485—that you can employ to easily communicate with and between your hardware (also known as device-to-device communication). While each of these standards serves roughly the same purpose, not all are created equal when it comes to making open source hardware accessible. When choosing the communication technologies you will use, it is important to continue to weigh the burden you are imposing on future developers who wish to extend or modify your designs. Considerations include whether the communication protocol requires any expensive or otherwise difficult-to-acquire external hardware. Are there any regulatory or IP implications in place if users wish to alter the hardware? How portable is the code required to communicate with the given technology if your end users want to move to different processors? Is the communication technology peer-to-peer or does it require a "master" node to coordinate communication with other devices?

Of course, how many existing devices you can communicate with is also an important consideration. For example, choosing to use USB in a design might mean it is easier to connect to personal computers, but might actually make it more difficult to interface with other open source hardware. This situation arises because USB generally requires specialized microcontrollers, introduces fees and bureaucratic oversight by the USB implementers' forum, and requires a master node (host) to control the bus. In cases where you must use USB, it may be advisable to add a secondary interface by simply exposing an unused UART from your hardware's microcontroller to lower the threshold for future communication. Remember to choose what your hardware says carefully and how it communicates just as wisely!

Hardware Interfaces

We covered software interfaces earlier as a mechanism that allows different implementations of the same interface to be swapped out, allowing much greater code reuse when only the code "hidden" behind the interface needs to be changed. We gave an example where a system could be designed with a simple push button and could be swapped out with a large floor pad simply by implementing the interface in software to communicate with the new floor switch. With hardware interfaces, we can extend this concept to allow new hardware implementations to be incorporated without writing a single line of code.

For instance, a MIDI-enabled keyboard can communicate with an external synthesizer through a standard cable and a standard protocol. The MIDI keyboard sends notes to the synthesizer, and the synthesizer responds by playing the notes through an amplifier connected with a standard ¼-inch audio cable. The owner of such a system is free to replace the synthesizer with an audio sampler while still retaining the keyboard and audio amplifier. This is because there are two standard hardware interfaces at play here: the ¼-inch audio "line-out" and the MIDI protocol and cable. The key point is that the interfaces define both the physical connections (MIDI and audio cables) and the data (analog audio and digital MIDI) sent over the physical wires. Enable a true plug-and-play experience by designing, contributing to, and utilizing standard hardware interfaces!

Modularity as a Design Principle

When we set out to design new things and are treading too much on something that already exists, we might think of the age-old warning not to "reinvent the wheel." But let's give ourselves more credit than that. As designers and developers, we know that the "wheel" already exists; hence I prefer to use the phrase "reimplementing the wheel," instead. This phrase points to some of the underlying reasons why we might attempt such an undertaking, such as existing wheels being too costly, or not having some functionality that we would like to add for a particular application. In such a case, we are forced to reimplement the wheel by inventing a cheaper production method or enabling a new functionality.

An end user of your open source hardware project might be thinking the same thing: that your wonderful widget lacks one piece of important functionality. Of course, by choosing open source, you've made it possible to take your design files and modify them—but doing so requires the new developer to get the new design manufactured. Certainly, 3D printing and circuit board manufacturing services are making this undertaking more accessible, but what about the user who needs to make that change before lunch time? By employing modular design principles, we allow our users to reconfigure their open source devices when and how they see fit. Remember, it's not necessary to reimplement your entire wheel if you let future developers pick a tire, pick a spoke, and pick a hub!

Other Standardization and Regulation

Because the open source hardware movement is so young, a great many ideas are laid out in this book for other types of standards. These topics include community-based standardization, such as attribution and documentation, as well as standards created by governing bodies, which are more along the lines of regulation. Another example where standardization offers benefits is found in Appendix B of this book: Open Source Hardware Security Do's and Don'ts. These recommendations can be thought of as standards for security and hardware.

Attribution in open source hardware is a form of personal currency and is included in several open source licensing structures. As yet, however, the etiquette and standard of how and where we do this remain to be determined. Because most circuit boards have a physical footprint too small to list the contributors on, it is standard to list them somewhere in the documentation, such as the README file and the product description. If you are giving a presentation about your open source hardware projects, perhaps it should be standard practice to list your fellow contributors and the original designers of your open hardware product at the end of presentations like movie credits. This would ensure the provenance is not lost.

The standards written into the Open Source Hardware Definition, such as what determines open source hardware, were foundational. Now that a standard has been set for defining open source hardware, we can delve into different areas of standardization. For example, one standard is defined for licensing source files: that source files must be licensed openly. But other types of documentation, such as tutorials and books, do not have to be open for a given piece of hardware to be considered open source. For more information on documentation standards, read Chapter 14.

Open source hardware has always dealt with external standards and regulations as well—for example, FCC regulations ensure products don't interfere with each other or with life-safety devices. As mentioned within this chapter, USB and Bluetooth are standards with which the electronics community, open and closed, is accustomed to. However, as open source hardware branches out, regulations are beginning to crop up in more places that affect open source hardware design and distribution, such as ITAR standards and FAA or FDA regulations. Although some standards are already in place, open source hardware could lead to new governmental standards for things such as sustainability from an ecological perspective, in which the focus is reducing e-waste. Other new standards might deal with creating "fair trade in hardware," thereby ensuring that hardware is built with certain humanitarian standards. Chapter 15 discusses how open source hardware is primed to establish these standards due to its transparent nature.

ITAR, Public Domain, and Fundamental Research
Stephen Murphey

Any U.S. citizen (or anyone interested in working with U.S. citizens) should be familiar with ITAR because it will potentially affect what you share and how you share any of your designs. ITAR stands for International Traffic in Arms Regulations. Open source hardware is all about sharing your designs—this an important point. ITAR, however, is about keeping U.S. military technology out of the hands of the country's enemies. Since most space technology could be used for military purposes, pretty much all space technology is classified under ITAR. This means you can't just share your rocket design with a friend in Europe or even post the design online, because that is considered exporting. You have to fill out the appropriate paperwork and manage a maze of federal regulations—probably more than you want to deal with for a small open source hardware project. So, if all of your project members are U.S. citizens (or none of them are), congratulations, you just made your life much easier!

There are two exceptions: public domain and fundamental research. First, anything that has been made publicly available in the public domain can be shared freely. The second exception is, in my opinion, more interesting because it enables the sharing of newer technology. Fundamental research (also called basic research) provides universities with the opportunity to publish and promote their work around the world. This is why the design for CubeSats have been made publicly available for more than a decade: They were designed at Stanford University. This exception is limited to projects associated with universities, however, and does not apply to personal or commercial projects.

Summary

This chapter asked you to consider both formal and informal standards, as well as existing and emerging standards within hardware and software. You now have a framework to think about how existing standards might help or hinder your users and how future standards should be considered to make open source hardware as strong as possible. Many standards deal with interfacing one platform to the next, be it software to hardware, hardware to hardware, or hardware to human. As an open source hardware developer, you're tasked with creating these interfaces as openly, transparently, and accessibly as possible.

II

Hands On!

5 The Design Process: How to Get from Nothing to Something

6 Making a Derivative

7 Modifying the Shape of an Arduino

8 Remix a 3D Print(er)

9 Wearables

10 Physical Materials

5

The Design Process: How to Get from Nothing to Something

Amanda Wozniak

"The only way of discovering the limits of the possible is to venture a little way past them into the impossible."

—Arthur C. Clarke

The creative process can be frustratingly existential. You have an idea for something you want to produce and the concept of going from idea to object seems straightforward enough—yet, it's never that simple. Every artist and maker knows the deep effort it takes to turn an ephemeral idea into that first functional prototype. In most cases, success comes only after several rounds of failure, backtracking, and reconsideration in a near-continuous cycle of elation and despair. But once you finally hold an object in your hands that does what you've designed it to do, the thrill is unparalleled.

Creative iteration is just one small step in making, producing, and shipping hardware. In full-scale product development, there are so many logistics to handle that if we were to design hardware in the purely creative mode, we would never be able to ship product. Even after the design is done, that's just the beginning. Consider the effort it takes for you to make one thing well, and now imagine that you're trying to make 100, 1000, or 10,000 things in the exact same way. You should feel a little panicked and overwhelmed. The key lesson here is that it can be impossible to support full-scale production if you don't carefully consider the process by which you're making that object (or 10,000 copies). A good process can also help you with more than just volume production. The challenges of system design become similarly difficult and impractical to manage when you—the maker—are trying to push your designs from making simple components to ever larger and more complex projects. You need tools to manage an engineering project (or commercial art business) if you want to succeed.

Managing that exponentially increasing creative effort is where the engineering design process comes in. Most large-scale projects employ some process, so you may have heard some of this jargon before. For example, "Agile" is a popular software development philosophy, and the most common hardware design process is a "waterfall" workflow. Either way, engineering best practices are just a formal way of breaking down a project into phases and tasks so that complexity and production become manageable. In addition to setting goals and holding reviews, best practices include and require making an investment in your tools (computer-aided design [CAD] software, circuit references, old designs, test methods) and having enough discipline (whether it's you working alone or in a team) so that you pass only those circuits and designs that are truly ready to graduate to the next phase.

This chapter discusses the overall engineering design process for hardware. Starting with the definition of a project's scope and purpose, it covers the different tasks required to go from the prototype phase, through concept refinement, through iterative development, and, once the final design is locked down, through the final checks before releasing the project to manufacturing. This chapter also defines which files to generate as source files to label as open source hardware for a printed circuit board (PCB) design.

The Phase of Projects

Hacking is fun! You already know that if you start hacking on a project before you have a plan, it can be fun, but there's no guarantee that it will be productive. If you have a goal and a deadline, yet you're relying on a seat-of-the-pants prescient, "I'll know it when I see it," feeling to tell you when your project is done, that's not engineering—that's art. And it's hard to make art on command.

Whenever you set out to begin a project, whether you recognize it or not, your workflow naturally follows a set of phases. In project management and engineering design, each of these phases gets called out explicitly.

First, you have a grand (possibly vague) idea for something you want to build. Perhaps you'd like to make a derivative of the Blinky Buildings project from the walk-through in Chapter 6. This is your project's over-arching **purpose.** When you begin to think about the resources you have available, you might realize that there's only so much you can build with the time, money, and skill you have. Understanding what you will (or won't) be able to do from a practical standpoint sets your project's **scope.** Whatever your scope is, you know for your project to really work out, it has to have certain key features. These features can be anything from design elements to production requirements, but you need to settle this information about what you need to do and to build for your project to be a success. Whether you think about these needs in terms of analytical metrics or "I'll know it when I see it," they're critical and are called your **specifications and requirements.** The back-and-forth negotiation where you nail down the specific details of your purpose, resources, scope, and critical requirements is called the **product definition phase.** What you're left with at the end of this phase is your **definition.** With your formal definition in hand, it's time to get hacking.

The **design phase** is just the flow of going back and forth between generating and testing ideas that naturally occurs while building something. *Designing* is often done on paper or in a computer simulation, and *prototyping* is always physical. The design process is always iterative, but it's not a chicken-and-egg scenario. Your first **design input** is always your formal definition. Every successive prototype you build (whether it works or not) is considered a **design output.** The way you iterate during the design phase is by checking whether your prototype meets the requirements listed in your product definition. This often-neglected step is called **testing** (or sometimes **validation and verification**). Of course, design doesn't occur in a vacuum, and no one ever perfectly defined the scope of a project before starting to work. Lots of different design inputs may emerge while you're in the middle of working, whether it's something you failed to consider during the definition phase, a critical part that happens to be made of *unobtanium* (an unobtainable part), or a problem you learned about only during testing. We'll get into how to handle those new needs in the next bit.

Once your design meets all of your critical requirements, you can launch into the **release phase.** During release, you start with your final preproduction prototype that's practically perfect in every way, and test it to the point where you have decided that you are ready to commit—that is, this exact version of the product is what you will sell to customers. Once you're in release, change *ist verboten*. All you should do during this phase is double-check the technical and ephemeral details for your project one last time and make sure that this version of your design is *the one.*

In the event that you catch a bug and need to change any part of your design that isn't something cosmetic (such as silk-screen color), then you need to think long and hard about the best way to fix it. If it's a major design change (and not, say, buying a different 0603 1k resistor to use), you absolutely need to stop where you're at, go back to the design phase, and make another preproduction prototype. Then start the release process all over again. This process may seem tedious, but the release phase is your last critical check to make sure you've caught everything before you commit a huge amount of time and money to go to **manufacturing.** Any last-minute, unchecked detail in design or something you've forgotten to check in testing can become a serious risk once manufacturing is involved. (If you don't believe me, check out Matt Bolton's chapter on manufacturing, Chapter 12, Accelerate from Making to Manufacturing.) Once you *honestly* feel there's no way your project can possibly fail, then and only then do you hit the big red button and release your design to production.

Figure 5.1 shows the process that industry follows (or should follow) for many products that have made it to market. There are different versions for different industries, and this example was adapted from the FDA's *Design Control Guidance for Medical Device Manufacturers* because medical regulatory approval is incredibly strict and tries to manage safety-critical complexity with the best of intentions. Notice the locks? Each one is a mandatory review point. You may not be making a medical device or a system that needs to pass CE Mark safety certification, but you're still taking plenty of business risks whenever your goal is to ship hardware. At these review steps, spend time to take a long, hard look at your project and your progress to date. Invite others to review your design, and make sure

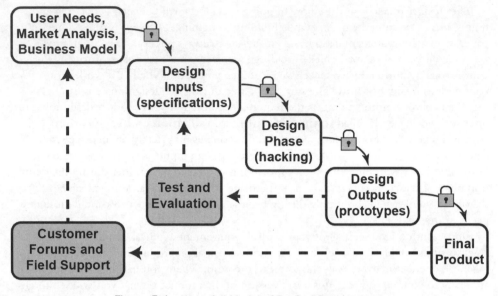

Figure 5.1   Waterfall Model of Product Development.
(Source: CC-BY-SA Amanda Wozniak)

everything looks good before you graduate to the next step. One common criticism of the waterfall workflow is that you have to go through the entire process before you iterate. In reality, it's the spirit that you want to follow. It's never too early to ask whether your design-in-progress will meet the target goals, and only solid and tested designs should move on to production.

Iterative Design and Concept Refinement

A good idea is just the beginning. In the previous section, we pretended every hacker and maker would have enough information to be able to make a winning product definition, just from a starting idea. That wasn't very nice. To help you decide exactly what to make, here are some leading questions that will give you a place to start (so that you can get down to the business of *how* you're going to make something and make it *profitably*):

- Is there a market for what I want to make?
- How big is that market?
- Who are my target users?
- What do my target users want?
- What do my users need this product to do?
- Which features do I need to add to make this usable?
- Which features are critical and which ones are optional?

- How much can I charge for this and still make a profit?
- How many of these will I make?
- What is my deadline? Will someone else scoop me by getting to market first?
- Do I want this to be a kit?
- (If assembled) Will I make this myself, or will I contract it to a manufacturer?
- Does this product require any regulatory certifications (e.g., child safety, FCC, FDA, CE)?

Answering these questions will give you an idea of your starting requirements such as target audience (useful for beta testing and good usability design), required versus optional functionality, maximum materials and assembly cost, timeline, and assembly method.

Many details can be worked out on paper or during the initial design phase, such as whether a specific type of amplifier IC (integrated circuit) is readily available in the volumes you'll need to buy. As mentioned earlier, however, a lot of different design inputs will inevitably crop up during your design phase that may impact your product, but that you won't learn about until after you've built the first prototype and either tested it yourself or given it to someone to try out. These issues include the following problems:

- Your prototype circuit doesn't work. At. All.
- Your circuit only works . . . sort of.
- Your circuit works, but it breaks easily.
- The LCD you were using isn't made anymore.
- The library part for your microcontroller had flipped pin assignments.
- You made the PCB's through holes for your LEDs too small.
- You misaligned your board-to-board headers. Your boards won't mate.
- You just realized your bill of materials cost is over budget.
- NASA called. Even they couldn't build your kit.

At this point, you should also recognize why some form of formal testing is a gatekeeping item in iterating through the design process. Whether it's a manufacturing test, a circuit performance test, a unit stress test, an interoperability test, or a user experience beta test, the only way to discover the shortcomings and limitations of your design is to see how well it works in all the ways you intend for people to use it. It should also be clear that it's not just users you have to worry about—you also need to beta test your production line. You'll never know if you have the right PCB footprint for your power supply capacitor until you run a manufacturing test, make a board, and solder that capacitor into place. Then you need to ensure that your contract manufacturer can solder 10,000 capacitors to 10,000 boards and have the process work every time.

Mistakes, bad design, sourcing scarcity, and manufacturing challenges are issues you can never escape. But by taking a methodical approach to design, they become the kinds of problems you can tackle while they're small—before they become showstoppers.

Setting up Your Workflow

No one ever makes a perfect PCB from scratch. Most projects start with bread-boarding bits and pieces together to make a proof of concept. The hardware doesn't have to be small, perfect, or manufacturable at this point: You just want to prove your circuit works and to determine which parts you need to build it.

Once you have that first proof of concept made, the next step is to move your design from the bench-top into CAD software so that you can make a PCB. This workflow is the same no matter which program you're using (e.g., Eagle, Cadence, Altium).

First: select your parts—and I mean, really select your parts. For anything critical (like microcontrollers or any nongeneric component), you should have both a **manufacturer part number** and a **vendor part number** for the specific part you're using. For generic parts you can buy anywhere, you can cheat and just specify the part as "MLCC Capacitor, Footprint: 0603, Value: 10 nF." Next, make sure you have each of those parts correctly entered into your **part library.** For extra credit, have a physical sample of the part on hand and use it to confirm that both the **schematic symbol** and the **part PCB footprint** are correct. One trick I use to check part footprints is to print out a 1:1 copy of the PCB on a paper; I then set the parts down on it to visually check the dimensions and placement.

Once your have a part in your library, you can place it in your **schematic.** In the **schematic capture** process, focus on reproducing the logical design of your bread-board circuit. While you're adding components to your parts library and schematic, you should also be adding them to a separate document called your **bill of materials** (**BOM**). Once the schematic is complete and you've passed the **design review,** you can start the **PCB layout** (in the same CAD program). All of these files should be shared as your source files for making open source hardware. The layout phase is where you focus on how all of your parts will physically be arranged and connected on your printed circuit board. During this phase, you'll want to think about all of the manufacturing rules that Matt will explain in more detail in Chapter 12, and you'll want to conclude this phase with a **layout review.** If you do not work at a company with a formal design review process, ask a friend in your field to review your board or make friends with your local hackerspace. If you can't phone a friend, many PCB fabricators and assembly houses provide **design for manufacturing** rule-checking services to flag errors in your final layout.

Finally, to get to your next prototype and have your ultimate design output, you'll need to generate **Gerbers** (board fabrication files that describe the layout of your board layers in a vector format). Your Gerber package (also called "artwork" or "PCB prints") will include a file for each physical layer of the board design. For a two-layer PCB, typical files are as follows: top copper (sometimes called the component-side copper); bottom copper (sometimes called the solder-side copper); top and bottom solder mask; top and bottom silkscreen; and top and bottom solder paste mask. The NC drill file contains the center coordinates for drill holes and the dimensions for each drill. Send your Gerbers off to a PCB fabricator, order your specific parts using the bill of materials as a guide, and, when everything comes back, assemble and test your PCB!

To avoid spending huge amounts of money on a single iteration, try to build a small number of prototypes for each design cycle (5 to 10 pieces). That way, you have enough samples for testing but not so many that you're broke. Each pass through the design cycle checks that your BOM is correct and your CAD library is correct. Lather, rinse, and repeat until you are happy with the final prototype.

Managing Constant Iteration

Managing iteration is just a matter of keeping track of the details. Every time you go through a design cycle, maintain an archive of the following:

- A copy of the parts library, schematic, and layout files
- A copy of the BOM
- A copy of the build package (Gerbers, drill files)
- Purchasing records for parts and PCBs
- Test notes (on both test procedures and test data)
- A bug tracker for new issues (and old)

Each iteration of the design cycle should generate a new "version" of your design, so you can keep track of what happened with MyThing v1.1 versus MyThing v1.25. If you record what you built, what you changed, and why you changed something between design iterations, it will be much easier to step back and revisit old designs. Formally, this information is collected in a **design history file.** You can keep track of this information on paper or in project management software, or you can even keep your design files and notes in a version control repository. How you manage documentation isn't as important as the fact that you do documentation. The lessons you learn during the testing phase might be fantastic inputs to your product's **user manual.** You might discover a new design requirement from the user beta testing. Either way, having that information conveniently captured in a design history file will give you an edge on both the competition and the inescapable forces of human error.

Every Master Plan Has an Exit Strategy

Normally, some external force (like a deadline) will compel you to wrap up your project before it's perfect. Even without a deadline, constraints always crop up. It's impractical to run a project under the assumption that all features, all requirements, and all details are created equal. If you are forced to wrap up with details left unaddressed, then *make an errata sheet,* clean up your manufacturing package as best as you can, and ship it.

Focus on Critical Features First

If at any stage of your process, you can't build a prototype circuit that satisfies your bare minimum requirements for functionality, go back to the drawing board and question your assumptions. Rope in other engineers. Be inventive. But if you revisit your scope and you still can't come up with a design that works, and you're frustrated and taking stabs in the dark, consider shelving the project. Sometimes as engineers, we have flawed premises, or we need more domain knowledge, or the integrated circuit we need doesn't exist yet. Either way, it's vastly important to recognize when you're spinning your wheels and call it quits.

Hail Mary Plays Only Work in American Football

If you are forced to wrap up a design that works functionally but has unaddressed manufacturability or cost problems, it can be worth your time to redouble your efforts, solve the issues, and get that project out to production. However, if you've gotten to the final last-minute deadline on a project, you have a design and fabrication files for a board that's untested, and you're about to place a $30,000 bet on getting something that works first-time-right—*don't*. Your best bet (if you absolutely have to ship something) is to step back and ship the last version that worked. Sending untested hardware to production is the stuff that nightmares are made of.

Preparing for Manufacturing

If you've done everything else correctly, preparation for release to manufacturing should be a breeze. All you have to do is put together your manufacturing package:

- Gerbers
- NC drill file
- Assembly drawings
- Pick and place coordinates (or kit assembly instructions)
- BOM, where the following information is provided for each part:
  - Part ID
  - Reference designators
  - Part type
  - Package footprint
  - Part value
  - Part tolerance (if important)
  - Part critical specification (if any)
  - Manufacturer part number
  - Vender part number
  - Alternate part sources (1, 2, 3, 4)
- Test instructions

Once you go to manufacturing, it's inevitable that there will be additional questions and inputs that will come back and change the design. If you've followed a good design process, you'll be responsive and ready to tackle them.

Summary

Using engineering best practices and following a waterfall workflow can help even small teams manage a lot of project complexity. If you take any lessons out of this chapter to put in your pocket and carry with you as you build hardware, believe in the utility of gate-keeping reviews and thorough documentation. More eyes on a design catch more issues. Having a plan helps you execute effectively. And the more you document about a design from theory to implementation and testing, the less you have to remember when it comes time to catch and fix bugs. Moreover, as the designer, you can always follow the spirit of formal engineering design, even if your company doesn't mandate formal design controls. If you want users to be able to use your hardware successfully, take the next step and thoroughly document your hardware. Chapter 14, Taxonomy of Hardware Documentation, by Addie Wagenknecht provides a walk-through of the appropriate documentation to include for open source hardware. For a series of checklists used throughout this chapter, refer to Appendix C, Design Process Checklist.

Good luck!

Resources

The following resources should be read in the light of helping you understand how quality management and process can improve your workflow:

Quality management principles: www.iso.org/iso/qmp_2012.pdf

Selection and use of the ISO 9000 family standards: www.iso.org/iso/iso_9000_selection_and_use-2009.pdf

6

Making a Derivative

Alicia Gibb

"Its province is to assist us in making available what we are already acquainted with."

—Ada Lovelace, on the Analytical Engine

This chapter gives an example of the source files and a physical object that you can copy, modify, make, and sell as a derivative under the Open Source Hardware Definition. This chapter first discusses derivatives and attribution, and then walks through a simple open source hardware kit named Blinky Buildings that readers are encouraged to alter or modify. Appropriate methods for creating a derivative are discussed. (The Blinky Buildings hardware kit can be purchased at www.bit.ly/blinkybuildings or at www.Sparkfun.com.) Readers can follow along with the instructions, thereby making their own derivative kit. You may have also noticed that this kit is referenced in other chapters throughout this book. The skills used in creating a derivative board consist of modifying the source files and understanding how to appropriately label derivative files and give credit. The Blinky Buildings kit is labeled with the open source hardware logo, meaning it is okay to copy and create derivatives from it. If you attempt to copy and create derivatives of hardware that is not open source, you may receive a cease and desist letter from the originating company. To be safe, look for the open source hardware logo, and stick to creating derivatives from what you know to be open.

Derivatives and Open Source Hardware

One of the reasons people open source their hardware is to allow derivatives to be built from that hardware. People create derivative hardware for many different reasons, ranging from personalized features to economic advantage. The Open Source Hardware Definition makes the following statement about derived works:

> *4. Derived Works. The license shall allow modifications and derived works, and shall allow them to be distributed under the same terms as the license of the original work. The license*

*shall allow for the manufacture, sale, distribution, and use of products created from the design
files, the design files themselves, and derivatives thereof.*

Clearly stated in the definition is the approval to create hardware from the original design files, to make copies and distribute the design files themselves, or to create a derivative
from the original design. Because open source hardware grants the right to make copies,
the terms "clone" and "counterfeit" get thrown around a lot when talking about derivative
works. Here are the definitions of these terms when referencing open source hardware
derivatives:

Derivative: A derivative is open source hardware that has been altered or modified but
is based on an original design by another person or company.

Clone or **Copy:** A clone or copy is an open source hardware product that has been
directly copied and conforms with the Open Source Hardware Definition because it
does not infringe on the trademarks of other companies.

Counterfeit: With a counterfeit piece of open source hardware, the trademark has
been copied onto a clone or derivative piece of hardware and does not abide by the
Open Source Hardware Definition because the trademark is not owned by the person
or company creating the derivative. Proper attribution does not include copying trademarks. Copying trademarks is illegal.

There are many examples of open hardware derivatives. In particular, the 3D printing
and Arduino communities are great places to find open hardware and their derivatives.
Keep in mind that Arduino itself is a derivative of Wiring, developed by Hernando Barragan, and Processing, developed by Ben Fry and Casey Reas. Some derivatives have small
changes from the original; others have large changes. Changes for derivatives generally
fall within four categories: (1) The function of the device is altered; (2) the form of the
device is modified; (3) the change is economic, with the creator selling the same product at a different—usually lower—price point; or (4) the change enables a better design
for manufacture (DFM), making it easier to manufacture or supply parts. Economic and
DFM changes often go hand in hand and can be difficult to separate. All of these changes
are permitted within the Open Source Hardware Definition, including a combination of
the four.

An example of a board that changed drastically in both form and function is the LilyPad,
which was created by Leah Buechley. The LilyPad was mashed up with the Arduino board,
altered in both form and function so that it could be sewn into textiles. This particular
derivative was quite extreme in the amount of changes made to the original Arduino
hardware. The reason the alterations were so drastic was that Leah invented a sewable microcontroller prior to the development of the Arduino product. (For more on the history
of the LilyPad, see the anecdote in Chapter 9.) When Leah's design was put together with the
Arduino board, one could argue that the Arduino's shape, the form factor of pinouts, the
thickness of the PCB, the typical construction materials used, and the main purpose of
the board were all altered. This particular Arduino derivative's function was to be embedded in wearables—a vastly different use than the Arduino team had previously imagined for

their microcontroller. The circular, thin (not to mention purple) LilyPad is to be sewn into wearables with a needle and thread rather than solder and wire.

Of course, not all derivatives are this different. In fact, some are even more or less copies of the original.

Let's take the Arduino example one step further by considering a derivative of the derivative. Adafruit's Flora is a derivative of the LilyPad (which is derivative of the Arduino board). The Flora derivative has the same form factor as the LilyPad—it is circular in shape and flat, and has copper petals around the exterior for ease of sewing—but has a different function, with a different chip on board than found in the original LilyPad. The Flora hardware introduced the ATmega32U4 chip into wearables with different functionalities than the ATmega328 on the LilyPad (such as allowing for a USB hookup rather than using an FTDI cable). Because these designs are all open source, the LilyPad developer was then able to roll the Flora's changes back into their design, and now LilyPad also offers an Atmega32U4 product. Naturally, both products can compete in the marketplace, because they are open source hardware, nobody is suing over rights; rather, everyone is focused on innovating. You can access the source files for LilyPad and Flora and compare and contrast the design files for yourself:

Original LilyPad files linked from SparkFun's product page: www.sparkfun.com /products/9266

Flora derivative files listed in Github: github.com/adafruit/Adafruit-Flora-Mainboard

New ATmega32U4 LilyPad design rolling in the Flora's ATmega32U4 improvements: https://www.sparkfun.com/products/11190

This is how derivatives of open source work! People build off improvements and ideas from others rather than reinventing the wheel each time. This process moves innovation forward at a more efficient and more productive pace.

Why the LilyPad Arduino Has "Arduino" in Its Name

The fact that the LilyPad carries the Arduino brand name is a very important point to note. The name Arduino is a trademark held by the Arduino company. Leah Buechley made an agreement with the Arduino company to license its Arduino trademark for a fee. This arrangement should *not* be confused with Leah giving the Arduino team attribution for their original board. Arduino has tried to make an important distinction in its trademark over the years. Although it is an open source project, the logo and company name are trademarked, much as any other company in the open source hardware space (and even in open source software, for that matter) can obtain a trademark for its products. We use trademarks because trademarks protect consumers and say something about the quality of the brand they are buying, rather than to protect the intellectual property of the hardware. Unless you obtain a license from Arduino, as Leah did to enable her project to be called a LilyPad Arduino, you cannot use the word "Arduino" in the name of your derivative as a way to give credit or attribution because it is a trademarked name.[1] You can

---

1. http://arduino.cc/en/Trademark

help the community understand correct attribution of Arduino derivatives by attributing Arduino in your README file or your project description.

Giving Correct Attribution

The Open Source Hardware Definition states the following about attribution:

> *The license may require derived documents, and copyright notices associated with devices, to provide attribution to the licensors when distributing design files, manufactured products, and/or derivatives thereof. The license may require that this information be accessible to the end-user using the device normally, but shall not specify a specific format of display. The license may require derived works to carry a different name or version number from the original design.*

When creating your derivative, you will want to give credit to the original design without infringing on the trademark of one of original creation. As Michael Weinberg reminds us in Chapter 3, "Including a 'share alike' provision in a CC license is not a polite request that anyone who builds upon the work contribute back to the commons; rather, it creates a legal requirement." This goes for attribution provisions as well. Due to the murky nature of licensing hardware, we tend to read the source files (which can be licensed cleanly with copyright or a copyright alternative) to understand the intention to list attribution or share it alike with the same license.

Attribution is like citing someone else's work in a research paper; it is not copying and pasting the logo of the original creator and applying it to your board. Attribution can also be thought of as giving the work provenance. In the art world, giving correct provenance means identifying who had a particular piece of art before you owned it. In open source hardware, the equivalent is who hacked on that particular design file or piece of hardware before you. List their names just as you would in a citation or provenance document.

Ego or Accuracy?

Call it ego or call it accuracy, but the open source community loves credit. Credit, or attribution, is one of the many benefits to sharing your project openly. Getting attribution for something you created is at the root of most open source licensing structures, be it in hardware or software.

Accurate attribution is important to the life of your project. Giving accurate attribution lets the community know what your project was built on. Contributors, be they original creators or makers of derivatives, may be known within the community for their quality, work style, community involvement, approach, knowledge on a particular subject, and so on. Listing creators for your derivative gives users more information and certain expectations about your derivative.

How far do you go back? Most projects don't include credit to the inventors of the transistor when using one on their board, or to the inventors of the C programming language when using Arduino. That practice is accepted within the community. We generally do not step further back than the first or second layer of original creators, although there will always be gray areas where credit is due. When in doubt, give credit. Even if your project no longer reflects any of the original design, you still may want to reference that previous versions were based on so-and-so's contraption so that people do not feel left behind or forgotten. No one will fault you for giving too much credit to other people who wrote code or built hardware before you. Perhaps the open source hardware industry will eventually grow in such a way that our README files will start to look like movie credits and go on for at least seven minutes after the movie is over.

Blinky Buildings Project

The Blinky Buildings project is a simple kit that you can use as an example of how to create an open source hardware derivative. My intention in creating this kit was to ensure that the community has something to experiment with and gives you the rights to create your own derivative. The goal of this kit is to inspire different derivatives of buildings, which together create a whole world of Blinky Building kits. My Blinky Building kit is shaped like the Empire State Building (Figure 6.1a); in its enclosure (Figure 6.1b), yours

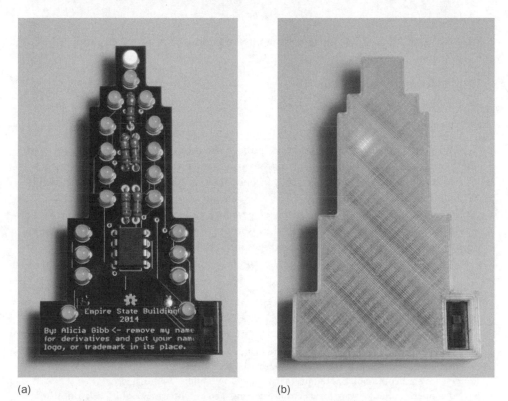

(a)   (b)

Figure 6.1   Blinky Buildings: Empire State Building (b) with enclosure.
(Source: Image CC-BY-SA Alicia Gibb)

can be shaped like a different building, city, or landscape structure. Your derivative Blinky Building may include any of the four alterations discussed earlier: modify the shape of the original, modify the function of the original, modify the economics, modify the DFM, or make your own copy.

Source Files

This section walks through which pieces of other people's open source material I used to create my kit; it also explores my source files that are shared with you. The source files include a circuit board created with the free version of Eagle and a 3D printing file for the enclosure. You can find all these files at www.bit.ly/blinkybuildings or in Appendix F. You will need PCB layout software, such as the following options, to be able to replicate or build off the derivative file:

- Fritzing[2]
- Eagle[3]
- KiCad[4]

You will also need a 3D printing software if you choose to print out or modify the enclosure, such as:

- Blender (reviewed in Chapter 8)
- OpenSCAD
- SketchUp

When making an open source hardware project, the most important thing to consider is whether people can rebuild the project from your source files. If so, you have a successful open source hardware project! If not, you need to release more source code or include more documentation.

As described in Chapter 5, I started my project by laying out the design process. My design purpose was to elegantly blink 20 LEDs in the shape of the Empire State Building. Given the scope and the specifications and requirements, I decided I would need a small, low-cost chip and would have to charlieplex the LEDs to drive 20 of them.

---

2. Fritzing is an open source project licensed under GNU GPL v3, which can take you all the way from a schematic to making the PCB.
3. Eagle offers a freeware version of its software that can be used for boards as simple as this example but is closed source software. However, this software is quite accessible in the open source hardware community, as the majority of users are familiar with Eagle.
4. KiCad is open source software for electronic designs such as schematics and PCB layout that is licensed under GNU GPL v2.

I discovered a project close to my needs that charlieplexed 20 LEDs in a falling snow-flake pattern. The file was licensed as CC-BY-SA. This designation means the schematic can be copied or used for a derivative, but the new schematic must give attribution to the original and must also share alike with the same terms. In addition, this schematic came with recommended code, also licensed as CC-BY-SA. Before I did anything else, I contacted both of the original designers—the hardware schematic designer and the code author—and asked if it would be okay to make a derivative of their work and include that derivative in my book. The open source hardware definition does not require this step, but the best practices recommend it.

I started with the schematic in Figure 6.2, which was created by Davy Uittenbogerd (daaf84). The file can be opened with Fritzing: fritzing.org/projects/charlieplex-snowfallshooting-star-20-leds.

A link to the code to run this circuit is included on the Fritzing page. The code was written by Geoff Steele (strykeroz). This code can be found in this GitHub repository: github.com/strykeroz/ATTiny85-20-LED-snowflakes.

When I copied and altered the code, I added a statement at the top of the code (known as the comment block) explaining where the original code was downloaded from and who the original author was: Geoff Steele. This gives Geoff attribution. I added a brief statement about which parts of Geoff's code I altered. I included comments throughout the code when I changed something as well. Geoff included which pin numbers correlate with which color of wire on the Fritzing schematic in the code. It is good practice to include basic instructions for the hardware pinouts in the comment block.

Here are the altered chunks of code, including the attribution in the comment block. To view the full code, refer to www.bit.ly/blinkybuildings.

```
----> /* downloaded from http://code.google.com/p/avr-hardware-random-number-
generation/ Original code by Geoff Steele. Alicia Gibb altered the code by
commenting out the fade functions so the building blinks LEDs on and off rather
than fade LEDs on and off.

The original code is still all there if others wanted to keep playing with it;
just take out the duty cycle comments.

The delays have also been changed, but can easily be reinstated by looking at the
original code:

https://github.com/strykeroz/ATTiny85-20-LED-snowflakes/blob/master/ATTiny85_
Charlieplex20Snow.ino

*/
```

I explained each of my code alterations by commenting that I altered the code from the original. I used a charlieOFF command rather than the original charlieON command in line 121.

```
------>

    if (current > 19) charlieOFF(19); //This is altered from the original code, to
turn LEDs off once the blink is over
```

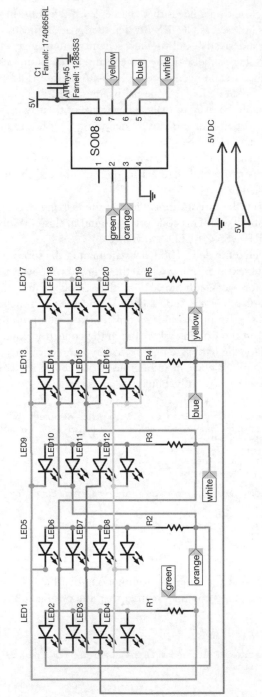

Figure 6.2   Schematic by Davy Uittenbogerd drawn in Fritzing.
(Source: Image CC-BY-SA Davy Uittenbogerd)

I explained in another portion of the code that I commented out the time delays for fading an LED so it blinks rather than fades:

```
current++;

if(current==23) { //// start over

    //Alicia commented out the below code to make the LEDs blink on and off
rather than fade out.

    //// now fade out the snowflake in that final position #19

  for(int dutyCycle = 3; dutyCycle <= 15; dutyCycle += 3) {

     //loopCount = 0;

     //timeNow = millis();

     //while(millis() - timeNow < (displayTime+current*2)) { //// fade out as
slow as animation has achieved by now

     // loopCount++;

      if(!(loopCount % dutyCycle)) charlieON(19);

     else charlieOFF(19);

    // }

   }
```

Once I had the code working on a bread-boarded prototype, I drew the schematic in Eagle following the Fritzing diagram. My schematic in Figure 6.3 is licensed as Creative Commons-By-Share Alike (CC-BY-SA), because the original schematic was licensed as CC-BY-SA. Due to the share-alike license, I must share it the same way. Any derivatives of this kit must also be shared alike as well, with the same Creative Commons license (CC-BY-SA) attached to the source files.

From the schematic, I created a board layout in Eagle (Figure 6.4) to be shaped like the Empire State Building. For instructions on how to give PCB boards an interesting shape, read Chapter 7. This board file is covered by a CC-BY-SA license: Because the schematic was posted under a share-alike license, and the board file is generated from the schematic, I must share it the same way. Note, however, that because Davy Uittenbogerd did not create this particular Eagle schematic or board file, it is licensed as CC-BY-SA Alicia Gibb and I will give him attribution in the README file and the product description. Labeling Davy as the creator at this point would cause confusion as to who produced and manufactured this product.

Bill of Materials

I am creating a kit for my Blinky Building that users will put together themselves. Since this is a kit, the bill of materials (BOM) will not go to a manufacturer, and it is not as detailed as the examples in Chapter 14. Generally, for a simple do-it-yourself (DIY) kit, the BOM serves the purpose of telling people what is in each kit. If the parts are standard, general parts that you could find at any hackerspace, there is no need to go into greater detail than the information shown in Table 6.1. In other documentation, it is advisable to include the data sheet of your chip as well.

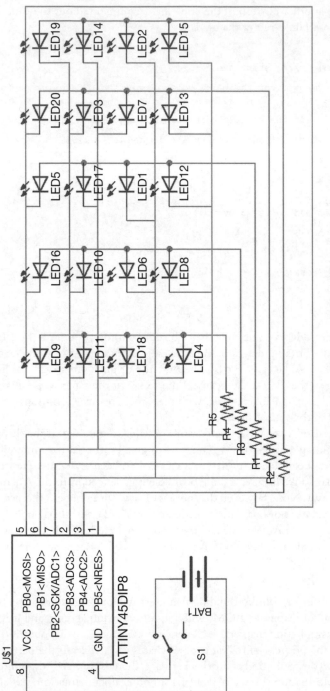

Figure 6.3   Schematic drawn in Eagle.

(Source: Image CC-BY-SA Alicia Gibb, derived from Davy Uittenbogerd's Fritzing diagram)

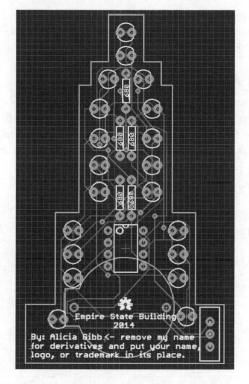

Figure 6.4   Blinky Buildings Board file in Eagle.
(Source: Image CC-BY-SA Alicia Gibb)

Table 6.1 **BOM List**

Quantity	Description	Package	Vendor Part Number	Manufacturer Part Number
1	Empire State PCB	Dimensions 1.7" × 2.95"	Golden Phoenix	
20	Round white diffused LED 8K MCD	3 mm	EBay	
5	RES 680 ohm 1/4W 5% carbon film	Axial	Digikey CF14JT680RTR-ND	CF14JT680R
1	8-bit microcontroller: MCU 8kB Flash 0.512kB EEPROM 6 I/O pins	PDIP-8	Mouser 556-ATTINY85-20PU	ATtiny85-20PU
1	Switch micro-mini slide 30V	Through hole	Digikey 679-1854-ND	MMS1208
1	Holder cell 2032 w/gold pins	Through hole	CTECHi BH32T-C-G-ND	BH32T-C-G
1	Battery lithium coin 3V 20 mm	CR2023	Digikey P189-ND	BH32T-C-G

In addition to my README file in Appendix F, this concludes the source files for this kit. With the schematic, board layout, BOM, and README file, others should be able to reproduce my Blinky Buildings Empire State kit.

Cost–Benefit Analysis of Suppliers

For complete transparency, the following lists include the suppliers from which I received quotes for each item listed on the BOM. Listing the results of the cost–benefit analysis of supplies is not required for open source hardware, but in teaching people how to make a derivative, it is important to know some economics behind what is created. As stated in Chapter 15: Business, typical mark-up on hardware is between 2.6 to 4 times your BOM

Board Manufacturer	Price/Unit	100 Pieces	Timeline
Gold Phoenix PCB	$3.11	$311	5 day turn + 8 day shipping
OHSPark	$5.00	$500	4 week turn + shipping
Advanced Circuits	$4.33	$433	4 week turn + shipping
Parts: ATtiny85	**Price/Unit**	**100 Pieces**	**Timeline**
Digikey	$1.95	$195.00	3–4 day shipping
Mouser	$0.75	$75.00	3–4 day shipping
Parts: Resistors	**Price/Unit**	**500 Pieces**	**Timeline**
Digikey	$0.008	$4.00	3–4 day shipping
Mouser	$0.33	$165.00	3–4 day shipping
Parts: LEDs	**Price/Unit**	**2000 Pieces**	**Timeline**
Digikey	$0.209	$418.50	3–4 day shipping
Evil Mad Scientist	$0.20	$400.00	3–4 day shipping
EBay: LED shop 2010	$0.02	$40.00	2–4 weeks
Parts: Batteries Holders	**Price/Unit**	**100 Pieces**	**Timeline**
Digikey	$0.60	$60.00	3–4 day shipping
CTECHi	$0.35	$35.00	5–7 day shipping
Parts: Batteries	**Price/Unit**	**100 Pieces**	**Timeline**
Digikey	$0.28	$28.00	3–4 day shipping
CTECHi	$0.35	$35.00	5–7 day shipping
Parts: Switch	**Price/Unit**	**100 Pieces**	**Timeline**
Digikey	$0.96	$96.00	3–4 day shipping
SparkFun	$1.20	$120.00	Pick up in CO or 3–4 day shipping

costs. I went with the cheapest possible BOM and marked up the Blinky Buildings kit 2.6 times the BOM.

> **Note**
>
> Pricing per unit were calculated based on the number of pieces being ordered. For example, a single switch at Digikey was $1.20, but buying 100 units brought the price down to $0.96.

Anecdote: Enclosure Case for Blinky Buildings

Jason Brownstein

An enclosure was made for the supplied Blinky Buildings board (Figure 6.5) in an effort to further illustrate the process of making a derivative including a 3D printed piece. This anecdote describes the design process and materials used. The enclosure described here was made using 3D modeling software, slicing software was used to produce G-code, and finally the enclosure was printed on an open source 3D printer. Chapter 8 provides links to the open source 3D modeling and slicing software packages.

Figure 6.5   3D printing the enclosure.
(Source: Image CC-BY-SA Jason Brownstein)

(continues)

When stepping through the design process, many iterations were made to the enclosure to improve its functionality, rather than the overall aesthetic. Beginning with the documents and Blinky Buildings board dimensions, constraints were established on the design of the enclosure. The purpose of this enclosure is to extend the current shape profile and complement the blinkiness. The dimension tool in the board's Eagle file can be used to obtain the exact dimensions of the board, which becomes the minimum dimension of the enclosure and forms the cavity. Keeping with the building theme, the enclosure profile was chosen to match the board dimensions, with a wall thickness of 2 mm or roughly 1/16 inch. This wall thickness allows for a rigid part, but permits some minor flexibility that will be utilized later in the design process.

Several iterations were made to enable the removal of the board from the enclosure, while still accessing the switch. The first iteration of the design had two full-length tabs on the top and bottom of the enclosure to hold the circuit board. However, with a full tab, the switch on the board would not allow the board to tilt into place. A modified route was then taken in the second iteration in which snap-fit features were used on the inner side walls of the enclosure. These lofted extrusions on each wall of the enclosure allow the board to slip over it and be retained. However, the snap-fit features were still too tight to get the circuit board in and out. Thus part of the bottom tab was removed so the board could slide into place.

Figure 6.6 contains three images of the iteration process, moving from the initial model to the final model. The files to print this enclosure for the Blinky Buildings kit are provided at www.bit.ly/blinkybuildings. The print files are licensed as CC-BY-SA Jason Brownstein.

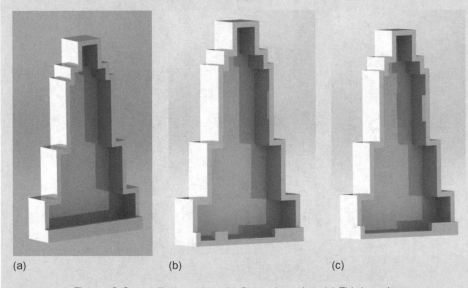

(a)   (b)   (c)

Figure 6.6   (a) First version. (b) Second version. (c) Third version.
(Source: Images CC-BY-SA Jason Brownstein)

To complement the blinkiness of the board, materials selection was considered as part of the design process. Clear plastic filament is available for use on 3D printers but it differs in transparency. A trial print was completed with standard clear PLA available from Lulzbot, and the result was considered acceptable. In the second iteration, T-Glase Nylon clear filament was used. This filament was chosen because of its optical properties, which enable it to carry light in much the same manner as fiber-optic cable. The T-Glase made the PLA look slightly dull in appearance. The appearance of the T-Glase diffused the light much better and provided an almost shiny finish to the enclosure. But with any change in the design process comes consequences, which may cause you to rethink another aspect of the design or manufacture. When using PLA, the settings are relatively standard for the Lulzbot, and the printing operation was executed with a high success rate. By comparison, the T-Glase nylon required reworking the settings, including increasing the extruded temperature, slowing the print head movements down by more than half the PLA speed, increasing additional cooling with use of the onboard fan, and adjusting the extrusion layer height. Each of these settings ensured the print layers fused together well, while minimizing shrinkage and unwanted slanted enclosure walls. Print one off for yourself or make a derivative!

Making a Derivative of This Kit

All of the files to re-create this kit or make a derivative of this kit live at www.bit.ly /blinkybuildings. These files are licensed as CC-BY-SA Alicia Gibb. (Remember, if you make a derivative of this project, you cannot include a noncommercial or no-derivatives clause to the source files or hardware.) Whether you change functions in the schematic, change the board form factor, or change the economics of the project, feel free to make derivatives! Turn your board into another building in your city or a landmark that is near and dear to your heart. Make the building roll away on wheels or create a glow-in-the-dark version by 3D printing a new case. Use it as a nightlight, a flashy model train landscape, or just a means to impress your friends!

Giving Correct Attribution: An Example

Earlier in this chapter, the "Giving Correct Attribution" section discussed what giving correct attribution means. This section shows you what correct attribution looks like.

Blinky Buildings is a communal descriptive title of this product that you can use—but be aware that having a communal project name is not always the norm. However, the same is not true of my name, Alicia Gibb; my company, Lunchbox Electronics; or my logo. Only I can use my name, along with other people named Alicia Gibb. But I'm the only person who can use my company name or my logo; even other people named Alicia Gibb cannot use my company name or logo. This is why the board contains the following text: By Alicia Gibb ← remove my name for derivatives and put your name, logo, or trademark in its place. Follow these instructions and place your own name or logo here and move my name (and the names of the other original creators) to an attribution section in the README.txt for your derivative.

When working on my Blinky Buildings projects, I leaned heavily on what has already been created within the open source hardware community. I have no idea how to figure out the code and schematics for charlieplexing, but I wanted to drive 20 LEDs off a small, low-cost chip. When I discovered a project close to my needs, I looked at the licensing to ensure I could use it openly, and I looked at who was behind the project to give correct attribution. I had to do a little Internet digging, but found both of the respective creators on Twitter and contacted them to ask permission to use their work (even though it was already licensed as CC-BY-SA, I wanted to ensure it would be okay to write about in a book) and for their preferred name/handle. When you contact someone to tell them you're using their open source hardware, you'll probably make their day. One reason to open source your hardware is to allow it to grow and change in ways you never expected.

Here is an example of how to correctly give another creator attribution on your project. This is the attribution section of the README.txt for my project:

```
Attribution -

The code for this project was downloaded from http://code.google.com/p/avr-
hardware-random-number-generation/ Original code by Geoff Steele, altered by
commenting some code out to blink LEDs on and off by Alicia Gibb.

The original Fritzing design of charlieplexing 20 LEDs was downloaded from
http://fritzing.org/projects/charlieplex-snowfallshooting-star-20-leds by Davy
Uittenbogerd. Alicia Gibb drew this schematic in Eagle and altered it into the
Empire State Blinky Building form factor.

The original code and the hardware files are both under a CC-BY-SA creative
commons license.

Code: CC-BY-SA: Geoff Steele

Fritzing layout: CC-BY-SA: Davy Uittenbogerd

Blinky Building schematic, board file, and BOM: CC-BY-SA: Alicia Gibb
```

I didn't take either source's names, logos, or trademarks and pass them off as my own. Instead, I gave credit for their work by acknowledging the work they created. The standard procedure for open source hardware is to include attribution both in the README.txt and in the software comment block. (For more information on README files, refer to Chapter 14, Taxonomy of Hardware Documentation.)

Onboard Byline

The physical board carries only my name, because putting the entire README file, or two other names, on the board file would take up too much space. Physical objects have a footprint with limited space for attribution, a fact that is well understood by the hardware community. There is usually not enough room on the piece of hardware itself to write the names of everyone who worked on it, including the original creators.

Figure 6.7 shows the open source hardware logo front and center on my board, so everyone who sees it will know it follows the Open Source Hardware Definition and can be copied under those terms. My board has the attribution text reflected in Figure 6.7: "By Alicia Gibb ← remove my name for derivatives and put your name, logo, or trademark in

Figure 6.7   Byline on the board file in Eagle.
(Source: Figure CC-BY-SA Alicia Gibb)

its place." These are instructions on what to do when creating your derivative. In other words, the attribution on the board you create should read: "By: [Insert Your name here]." But unless you are Alicia Gibb, do not use that name!

Notice that on the board I used the open source hardware logo and the word "By" instead of CC-BY-SA. This usage is meant to alleviate any confusion about copyright claims. The physical hardware is not under copyright, so a CC license would not be applicable. CC licenses can be applied only to the source files and documentation, so I did not reflect the CC-BY-SA terms on my board for clarity of separating the IP that protects written documents and hardware. The term "By" does not close down my board, but patenting it would. Generally, creators do not bother to include "By" on their boards, but for the exercise of creating derivatives I wanted to spell out all the elements associated with attribution.

The open source hardware community does not yet have a standard for applying an attribution icon with the open source hardware logo. Over time, the community will most likely come to some sort of consensus as to how the open source hardware logo and other terms should be displayed, along with other conditions such as attribution.

Summary

By now, you should understand how to make a derivative of open source hardware, and be aware of the issues and benefits surrounding derivatives. You can create your own derivatives of the Blinky Buildings kit using the source files highlighted in this chapter and available at www.bit.ly/blinkybuildings. If you create a Blinky Buildings derivative, please email me at amgibb@gmail.com so that I can link to your building as well!

Remember to read the licenses of the original creators when making derivatives and follow the license terms. The most important issue that open source hardware faces with respect to derivatives is giving correct attribution without copying a trademarked logo or name. You can help open source hardware become a stronger brand by taking care to give attribution without infringing on another person's trademark.

7

Modifying the Shape
of an Arduino

Tiffany Tseng

"Design is the method of putting form and content together."
—Paul Rand, American modernist and designer

This chapter presents a practical guide to modifying the shape of your custom Arduino derivative, covering early design considerations that will drive the size and shape of the board, tools for determining the board outline, and processes for designing and proto-typing a custom-shaped board using Eagle. Changing the shape of your circuit board becomes an important process particularly if you're designing electronics to fit within a custom, non-rectangular enclosure. Additionally, creating a shaped board is a useful technique for showcasing the functionality and aesthetics of your design. This chapter is intended to help designers think about modifying the Arduino board not only on the component-level but also on the form level and ultimately to think outside of the Arduino box.

This guide will be most useful if you already have some familiarity with the Arduino microcontroller platform (discussed in Chapter 11) and a general understanding of the functional requirements of your design (discussed in Chapter 5), including the types of electronics you will need to consider (such as sensors, actuators, or other electronic components). We also assume that you already have a schematic drawn for your board and have working knowledge of board layout using Eagle. (Refer to online tutorials for designing a circuit board in Eagle, as that skill is not covered in this book.)

Shapes of an Arduino Derivative

Off-the-shelf Arduino boards come in many sizes, but not many shapes. Most are rect-angular, which leaves three options for those who want more control over the shape of their physical computing projects. The first option is to house the off-the-shelf Arduino in a custom-shaped container, which often leads to boxy cases. The second choice is to separate the form factor of embedded sensors and actuators from the microcontroller that controls them—the iconic, messy Arduino board hidden from view with wires connecting it to the more carefully crafted physical design. The third option is to design and manufacture your own Arduino derivative, which provides the most control over the form of your board.

Designing your own Arduino derivative lets you optimize three interrelated parameters: size, cost, and shape. For example, eliminating unused components from a commercial Arduino board in an Arduino derivative can reduce the cost and size of the board, which in turn provides more flexibility for adjusting its shape.

The shape of a board becomes an important factor for projects where the aesthetics and function of the object are largely dependent on its form factor. Custom-shaped boards can be **stand-alone boards** used to signal the board's function or highlight the aesthetics of the electronics (Figure 7.1). Alternatively, **housed boards,** or boards housed within an enclosure, may need to be shaped to fit within a custom-designed form (Figure 7.2b).

In this chapter, we'll walk through the creation of a custom-shaped housed Arduino derivative using the Replay construction kit as an example (Figure 7.2). Replay is a self-documenting construction kit developed by the author as a way to explore automated ways to capture how a physical construction kit is assembled.[1] It consists of a set of angular pieces, each with a microcontroller and embedded sensors, that record how the pieces are connected in a way that can be played back using a three-dimensional, digital model. The shape and size of the construction kit pieces lead to the development of a custom-shaped Arduino derivative housed within each piece.

Before You Begin

Designing a custom-shaped Arduino derivative often begins with gaining a general sense of the desired size and shape. For example, in designing a housed board for Replay, clay and foam form models completely void of any electronics were prototyped to help spark ideas around the use of the toy itself. This exploration ultimately led to a shape that enabled the construction of interesting structures using a limited number of pieces.

Once you gain an understanding of the physical constraints of your design, ask yourself the following questions regarding the electronics:

- How complex is the program you need to run (in terms of memory usage and storage)?
- How many input and output pins do you need?
- Will the sensors, actuators, and power reside on or off the board?
- How do you plan to manufacture the board (e.g., double-sided or single-sided, in-house or using a service)?

1. Tseng, T., Hemsley, R., and Resnick, M. (2012). Replay: A self-documenting construction kit. In *Proceedings of IDC,* Bremen, Germany.

(a)

(b)

Figure 7.1   (a) Speedometer board from LuciTronix.[2] (b) Christmas tree
ornament designed by Neonsquirt.[3]
(Source: Speedometer Image CC-BY-SA LuciTronix. Christmas tree
image CC-BY-SA Brian Schulteis.)

2. http://www.lucidtronix.com/tutorials/13
3. http://www.neonsquirt.com/xmas_ornament2012.html

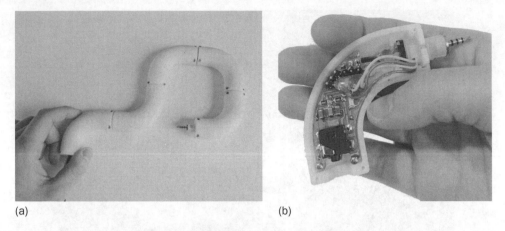

(a)   (b)

Figure 7.2   (a) Physical design of the Replay construction kit.
(b) Replay hardware.
(Source: Images CC-BY-SA Tiffany Tseng)

Your answers to the first two questions will help determine which type of microcontroller you use for your Arduino derivative. If you're running a relatively simple program with few input or output pins, you may be able to incorporate an ATtiny microcontroller, which is less powerful but also smaller and less expensive than the ATmega328 used on Arduino Unos.[4]

Deciding whether the sensors, actuators, and power will be offboard or onboard components further determines your size constraints. Offloading components enables the board to have a smaller footprint but also requires the design of connectors between the board and the sensors, actuators, or power source. For example, for Replay, the power and signal were passed between pieces using a 4-pin audio connection. While the audio jack was a surface-mounted component securely fixed to the board, the audio connector was an offboard component that was connected via ribbon cables, thereby conserving space on the custom board.

After you determine which components are needed for your application, identify space-limiting components—that is, components that dimensionally take up the most space. Remember to account for the headers used to program your microcontroller. If you're using an ATtiny microcontroller, you have the option of using a small outline integrated circuit (SOIC) clip programmer, which eliminates the need for separate programming headers. If you are trying to minimize the footprint of your board, consider using surface-mounted components rather than through hole, and use the smallest package size for each component that will work with whatever manufacturing process you choose.

---

4. For more design considerations regarding the ATtiny family of microcontrollers, refer to http://highlowtech.org/?p=1695.

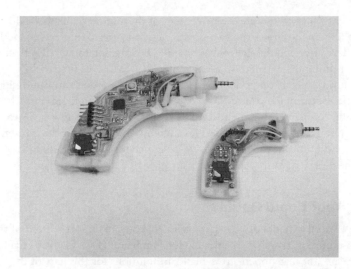

Figure 7.3   Size reduction resulting from transitioning from a single-sided
board (left) to a double-sided board (right).
(Source: Images CC-BY-SA Tiffany Tseng)

How you ultimately decide to manufacture your boards will drive many of your de-sign decisions. If you have the resources to create double-sided or multilayered boards, you can drastically reduce the footprint of your board. For example, with the Replay construction kit, double-sided boards enabled the pieces to be cut in half relative to their single-sided counterparts (Figure 7.3). Take careful note of the trace size limita-tions for the manufacturing process you use. Additionally, if you plan to manufacture your boards with an external service, factor in additional costs created by cutting from a non-rectangular board.

Determining Your Board Outline

After sourcing your electrical and mechanical components, it's time to generate a board outline!

If you're designing a stand-alone board, you can design your board outline in any software that enables you to export a DXF file; this includes most three-dimensional modeling tools (e.g., OpenSCAD, SolidWorks, Rhino) as well as two-dimensional vector graphics software (e.g., Inkscape, Illustrator). If you're designing a housed board, you can employ the same software tools, but it is often most beneficial to use three-dimensional modeling software for visualizing physical constraints. Whatever software you use, defining your model parametrically will allow you to make any adjustments down the line much more easily.

As the board size is determined by the physical components on the board, it makes sense to start by modeling any mechanical constraints for your space-limiting components.

For example, with Replay, the precise placement of the audio connector and jack was modeled first. Figure 7.4 shows the two boards necessary for each piece of the Replay kit: the Arduino derivative and the hall-effect board (a board containing hall-effect sensors used for determining the orientation of each piece relative to its neighbor).

Once the fundamental components are placed in your model, you can design the widest-possible footprint for your custom Arduino derivative. In designing a housed board, it's often helpful to include alignment features such as bosses, or screw posts to screw your board into the housing, or keyed-features (as shown with the slot in the hall-effect board in Figure 7.4). Additionally, you should leave clearance for a programming cable and connector if it's necessary to easily reprogram your boards.

Importing Your Board Outline

Once you've created a model of your circuit board, you can export a DXF of the board outline and use one of several tools available for importing DXF files into Eagle. Unfortunately, there are not many open, cross-platform solutions for this part of the process. The most straightforward is **Eagle PCB Power Tools**[5] (Figure 7.5a), which generates an Eagle script (SCR) file from a DXF file, but is a Windows-only stand-alone application. The Eagle User Language Program (ULP) **Import DXF Polygons**[6] (Figure 7.5b) generates a board outline directly in Eagle given a DXF file, but the tool imports only straight lines. Thus, you must add anchor points to any curved outline via a vector graphics editor

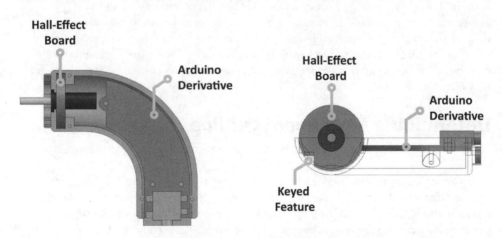

Figure 7.4   Board outlines in the Replay construction kit.
(Source: Images CC-BY-SA Tiffany Tseng)

---

5. ftp://ftp.cadsoft.de/eagle/userfiles/misc/eagle_pcb_power_tools5_09beta.exe
6. http://todbot.googlecode.com/svn/trunk/eagle/import_dxf_polygons_v4.ulp

prior to importing the DXF file. Tod Kurt has put together a helpful guide for using Illus-trator in combination with this ULP.[7]

Those looking for a cross-platform, free method for importing DXFs into Eagle can use a process identified by *badcafe* that involves converting your DXF file to a HP Graphics Language (HPGL) file, running a C++ script to generate an Eagle script file, and executing the script in Eagle to create the board outline on a specified layer of your board.[8] The open source graphics editor Inkscape[9] is capable of exporting HPGL files from a DXF file. The resulting HPGL file representing your board outline can then be used as an input to a C++ program designed by *badcafe* to generate an Eagle script file.[10] After downloading the source code *hpg2eagle1.c*,[11] you will need to compile it, being sure to specify the units (metric or inches) used.

Finally, after generating an Eagle script file, you're ready to execute the script in Eagle. The script will place the board outline on the selected layer, which you typically want to be the **Dimension** layer. After clicking **execute script** (Figure 7.6a) and selecting your script file, you should see your board outline in Eagle (Figure 7.6b).

Lay Out Your Arduino Derivative in Eagle

While the details of laying out a board in Eagle are beyond the scope of this chapter, some general techniques can be applied when arranging components, particularly on non-rectangular boards. Components used to build Arduinos are available through the Arduino schematic: arduino-uno-Rev3-reference-design.zip. You can see the final Replay board in Figure 7.7. This section highlights the process of placing mechanical components, headers, and parts that require clearance.

Place Mechanically Constrained Components First

Any components with mechanical constraints in your assembly should be placed precisely in the model, and the remaining components should be organized around them. For example, with the Replay boards, the position of the audio jack was critical, so it was the first component to be added to the board. Additionally, if you're designing a housed board, place components that you need quick access to accordingly so that you can easily access them once the board is fully assembled into its enclosure.

Leave Space for Any Necessary Programming Headers

Burning a bootloader onto your microcontroller is much easier when you have headers that you can easily connect to your ISP, so make sure to reserve room for these headers.

---

7. http://todbot.com/blog/2011/06/06/from-illustrator-to-eagle-vector-graphics-in-circuits/comment-page-1/

8. http://badcafe.co.uk/2011/03/20/dxf-hpgl-to-eagle-script-conversion/

9. http://www.inkscape.org/

10. http://badcafe.co.uk/2011/03/20/dxf-hpgl-to-eagle-script-conversion/

11. http://badcafe.co.uk/wp-content/uploads/2012/12/hpgl2eagle1.c

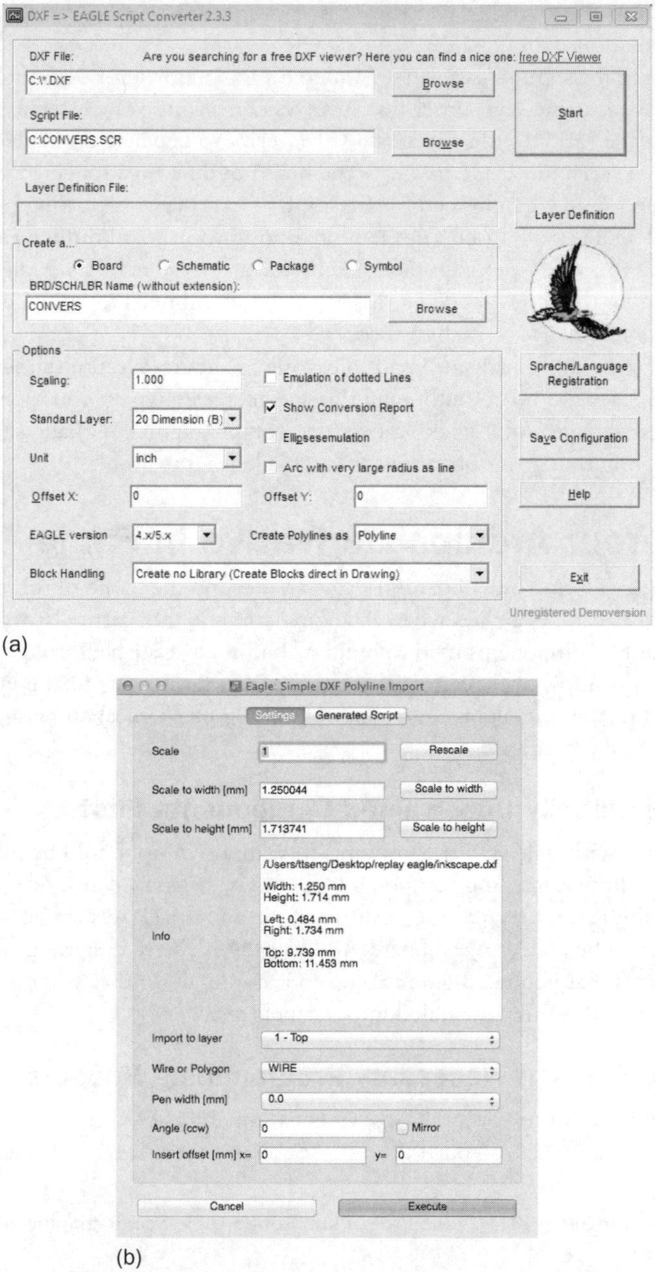

(a)

(b)

Figure 7.5   (a) Eagle PCB Power Tool's DXF Converter.
(b) DXF Polyline Import ULP.
(Source: Images CC-BY-SA Tiffany Tseng)

The downside of incorporating these headers on your Arduino derivative is that they unnecessarily take up space after the bootloader is downloaded. Alternatives for conserving space include designing the board so that the headers can be easily detached and physically separated from the board and designing a separate board solely for burning the bootloader on the microcontroller before it's transferred to your custom Arduino derivative.

Leave Clearance for Screw Caps

If you plan to use screws to fasten your board to the enclosure, ensure that you leave enough clearance for the screw caps to prevent shorting traces on your board. A manufacturing process that incorporates a solder mask can assist in preventing shorted traces on your board.

Double-Check by Creating a Printout to Scale

As Amanda Wozniak pointed out in Chapter 5, once you've finished your board layout, you can print out a 1:1 scaled drawing of the board directly from Eagle. Printing your board layout and cutting it out is an incredibly useful way to test whether your board and its components fit as you expect. It is especially helpful if you have a prototype of the enclosure on hand and can check whether the board outline fits inside of it.

Moving from Eagle to CAD

If you prefer to start from Eagle rather than a CAD package, you can export a DXF file of your board directly from Eagle (under **File > Export > DXF**). This requires that you draw the board outline in the **Dimension** layer of the Eagle program. After specifying the units of the file, you can then import the DXF file into your CAD package and build your model around the board.

If you're unable to fit all of your components and routes within your board outline, you may need to repeat the process by redefining your board outline in your CAD package and re-importing it into Eagle, or consider a smaller part package, if possible. Ideally, you will have used a parameterized model that will enable you to easily accommodate dimensional changes!

Manufacturing Your Board

The process used to prepare your board for manufacturing heavily depends on the manufacturing process you select (e.g., chemical etching, milling, or using an external service). Read Chapter 12 for tips on how to prepare your newly designed board for manufacturing. Make sure you send the .oln file with your Gerbers to the manufacturer. The .oln (outline) file tells the machine to route your board with that outline. Many manufacturers will send you a confirmation email to double-check your board details. Before you give them the green light to continue with manufacturing, verify that the image sent shows the dimensions of your board or that your irregular shape has been communicated correctly.

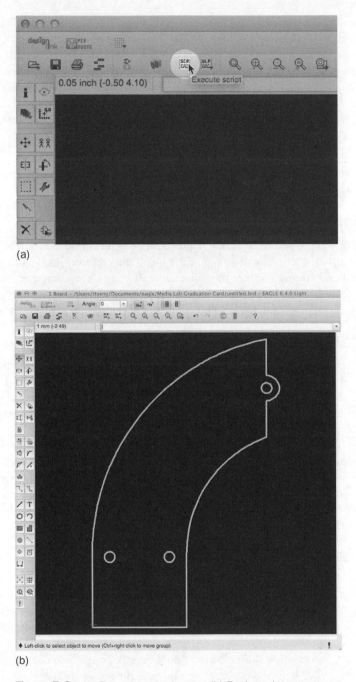

(a)

(b)

Figure 7.6   (a) Execute script button. (b) Eagle script output.
(Source: Images CC-BY-SA Tiffany Tseng)

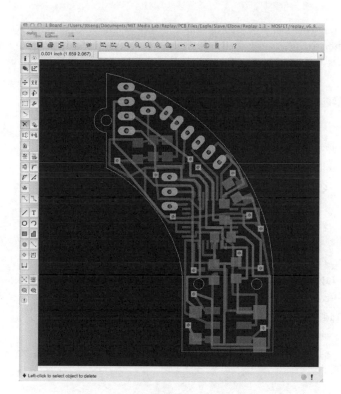

Figure 7.7   Replay Eagle board layout.
(Source: Images CC-BY-SA Tiffany Tseng)

If you're creating a housed board, it is often helpful to put together and program a single, fully assembled product (including the housing and electronics) to ensure that your mechanical constraints are respected before you invest in manufacturing a complete set of boards and enclosures. Check that you have enough clearance to turn on, reset, and reprogram your board. If you are incorporating any moving parts, ensure that there is enough clearance between your enclosure and the actuated components. You certainly don't want to waste time and money on manufacturing a set of parts before you know for sure that everything fits!

Summary

Whether you're designing the shape of your board to communicate its function or simply to integrate it within an angular form factor, modifying the shape of your circuit board creates new possibilities for aesthetics and personalization. The process of designing your board shape involves a careful interplay between understanding mechanical constraints and accommodating aesthetic concerns. While this process is generally a multi-tool endeavor, each step can be done using freely available software. Remember to name your derivative something other than Arduino. We hope this guide will inspire you to create boards of all shapes and sizes and consider the form as well as function of your next circuit board!

Resources

For more information, refer to the following sources:

ATtiny Programming Tutorial: www.highlowtech.org/?p=1695

Board manufacturers: www.oshpark.com and www.goldphoenixpcb.com

DXF Script Conversion: www.badcafe.co.uk/2011/03/20/dxf-hpgl-to-eagle-script-conversion

Eagle PCB Power Tools: ftp://ftp.cadsoft.de/eagle/userfiles/misc/eagle_pcb_power_tools5_09beta.exe

Eagle Tutorials: www.cadsoftusa.com/training/tutorials

Importing DXF polygons: www.todbot.googlecode.com/svn/trunk/eagle/import_dxf_polygons_v4.ulp

Arduino Trademark Policy: www.arduino.cc/en/Trademark

8

Remix a 3D Print(er)

Steven Abadie

"If I can't dance, it's not my revolution!"

—Emma Goldman

In the last three years, 3D printing has exploded into the mainstream. You've likely seen it covered on national and local television or in print media, discussed on radio, and plastered all over the Internet. 3D printing is transforming the way we design, manufacture, and repair objects. You can see 3D printers currently in use in scientific research labs, manufacturing facilities, classrooms from K–12 to colleges and universities, and your local community hackerspace. What you may not have seen in the 3D printer media rush is how 3D printing is spreading the use and creation of open source hardware. Not only are many of the desktop 3D printers in use today based on open hardware designs, but they also greatly facilitate the creation of new open source hardware.

Dawn of the Desktop 3D Printer

3D printing is not as new of a technology as it would seem from the recent publicity accorded to this form of printing. The first 3D printers appeared in the 1990s. In the 1990s and into the early 2000s, you could find 3D printers in research departments of large manufacturers, a few research labs in colleges and universities, and at prototype service bureaus. At that time, 3D printers and 3D printing were both cost prohibitive for most companies and organizations. Even for the lowest entry-level 3D printer, it might be necessary to spend tens of thousands of dollars to purchase one. Due to the high entry cost of 3D printers and high materials costs, bureaus that offered 3D printing services generally charged a high rate for these services.

In 2005, a project was started with the goal of making an open source self-replicating 3D printer. Started by Dr. Adrian Bowyer, the RepRap project quickly built 3D printers and interest around the world.

The 3D Printer Derivative

The greatest result of the RepRap project is the fast development of 3D printers as open source hardware. The name of the project, *Replicating Rapid Prototyper,* means that many of the components of a RepRap printer are printable on a 3D printer. Replication meant that every new printer that was printed and built could then also print parts for additional printers. Early advancements could be quickly printed, tested, and implemented among the RepRap community.

This fast development curve rapidly led to more stable and more efficient designs. Because most early developers worked out of their homes or in small groups, a lower-cost printer was a common goal. Finding cheaper alternatives to materials and components drove much of the design principles of the early RepRap designs. By 2009, a RepRap printer could be built for less than $2000. Only one year later, that cost had been cut in half by further design changes.

The community's exponential growth led to rapid development in all areas of 3D printers. Open source hardware electronics specifically for 3D printers were quickly developed and put into use.[1] Free source software was also developed for 3D printing, including firmware to control the printer, hosts to communicate with the printer from a PC, and slicer software to generate print files from common CAD and 3D models.

After starting with the release of the first RepRap 3D printer design in 2007, the RepRap project, as of early 2014, had spanned almost 500 derivatives (Figure 8.1).[2]

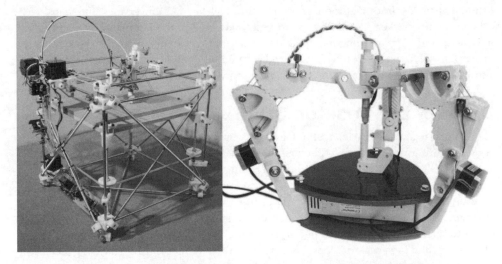

Figure 8.1   The first RepRap design, Marlin, and a recent design, Simpson.
(Source: GNU General Public License, version 3, RepRap project)

---

1. For a list of current RepRap open source hardware electronics, see http://reprap.org/wiki /List_of_electronics.
2. http://reprap.org/wiki/RepRap_Family_Tree

The project has now spread out into many types of 3D printers, including fused filament fabrication, photo-polymerization, and selective laser sintering.

Desktop 3D Printer Explosion

Directly tied to the development done by the RepRap project and community, 3D printing is here to stay. As an outgrowth of the RepRap work, 3D printer parts and printer manufacturers and retailers have formed. Before the rapid expansion of 3D printing, a person or organization had only a handful of choices available for purchasing a 3D printer and materials. Now, 3D printers can be purchased from numerous manufacturers around the world.

The cost of 3D printing has also vastly decreased. A fully assembled 3D printer can be purchased for less than $3000; starter DIY 3D printer kits can be found for as little as $350. This reduced price now allows people, organizations, and manufacturers that were previously locked out of the technology because of cost to access 3D printers or high-cost 3D printer services.

3D printer materials have also come down in cost. Before the spread of open source 3D printers, such materials were generally proprietary and expensive. Because of open source designs, materials can now generally be used across multiple printer models and sourced from multiple filament manufacturers. Materials for open source 3D printers can be found for as little as one-fourth the cost of the proprietary materials.

Finding an Open Source 3D Printer

The rest of this chapter pertains to making open source hardware designs by using a 3D printer. If you do not currently have access to a 3D printer, you will need to find one. You have a few choices available.

First, you can purchase a fully assembled 3D printer or a 3D printer kit that you can build yourself. It is highly recommended that you get an open source or open hardware 3D printer.[3] Such a choice means that you will save on filament costs and any maintenance or repair costs. Preferably, you should pick a printer that has accessible source materials and a defined community of users.

Second, you can find a 3D printer that is available in your community. If your community supports a hackerspace/makerspace, chances are high that it has a 3D printer available for members. Check colleges, universities, and libraries near you, as they may provide 3D printing services.

Third, you can use a 3D printer service bureau.[4] This option carries the lowest initial cost but will be the most expensive choice over time. Large 3D printer bureaus generally use high-cost proprietary 3D printers, which in turn make for high-cost prints. An alternative to the large 3D printer bureaus is www.makexyz.com. Using this website,

---

3. Shameless plug: Aleph Objects' LulzBot 3D printer models are currently the only 3D printers to have received the Respects Your Freedom certification by the Free Software Foundation.
4. You can find a list of professional 3D printer service bureaus at www.3ders.org/3d-printing /3d-print-services.html.

you can search for local people or companies that own a 3D printer and provide 3D printing services.

Open Hardware Design for 3D Printing

The usual response when someone, for the first time, sees and understands how a 3D printer works is, "How do I find designs to print?" For some, answering this question is easy: Create your own design in a CAD or 3D modeling software. For many others, learning to use CAD or 3D modeling software can represent a large hurdle. Luckily, for those who are wary of design software, many of the developers and users of open hardware 3D printers have also been creating open hardware designs for other purposes.

With more users joining in to boost the popularity of desktop 3D printers, more users have also been creating 3D printable designs. The majority of these designs have been posted to websites available under free software and/or open hardware licenses. In 2013, a large number of new websites appeared offering new features for posting, version control, derivatives, and selling of 3D designs and models. A selective list of web sources for 3D designs includes the following sites:[5]

- www.bld3r.com
- www.yeggi.com
- www.cubehero.com
- www.repables.org
- www.sproutform.com
- www.github.com
- www.thingiverse.com[6]

Using Existing Designs

On any of the 3D design resource websites mentioned previously, you will find designs covering a wide range of interests and styles. Among the tens of thousands of designs available, you can find designs of human figures, cell phone cases, parts to repair appliances, toys, and useful inventions.

For those individuals who are not accustomed to using free software or open hardware, building off existing work in open source hardware design is a major advantage. When starting a project, you should always research existing designs to identify any previously

---

5. For a more extensive list of 3D design web resources, visit http://reprap.org/wiki/Printable_part_sources.

6. Currently, www.thingiverse.com is home to the largest variety of 3D printable parts and models. However, www.thingiverse.com is owned and maintained by a now closed source 3D-printer company, and its terms of service and ownership of models should be carefully read by any would-be users. This company's change to closed source status was in part responsible for the sudden boom in new 3D design repository websites in 2013.

done work that pertains to your project, in whole or in part. If you find existing work that completely fills the needs of your project, you can use it to quickly accomplish your goal.

Be Aware of Licensing

When downloading and using design files from 3D design websites, be aware of the various licenses that may apply to designs. Most designs' licenses allow you to download, use, edit, and redistribute the design source freely.

Some licenses, however, specify particular sets of rules that users must follow. For more information about open hardware and licensing, see Chapter 3, Licensing Open Source Hardware, by Michael Weinberg, or the resources on OSHWA's website (for example, the FAQ at www.oshwa.org/faq/).

- **Attribution:** When using a design with this license, when you publish or redistribute the original design or a derivative design, you must always give credit to the author of the original design.
- **Share Alike:** With share-alike licenses, any future derivatives of the original design must also be filed under the same share-alike license. This license is commonly used, but should be noted when setting a license on derivative designs you have made.
- **Noncommercial:** Any derivatives made from a design listed under a noncommercial license cannot be used for commercial advantage or monetary exchange and are not considered open source.

To use an existing design, download the .STL file from your 3D design resource website of choice. The vast majority of current 3D printer software packages use the .STL file type as the source 3D model. Let's try an example.

Suppose I've just purchased a new Beaglebone Black[7] that I plan to use to create a few projects. Before starting, I want to make a case to protect the board and components. Two great websites to search for existing work before I begin are www.bld3r.com and www.Yeggi.com; both function as search engines for multiple 3D design resources. Upon doing a quick search on www.bld3r.com, I find a design that looks great (Figure 8.2), www.bld3r.com/obj/5848156587687936.

The Beaglebone Black case design by Guyc is licensed under Creative Commons—Attribution, which means that I can use the design as long as I give credit to the author. I can download the design, print, and install the board in the case and move on to the projects I have planned, using the Beaglebone Black. This is a great example of how using an existing open source hardware design speeds up development. The time that I would have spent designing a case can now be spent on other development tasks.

Spend some time browsing all of the 3D design resources. When you find something that piques your interest, download the design. Once you have the .STL file, follow the directions for your 3D printer software on importing and processing the design for printing. The software will turn your source 3D model into a file that is usable by your 3D printer. See the instructions included with your 3D printer for further instructions on processing the .STL file.

---

7. Beaglebone Black is an open source hardware single-board computer. See www.beagleboard.org for more information.

Figure 8.2   The first shot at printing the Beaglebone Black case.
(Source: CC-BY-SA 3.0 Steven Abadie)

Remixing a Design

As you've likely noticed while browsing 3D model websites, there is an abundance of 3D printable designs available. Even so, you may not always be able to find exactly what you need. You may have found a design that is very close to what you want for your project, but is missing a few features. This is where open source hardware really shines—in the use of derivatives.

A derivative design is a design that builds onto or from an existing design. Open hardware licenses permit you to create derivatives of the existing design file, allowing you to edit it to add new features, remove features, or even copy parts of the existing design into your own design. Derivative licenses also allow non-associated people to collaboratively work on a project. While one person or group works on adding one feature, another person or group can work on another feature of the project. This allows for rapid development in a group that is not necessarily strictly organized or directly related.

To remix a design, you have to step into the software world. CAD and 3D modeling software can have a steep learning curve for anyone not accustomed to using graphic software. Do not worry, though: There are many great software packages out there with a seemingly endless number of tutorials and guides.

Blender

One of the more widely used free and open source 3D modeling software packages, Blender (Figure 8.3), is a 3D graphics powerhouse. Blender is used for animation, digital sculpting, video game modeling, particle simulation, and a number of other purposes.

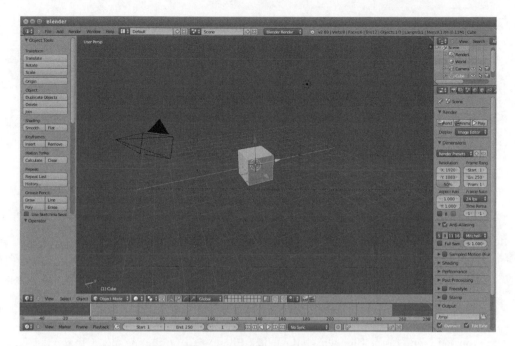

Figure 8.3   The Blender software interface.
(Source: CC-BY-SA 3.0 Steven Abadie)

It turns out that it also works great as a modeling and mesh editing software for creating and editing designs for 3D printing.[8]

I will not deny that at first glance Blender can appear daunting. But don't let that first impression stop you from learning it. The Blender community has created numerous high-quality tutorials and documentation to get you started with creating your design in this software.

I know, you're thinking: "I thought this was for beginners?" Trust me, this will be easy. In just a few steps, we're going to make a derivative. To get started, go to www.blender.org to download and install Blender.

When you first open Blender, a default project will be opened. In the 3D workspace, you will see three objects: a cube, a dot with dotted circles around it, and a pyramid shape. If you have a mouse with a middle mouse button, click and hold it down when in the 3D workspace. With the middle mouse button clicked, move the mouse cursor to rotate the

---

8. As of version 2.67, Blender includes a great 3D printing toolbox add-on. The toolbox includes a number of features to check the quality of your 3D model. One great feature will highlight the areas in the model that could be hard to print. For more information, search *3D printing* in the Blender user preferences Add-on tab.

3D workspace. You can also zoom in and out by holding the CTRL key on your keyboard and the middle mouse button, or by scrolling the mouse wheel if it has one. Holding the Shift key and middle mouse button will pan across the workspace.

Now that you have seen those three objects rotating within the Blender 3D workspace, it is time to delete them. The cube is generally used when starting a design from scratch, which will not be covered here. The other two items are a light source and a camera; both are used for creating still renders or 3D animation. First select the cube by right-clicking on it. When an object is selected, it will be highlighted orange. Once you are sure the cube is selected, press the X key and then press Enter to delete the cube. Go through the same steps to delete the camera and the lamp. Now that you have a clean workspace, it is time to import some models.

Importing a 3D Model

Earlier, I found a great printable case for a Beaglebone Black. The case is nice, but it would be even better if I added a new feature. A vent in the top of the case would be useful. While we're at it, we can make the vent a fancy graphic. I've already downloaded the .STL file for the case; now I just need to find a graphic. I happen to know there are a number of Open Hardware logo 3D designs and have found one with an appropriate license: www.thingiverse.com/thing:27097.

Once both files are downloaded, we will first import the Open Hardware logo. In the top-left menu of the Blender window, click **File** to expand the file menu. In the file menu, locate and click **Import** and then the revealed **Stl (.stl)** option. You will then have the option to locate and select the Open Hardware logo .STL file. Once you have found and selected the file, click the **Import STL** button at the top right of the window. The 3D model now appears in the 3D workspace. It will likely be quite large in the workspace; zooming out will make it easier to see the entire model.

Moving and Scaling a Model

Now that you have a model in the workspace, you can use a number of basic tools to move and change it. Many of the basic tools in Blender have keyboard shortcuts that are faster to use than the menus of the graphic interface. When a key is noted here, the reference is to the keyboard key.

With the logo model selected (remember the orange outline), press the G key on your keyboard. The G key activates the grab tool, which will allow you to freely move the model around the workspace by moving the mouse cursor. When the grab tool is active, you can also move the model more precisely by moving in just one or two axes. Press the X key to move the model on just the x axis. You can also press the Y or Z keys to move in those single axes. To move in two axes, press the key for the first desired axis; then, while holding down the Shift key, press the second desired axis. Once you have found a good location where you would like the model moved to, click the left mouse button to confirm the grab move. You can also click the right mouse button to cancel the grab move.

Another useful tool is the scale tool. With the logo model selected, press the S key. Now, when you move the mouse, the model will shrink and expand. The X, Y, and Z keys can also be used with the scale tool. In this case, pressing one of those keys will set which axis to expand the model. For our purposes, press the Z key so the model will scale only in the z axis. Move the mouse cursor upward until the logo model is about twice as tall as the original height. Click the left mouse button to confirm the scale change.

Although this function will not be needed in this exercise, pressing the R key allows you to rotate your model in all three axes or in a selected axis or axes.

Now that you have used the basic tools to move and resize a model. we can make some edits to the Beaglebone Black case.

Cutting a Shape

With the Open Hardware logo still in place, go through the **Import** menu to locate and import the Beaglebone Black case file. When the model appears, notice that it overlaps the logo model, as shown in Figure 8.4. This is okay: We know how to move the models. We will use the Open Hardware logo to cut away part of the case lid. To do so, we first need to move the logo model to the place where we want the logo cut out of the case lid.

Select the logo model and press the G key to begin moving the logo model. Press the X key and then press Shift + Z key to move the model only on the horizontal plane. Using the mouse cursor, place the logo model in the center of the case lid. Click the left mouse button to confirm the placement. Because we want the logo model to cut completely through the case lid, the logo model needs to be moved down a small amount. Select the logo model and press the G key again to activate the grab tool. Press the Z key

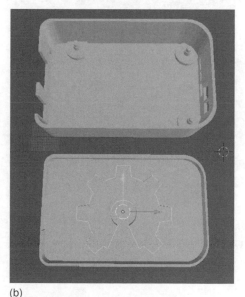

(a)   (b)

Figure 8.4   Both models imported and the logo model put in place.
(Source: CC-BY-SA 3.0 Steven Abadie)

to allow the model to move only along the z axis. Move the logo model so it can be seen through the top and the bottom of the case lid. You may need to rotate the workspace to see the bottom of the lid. Once you are happy with the placement, confirm the move.

With the logo model in place, first select the case. With the case selected and high-lighted, look at the menu to the right. In the second menu down, you will see a row of buttons with icons. Select the button with a small wrench to reveal the modifier menu (Figure 8.5). In the modifier menu, click the **Add modifier** button to bring up the mod-ifier selection menu; select the Boolean option.

In the modifier menu, you will now see additional options for the Boolean modifier. In the new options, click the **Intersect** button to reveal a selection menu. Select the **Difference** option. Just to the right, click in the empty box with the small cube. This will reveal a menu of available objects that can be used to cut away at the selected lid. Select the Open Hardware logo object/model. Finally, click the **Apply** button in the Boolean modifier to apply the difference modifier. To see the cut that has been made, select the logo model and delete it. You should now see an Open Source Hardware logo cut out of the lid of the case (Figure 8.6).

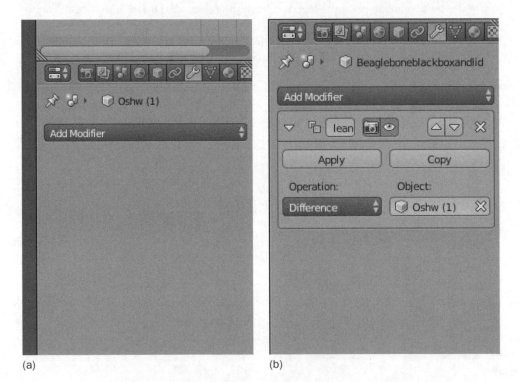

(a)   (b)

Figure 8.5   The modifier menu (left) and the Boolean modifier (right).
(Source: CC-BY-SA 3.0 Steven Abadie)

Figure 8.6   The completed derivative.
(Source: CC-BY-SA 3.0 Steven Abadie)

Now that you have a modified design, you need to export a new .STL file. With the case model selected, go to the **File** menu and select **Export** and then **Stl (.stl).** Use the file manager to name your new file and select the save location. Click the **Export Stl** button to complete the export operation. You've now created a derivative 3D model that you can process through your 3D printer software and use to print out a physical copy.

Creating a Design from Scratch

The quick example you have just completed using Blender offers just a tiny sliver of the many possibilities for creating your own open source hardware. To learn more about Blender and its capabilities, visit www.blender.org/support/tutorials/. There you will find video and text tutorials that will take you step by step through the Blender interface, introducing you to tools that will allow you to create your own designs.

As you continue to think of new things to design and 3D print, you may eventually reach a point where you cannot find any existing designs to use for a project. Ideally, by then you will have been using Blender or other beginner 3D design software to make derivative works. That practice will help you when you need to start a project from scratch or learn a new software package. However, do not fret if you have not been practicing reworking existing designs.

Free and Open Source 3D CAD Software

In general, I would rather mention only free and open source software (FOSS). However, free and open source CAD software is lacking for users who have little or no computer graphics software at their disposal. A few promising early-development software packages are available. Those packages are not quite feature-full enough to do some of the tasks a beginner would need, but are worth mentioning.

In the near future, a number of FOSS packages will offer new advanced features and will be able to serve as the go-to 3D CAD software for beginners. For now, I will mention a number of non-free source software. Any non-free source software will be noted as such in the following list of software.

If you are in the early stages of learning CAD and 3D modeling, there are a few software packages aimed at learning the basics:

- **Tinkercad** (Non-Free). No doubt, Tinkercad is the easiest and most well-documented software for beginners. Tinkercad is aimed at younger users and adults with little to no computer graphics experience. The software is also web based and requires no software install.

One large negative: Tinkercad is a closed source cloud service. There was already one scare about the website closing and all users losing their designs. Tinkercad has since been purchased by a larger company, but I would advise using it only as an early learning tool before moving on to more advanced software.

- **Sketchup Make** (Non-Free). Despite having been a Google product for only a short time, Sketchup has a wide base of users. The user interface is easy to use for beginners, and a number of tutorials are available to help you get started. Sketchup also has a number of plugins that allow importing and editing .STL files. Sketchup is closed source, and the free ($) version, which is available for use only for home, personal, or educational purposes, is missing some of the better features that are included in the non-free version.

- **Shapesmith.** A free and open source software package, Shapesmith could be a replacement for Tinkercad and Sketchup in the future. Similar to Tinkercad, Shapesmith is web-based software. Currently, the web version of the software allows you to create basic geometric shapes and join and subtract with those shapes. You can also export .STL files. If Shapesmith had a way to import .STL files, it would have been the software highlighted in this chapter to use for beginners. It is very close to being ready for widespread use.

After you've spent some time on the beginner software, you will likely start to notice that you are unable to create more complex designs because of constraints imposed by the software features. Once your skill level has reached beyond the scope of the beginner-level software, it is time to move on to more advanced software.

- **FreeCAD.** Following the format of traditional CAD software, FreeCAD is a fast-developing free source CAD software package. Although still in the early development stage, FreeCAD is more than capable of creating quality designs. The software allows you to quickly create designs using geometric shapes and 2D line sketches. If you enjoyed using Tinkercad or Sketchup, you will find FreeCAD similar in work-flow but with many more tools and features.

- **Other Choices.** There are many other 3D modeling and CAD software packages out there. I highly recommend that you give Blender and FreeCAD a try, but if you already know another software package, feel free to use it. If the software can export .STL files, then you can use it for 3D printing. For a list of software packages, see reprap.org/wiki/Useful_Software_Packages.

Next Steps

You now have (or soon will have) access to a 3D printer, have sifted through the thousands of available designs, and maybe have made a few designs yourself. The broad question some may have at this point is, "What do I do now?" The answer to this question will differ depending on your interests.

For some, the activity of 3D printing becomes the central interest. You may enjoy printing parts and trying new ways to print designs. If that is your interest, make sure to see the previously mentioned www.makexyz.com. You can create a free account to offer your 3D printing services. By offering 3D printing services, you can either fund other projects or build a 3D printing service of your own.

If you have access to or have purchased an open source hardware 3D printer, you have likely seen available modifications that can be done to your printer. In some cases, you can print upgrades or add-ons for your printer. While you're at it, you could also print parts for a second printer. In a number of RepRap design 3D printers, large portions of the design are made from printable parts. Buy a reel of plastic and the additional hardware, and you can print twice as many parts.

Research and Production

The roots of 3D printing are found in research and development. Specifically, 3D print-ing has a long history as a highly useful tool for prototyping. With the drop in cost of 3D printing, research and development has become less expensive and more accessible to many more people and organizations. If you have an idea, it can be quickly designed and printed, even sitting on your desk that afternoon. The turnaround time when using a 3D printer in development is blazingly fast.

A new trend that is rapidly evolving is manufacturing using 3D printers. Previously, if you wanted to create a product, you would likely resort to high-cost machining or high-upfront-cost injection molding. Compared to machined prototypes, 3D printers are cheaper in terms of both equipment and materials costs.

Injection molding is more complex, but the materials cost associated with an injection-molded part makes this generally the cheapest option. However, the upfront cost of having the molds produced is very high. That upfront cost is spread across the high volume of low-cost parts produced. Unless you want to incur additional costs to modify or produce a

Figure 8.7   3D printer cluster at Aleph Objects, Inc.
(Source: CC-BY-SA 3.0 Aleph Objects, Inc.)

new mold, however, you are stuck with that design until the end of life of the project, the product version, or the mold. If you plan to make a small volume of your product, injection molding is out of the question.

In manufacturing, 3D printers offer the advantage of being an expandable production system. You can start with a few printers, printing parts while you begin building up your product, business, and/or brand. If you need to ramp up production, simply add more printers (Figure 8.7). Many of the 3D printer manufacturers that use 3D printed parts in their printers have large clusters of 3D printers, or bot farms, that are constantly churning out parts to build more 3D printers. This kind of manufacturing system could be used to produce many other products.

Using 3D printers also gives you the ability for you to make incremental or version changes in your product at very little cost. Simply make the changes to your 3D model and push the new files to your cluster. In a single day, you could make a quick correction or revision to your product.

Summary

Run free and make! 3D printing is widely covered in the media as a new technology that is now changing, and is poised to further change, the world. This fact cannot be denied when you consider some of the development being done in the prosthetics and medical fields with 3D printing. Although these developments are telling in regard to the possibilities of 3D printers, do not let them dictate what can be made in your kitchen, office, friend's garage, research lab, hackerspace, or classroom.

Their broader availability explains why 3D printers are popular. Due to the freedom created by open source hardware, this technology is now finally real to many who would have previously not been introduced or interested in the technology. This is your chance to make something and share it.

Resources

Open source hardware 3D printer resource:

- RepRap: www.reprap.org

Repositories of 3D designs:

- Bld3r: www.bld3r.com
- Beggi: www.yeggi.com
- Cubehero: www.cubehero.com
- Repables: www.repables.org
- Sproutform: www.sproutform.com
- Github: www.github.com
- Thingivers: www.thingiverse.com

3D modeling software:

- Blender: www.blender.org
- Tinkercad: www.tinkercad.com
- Sketchup: www.sketchup.com
- Shapesmith: www.shapesmith.net
- FreeCAD: www.freecadweb.org

9

Wearables

Becky Stern

"Change the world one sequin at a time."

—Lady Gaga

Electronics get out into the world when you wear them on your body. Creating a wearable device poses unique challenges in construction, durability, safety, and usability. As more wearable electronic products come to market, it's increasingly important for the open source hardware community to publish project tutorials that make wearable technology reachable for hobbyists. Our bodies are personal real estate, and we should be able to create and understand the technology that's used to augment them. Furthermore, the wearables field has a huge fashion component, which is uniquely suited to gain the attention of textile craftspeople who otherwise wouldn't venture into electrical engineering or computer programming. Wearables are a bridge between hardware and textiles, and open source hardware makes it possible to cross that bridge. This chapter addresses the most common elements of successful open source wearables projects.

History of Wearables

The wearable electronics revolution started in academia in 2005. Only in recent years have creativity, the DIY ethos, and low-cost electronics components all come together to create a truly definable movement. The huge coffers of the U.S. military created a demand for small parts and sensors that had been previously bulky and unaffordable, such as accelerometers, GPS modules, and microprocessors. The smartphone revolution has accelerated the demand for smaller, more energy-efficient electronics components that make it possible to have live video chats, play music, and find your way to that new restaurant. DIY projects that would have previously been limited to university research labs or technology firms are now affordable to just about anyone. Open source hardware companies that create easy-to-use breakout boards and sample code for these sophisticated sensors are enabling the bleeding edge of creative engineering in electronics.

Before the Internet became mainstream, Steve Mann was fostering the beginnings of wearable computing, with his cyborgish modules strapped onto his person like something out of *Snow Crash*. Phone companies now have an economic incentive to connect the objects around and on you to the Net as we carve out new data and advertising markets around the real estate of our bodies. A sign of the times is Google Glass, reaching far in the heads-up display category. A truly good idea, no matter how clunkily executed it is initially, will be refined until it eventually catches on.

Media and tech in art and fashion have simultaneously taken off in the 21st century. For example, 3D printing and animatronic illuminated fashion are in vogue for celebrity performance wear and red carpet fashion alike. Couture price tags accompany these custom designs seen on Katy Perry, U2, Kanye West, Lady Gaga, Madonna, Rihanna, OK Go, and more.

Phones are the ultimate wearable electronic device. We carry these devices with us everywhere, and their development fuels many technological developments, not the least of which is the miniaturization of batteries. Hackers won't be satisfied with off-the-shelf hardware: we seek to mod for both flair and function, such as illuminating the logo on the back of an iPhone or unlocking an Android phone with an NFC tag in the user's manicure. Phones can also connect to other hardware a person carries via Bluetooth. In fact, you can expect to see a lot more development of wearables communicating with phones via Bluetooth in the next few years.

Bike projects have a special allure for wearables makers because they (arguably) improve safety while looking fly at the same time. Leah Buechley's turn signal bike jacket got imaginations churning on Instructables; you can now find at least 100 wearable bike safety projects on that site.

The accessibility of components and sample projects coupled with the democratization of media on the Net have brought success to niche companies like Neurosky, the makers of the Necomimi brainwave-reactive cat ears.

Anecdote: LilyPad History

Leah Buechley

I discovered that threads and fabrics could conduct electricity in 2005 when I was a graduate student at the University of Colorado. I was instantly enchanted. The idea that it was possible to build interactive electronics from textiles seemed deliciously subversive—subverting traditions of design, engineering, and, even more powerfully, culture. It was delightful to mash up and juxtapose soft and hard, masculine and feminine, decorative and functional.

I began to build my own e-textile projects and to share my enchantment with others. I published lots of DIY tutorials, and fellow graduate student Nwanua Elumeze and I designed an e-sewing kit that we used to introduce young people to electronics.

In early 2006, I added a microcontroller and a collection of sensors and actuators to this kit. This was the first prototype LilyPad set (Figure 9.1). Components were soldered to circuit boards I made by laser-cutting conductive fabric. These circuit boards could be stitched into textile projects like a fabric patch. Conductive thread made electrical connections between pieces. I began to hold workshops, using my e-textile construction kit to teach people programming, design, and engineering with the materials pictured in Figure 9.1.

Everyone, especially young women, was excited about the medium. Unfortunately, the kit pieces were bulky and not terribly attractive. I wanted to work with smaller surface-mounted components, but I wasn't able to make fabric circuit boards that were durable enough. In mid-2006, I realized that if I built my circuits in a different way—using traces

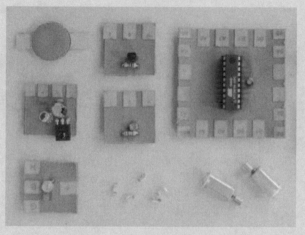

(a)

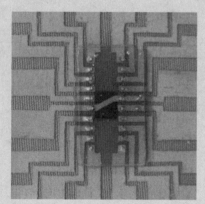

(b)

Figure 9.1   First prototype LilyPad set.
(Source: Images CC-BY-SA Leah Buechley)

(continues)

that looked like flower petals—I could make robust fabric PCBs for tiny electronic components. The first "LilyPad" was born (Figure 9.2).

Around the same time, I discovered a new project called Arduino whose software made it much easier to program the AVR microcontrollers I used in my kit. I made a few tweaks to the open source Arduino software to make it work with my boards. With new pieces and the new programming environment, my workshops improved tremendously. Students built beautiful, funny, and gorgeously crafted projects—a fortune-telling tank top, a handbag with a twinkling map of the stars, a hoodie that glowed in greeting.

(a)   (b)

Figure 9.2   First LilyPad.
(Source: Images CC-BY-SA Leah Buechley)

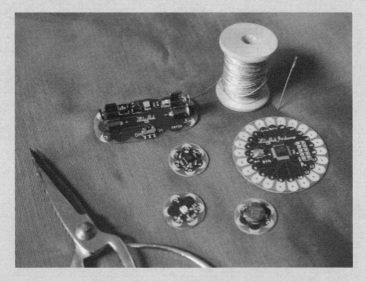

Figure 9.3   LilyPad commercial kit.
(Source: Images CC-BY-SA Leah Buechley)

I got tired of soldering fabric PCBs, and I wanted more people to be able to play with e-textiles. In 2007, on a whim, I brought one of my fabric boards to a small electronics company that had just started up in Boulder. SparkFun said it would be happy to collaborate with me on a commercial version of my kit, and after a few months of prototyping, we released the first commercial LilyPad set (Figure 9.3).

We've been iterating on and adding to the platform ever since. It's been a delight to see the ingenious, gorgeous, elaborate, and marvelously strange things people keep making with LilyPad. The examples pictured here include the Pollution sensing gown by Diffus Design (Figure 9.4), a POV bracelet created in Kylie Peppler's research lab (Figure 9.5), and under(a)ware developed by Mark Shepard (Figure 9.6).

Figure 9.4   Pollution sensing.
(Source: Image by Diffus Design)

(continues)

Figure 9.5   POV bracelet.
(Source: Image by Kylie Peppler)

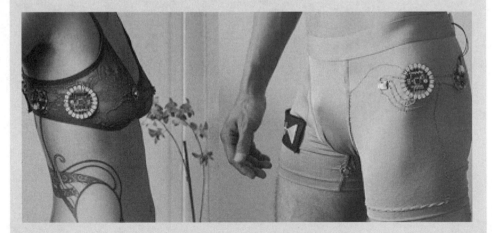

Figure 9.6   Under(a)ware.
(Source: Image CC-BY-SA Mark Shepard)

Conductive Textiles

Not all conductors are created equal! Conductive thread is quirkier than wire and sometimes deceptively simple and heartbreakingly frustrating to work with. Silver-coated fibers can tarnish over time, rendering circuits inert after a few years. Stainless steel thread (shown in Figure 9.7) doesn't tarnish, but it's so springy that its knots have to be sealed with strong adhesive (clear nail polish or super-glue) to keep them from coming undone.

When shopping for conductive thread and ribbon, look for solid metal fibers over plated ones. Small-gauge threads can be used in the bobbin of your sewing machine, while fuzzy yarns are great for knitting or felting sensors or modding up your own pair of touchscreen gloves. Conductive fabrics are mostly plated in silver or copper (not solid metal), and conductivity will vary depending on the fabric's metal content and whether the textile is knit or woven. There is even conductive hook and loop material (Velcro).

Conductive textiles are great for making slim, flexible fabric circuits and soft sensors and switches, but they are not ideal for projects that might get wet or overly sweaty. If you need insulated connections, it's far better to use thin-gauge stranded wire than to try to insulate conductive thread traces.

Figure 9.7   Conductive Thread.
(Source: Image courtesy of adafruit.com)

Sewable Microcontrollers and Components

When designing printed circuit boards for wearables, creators often use double-sided pads with holes large enough for a needle to pass through. This way, the boards can be stitched into clothes with conductive thread (as in Figure 9.8) or soldered. Using gold-plated pads will slow oxidation. Circuit boards often have rounded corners so as not to poke the wearer. Dedicated wearable PCBs are easier when beginners are getting started, and the resulting projects are a bit more flat and refined. Nevertheless, standard through-hole components like LEDs and photoresistors can also be made wearable by coiling the leads with pliers.

The most commonly used sewable microcontrollers are Arduino-compatible, likely because it was easy to modify the open source files to transform the standard Arduino microcontroller into a sewable format while still using the now-familiar toolchain. SparkFun's LilyPad product line and Adafruit's FLORA line (Figure 9.9) both have plenty of Arduino-compatible sewable accessories like LED sequins; I2C sensors for motion, light, and color; a sewable GPS; and more. In many cases, these parts are wearable/sewable versions of breakouts already created in more standard configurations for bread boards. Although Arduino-compatible sewable microcontroller platforms are the most widely adopted and have the most source code and sample projects available online, other open source platforms are also available based around PIC and .NET, for example.

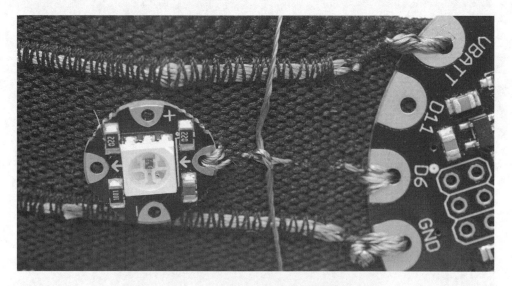

Figure 9.8   Sew hardware with conductive thread.
(Source: Image courtesy of adafruit.com)

Figure 9.9   Flora sewable microcontroller.
(Source: Image courtesy of adafruit.com)

EL Wire/Tape/Panel

Electroluminescent (EL) wire is a stiff wire coated in an electrically sensitive phosphor (Figure 9.10). Smaller wires wrap around the phosphor inside the PVC sheathing, called corona wires, and alternating current applied across the inner and outer wires makes the phosphor glow. EL tape and panel work in a similar way; that is, two layers of a dielectric material sandwich a layer of phosphor.

EL glow is evenly distributed along the entire wire/tape/panel, which is a difficult effect to achieve with LEDs. EL panel can be cut into the desired shape or masked with opaque vinyl. All EL materials require an inverter to create the low-amperage, high-voltage alternating current that drives the glow, and most inverters make a high-pitched noise. Inverters are available in different sizes and battery configurations depending on the application; some are even small enough to fit on the tongue of your shoe.

While it is possible to control segments of EL panels with a microcontroller, EL materials are most commonly used in wearables when no microcontroller is needed or desired.

Figure 9.10   EL bow with inverter.
(Source: Image courtesy of adafruit.com)

Over time, repeated flexing stress can crack or break EL materials, so it's recommended that they be limited to areas of garments/costumes that do not experience repeated bending.

Tools and Techniques

Many craft and electronics techniques can be researched independently online. Sometimes, however, a weird hack or extra step is required when working with wearables, and documenting those "gotchas" effectively is key to the user/viewer/reader's success.

For example, to carry current over a long distance, many strands of conductive thread can be affixed to a textile by using a zigzag stitch (and plain thread) on a sewing machine to capture conductive threads (Figure 9.11). You can then hand-stitch components to this "bus." When documenting your project, make sure that you show your techniques in action and provide resources to help would-be users obtain more background information if necessary.

Documenting for Wearables

Just like the traditional electronics industry, the craft/construction field has special terminology to describe its tools and techniques. When you are sharing information about your project, you should make a list of every tool you touch while making that project.

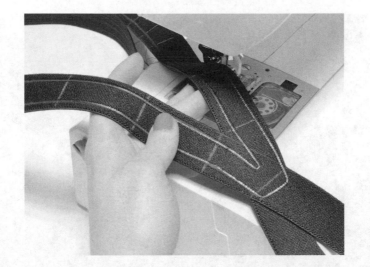

Figure 9.11   Zigzag stitching over multiple strands of conductive thread.
(Source: Image courtesy of adafruit.com)

Do not assume that the potential user shares your adhesives hoarding behavior or art supply addiction. Clarify which type of tool you're using if multiple options exist (as shown in Figure 9.12). If you use any specialty equipment like a serger or 3D printer, suggest an alternative for those users who do not have access to these devices. Provide resources for obtaining and using all tools and equipment, and make a point to mention any safety measures necessary to carry out the task at hand. You may have to include pictures of specific tools used for crafting and construction; Figure 9.12 shows an example of the various scissors used for different jobs.

Always provide a clear circuit diagram with your documentation. Photos alone don't always paint the most concise picture of what's going on inside the folds of fabric. It can be useful to draw a circuit diagram on top of an image of the garment, as shown in Figure 9.13.

As described in Chapter 14, Taxonomy of Hardware Documentation, clear photos and videos are key to documenting any project, and that applies to wearables, too. Photograph each step along the way. Work in a clean, well-lit area. You can even use a foot pedal to trigger the camera's remote trigger for those two-handed action shots. Choose only the clearest photos to document your process, and use editing software to crop and adjust levels before uploading the photos to the web or otherwise including them in your documentation. Businesses might find it highly worthwhile to hire a professional photographer for this purpose.

Video is also important for documenting your wearables project/product. Video puts everything in context, makes your work relatable, and can provide quality instruction for tricky techniques that are tough to capture in photos, such as turning a pocket inside out.

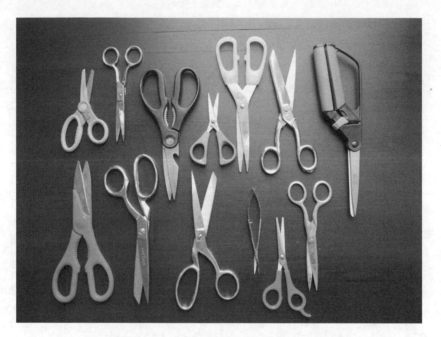

Figure 9.12   Different scissors for different jobs.
(Source: Image courtesy of adafruit.com)

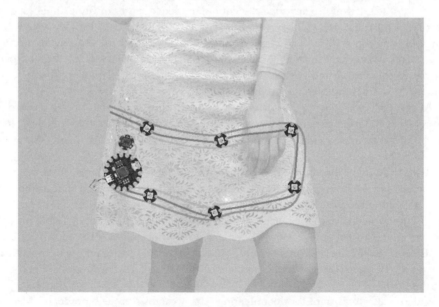

Figure 9.13   Circuit diagram.
(Source: Image courtesy of adafruit.com)

Always use a tripod or clamp arm (Figure 9.14), and capture shots while you're making the wearable. Also grab some "hero shots" of the project/product in action. Videos are easy to share online, of course. Remember, good information is good advertising.

Readily Available Resources

Instead of constructing skirts, jackets, bags, and other base garments from scratch, in most cases it's much easier to modify an existing item (Figure 9.15). Providing shopping tips and fabric/garment qualities to seek out (e.g., pockets, layers of fabric, material choice) will teach users the type of outside-the-box thinking required to create their own projects down the line.

Batteries and Power

Powering DIY wearable electronics projects is one of the more challenging aspects of this new field in emerging tech. How do you choose the right power source? Will it be safe? Beginners need clear instructions about which batteries to use, how to use them safely, and why. Alkaline battery packs with hard shells are the safest and most straightforward option (and can hold rechargeable NiMH batteries, too), but they can be clunky. Three AAA batteries are too bulky for a hat, for example.

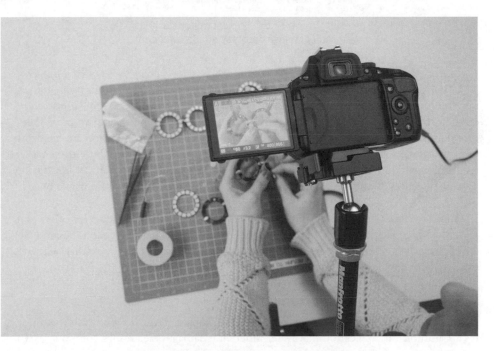

Figure 9.14   Capturing while making.
(Source: Image courtesy of adafruit.com)

Figure 9.15   Project materials.
(Source: Image courtesy of adafruit.com)

Lithium ion polymer rechargeable cells are power-dense, lightweight options, come in many shapes and sizes, and require a special charger to fill them up. Some are small enough to wear on earrings or other jewelry (Figure 9.16). Lithium cells are more delicate than alkaline battery packs and for this reason more care and attention are needed to prevent damage. You should never bend, puncture, crush, or otherwise abuse these batteries. Also, they don't come in a protective hard shell. Lithium batteries can get hot during charging, so they should be charged off of fabric or the body to prevent possible burns or fires.

Another widely used power option for advanced wearables that draw a lot of current, such as a video jacket, is a USB battery pack designed for recharging cellphones and tablets. These packs often have beefy amperage output in a portable hard case that's easy to store in a coat pocket or handbag.

Washing Wearable Electronics

A common question arises when talking about wearables: "How do you wash that thing?" It's a common misconception that water inherently damages electronics components. In fact, it's the power shorting out that can cause damage. Thus, after removing the batteries, many wearables can go in the wash as usual. Hand washing may also be recommended so

Figure 9.16   LiPoly-powered watch.
(Source: Image courtesy of adafruit.com)

as not to unnecessarily agitate or loosen any connections. Circuits should be allowed to dry completely before power is reapplied.

Some components, such as microphones, can fill with water, so they shouldn't be submerged (Figure 9.17). Stainless steel thread, fiberglass circuit boards with metal traces, and even EL wire can get wet and work just fine once dry. Silver thread and some circuit board metals can oxidize over time. Manufacturers often choose slim PCBs with gold-plated contacts for wearables circuit boards for this reason.

Dry cleaning is tough on circuits. This cleaning method often uses high heat and harsh chemicals, which can damage wearable electronics. Since we tend to think of dry cleaning when we think of delicate garments, it is a common misconception that it is better for wearables than simply hand washing them gently in the bathroom sink. Dry cleaning should be avoided unless it is the only option (as with a big wool coat, for example).

Managing Expectations

As part of your documentation, provide information about keeping your wearables in working order for as long as possible. Help others benefit from your own mistakes by issuing warnings and callouts for any sticky spots or commonly overlooked problems. Many homemade creations aren't durable enough for everyday wear; others require routine maintenance. Omitting this information when documenting a wearables project can lead

Figure 9.17   Hand washing a circuit.
(Source: Image courtesy of adafruit.com)

to unrealistic expectations of performance and dissatisfaction in execution. Set your user up for success!

Include photos and instructions for troubleshooting when things don't work as planned. This can be the most difficult part of writing a tutorial, because everyone comes to the table with a different set of experiences informing their work. You might simply not think of all the things that could possibly go wrong. Publishing frequently and interacting with the community online can help you build your skill in thinking of potential mistakes before other users make them.

Future of Wearables

Wearable electronics is a very creatively fertile field, with new companies starting up with wearable devices seemingly every day. It's clear that the next great technology frontier is the human body, where options range from medical devices to high fashion, and everywhere in between. Sensing technology will be constantly gathering data about humans' every move, wirelessly communicating with our other devices, and communicating with the Internet to give us assessments and instructions.

Given that wearable electronics are so close to our physical selves, they must inherently express our personal styles. Mass-market gadgets like MP3 players and phones usually let you customize the color of the device, either with a limited set of options or an accessories/case market. These limited customization options won't fly when it comes to integrating electronics into the fabric of life and style. Thus the future must hold more mass customization for the look and feel of devices that augment our senses of self.

Open source technologies are likely to play a gigantic role in the future of wearable electronics. Who owns the data collected by your fitness tracker? The intensely personal nature of wearables implies a similarly intense controversy over proprietary systems interacting with the body. In the future, wearable devices might even be considered part of the body—it seems natural to want to open and repair that device yourself. Just like putting together an outfit from disparate pieces, it will be necessary to have open standards for common wearables functions such as sensing and displaying information/color. It will be commonplace to program your wardrobe to do your bidding.

On the hardware end of things, we're seeing ever smaller and less expensive sensors, batteries, and wireless communication technologies. Wireless charging will be huge in medical applications, and Bluetooth low-energy technology is already making it easy and inexpensive to control your garment from your phone. Fashion companies will have to become tech companies, and the future is looking weird, blinky, and awesome.

The dream of a video jacket, a gown dripping with pixels, and other garments-as-displays is getting closer. CuteCircuit's over-the-top galaxy dress impresses on a mannequin; in the future, open source hardware will help us get closer to building our own versions at home without the $20,000 price tag.

Summary

This chapter has addressed the most common elements of successful open source wearables projects. Building your own wearable electronics can be fun and rewarding, but teaching others to do the same requires some special considerations outside the standard circuit diagram and source code documentation. You're teaching textile crafts, interaction design, and fashion at the same time as electronics, after all! From teenage girls to quilting grandmas, the wearables field has something for everyone.

Resources

For more information and to get involved, refer to the following sources:

Adafruit Learning System (http://learn.adafruit.com/): Adafruit's tutorial site hosts dozens of step-by-step wearables tutorials and videos, including projects with the FLORA and GEMMA microcontrollers as well as construction techniques for incorporating electronics into garments and accessories. Adafruit also publishes tear-downs of popular wearables products.

Wearable Electronics with Becky Stern weekly web show (http://www.adafruit.com/beckystern): Each week Adafruit's director of wearable electronics discusses materials and tools, and answers viewer questions about Adafruit's wearable endeavors.

Fashioning Tech (http://www.fashioningtech.com/)

Kobakant DIY (http://www.kobakant.at/DIY/): This source "aims to be a comprehensible, accessible, and maintainable reference resource, as well as a basis for further exploration and contribution." It offers oodles of textile tutorials and fun sensor ideas and materials exploration.

SparkFun ElectriCute (http://www.youtube.com/sparkfun): SparkFun's textile specialist, Dia Campbell, demonstrates projects with e-textile materials and techniques.

Instructables (http://www.instructables.com/): Search "wearables" for a fun grab bag of tutorials and projects created by users in the Instructables community.

Electric Foxy (http://www.electricfoxy.com/blog/)

Sew Electric by Leah Buechley, Kanjun Qiu, Sonja de Boer, and Jocelyn Goldfein

Textile Messages: Dispatches from the World of E-Textiles and Education by Leah Buechley, Kylie Peppler, Michael Eisenberg, and Yasmin Kafai

Make: Wearable Electronics: Tools and Techniques for Prototyping Interactive Wearables by Kate Hartman

Getting Started with the Adafruit FLORA by Becky Stern and Tyler Cooper

Fashion Geek by Diana Eng

Switch Craft by Alison Lewis

Fashioning Technology: A DIY Intro to Smart Crafting by Syuzi Pakhchyan

Fashionable Technology: The Intersection of Design, Fashion, Science and Technology by Sabine Seymour

Physical Materials

Gabriella Levine

> "People who are really serious about software should make their
> own hardware."
>
> —Alan Kay

Open source hardware pertains to industries that encompass multiple hardware platforms and a wide variety of physical components, tools, and materials. This chapter highlights numerous fields of open source hardware products in cross-disciplinary domains, including mechanical engineering, environmental preservation, disaster relief, and biotechnology. Some open source hardware products embrace multiple layers or types of hardware. When designing such products that combine multiple elements of design (i.e., mechanical fabrication, electronic design, and source code), there are some standard practices for releasing information and designs that can encompass all layers of the product.

This chapter introduces open source hardware products in a range of industries, and it serves as a lesson on applying the definition of open source hardware to various fields of hardware. It outlines some of the benefits for designers and users in different fields, and it outlines each layer of open source hardware projects as a means to standardize documentation of open source hardware products across varied industries.

Centralized Online Hub for Information Sharing

The common thread that ties together open source platforms is open access to an online centralized hub for information exchange through a community website. Such websites provide a forum for conversation, a wiki for detailed plans for construction, source code, fabrication, and an open online database, which can be upgraded by the community. Access to information and the efficient transport of goods and tools globally ensures that users can obtain tools that were never before available. Moreover, through the sharing of digital files, designs can be replicated and improved from anywhere in the world. Open source hardware debuted in electronics, but it has since proliferated into a number of fields that rely on different materials and documentation formats. As a guide, providing source files, a bill of materials or parts list, an assembly guide, and any required software will ensure your hardware can be reproduced. This chapter walks through several examples of the design files required for different types of hardware.

Benefits for the Designers and Customers

Open source hardware facilitates inventors, manufacturers, academics, and corporations in innovating together. Inventors benefit from releasing technology through open source hardware by achieving crowd-sourced development, formation of online centralized knowledge hubs, and massive citizen-driven data sets. Entrepreneurs also benefit from getting their names publicized when they specify licenses for their work that require attribution for all derivatives.

The consumer benefits from the empowerment of user-driven innovation through testing, alteration, and iteration upon the product. The resulting competition within the free market opens up a wider market for derivative products and modular tools in different iterations, which in turn promotes healthy competition and free flowing of ideas that spawns further innovation. For more benefits and discussion of business practices, refer to Chapter 15, Business. This simultaneous cross-development of technology across multiple sectors (Figure 10.1), facilitated by the sharing of information, creates a network of simultaneous innovation among local communities, hobbyists, corporations, government, and nongovernmental organizations (NGOs).

Flexing the Open Source Hardware Definition to Fit Other Physical Objects and Products That Require Multiple Types of Manufacturing

The open source hardware community created a definition of open source hardware that specifies which parts of a hardware product must be documented openly to warrant its designation as "open source." The definition can be found in Chapter 2 of this book or

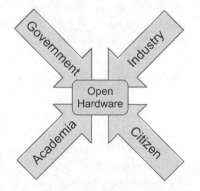

Figure 10.1   The network of innovation that open source hardware facilitates through cross-disciplinary collaboration between various sectors of academia, government, corporations, and civilians.
(Source: Image Public Domain by Cesar Harada)

online at oshw.org/definition. Many products are released as open source hardware that incorporate multiple types of materials, which means that the methods of production vary and the manufacturing processes are more complicated than simply printing PCB electronic boards from Gerber files. Documenting open source hardware designs that encompass varied methods of production is a more complex endeavor because production includes mechanical fabrication, hardware design, schematics of the electronic boards, and the layout and assembly of all the hardware combined.

Designers and inventors must be aware of these considerations when manufacturing and releasing products that combine multiple platforms and materials. This section outlines some of the parameters that should be taken into account by the inventor and manufacturers for applying the Open Source Hardware Definition to a diverse range of physical products for different fields and industries.

Parts of the following section are derived from an Adafruit presentation outlining open source hardware[1], the slides of which are available online.

A designer, inventor, or entrepreneur who releases an open source hardware product is obligated to provide design files in an optimal format for making modifications. The creator must satisfy the following conditions:

- Allow modification and redistribution of the design files

- Allow manufacture, sales, distribution, and use of the product from the design files

- Publish any documentation or software that is essential to use the product

Depending on the license used for the design files, the designer or manufacturer of a derivative open source hardware product might have to do the following:

- Provide attribution when distributing or manufacturing a derivative product and when distributing design files of a derivative

- Release the product and documentation (that are based on the original design files or any derivatives thereof) as open source

- Cannot imply that the device is manufactured, tested, warrantied, or guaranteed by the original designer, and cannot make use of trademarks owned by the original designer, without permission

When designing an open source hardware product, it is best to use open source design tools and components, standard materials that are accessible locally, and standard processes. This maximizes the ability of consumers to make, use, and improve the hardware. When a designer shares and documents more information about the work, this openness benefits the consumer and leads to a higher likelihood that the open source hardware community will adopt the product.

With a complex physical product that combines mechanical systems, electronic elements, firmware for the hardware, and software for a user interface, there are many layers of information pertaining to the documentation of the hardware. This section aims to lay

---

1. www.adafruit.com/blog/2009/03/28/open-source-hardware-overview-slides/

Hardware Layer	What It Includes	Model/Image Type	Preferred File Type
Mechanical designs	Physical assembly, materials used, enclosers	2D/3D models	.dxf, .dwg, .ai, .pdf, .3dr . . .
Electronic schematics and circuit diagrams	Diagram of the electronic circuitry, physical layout for the circuit board, list of electronic components	2D images	.pdf, .jpg, .pdf, .gif, .tiff
Bill of materials	Detailed parts list, cost of each item, part numbers, data sheets	Spreadsheet or text file	.pdf, .xls, .txt, .csv
Diagram of physical layout of the circuit	Layout of the physical elements for the PCB	Gerber files	Gerber files
Firmware for the processor	Firmware for the microprocessor	Source code (C, Linux . . .)	Text or binary
Source code for user interface, API, or drivers	Source code for computer graphical user interface layer, drivers, API's, and any requirements for running the software on a computer	Source code in whatever programming language it is written	Text or binary

Figure 10.2 Hardware layers of an open source hardware device, and the
corresponding documentation that should accompany the design files.
(Source: Image CC-BY-SA Gabriella Levine)

out a standard for organizing the layers of documentation released with an open source
hardware device. There are six stacks, or layers, of a hardware project (Figure 10.2), and
each stack should be documented accordingly and appropriately to the materials in that
particular field:

1. **Hardware and mechanical designs that demonstrate how to physically
   make the product:** This stack includes 2D and 3D models, in vector graphics files
   (e.g., .dxf, .dwg, .ai, .pdf, .3dr). It identifies materials used, dimensions for any enclosures, and a list of mechanical subsystems.

2. **Electronic schematics and circuit diagrams:** This stack includes diagrams of
   electronic circuitry, the physical layout of the circuit board, and a parts list (i.e., the
   components for the circuit). The physical layout diagram demonstrates how components are physically laid out on the circuit board itself. Formats for electronic schematics and layout diagrams are often 2D images (.pdf or .png), Eagle files (.sch .brd),
   or Fritzing files (fritzing.org).

3. **Bill of materials (BOM), parts list, or recipe:** This stack includes a detailed list
   of the parts used, places to source those parts, part numbers, cost of each item, and

relevant data sheets for each part. It can also include notes about each part as well as an indication of whether it can be supplemented by a more generic part. Generally, this stack takes the format of a text file or a spreadsheet, but it can also take the form of a recipe and list ingredients.[2]

4. **Diagram of the physical layout of the electronic circuit:** This is the layout diagram, or board file, of the physical elements of the electronic circuitry. It includes information about placement of the parts, paired with a schematic of the circuit diagram, as well as information about how to make the PCB copper prints for the electronic schematics. Gerber files give information about the physical layout and generate the PCB electronics board.

5. **Firmware for the microcontroller or processor:** This stack documents the source code and core firmware that runs on a microcontroller chip or the processor itself, which acts as the brain of the entire system. This is often written in C or as Linux utilities. Generally, the source code is released as a text file, and it can be downloaded directly, or from code repositories such as GitHub.[3] Precompiled executable binary files are sometimes provided so users don't need to compile from source.

6. **Source code for the user interface software stack (e.g., APIs, drivers):** If there is a computer application layer with a graphical user interface (GUI), the source code that communicates with a computer must be documented, as well as any drivers necessary for running the software interface.

7. **Assembly guide:** This layer demonstrates how all pieces fit together. Complex designs may require an assembly guide to make the hardware replicable.

Along with the just-mentioned layers, depending on the materials used in your hardware, you may need other files as well. For example, in Chapter 16, Joshua Pearce outlines scientific principles, equations, cultural context, and technical specifications as layers needed in reproducing scientific equipment and learning services. Because open source hardware is new, layers may be missing for some materials. The most important take-away message about layering open source principles is to ensure that every part of your source design is replicable.

A designer can also choose to release additional design files that can help the user make, use, or modify the device. This can include a handbook, photographs, drawings, written instruction, use-case scenarios, or other explanations that can assist users.

Documentation for multiple types of design files can be hosted either directly on the company/product website or on repositories that pertain to different physical elements. For example, Thingiverse[4] is an online repository for sharing 3D design files, generally for

---

2. View the recipe to make conductive dough from Squishy Circuits here: http://courseweb.stthomas.edu/apthomas/SquishyCircuits/conductiveDough.htm.

3. www.github.com

4. www.thingiverse.com

3D printing. Instructables[5] is a website used by designers to share their inventions; here, they can document their design processes in a step-by-step manner. Instructables also hosts video, photo, and written documentation for products. GitHub,[6] a website for sharing source code, encourages social coding through the ability to branch, merge, and fork projects. To read more about documentation, refer to Chapter 14.

A Range of Products and Industries

Open source hardware projects span many sectors, including industrial machines, agriculture, mechanical engineering, manufacturing, distributed sensing, environmental mapping, disaster relief, space exploration, biotechnology, transportation, education, sustainable energy, and robotics. Various companies and inventors choose to use open source hardware for different reasons.

This section covers some open source hardware projects that are being developed across specific industries and describes products that incorporate elements of mechanical fabrication, electronics design, and software stacks.

Industrial Machines and Agriculture

Open Source Ecology[7] is developing open source industrial machines that can be made for a fraction of their commercial costs, with the ultimate goal of creating an efficient open source process to increase innovation through open collaboration. Open Source Ecology is an international collaboration of people who come together in different configurations for development opportunities, including design sprints and workshops. They aim to develop accessible blueprints for industrial and agricultural machines, called the Global Village Construction Set (Figure 10.3).

The members of Open Source Ecology aim to ultimately spur a cultural revolution, by creating accessible tools and interdisciplinary development processes that enable people to co-develop tools, systems, and processes. The source files for machinery differ greatly from those for electronics. Thus Open Source Ecology's documentation includes file sets of hydraulic plans for tractors (Figure 10.4a), power details for the MicroTrac (Figure 10.4b), and parts builds for the compressed earth brick press (Figure 10.4c).

Urban Farming

Windowfarms[8] is a hydroponic urban indoor gardening kit made from repurposed water bottles and accessible plumbing supplies that delivers liquid nutrients to plant roots. The kit allows for year-round growing of plants in the window of any house or apartment, and the plants thrive on natural light from the sun coming into the window.

---

5. www.instructables.com
6. www.github.com
7. http://opensourceecology.org/
8. www.windowfarms.com/

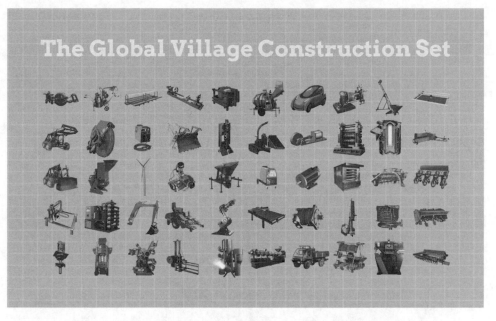

Figure 10.3   The Global Village Construction Set, a life-size, scalable, modular, low-cost construction set that can be used to produce more than 50 different industrial machines.
(Source: Image CC-BY-SA Open Source Ecology)

Along with a store for purchasing Windowfarms and an online wiki detailing how to build, set up, and maintain Windowfarms, a centralized social media community sharing website[9] allows users to share their improvements to the design. To date, the Windowfarms community has grown to more than 42,000 users worldwide who have contributed to the online forum about modifications to the technology. This crowd-sourced development has facilitated rapid technology advancement to the point where it is today inexpensive and effective.

Household Plant-Monitoring Systems

Botanicalls[10] is an open source hardware sensor that integrates the Arduino microcontroller. It facilitates communications between humans and their houseplants, by monitoring the moisture level of the plant and communicating to its owner via Twitter when it needs water. The plant (through the sensor) also thanks the owner when it has been watered. This collaborative DIY project was facilitated by students at the School of Visual Arts and the Tisch School of the Arts Interactive Communication Program at NYU.

---

9. www.our.windowfarms.org
10. www.botanicalls.com/

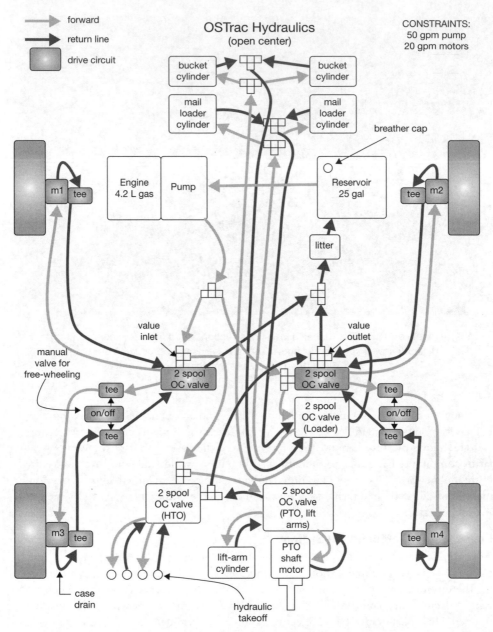

Figure 10.4   (a) Hydraulic plans. (continues)
(Source: Images CC-BY-SA Open Source Ecology)

CEB Press Prototype 2 Hydraulic Power Detail from Micro Trac
(manual control valve)

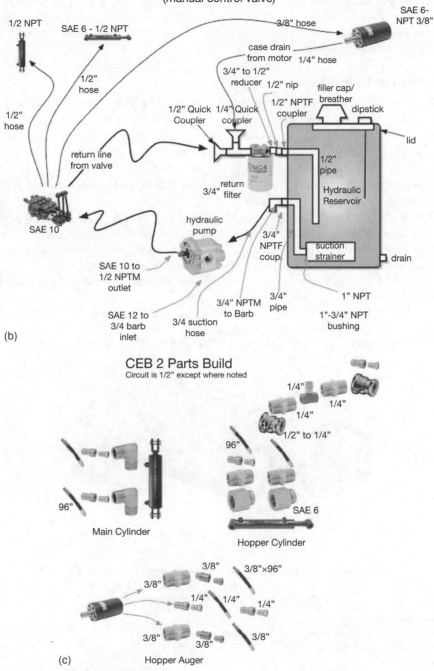

(b)

CEB 2 Parts Build
Circuit is 1/2" except where noted

Main Cylinder

Hopper Cylinder

Hopper Auger

(c)

Figure 10.4 (continued)   (b) Power detail. (c) Parts build.

Because Botanicalls is open source and hackable, it is easy to modify the hardware and the software to do things like integrate Wi-Fi connectivity or change the Twitter messages. This gives control to the consumers and users to modify and repurpose the platform to fit different use-case scenarios. There is an online forum[11] where people ask questions or share ideas about Botanicalls.

Automotive Industry

Tabby is a small open source hardware vehicle[12] made by an Italian company, OSVehicle (Figure 10.5). All of the assembly plans for the car are available to download online. According to the company, it can be assembled in less than an hour in a customer's garage for less than 6000 euros. In the centralized community forum, customers can share improvements and make modifications to the design, which facilitates crowd-sourced research and development. This forum also serves as an online hub for communication and global collaboration.

Velocar[13] is a platform for an open source bicycle that has a protective shell to shield the rider from the elements (i.e., rain, cold, and wind). It takes the form of a Velomobile, which is a tricycle covered by an aeroshell. Velocar and Open Source Ecology have collaborated in this attempt to reinvent the bicycle and car by combining them into a sustainable and affordable platform that provides efficient human-powered transportation but also protects the user from the elements.

Figure 10.5   Tabby, an open source framework for designing
and constructing vehicles.
(Source: Image CC-BY-SA osvehicle.com)

---

11. www.botanicalls.com/forums/forum/community/
12. www.osvehicle.com/
13. www.velocar.cc

Mechanical Engineering and Manufacturing

With open access to online information, high-speed communication, and rapid transport of goods and tools, machining and manufacturing capabilities have penetrated the household, personal studios, educational facilities, corporate offices, and public spaces. The following are examples of open source hardware fabrication tools whose crowd-sourced designs, accessible materials, and inexpensive replacement parts are allowing hackers, artists, entrepreneurs, and even children to have access to sophisticated machines for prototyping and manufacturing.

Laser Cutting

The **Lasersaur**[14] is an open source laser cutter designed for makers, artists, and scientists by Nortd Labs,[15] an international R&D lab founded in New York City. The intention is to provide an inexpensive DIY laser cutter that can be produced using modular parts that can be sourced directly or bought locally by referencing the bill of materials (which can be viewed in Chapter 14, Taxonomy of Hardware Documentation). Lasersaur relies on distribution through its BOM, meaning costumers are intended to build a laser cutter for themselves from locally sourced parts. A free and thorough document outlines the resources needed for building and maintaining the Lasersaur, including hardware/software specifications, the source code and a software application with a GUI, a bill of materials, the building process, and instruction on how to run and operate the laser cutter. There is also a community mailing list, a map of users, and a Flickr group.

The benefit of using open source hardware during the development process is that the Nortd Labs team was able to release the design sooner to the public. The hope was that open collaboration would help its design improve over time as people used it, contributed to the development, and documented improvements. Instead of putting years of effort and money into R&D, Nortd Labs shared the designs with the public at an early stage in the development. In turn, hackerspaces and universities participated in the collective research and development. This crowd-sourced R&D enabled tools that were typically created in a hierarchical development cycle to be developed by an international online network composed of academics, hobbyists, artists, and scientists.

CNC Milling

Shapeoko[16] has created an open source hardware, modular, upgradable, easy-to-assemble, low-cost CNC (computer-numeric control) router. The parts required to build it are available online through a bill of materials. The CNC router can also be purchased as a preassembled consumer-friendly kit ($649) or as an online DIY kit ($299). The assembly process is well documented, and setup requires accessible hardware components (nuts and bolts) from any local hardware store. The device's shape and bed size can be expanded or

---

14. www.lasersaur.com/
15. http://labs.nortd.com/
16. www.shapeoko.com

remodeled based on the original design. The control unit is Arduino based, so the micro-controller is well known and accessible. Because it is open source hardware, the Shapeoko CNC router is customizable, low cost, and accessible to artists, designers, hobbyists, and schools, enabling them to fabricate precisely designed machine parts as well as to carve works of art.

Shapeoko hosts a community web forum with more than 1000 members, and the community input has contributed to the low cost of the CNC router—such machine typically costs orders of magnitude more when purchased from closed source vendors. The crowd-sourced R&D means that the costs of research and development can be eliminated from the price tag: the centralized community forum has provided an outlet for the community to contribute back new improvements, as well as undertake testing and troubleshooting. The engineers behind Shapeoko were able to crowd-source the testing and research for the Shapeoko 2 by responding to community needs just two years after releasing the design for the Shapeoko 1. Shapeoko relies on distribution through its BOM, meaning costumers are intended to build the hardware themselves from locally sourced parts.

3D Printing

Numerous examples can be cited of open source 3D printers on the consumer and hobbyist market being developed and sold globally. A wealth of derivatives has emerged, and newer models continue to be built, derived, modified, and rebuilt. It is important to note the consumer 3D printing market would not exist as it does today without the RepRap 3D printer being open source hardware, as the vast majority of consumer printers on the market are derivatives of the RepRap.

The **Lulzbot TAZ** 3D printer (Figure 10.6) is one example of an open source hardware 3D printer; it is priced at $2194. TAZ is based on the RepRap[17] 3D printer, and it claims to be the most dependable desktop 3D printer on the market. It requires minimal maintenance, so it is a good choice for consumers as well as engineers, hackers, and artists both for creating prototypes and for small-scale manufacturing. Because of TAZ's open source design, this 3D printer can be modified or adapted. Lulzbot also hosts an online store selling parts and accessories. It provides customer support as well as a community forum where members can discuss, troubleshoot, and collaborate on projects. The TAZ 3D printer is so well documented that its source files even include a quality checklist and test acceptance record.

Many more open source hardware 3D printers are being developed, and many of them are raising money on Kickstarter and other crowd-source funding venues such as Indiegogo.[18] For example, Fabtotum is an open source 3D printer that aimed to hit the market in September 2014, selling for $1099 as a preassembled device and $999 as a kit.

Open source parts and accessories for 3D printers are also reaching the market. For example, the Filabot[19] is a filament extruder that can transform pellets into plastic

---

17. http://reprap.org/
18. www.indiegogo.com
19. www.filabot.com

Figure 10.6   Lulzbot Taz 4 from Aleph Objects.
(Source: Image CC-BY-SA Aleph Objects)

filament, thereby allowing users to make their own materials for 3D printing. This gives designers the option to mix colors and combine materials or shavings; thus they can potentially make things like magnetic, conductive, or glow-in-the-dark objects.

3D printers have enabled hobbyists to do things like custom-fabricate their own machine parts, engineer their own tools, and conduct local small-scale manufacturing. DIY fabrication techniques could potentially lead to larger-scale local manufacturing. Open source tools for manufacturing and mechanical engineering have spawned into projects that are penetrating into various industries, including automotives, civilian drones, and even health care.

One example is the **Robohand**[20] project. Robohand was developed by Richard van As (@Robohand on Thingiverse), a South African construction worker who lost two of his fingers during an injury on the job. Due to financial limitations and the type of injury he suffered, there was no preexisting prosthetic hand within his price range that could fit his fingers. Richard found the website of Ivan Owen, a mechanical special effects artist from Washington state who had recently developed a robotic hand. Richard began collaborating with Ivan online, and the pair began exchanging design files for a robotic hand that could fit Richard. Eventually Richard got access to a 3D printer and was able to cut down production time from what used to take weeks to just hours. He no longer had

20. www.robohand.net

to wait a week for parts to arrive in the mail. If he broke a part, it took just 20 minutes to print a new one. Richard posted his designs online on Thingiverse,[21] a repository for storing and sharing 3D printed design files. Others saw his work online. For example, the mother of a young boy named Liam, who was born without fingers on his right hand, asked Richard to print him a new hand. In addition, because Richard had shared his design files online, people began printing their own hands and requesting prints from Richard. To date, more than 200 people all over the world have 3D-printed derivative prosthetic hands based on Richard's designs.

Projects like Robohand are made possible with open, scalable, customizable, and hackable technologies, so that each user can tweak and improve the design to fit his or her own body. Using a few accessible tools such as a 3D printer, a computer, and some inexpensive hardware components, people all over the world have been exposed to personal accessible tools that have the potential to improve the lives of communities and individuals.

Air and Space Exploration

Mach30[22] is an open source hardware space initiative. Contributors to the Mach30 project have created a Shepard Test Stand and a Ground Sphere CubeSat Ground Station. The Shepard Test Stand is one part of a larger Arduino-driven system for safe rocket engine operation. The Ground Sphere CubeSat Ground Station communicates with space-bound things. Among its design files, the Shepard Test Stand provides documents for thrust calibrations. The documentation for the Ground Sphere CubeSat Ground Station contains calculation worksheets as well as instructions on how to size and sew fabrics in the assembly guide.

DIYdrones[23] is the largest web-based community for modular flying robots, founded by Chris Anderson, who is also the co-founder of the largest DIY drones distributor, called 3D Robotics.[24] The DIYdrones website has spawned a growing group of enthusiasts, composed of hundreds of developers, who have developed one of the largest Arduino programs collaboratively. Companies are now sprouting up all over the world that use the 3D Robotics drone platform for things like unmanned aerial photography, mapping, data collection, and transportation.

The collaboration between the distributor (3D Robotics) and the online community (DIYdrones) relies on open source hardware and software, as well as sharing of information. 3D Robotics collaborates directly with online developers (to whom the company pays royalties), thereby outsourcing the research and development to community enthusiasts who are developing software on multiple hardware platforms for the drones. This collaboration between the community and the company increases the speed of innovation and cross-platform capabilities, by providing the communities with accessible software and the capability to purchase prefabricated drones or parts to make their own.

---

21. www.thingiverse.com
22. www.mach30.org
23. www.diydrones.org
24. www.store.3drobotics.com

Through the community web forums of the DIYdrones website, tools such as drones and quadcopters that were once accessible only to military and government have now begun to penetrate the civilian space through massive online collaboration and cross-platform development. As platforms for drones have proliferated in the hobby market, inventors and designers have started using these platforms as creative new solutions to widespread global problems.

Anecdote: Open Space Initiative
Stephen Murphey

Exploring outer space has been, for the longest time, the domain of governments and large corporations. This situation is now changing dramatically thanks to new technologies and ideas like the Internet, open hardware, and crowd-source funding. Just as open software helped usher in the dot-com era, so open hardware is helping to launch a new space era—and it's one that we can all participate in. The following is a brief introduction that is intended to inspire you to seek out more information.

CubeSats

A CubeSat is a small open source satellite design that was released in 1999 and has exploded in popularity as electronics have become cheaper, smaller, and more powerful. The basic design of a 1U CubeSat is a 10-cm cube that weighs no more than 1.33 kg. The design can be stacked to create larger satellites. A 2U CubeSat is 20 cm long with 10-cm sides; a 3U CubeSat is 30 cm long with 10-cm sides (you get the idea). CubeSats are typically launched from a Poly-PicoSatellite Orbital Deployer (P-POD), although a company called Nanoracks now launches them from the International Space Station (ISS).

Because of the small size of the P-POD and the common design requirements for CubeSats, it is much easier and cheaper to build and launch a CubeSat than a traditional microsatellite. Several companies provide ready-made satellite parts, and new companies like Planet Labs and Ardusat have actually launched CubeSats to offer satellite services.

Nanoracks

Nanoracks is the FedEx of space companies. This company works with NASA to launch small satellites and experiments to the International Space Station for a fee. If you wanted to launch an experiment in space before Nanoracks came into being but you didn't have millions of dollars, you had to convince an organization like NASA that your experiment deserved a launch. This could take years, if it ever happened at all. Nanoracks realized the market needed a second "pay to play" option and worked with NASA to install science modules on the ISS. Customers pay the fee and ensure their experiment meets the design and safety criteria; Nanoracks handles the rest.

The NASA/Nanoracks collaboration has been one of the most successful public/private partnerships in the space industry. The company is building the much-needed "space infrastructure" to enable affordable micro-gravity experiments and small satellite launches. Both Planet Labs and Ardusat have used Nanoracks to launch their spacecraft

(continues)

from the ISS. In case you're wondering how expensive the service is, note that one of Nanoracks's first customers was a high school.

Copenhagen Suborbitals

One of the most daring projects I've ever seen is Copenhagen Suborbitals. This all-volunteer group located in Copenhagen has the audacious goal to send a person into space on a home-made rocket. They post all of their designs on their website so anyone else can follow along and duplicate their efforts (Denmark doesn't have export controls like ITAR). Although Copenhagen Suborbitals is a volunteer group, it could easily be mistaken for a government backed program. The group even accepts donations on its website (www.CopenhagenSuborbitals.com) in case you want to contribute.

Environmental Preservation, Disaster Relief, and Mapping

OpenRelief[25] is a platform that aims to enhance disaster relief efforts by developing communication tools to facilitate getting aid to the right place at the right time. Open-Relief is designing an inexpensive, semi-disposable open source hardware drone that can map disaster zones; the device can be launched from a small road. The drone is modular so that it can be integrated with other software and hardware platforms. Using computer vision, the drone can recognize topography and people, and it can measure weather data as well as radioactivity and smoke. The data can then be uploaded to disaster management systems, such as Sahana Eden,[26] a real-time open source mapping platform for disaster management and mitigation. Additionally, OpenRelief has developed a small open source hardware radiation sensor that can be placed in disaster zones and will broadcast information directly to the OpenRelief drone. Sometimes open hardware revolves around very traditional, nondigital tools, but labeling the project as open source hardware gives a clear definitive solution to a problem that it is allowed to be copied. One of the OpenRelief simulations states the supply list as follows: "You just need this guide, pencils, paper and a map of the area where the disaster is being simulated." Through the use of open source hardware, OpenRelief ensures that anyone in the world can access this humanitarian drone technology, for the sake of building their own platform, integrating other software and hardware technologies with the OpenRelief airframe, inspiring the development of other modular sensors that can be integrated with the OpenRelief platform, and accessing the data to aid with disaster relief.

The Public Laboratory for Open Technology and Science (**Public Lab**[27] for short) is a community supported by a nonprofit company operating in various cities in the United States. Public Lab aims to develop and apply open source tools for environmental exploration and investigation. Through the distribution of hardware and software tools to the public, and by providing web platforms for aggregating the environmental data collected

25. www.openrelief.org
26. http://eden.sahanafoundation.org/
27. www.publiclab.org

with these tools, Public Lab assists in the proliferation of civilian science so as to generate distributed networks of knowledge and information. Some of its products include a mass spectrometer that can optically measure contaminants in liquids, such as drinking water, and balloon and kite mapping kits that provide affordable, easy-to-use, and safe tools for taking aerial images for mapping purposes. Public Lab comprises a collaborative community of contributors; experimental, inexpensive, easy-to-use tools; networks of local groups working in chapters; an open access online data archive; free and open source software; and an online platform to build collaborative communities. By leveraging open source DIY techniques and tools, Public Lab aims to empower underserved communities to take a hands-on approach to environmental sensing.

Safecast[28] is a Tokyo-based nonprofit organization that aims to empower people globally through available data. In response to the lack of available data about radiation levels in Japan after the Tohoku earthquake in 2011, which resulted in a tsunami and a nuclear plant (Fukushima Diaichi) meltdown, Safecast developed a platform for a distributed sensor network to collect and map radioactivity data. Safecast distributes and sells open source hardware Geiger counters (Figure 10.7) to measure radiation levels, and it has developed its own mapping platform online that makes it easy for individuals to contribute to and freely use the radiation level data. Since 2011, when Safecast was founded, Safecast and its community of users have amassed more than 15 million data points. Through open source hardware and open access to information, Safecast has been able to create a distributed sensor network and amass large amounts of useful environmental data for global communities. Its design files include templates for laser-cut plates, an API for data, and pre-uploaded board files (sent to OSH Park) for easy manufacture.

Educational Modular Toolkits

HacKIDemia[29] is an organization that trains mentors in local communities to teach young people the skills needed to invent new technologies, participate in science, technology, engineering, and math (STEM) education, and enable change. HacKIDemia is composed of three parts, reflected in its name: hacking, kids, and academics. The organization hosts global workshops using its Maker Box, which uses open source hardware tools to foster STEM initiatives and inspire research. The Maker Box will also be used in a new initiative called Afrimakers. Afrimakers is a program that will set up 10 hubs in Africa where local residents can teach workshops, disseminate information, and share local skills. In addition to workshops, HacKIDemia runs makehub.io,[30] a repository of HacKIDemia projects on GitHub. Projects from this initiative range from video game production and extracting strawberry DNA to sensor networking and building oscilloscopes out of moss.

LittleBits[31] is a partially open source hardware project that supports kits of electronic modules that snap together with tiny magnets to make cool prototypes, projects, and

---

28. www.safecast.org
29. www.hackdemia.com/
30. www.makehub.io
31. www.littlebits.cc

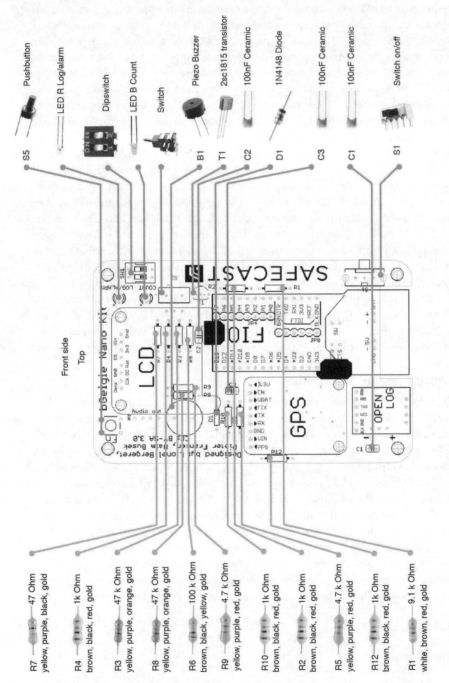

Figure 10.7   Safecast Small Parts Assembly Guide designed by Jurgen Westerhoff.
(Source: Image CC-BY Safecast)

assemblages of electronic elements. There are actuation elements, such as lights, speakers, and motors, as well as sensing elements, such as buttons, switches, and sensors. LittleBits aims to get electronics into the hands of children, artists, designers, makers, and students, for prototyping, play, and learning the fundamentals of electronics. Using the simple, intuitive platform for connecting sensors and actuators, users can build existing tools like light dimmers and invent new tools by plugging the little bits together. LittleBits is an example of a project using dual licensing, as described in Chapter 15, Business. The electronic schematics are open source hardware, but the connectors are patented. While you can reproduce the circuit boards of the LittleBits design, you cannot remake the completed product with connectors.

Fashion

OpenKnit[32] is an Arduino-controlled, RepRap derivative, open source hardware knitting machine that can knit clothing from CAD files. It carries a low price point, approximately $700, and knits a sweater in less than an hour. Digital fabrication of garments from CAD files had previously been possible with other tools, but has been prohibitively expensive for the hacker/DIY community. Thus this open source design of OpenKnit increases accessibility and affordability of such a tool. Online, OpenKnit hosts tutorials focusing on using the software, learning how to knit, and replacing the microcontroller. The software and the hardware are documented and modular enough for others to use and modify them. OpenKnit aims to bring open source digital fabrication to the DIY fashion industry, give hobbyists, fashion enthusiasts, and artists enough control to make their own fashion clothing.

One benefit of releasing OpenKnit with open source hardware is that the research and design can be crowd sourced and, therefore, can evolve organically with and for the community. Additionally, the community of users will drive some of the use-cases, as the hardware is modular and can be adapted to many different configurations for combining 3D modeling with fashion design.

Anecdote: OpenKnit
Gerard Rubio Arias

Walking around the corridors of the design university and seeing some schoolmates from the fashion design specialty using old commercial knitting machines from the 1980s, moving the carriage manually back and forth for their assignments, made me wonder if I could find a way to automate that process and make their life a bit easier. I started to imagine which mechanisms could make it possible and how people would use that capability. I mulled the idea around until one day I connected with the RepRap project, and the OpenKnit project was born. If it's possible to print objects from digital files, why not do the same with garments?

(continues)

---

32. www.openknit.org

I thought that someone would already have taken that step, but after doing some research I couldn't find anything similar. There were too many reasons to not start working on the project right away. I didn't create anything new—a digital fabrication tool for creating ready-to-use garments had been on the market for many years, albeit exclusively for the professional industry due to its high price. However, I opened up this technology and lowered its cost. The process of building a knitting machine from scratch consisted of learning how to use a knitting machine, researching as many machines as possible to get ideas, copying to create, and finally starting the tough process of making it real. Every single part had to be tested in depth (and I am still testing!), but after a few months the puzzle started to take shape.

An OpenKnit machine is not able to obtain the remarkable results the industrial machines do, but that's something we have to keep reviewing, and that's why I decided to go open source. I started working on this project a year ago, and I'm happy and surprised how far I got by myself. Nevertheless, I reached a certain point where making the project evolve further to create a more reliable system required many, many hours of testing and knowledge that I don't have. Making the project open source can only make it better. Because everybody is welcomed, a community is being created right now, and the excitement is pretty high. I can imagine many future applications.

Open Source Biotechnology

Many organizations globally are collaborating to produce open source hardware toolkits for biological and chemical experimental platforms to allow for inexpensive and accessible means to study health and biology, and to empower people through a greater understanding of biotechnology. The goal is to spawn a vibrant, productive, and safe community of DIY biologists. Much of this work is happening in countries where citizen science and grassroots activism can empower local communities through the use of open tools and technologies. Hackteria is one example of a global community platform to engage scientists, academics, hackers, and artists to collaboratively proliferate tools and platforms for research and innovation. Other organizations are collaborating on a global scale to bring open source hardware tools to the biomedical space, such as DIYBio[33] (United States), GenSpace[34] (New York City), BioCurious[35] (San Francisco), LifePatch[36] (Indonesia), Kharkhana[37] (Nepal), Art/Science Bangalore[38] (India), Labitat[39] (Denmark), and more. These grassroots organizations are gaining fast traction and collaborating with academia and corporations to penetrate the civilian space and popular mainstream.

---

33. www.diybio.org
34. www.genspace.org
35. www.biocurious.org
36. www.lifepatchsystem.org
37. www.karkhana.asia/
38. www.artscienceblr.org
39. www.labitat.dk

OpenPCR[40] (Figure 10.8) is one example of a biomedical research machine, developed collaboratively in hackerspaces internationally, that can amplify DNA for analysis through polymerase chain reaction (PCR) technology. Such a machine typically costs thousands of dollars and is inaccessible for general public use. OpenPCR is available for $599 and is made out of laser-cut wood and accessible electronic components. It is easy to build and use, thanks to the PDF assembly guide available on OpenPCR's website.[41] In addition to the assembly guide, the project source files include code for an air client and technical specifications for thermal purposes. The design files are hosted online, as are the instruction manuals, software, and bill of materials. OpenPCR is also available as a prefabricated kit.

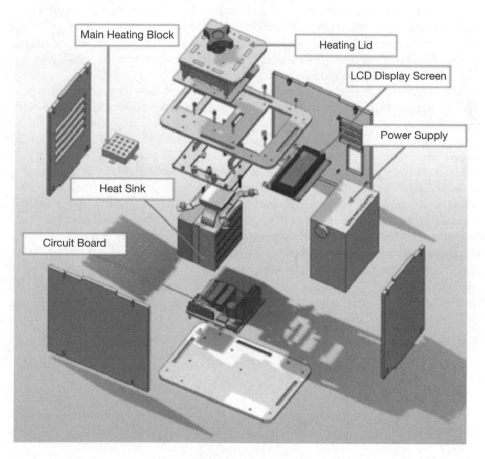

Figure 10.8   Open PCR.
(Source: Image CC-BY-SA OpenWetWare)

40. http://openpcr.org/
41. http://openpcr.org/build-it

Dropbot[42] is another example of an Arduino-based open source hardware platform for lab automation. It was developed in a laboratory in the University of Toronto. The digital microfluidic (DMF) system is driven by custom software that is intuitive, user friendly, and customizable. Dropbot's designs are published online, along with video tutorials, bill of materials, downloadable firmware, and calibration instructions. Detailed build instructions are available online, as well as a wiki and a place to submit tickets.

Summary

Open source hardware depends on proliferating technology through sharing the documentation and source files that are needed to build and modify the hardware itself. The open source hardware community is continually trying to standardize documentation and efficient sharing of work related to a piece of hardware so that others can use and modify the work, and it encourages the development of a vibrant community of people who use and improve on other open source hardware projects.

The rise of the Internet has allowed for rapid sourcing of tools for prototyping, designing, and manufacturing, as well as the creation of centralized online knowledge hubs in the form of wikis and forums. This allows for information exchange among people in remote locations, rapid distribution of design files, and a place to get questions answered fast. As more designs are shared that can be built and modified from anywhere in the world, manufacturing chains are becoming more distributed in networks of innovation at global levels. With the rise of open source hardware and digital fabrication and assembly techniques, automation will inevitably increase, as well as more abundant large-scale local manufacturing. In addition, many of the projects described in this chapter have physical locations, their own community chapter, or a hackerspace where they work. These physical spaces provide in-person collaborations and hands-on involvement with the hardware, also furthering innovation with open source hardware.

---

42. http://microfluidics.utoronto.ca/dropbot/

III

Production Bits

11 Personal Manufacturing in the Digital Age

12 Accelerate from Making to Manufacturing

13 Troubleshooting from Your Design to Your Manufacturer

14 Taxonomy of Hardware Documentation

15 Business

16 Building Open Source Hardware in Academia

Personal Manufacturing in the Digital Age

David A. Mellis

"From my point of view, the greatest developments to be expected
of technics in the future . . . will not be, as we are usually led to
think, in the direction of universalizing even more strenuously the
wasteful American system of mass production: no, on the contrary,
it will consist in using machines on a human scale, directly under
human control, to fulfill with more exquisite adaptation, with a higher
refinement of skill, the human needs that are to be served. . . . Much
that is now in the realm of automatism and mass production will come
back under directly personal control, not by abandoning the machine,
but by using it to better purpose, not by quantifying but by qualifying
its further use."

—Lewis Mumford, *Art and Technics* (1952)

Digital technology is enabling new alternatives to industrial production. Computer-aided
design (CAD) tools encode objects as information, allowing their designs to be freely
shared online—the practice of open source hardware. Digital fabrication machines turn this
information into objects, allowing for precise, one-off production of physical goods. A variety of sophisticated off-the-shelf electronic components enable complex sensing, actuation,
communication, and interfaces. Together, these technologies enable individuals to produce
complex devices from digital designs, a process we can think of as *personal manufacturing*.

Because open source hardware involves treating physical objects as digital information,
it suggests that we may be able to apply principles and practices from other kinds of online collaboration to the design of hardware. Open source software, Wikipedia, and other
digital artifacts incorporate the creativity of many different individuals working without
the direction of markets or firms, a process known as peer production. It works because
the means of production of digital goods—computers and software—are widely distributed, the Internet makes communication and coordination efficient, and the work can be

divided into pieces that individuals can choose to work on based on their own interests, needs, and abilities. The extent to which peer production can apply to hardware will shape the extent to which this approach can provide a viable alternative to mass production for the technology in our lives.

To make electronic devices amenable to these peer production approaches, we need to design with them in mind. This process yields devices that look very different than ones that are industrially produced. Such devices are optimized for translation from the digital design to the physical object. They make use of a variety of processes, from the much-hyped 3D printing to the more prosaic (but potentially more useful) techniques of laser cutting, CNC milling, and circuit board fabrication. They allow for a variety of materials and aesthetics. They can be adapted by individuals for their own needs and interests. They allow for different business models, in which objects can be made on demand or in small quantities to serve specific markets or particular individuals.

Of course, none of this eliminates the need for individual skill, whether in the design process or in the use of the fabrication machines. Good CAD tools can make the process easier, but translating an idea into concrete form requires many decisions and compromises that rely on human skill, experience, and intuition. Similarly, making effective use of a fabrication machine relies on knowledge of its configuration, operation, limitations, and quirks. Technology offers possibilities, but people turn those possibilities into reality. Similar considerations exist in open source software, where peer production doesn't eliminate the need for expertise on the part of contributors but rather provides new ways of organizing and combining those individuals' skills and efforts.

The two case studies discussed in this chapter—dealing with Arduino boards and my own consumer electronic devices—illustrate different possibilities and limitations of working with these techniques. Together, they illustrate this new personal manufacturing ecosystem, highlighting its implications for product design, for collaboration, and for business. They show some of the ways that digital technology can transform the production of objects, but also indicate some of the constraints derived from industrial systems that persist in personal manufacturing. They provide some hints of what a peer production ecosystem for electronic devices might look like, yet also point out some of the difficulties to be overcome in creating one.

The next section gives an overview of personal fabrication and the considerations involved in going from an open source hardware design file to an actual physical object. This discussion is followed by the two case studies. The lessons from the case studies are used to derive some general principles for open source hardware and personal manufacturing. Finally, I conclude with some questions and thoughts for the future.

Personal Fabrication, Processes, Parts, and Materials

Digital fabrication machines translate open source hardware designs into actual physical objects. In theory, this process depends only on the digital file and the choice of fabrication machine, allowing for iteration and refinement through successive changes to the file. In practice, though, the constraints and intricacies of various fabrication processes mean that a certain amount of skill is required to use the machine and that the results can vary each time. As a result, open source hardware depends on the selection of appropriate processes and effective use of them. This section discusses some of the considerations involved in various popular fabrication processes.

3D Printing

The purest of these digital fabrication processes are the various forms of 3D printing. These turn digital design into physical objects by gradually adding material in the desired locations, allowing for a wide range of possible geometries. The term *3D printing* encompasses a broad range of machines, from personal plastic printers costing a few hundred dollars to industrial machines that sinter metal and cost hundreds of thousands of dollars. Different machines work with different materials and offer different resolutions and tolerances. The materials may have different strengths, optical properties, appearances, finishing possibilities, and so on. Depending on the object being fabricated, some or all of these characteristics may be crucial to creating a useable result. In designing and sharing objects for 3D printing, therefore, it's important to specify not just their geometries, but also the required tolerances, materials, and other characteristics—most of which are less easily captured in digital form. In addition, many 3D-printing processes need some form of manual post-processing, such as removal of support material, finishing, or curing. These require an operator with appropriate knowledge and skill—and can create variations from one print to the next, even with the same file and machine. Finally, 3D printing technology is evolving and diversifying rapidly. For all these reasons, it's important not to think of 3D printing as a way to automatically create things from information, but rather as a material process with specific qualities and affordances.

Milling and Cutting

Other fabrication processes work by cutting or removing pieces of a larger stock material. Laser cutters cut 2D shapes out of plywood, cardboard, acrylic, and other flat materials. Vinyl cutters do the same, but with a knife that cuts through thin materials like paper or adhesive-backed vinyl. The water-jet cutter handles stronger and thicker materials like wood, metal, and glass, cutting with a stream of hard particles in a powerful jet of water. CNC (computer-numeric control) machines, like mills or routers, work in three (or more) dimensions, removing material from solid blocks of stock with a variety of cutting bits. They are often capable of very precise operations, albeit only within specific axes of movement. Compared with 3D printers, these cutting and milling tools have the advantage of being able to work with a variety of existing materials, including natural ones with complex structures that are difficult or impossible to replicate with the homogenous stock of most 3D printers. They are more limited in the geometries they can produce, however, and often require more steps in fabricating or assembling the parts.

In addition to specifying the geometry of the design itself, it's important to be explicit about the nature of the stock material and the characteristics of the cutting process. Whether two parts press-fit tightly together, slip past each other, or don't fit at all depends as much on the precise thickness of the stock (which can vary even across nominally equivalent materials) and the thickness of the cut as on the shape in the file. Some constructions may be infeasible to achieve given the tolerances of a particular machine. (Laser cutters may yield slightly different cut thicknesses on different sides of their working area; water-jet cutters can give rough, nonvertical edges, for example.) Traditional engineering drawings often capture the required tolerances for various surfaces and the material to be used. A quickly created CAD file used for a prototype and then thrown up on a webpage may not. Parts might be sanded, glued, pounded together, or otherwise tweaked in ways not reflected in the design files. Generating tool paths for a CNC machine is a complex process with a significant impact on the form and finish of the resulting object; this complexity may not be possible to capture in a way that can be easily shared with others, particularly if they are using a different machine. Finishing and assembling parts created with CNC devices requires careful craft, which might be difficult to communicate or learn. All of these factors need to be kept in mind when designing or sharing a digital file for someone else to replicate.

Other Fabrication Machines

A variety of other digital fabrication processes exist, each with its own affordances and constraints. For example, a host of machines are available for working with soft materials: CNC embroidery machines apply custom designs to fabric, knitting machines generate colors and constructions based on digital files, and Jacquard looms are possibly the oldest digital fabrication machines in existence. Industrial production uses a variety of automated machines, including robot arms and other adaptable parts of an assembly line. Furthermore, as digital fabrication becomes more established, more people are creating their own machines for custom purposes of various kinds.

Printed Circuit Boards and Electronics

The production of printed circuit boards (PCBs) can also be considered a digital fabrication process—and a relatively mature one. Digital designs are etched from copper or other materials using a photographic process, then covered with an isolating layer and text and other annotations. While the processes for creating circuit boards in this way are generally toxic and the automated systems for doing so are expensive, many services will produce PCBs on demand for individual customers with small or nonexistent minimums and standard specifications and tolerances. (As a board's specifications get more demanding, however, costs can increase, sometimes dramatically.) Circuit boards can also be manually etched or milled on a CNC machine, processes that are more directly accessible to individuals but also less robust and precise. While some circuits are sensitive to the precise characteristics of circuit board's substrate or the exact tolerances of the fabrication process, a great many can be shared with relative confidence that they will work when made on a different machine from a different provider.

In reproducing circuits, then, the main difficulties are typically getting the necessary parts and assembling them. While vast quantities of components are available to individuals—and many distributors specifically target hobbyists—advanced parts with specific functionality may not be accessible. These may be simply impossible to purchase, require an extended procurement process that makes replication infeasible, or be difficult or impossible to assemble with the processes available. As parts are optimized for size and automated assembly, they become harder for individuals to work with. Even easier-to-solder parts rely on manual skill and the knowledge to troubleshoot problems. Different electronic components may be available or preferred in different locations. Parts may go out of stock, become obsolete, or cease being made altogether. All of these factors mean that while making a PCB may be a robust and accessible process, much work must be done to ensure that individuals are able to replicate a complete electronic circuit for themselves. (It's also worth noting that while the problem may be worse for electronic components, other materials—such as plywood or 3D printer stock—are also industrial products and may not be available everywhere or all the time.)

Access to Fabrication

Access to digital fabrication processes comes in a variety of forms. Some machines, particularly 3D printers and vinyl cutters, are being targeted at individual consumers via low-cost, easy-to-use models. Local workshops, whether at schools, libraries, community centers, or commercial locations, provide access to larger, messier, and more expensive machines. They also offer opportunities for people to learn how to use the machines and can provide a community of like-minded individuals. Online services offer an alternative for those without local, hands-on access. They can provide a larger variety of processes and materials than those found in a single workshop and obviate the need to learn to operate the machines directly. On the downside, the time required for parts to be produced and shipped—and the lack of direct control over the process—can make it harder to iterate and refine designs when using an online service. Additionally, online services generally involve higher per-part prices than direct machine access, since they need to cover the cost of the machines, labor, and infrastructure required to support the service.

Case Studies

There's a lot more to open source hardware than just the fabrication and electronics technology. The following case studies draw on my personal experiences with open source hardware to discuss some of the real-world issues involved. The first case study looks at the Arduino electronics platform, a well-known open source hardware project. The second case study discusses my research at the MIT Media Lab, building open source and DIY consumer electronic products.

Case Study: Arduino Microcontroller Development Boards and Their Derivatives

Arduino is a platform for building interactive objects. It consists of microcontroller-based circuit boards and the software for programming them (both of which are open source), along with relevant documentation and community support.

Arduino builds on the work of many other projects, including the Wiring electronics prototyping platform, the Processing development environment, the GNU C Compiler (gcc), AVR libc, avrdude, and more. Since the Arduino electronics prototyping platform started in 2005, it has spawned and participated in a diverse ecosystem of software, hardware, communities, and companies. The relationships between the various actors in the Arduino ecosystem take many different forms: some specifically relate to the open source nature of the Arduino hardware, others reflect its open source software, and still others are based on more traditional business factors. As a co-founder of Arduino, I've witnessed many of these stories over the years. This case study attempts to make sense of the lessons of Arduino for open source hardware and personal manufacturing.

Because the original Arduino circuit boards are relatively simple, were created with a low-cost circuit design tool (Eagle), and use widely available parts, it's relatively straightforward for someone to make their own versions of them. This has led to a proliferation of Arduino derivatives, with a number of different modifications. These boards reveal an open source hardware ecosystem with a very different structure than that of most open source software projects. Successful open source software projects typically involve decentralized collaboration efforts, in which a number of individuals contribute to a single body of source code. The derivatives of the Arduino hardware, in contrast, tend to be produced by a small group of people, often the same ones who sell the resulting product. These derivatives often undergo few public revisions, even though some have remained available for purchase for a number of years. Moreover, relatively few changes have been contributed back to the design of the official Arduino boards. Overall, the derivatives constitute a diverse set of alternatives from different producers, in contrast to the centralized codebase that seems to prevail in most open source software projects (including, in many respects, the Arduino software itself). While some derivatives (like the LilyPad Arduino) have been incorporated into the official Arduino product line, very few (if any) modifications have been contributed to existing boards.

There are multiple obstacles to collaboration on centralized hardware designs that go beyond the need for human skill and motivation common to other domains (like open source software). One is the difficulty and expense of fabricating and assembling boards. Soldering them by hand can be done in small quantities (facilitating changes and the creation of unique variations) but is time consuming, error prone, and limited in the parts it can work with. Automated assembly is more efficient but typically requires larger quantities, limiting the frequency of changes to the circuit's design. Even worse, it can be difficult to switch between these approaches because they may require the use of different components.

Another obstacle is the relative unavailability of tools for tracking and merging changes to the design of circuit boards. Open source software has robust version control tools that allow the tracking and merging of changes by many different people. The free and low-cost circuit design tools used by most of the people designing Arduino derivatives don't provide automated methods for viewing or merging changes. Without these capabilities, the process of proposing changes to the design of an Arduino board is one that in many ways fails to take advantage of its digital nature. That is, you describe the change you'd like to see and rely on the original designer to re-create it for themselves, if desired, rather than providing a digital encoding of the change that can be automatically previewed and merged. This lack of easy methods for merging the efforts of multiple individuals reduces the viability of peer production for electronic circuits.

A final obstacle to centralized collaboration is the complications relating to the role of money and business in the production of hardware. When developers have to invest money and time in making and testing changes to the design of a circuit, they may be motivated to recoup those investments by selling their own version of a product rather than contributing their changes back to the original producer. This can create confusion around identity and branding as well, as it can become challenging to distinguish between boards of similar or identical design from different producers. As a result of these complications, Arduino has trademarked the Arduino name, using it to identify only products made by the company. This decision was initially contentious but since seems to have become an accepted practice.

The Arduino ecosystem also points out the importance of open sourcing the complements to the hardware itself. Because the Arduino software is open source (as are its underlying software tools), it gives the makers of derivatives a platform that people can use to program their boards. This factor has slowly pushed the Arduino software to become ever more general; it originally supported only a single AVR processor, then spread to most of the AVR product line, and now can support multiple processors with completely different architectures. This provides a uniform, centralized software platform for the whole ecosystem of derivatives. It also allows others to customize the software along with the hardware, adopting it to both specific uses and available resources. Online documentation (especially if liberally licensed) also makes it easier to support a new board, as that product doesn't need to be documented from scratch. This open source software and documentation, combined with accessible circuit board fabrication and electronic components, together yields a healthy ecosystem of Arduino derivatives and alternatives.

It's not clear what the relative importance of these various factors has been in promoting the vibrant Arduino ecosystem that exists today. Certainly, the Arduino software is more sophisticated (and, therefore, would be more difficult to re-create from scratch) than the basic Arduino circuits—and, in many cases, the derivative circuit designs have been re-created from scratch rather than derived from the files for the original Arduino. In theory, if the Arduino software were simply flexible and extensible, but not actually open source, it could still support a variety of derivatives of the Arduino hardware. In practice, it seems clear that many of the improvements that have been contributed to the software (including those for better support of third-party hardware) have relied in various ways on the fact that the code for the software is available. It's hard to guess which kinds of extensibility people will need, and we probably would have done a bad job if we had tried to predict those directions; instead, individuals have been able to modify the Arduino software in whatever ways they needed and the most useful of these changes have been merged back into the main codebase.

In short, it's difficult to separate electronic devices from the software that works with them. On the one hand, open sourcing just the hardware limits the modifications that can be made (without requiring reimplementation of the software). On the other hand, if the software is open source but the hardware isn't, it might not be clear that derivative designs are allowed. Thus open sourcing the hardware can help make it clear that it's acceptable to create derivatives of or add-ons to an electronic device. In addition, the design files can serve as a de facto specification and reference, facilitating the creation of compatible products. In general, the more aspects of a device's design are shared, the more likely it seems that others will reproduce or modify it.

Case Study: Open Source Consumer Electronic Products

While Arduino has demonstrated that open source hardware can create a thriving eco-system, it's sobering to note that the vast majority of devices that people use remain proprietary. In my research at the MIT Media Lab, I've been researching the possibilities for people to build devices for use in their daily lives. I started with well-known consumer electronic products: a radio, speakers, a mouse, and, most recently, a cellphone (Figure 11.1).

(a)

(b)

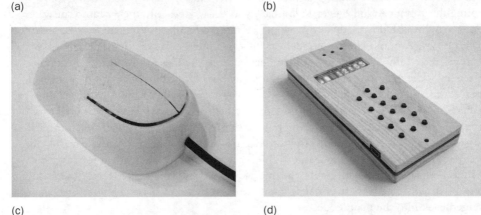
(c)

(d)

Figure 11.1   (a) A radio. (b) Speakers. (c) A mouse. (d) A cellphone.
(Source: Images CC-BY 2.0 David A. Mellis)

I design the products, prototype them, and use them in my life. In workshops, I help others to make and modify the products for themselves. In general, I try to start from technologies that are accessible to individuals and find ways to put them together into robust and attractive devices. This requires integrating the enclosure, electronic circuit, and embedded software into a complete product—and doing so in a way that lends itself to replication and modification by other individuals. It also means designing specifically for personal fabrication, which has very different opportunities and constraints than the mass production that creates most of our electronic devices.

Electronics

For the electronic aspects of a device, determining the core functionality, interface, and components is an important first step in the design process. Knowing the parts that will compose a device gives a general sense of the required form and shapes the specifics of the electronic circuit. For example, in the speakers, the decision to use three AAA batteries as the power source placed constraints on the size and shape of the speakers and on the design of amplification circuit. Component selection is also crucial for mass-produced devices, of course, but many additional constraints apply when designing devices for personal fabrication. The components have to be available to individuals and possible to assemble without expensive machines or processes. Often, there are limited possibilities available, especially for key components. The radio, mouse, and cellphone all have, at their core, an electronic part that performs much of the basic functioning of the device (receiving radio signals, interpreting the mouse movements, or communicating with the cellular network). For all three, I've had problems finding or maintaining a supply of these core components: the radio receiver and mouse chip that I used have since become unavailable and the cellphone module may become obsolete as cellular networks are upgraded.

This experience points out the essential role that industry can play in DIY: the components it makes available shape the devices that individuals can make for themselves. (There are efforts to produce open source or DIY implementations of core technologies like microcontrollers and cellular baseband modules but, in general, these don't yet seem to offer a feasible alternative to commercial components.) For these reasons, the personal fabrication or DIY process is perhaps better viewed as an individual's ability to assemble the available technologies into a desired product rather than the ability to make everything oneself, from scratch.

The limitations on component selection need to be considered when designing the circuit. For example, with the cellphone, I had to carefully balance the functional requirements against the overall size of the circuit board to yield a usable device. This imposed severe limitations on the functionality: the screen (an LED matrix) shows only eight characters at a time and there's no headphone jack, loudspeaker, removable storage, or many other common features. Even so, the phone can send and receive calls and text messages, keep time, and function as an alarm clock, which is enough functionality for me to have used it as my main phone for the past year. Cramming in more functionality may have made the device too big or fragile to actually use.

Being selective about the functions I needed (and being able to choose them for myself) allowed me to find a compromise that worked for me. In addition, because I faced similar constraints on component selection as many other hobbyists, I ended up using components for which I could download open source libraries. I was also often able to find existing circuit designs incorporating the same parts, which I could use as a reference in designing my own board.

Developing successive versions of my devices has also shown me that it's important to design your circuit boards with iteration in mind. Building extra flexibility into a design speeds up the process by making it possible to try out different forms and functions without having to fabricate a new board. For example, breaking out additional microcontroller pins, allowing for multiple types of power, and providing different mounting options can allow the board to be used in new and unexpected ways. Another approach that's sometimes useful is to provide a footprint on the board for some parts but not actually solder them on unless they're needed. These development techniques mean that you can try out new variations on a device's form and function without having to wait for a new circuit board to be fabricated, assembled, and tested.

Finally, while the design files for a device capture the components selected, they don't necessarily document the requirements or tradeoffs that led to those decisions, which may make it more difficult for others to create their own modifications of the device. In the cellphone, for example, I restricted the circuit to components shorter than 6 mm so that they'd fit within the laser-cut enclosure. This decision isn't shown in the circuit's design file but is an important constraint on the components that can be used.

Enclosures

Most of my devices have been housed in cases made on the laser cutter. This has allowed me to use natural materials, such as wood and fabric, that are rarely seen in commercial devices. It has, however, required finding clever ways to combine the flat pieces made by the laser cutter into three-dimensional objects. The radio and speakers use two parallel laser-cut plywood faces connected by struts. The faces are then wrapped with another material (either fabric or veneer). For the cellphone, I've sandwiched the circuit board with two pieces of plywood and then covered them with veneer. (In general, I'm not a fan of the finger-jointed boxes found in many laser-cut projects.) All of the designs have fairly simple contours, making it fast to laser-cut them. That constraint has allowed me to quickly iterate through designs by actually making them and seeing how well the parts fit together and how they relate to the electronics. Because the parts are designed in a simple, open source 2D drawing software (Inkscape), they are relatively easy for someone else to modify, whether by simply adding personal text to be engraved or by changing the overall form.

Another approach, which I used for my computer mouse, is to model the circuit board in 3D (using Rhino or similar software) and then use it as a reference when designing the enclosure. This strategy takes advantage of the relative flexibility of 3D printing and the resulting ability to visualize the desired object in software. In addition, 3D-printing parts can be relatively slow, particularly if you are using a high-end machine via an online service. By working in CAD before printing the enclosure, it's possible to experiment with various designs and iterate on their form and relationship to the electronics. Because this process uses more sophisticated 3D modeling software, it tends to be more difficult for a novice to modify the design of the enclosure, even in a simple way. Conversely, experts can capture more of their work in the 3D model, potentially achieving greater leverage of their skills as they share those models with others.

Assembly

I've tried to take advantage of the manual assembly required for my devices by using this step as an opportunity to engage people in their design and production. The radio and speakers include a fabric element that can be chosen by the individual making the device, giving it a unique appearance and personal significance. Other users, particularly those with prior CAD experience, have created more distinctive variations on the design of the products—creating an owl-shaped pair of speakers, in one case, or producing cellphone enclosures from a variety of materials. Assembling a device offers an opportunity and an engaging context for learning or practicing various skills, such as soldering or hand work. Many of the participants in my workshops are motivated by the desire to create a finished device but, in the process, gain experience with and appreciation for the skills involved in the process. In addition, the mere fact of putting an object together for oneself can invest it with a meaning not present for purchased products.

General Principles

The case studies suggest that there is more to making an open source hardware project successful than simply sharing its design files. These guidelines attempt to distill their lessons in ways that can be applied to other open source hardware efforts:

- *Use standard parts and materials (in conjunction with your open source design files).* For others to make use of an open source design, they need to be able to get the parts that it relies on, whether those are electronic components, screws, stock material, or something else. The more standard and widely available the parts you use are, the easier it will be for someone else to reproduce your design. That might require foregoing components that are convenient for you if they're not available to others. Note that this guideline is in some ways opposed to some quick prototyping techniques, which may favor the materials at hand regardless of their future availability.

- *Understand and design for the fabrication process used.* Different fabrication processes are good for different things—and they also have different processes and constraints. By designing for a specific fabrication process, you can take advantage of its strengths, avoid its weaknesses, and optimize for its parameters. Be specific: different kinds of 3D printers have very different possibilities, as do different stock materials that you might cut with a laser cutter or CNC machine. Working with a particular machine or process as you iterate on your design allows you to learn the capabilities of the machine and ensure that your designs are compatible with it. Of course, other people trying to reproduce your design might not have access to exactly the same machine or process, so try to find ways to avoid relying too heavily on individual quirks or features. Pay special attention to the tolerances of your chosen fabrication process. Don't create designs that rely on a precision that's not possible to reliably achieve with the machine (e.g., if you have to laser-cut 10 parts to get 2 that actually work, you might want to rethink your design). Hand-soldering is not a particularly exact process; when designing enclosures for a circuit, remember that some components may not end up exactly where the design file specifies they should.

- *Pursue unique meanings, functions, and aesthetics.* The power and efficiency of mass production make it difficult to compete with this approach on its own terms. Instead, try to find unique values for your open source devices. Those might come from solving a problem that's of interest to only a small group of people, albeit possibly of great value to them. It might mean using unusual materials or aesthetics to differentiate your devices in ways that might not appeal to a mainstream consumer but might be appealing to someone looking for an alternative. Or the unique value might simply flow from finding ways to meaningfully involve individuals in the production of the devices. Take advantage of the fact that personal fabrication allows you to make devices in small quantities to find audiences that aren't well served by existing commercial products.

- *Find ways to make iteration faster, cheaper, and easier.* A key benefit of digital fabrication is that every part it produces can be different. To take full advantage of this ability, find ways to iterate on your design rapidly. Getting direct access to a laser cutter, for example, might mean you can try out a few designs in an afternoon instead of waiting a week or two to get a single one in the mail. Similarly, having the electronic components on hand to solder them to a newly fabricated circuit board will allow you to test that board more quickly and update its design accordingly. Identify the biggest barrier or barriers to iteration and try to find ways to remove them, whether by getting hands-on access to a machine, using software tools to refine your design before fabricating it, or being able to modify or update a part after it's been made.

- *Open source the complements to the hardware itself.* Someone who wants to re-create or modify your design will likely need more than just a raw CAD file. Provide whatever additional information seems likely to be useful—for example, parts lists, assembly instructions, firmware, and user documentation. Furthermore, by providing the original sources for these additional resources (not just compiled binaries or hard-to-edit documents like PDFs), you enable others to update them together with your hardware files when creating new variations on a design.

- *Clearly distinguish between open source design files and the products based on them.* Selling a physical product is very different from sharing a hardware design file, even if the former is based on the latter. Someone who buys a product may have higher expectations for its functionality, reliability, and safety than someone who makes a device for himself or herself based on your design. If you make and sell products based on someone else's design, be sure to distinguish between the two, making it clear that the product is from you but giving credit to the original designer.

Questions for the Future

Even if we continue to improve our practices along the lines suggested in the general principles, it's not clear what the future holds for open source hardware and personal manufacturing. The pace at which technologies of digital fabrication and embedded computation are evolving shows few signs of slowing down (notwithstanding the impossibility of the exponential growth of Moore's law continuing forever). The extent to which these improvements will extend the capability of individuals and the possibilities for open source hardware, however, is not so easy to predict. Here are three questions about the future of open source hardware and personal manufacturing—questions that I hope will encourage us to think about the future we'd like to see and to work toward making it a reality:

- *Will the technologies that can be made by individuals keep pace with those produced by large companies?* Although technology continues to improve, it doesn't necessarily do so in ways that are accessible to everyone. As a result, it's unclear to what extent open source, DIY, and peer production will be able to keep up with the devices that are produced and sold by large companies. While the potential scope of open source hardware continues to expand as technology improves, the gap between it and proprietary products may limit the extent to which it can serve as a feasible substitute for them. We should remember that the decisions we make influence the potential scope of open source hardware. If we encourage manufacturers to make their technologies available, support open tools, make use of open standards, and make our own hardware open source, we can expand that extent to which individuals are able to create, modify, and control the technologies they use in their lives.

- *Will peer production of open source hardware improve?* Although there are exceptions, open source hardware currently seems less likely than other domains (e.g., open source software) to involve collaboration between many individuals on a centralized design or repository, in which small contributions are combined together into a complex whole. Although there are many reasons for this pattern, if open source hardware is to thrive, it seems crucial to facilitate better collaboration between large numbers of distributed and diverse individuals. This will require improved tools, more efficient processes, and, perhaps most importantly, a focus on fostering communities that have a shared interest in the development of open source hardware.

- *Will the culture of open source hardware expand to include new people and applications?* Although digital fabrication and embedded computation allow for a wide variety of activities and outputs, it's easy to get caught up in the technologies themselves as opposed to their many contexts and applications. For early adopters, an interest in the technology itself can be helpful, as its uses may not be immediately clear or accessible. Even so, this emphasis on technology for technology's sake will not appeal to everyone. Thus, as we think about the future of open source hardware, we should remember to not just play with the technology, but also find ways to make it relevant and useful to new people and situations. In part, this evolution may happen naturally as technologies mature and we come to take them for granted, but it also relies on those of us with early access to and expertise in technology to think about how to make it relevant and useful to others.

Depending on the answers to these questions, the future of open source hardware and personal manufacturing may look very different. My hope is that we will find ways to make them increasingly relevant and valuable, by expanding the technologies they can make use of, the collaborations that can produce them, and the applications and contexts to which they can be applied. If our practices can keep pace with the growth of technology, open source hardware should offer a powerful alternative to mass production for the technology in our lives.

Summary

Personal fabrication offers a potential alternative to mass production for the creation of hardware. This requires effective use of the available fabrication processes, such as 3D printing, laser cutting, and printed circuit board fabrication. As the Arduino case study demonstrates, the success of open source hardware also depends on a number of other factors, like the complements of the hardware itself and the business decision of various actors. Bringing open source hardware into our daily lives (as I try to do in my research) requires careful design of the devices themselves and the process of involving people in their production. Personal fabrication suggests new design principles. The effectiveness of these, and broader questions about the future of technology, will determine the extent to which digital technology can make peer production feasible as an alternative to mass production for hardware.

12

Accelerate from Making to Manufacturing

Matt Bolton

"Necessity is the mother of all invention."

—English proverb

Manufacturing a product—any product—is a great challenge, but one that can be highly rewarding. There is something wonderful to be said about retaining full control of your designs, from concept to customer delivery. Retaining full control allows you to open source not only the design but also the process for mass producing that design. Working side by side with your manufacturing team is likely to produce innovative improvements to your designs as the manufacturer, with a vested interest in your product, develops more efficient assembly methods and discovers tiny design defects that are reported directly back to you.

Once written off as simply a nostalgic element of America's past, manufacturing has become possible in the United States once again thanks to the reduced cost of entry-level equipment; the shift in consumer desires to more customized, niche products that do not require high-volume manufacturing on a grand scale; and a strong desire within many organizations to live out their do-it-yourself (DIY) dreams.

One thing to be aware of when committing to fully owning the manufacturing of your product is the fact that manufacturing is likely to be the most costly part of all hardware design and distribution. Many people often underestimate this cost. When said out loud, the expense linked to this step sounds entirely logical; however, many hardware start-ups, time after time, make the mistake of not planning a sufficient amount of capital for all of the expenses involved with building up their product design(s) at an acceptable quality level and in ample quantities. Be prepared for manufacturing to cost more than you originally thought.

Many local contract manufacturers are highly skilled and would make excellent partners should you choose to lean on someone else to help you manufacture your design(s). Regardless of whether you choose to manufacture your own product or outsource that step, a large number of detailed checklists must be worked through before your product is ready to be shipped out to the excited masses awaiting your latest and greatest innovation.

Manufacturing Partner Decision

To DIY or not to DIY—that is the question. You can choose to DIY manufacture or select a trusted **contract manufacturer** (CM) to build your product for you. One of the great things about producing your own designs in this day and age is that there are a vast range of options for building new innovations at practically all points on the demand spectrum, from building single units to mass-producing many millions of units. In the world of electronics assembly, an electric skillet purchased at your hometown general store and a set of tweezers can get the job done, depending on the complexity of the components required for the circuit board you are building. Should you ever need to manufacture that board in the same volumes as the latest iPhone or Galaxy Nexus model, you can certainly set up factories with complete assembly lines of specialized equipment that will help you fulfill that quantum leap in demand. Of course, a plethora of options are available for anyone needing a solution that falls somewhere in between those two extremes.

Should you elect to contract your manufacturing out to someone else with expertise in building products in large volume, it is important to ask the right questions that will help you determine what you want and need out of your manufacturing partnership. Of equal importance, you should ask any potential manufacturing partner the questions that will give you the peace of mind that the manufacturer can and will deliver the results that you desire. Though by no means exhaustive, the following questions should set you off on a course for finding the right CM:

- Can the CM provide a fully turnkey solution, including the procurement of all parts? What is the difference in total unit cost between the turnkey solution versus the "assembly only" cost?

- What is the CM's average turnaround time once an order becomes official? If working with an international contractor, has the company verified that its quoted turnaround time includes shipping?

- What are the CM's minimum order quantity requirements? Does that requirement differ depending on who is supplying the parts for the production run?

- Is the CM capable of sourcing bare printed circuit boards (PCBs) in any color desired?

- Does the CM have a non-disclosure agreement (NDA) and/or a documented policy on intellectual property to govern the partnership and give you the protections you desire for open source hardware?

- Does the potential CM have any current or former customers that can be independently contacted for their opinions on working with that particular CM?

- Will the CM accept orders without requiring its own design for manufacturability (DFM) engineering be applied to the design, especially if that engineering service comes at an additional cost?

- Can the CM support your materials and process requirements (e.g., solder and flux type, Restriction of Hazardous Substances [RoHS] or conflict-free compliance, 100% testing of each solder joint)?

- Is the CM accepting of both infrequent and unpredictable orders with potentially varied unit quantities in each order?

Of nearly equal importance to selecting the right contract manufacturer is the decision of whether to supply that CM with all the inventory for each production run or ask the CM to handle this task for you (typically known as a **turnkey** solution). If you have chosen a reputable CM to work with, it will more than likely do a great job of sourcing all your bill of materials (BOM) components for you. Understand, however, that the CM will be providing this service at an additional cost to you. Also, be prepared to hear its ideas for how your design can be improved to better optimize your product for efficiency gains when being built with the manufacturer's production processes.

In contrast, making the decision to set up your own supply network and provide your CM with inventory *can* deliver some very tangible benefits, including some significant cost savings. Be aware, however, that this route will require a lot of hard work spent contacting potential suppliers to establish a network for procuring the components needed for your design.

Anecdote: Innovate with China
Momi Han and Seeed Studio

The concept of "innovate with China" is situated parallel to Chinese Shanzhai culture. China has grown to be a manufacturing giant in the past 50 years—hence the "Made in China" stickers attached to the vast majority of products around the globe. A new shift is occurring where China wants to innovate with the rest of the globe and use its people's creativity, rather than simply manufacturing other people's products. With the global demand for mobile phones, tablets, and anything electronic, Shanzhai culture helps lower the costs of commonly used components, making them accessible to makers in a convenient, quick way. The usual production timeline of a hardware start-up is seven to eight years; with the advent of open source hardware, the average time to shape the first prototypes is highly shortened. If you are in China, especially in Shenzhen, you'll also find that it's much easier to actualize your ideas into solid hardware products. The ecosystem in Shenzhen provides makers with advantages in aspects such as sourcing, manufacturing, and logistics to make hardware start-ups scale more easily.

Seeed Studio, an open source hardware company located in Shenzhen, is also accelerating the maker movement by helping people in mainly three aspects. First, the company makes technologies accessible to makers by providing corresponding open hardware modules for makers to build projects. Second, it helps makers turn ideas into products by providing Agile manufacturing services, including sourcing, design, cutting costs, and logistics, among others. Last but not least, Seeed Studio has helped spread the culture by building the first maker space in Shenzhen, thereby providing a physical space and

(continues)

platform for cross-field cooperation; as well as bringing Maker Faire to Shenzhen, and encouraging communication between makers within China and abroad.

As to the outcome of this movement, we hope to fill the gap between makers and the supply chain system, making it easier for makers to materialize their creative ideas. We'll continually strive to build an open, cooperative open source hardware ecosystem with global peer companies and partners from other fields. In the future, we hope those "Made in China" stickers will turn into "Innovated with China" stickers.

How SparkFun Electronics Grew to Scale

SparkFun Electronics was created to be a source of electronics components and tools for students studying electrical engineering. Over time, that business model morphed into one that delivered uniquely easy access to electronic components that were often difficult to "play" with because the only package type they were manufactured in were surface-mounted devices (SMD), which the electronics industry has continuously adopted with greater frequency in the name of smaller, faster, lighter, and more energy-efficient devices. SMD components have been a fantastic development for the electronics industry and have been one of the driving forces behind technology being delivered in ever smaller platforms. However, the more tightly packed and diminutive this technology became, the more difficult it became for the lay person to access, at least without having access to high-end, expensive assembly and testing equipment. Recognizing this challenge to access the day's technology, Nathan Seidle, founder of SparkFun, and his early engineering cohorts saw an opportunity to chop down the barriers to entry for interacting with that technology. They were interested in bringing SMD components and other technologies back to a human scale, where the units could be worked with low-cost tools that were readily available in household workspaces. The solution was to design and build circuit boards, such as breakout boards, that would make it easier to embed those technologies into whatever unique and custom-built projects inventors could dream up.

Early on, and without the capital to invest in the machinery that large circuit board assembly manufacturers utilize, Nathan learned how to utilize some very basic tools to assemble circuit boards and developed a method of reflowing circuit boards using an electric skillet (Figure 12.1). Reflowing is the process of melting a solder paste that has the consistency of peanut butter at high temperatures until the paste turns into a liquid state; this liquid then becomes a solid metal alloy when cooled. The hardened alloy acts as the conductive material connecting electronic components to the conductive circuitry within the circuit board substrate. The reflowing process is the most common way of putting together a working circuit board and it is the process used by most electronics manufacturers, no matter how large or small.

The electric skillet reflow technique didn't always produce functional circuit boards and sometimes resulted in solder connections that would never pass even the most lenient of **IPC standards** (IPC stands for "Interconnecting and Packaging Electronic Circuits,"

Figure 12.1   Reflowing a panel of 12 Bluetooth modules in an electric skillet.
(Source: Image CC-BY 2.0 Matt Bolton)

the dominant accrediting organization for the electronics manufacturing industry). Even so, SparkFun was able to get enough boards successfully built this way to use in personal electronics projects and to sell to others who would be using them in the same DIY, hobbyist fashion. Fortunately, there were no aerospace, military, or medical contracts coming SparkFun's way in those days that would have required a much higher quality level of circuit board assemblies than what was possible with less precise, repurposed tools.

It can't be emphasized enough, though, that simply getting functional boards out into the world, which made previously difficult-to-access technologies more accessible, was the goal of SparkFun back then. A burgeoning market of creative and talented innovators lay in waiting, ready to embrace the extensive lineup of sensors and microcontrollers that could interact with, speak to, and control any number of things, both abstract and physical. SparkFun is still excited to bring these technologies to the curious and creative masses, but it also seeks to share its stories and advice on open source hardware development and manufacturing.

As it turned out, the market for these electronic shortcuts and the tools to work with them was far larger than Nathan had envisioned at SparkFun's inception. In turn, Spark-Fun had to scale up its circuit board assembly operations to meet that demand. It became clear that we weren't going to be able to do so with a few tweezer-equipped assembly technicians and that electric skillet. Instead, the scale-up would require the right tools, clever yet practical designs, a little luck, and a lot of effort to pull it off. The following subsections lay out how SparkFun learned to dial in and scale up its operations over time to continue to meet that ever-growing demand.

The Process

As any manufacturer will tell you, and as you read in Chapter 5, The Design Process: How to Get from Nothing to Something, it can takes months—if not years—of trying, failing, redesigning, reconfiguring, and trying again to make any assembly or manufacturing process a successful endeavor. If you decide to try your hand at manufacturing your own product and owning every aspect of that design, five critical manufacturing focal points must be given serious consideration as your production plans take shape:

- Design for manufacturability
- Equipment selection and implementation
- Supply chain/purchasing
- Resource planning and scheduling
- Testing and quality control

Each of these principal elements must be continually revisited and refined, as the circumstances surrounding each will change more often than expected, no matter how good your implemented control processes are. These five manufacturing design components are discussed here by highlighting how each was addressed when SparkFun agreed to work with two talented and creative designers, Jay Silver and Eric Rosenbaum, when the Kickstarter campaign for their MaKey MaKey kit grew beyond their expectations.

In early 2012, SparkFun agreed to collaborate with Jay and Eric. The MaKey MaKey kit is an interactive and educational circuit board leveraging resistive touch. SparkFun's role in the project was to serve as a guide for Eric and Jay in designing their circuit board and associated electronics kit for ease of manufacturing and, in addition, to assemble the first production run of MaKey MaKey boards and kits for them. Early planning for the project assumed that this idea would raise $25,000, their original funding goal, on Kickstarter. This amount was considered sufficient to manufacture 300–400 MaKey MaKey boards and kits, a number easily in line with the volume that SparkFun was equipped to handle at that time.

As it turns out, the MaKey MaKey team had no problem hitting that funding goal, achieving it within the first 48 hours of the Kickstarter campaign with still another 28 days of fundraising to go. By the end of the first week of fundraising, it was obvious that the project would be far more successful than had originally been anticipated. It also became clear that SparkFun would have to make some decisions about how to build the MaKey MaKey boards and kits if it wanted to meet its goal of delivering *all* of the kits to Jay and Eric's Kickstarter backers on time—a decision that had been made early on to show the world that Kickstarter-backed products need not always ship late if good planning has been done by the developers.

When the Kickstarter campaign ended on June 12, 2012, Jay and Eric had raised more than $560,000. The clock immediately began ticking down for SparkFun to assemble and ship 13,802 MaKey MaKey Invention Kits by the estimated delivery date of August 2012. Having only 80 days to pull this feat off posed a much greater challenge given that the volume was at least one order of magnitude greater than anything SparkFun was accustomed to at that time.

Although SparkFun was not starting from scratch in setting up its own manufacturing operations, it was being challenged to scale capabilities to an entirely new level in a finite amount of time. As a result, we had to revisit each of these five manufacturing design elements if we wanted to succeed in shipping out kits on time that were both designed and built to the highest quality level possible.

Anecdote: My Watercolor Bot Kickstarter

Sylvia Todd ("Super Awesome Sylvia")

In January 2013, I really wanted to compete in RoboGames, so I came up with an idea for a watercolor painting art bot. I worked out with my parents that I could spend a week off school. With help from Lenore and Windell at Evil Mad Scientist, I went from an awesome idea to a working prototype in only one crazy, caffeine-fueled week. Right before Robo-Games, I got invited to the White House Science Fair, and decided I might as well bring the project. When RoboGames finally arrived, I won second place. The next day I flew to the White House and showed off my invention to hundreds of important peeps, including President Barack Obama himself. He liked it, I think.

In the two months we had to build the bot, Windell and I decided that we could totally make this into a kit that we could sell. We continued to build and improve the bot over the next six months until it was customer proof. We launched a Kickstarter campaign that July with a goal of $50,000, but eventually got $90,000. It was a success!

At every step of the way, we made sure the project was open source. I think the real reason we kept everything open was because one of my whole points of making it into a kit was so my idea could "be out there"—that is, so it could just exist in the world. The kit was geared toward people who wanted to get their hands on something and experiment with it or who were just starting and were curious. Keeping information closed and hidden can be really stupid, and it almost never really works anyway. Making the hardware open source also meant that we could borrow and use other ideas inside of the Watercolor bot. It's like a pen plotter mixed with an Etch-a-Sketch made robotic, with a paintbrush thrown in! It's not rocket science or brain surgery, but it's still *my* idea: it's my very first "real" robot, and I'm proud.

Back in 2012, only two years after I started making my Super-Awesome Maker Show on YouTube, I was invited to talk at the Open Hardware Summit. I got on stage and talked about something that is *really* hard to talk about or understand, especially if you're only 11 years old: what open source hardware means to me. I hadn't made any open source hardware yet, but with everything else I'd made, I tried to be open source because that is what my dad and I learned from what people were sharing online. Share what you can back to your community and people will learn more, and maybe they'll want to share, too! Copyright law? Patents? All of that seemed a little crazy when the answer was right in front

(continues)

of us: sharing and openly building off the ideas of others helps everyone learn and create things we could have never dreamed up. And, of course, as long as your documentation has a home on the internet, your creation can never truly die.

I'm 13 years old and only just getting started making hardware, but I plan on releasing everything I do in the future as open and documented as I can, and so should you. No matter how small a thing it is, it'll help someone somewhere. What are you waiting for? Get out there and make something . . . open source!

Kitting

Many open source hardware products have an aspect of kitting. The open source hardware community normally thinks of a kit as having loose parts that are intended to be put together by the end user. Kits generally require less manufacturing due to the DIY nature—that is, the end user is responsible for building or assembling the kit. But do not underestimate the difficulties and complexities behind kitting. A kit has to be counted carefully *every single time*. Imagine you received a LEGO kit as a gift: How would you feel if you discovered some of the blocks were missing? An incomplete kit is a horrible user experience that can tarnish the initial impression of your product.

Kitting takes time and considerable amounts of checks and balances along the way. Build your kit in 50- or 100-unit batches. Pre-count all of the components necessary to complete the batch. If you end up with an extra screw, you will know there is a kit missing a screw. Use plastic cups or bins to help divide up the kits. If you can create a location for each part of the kit within the box, it will make visual inspection much easier. We laser-cut foam with holes and tabs for the specific components like stand-offs, buzzers, and ICs within our kits. It's much easier and faster to see a void than it is to count to 17 over and over. At SparkFun, we even go so far as to create a kit photo showing the location of the pieces within the box for our employees. This gives the end user the same box-opening experience no matter who built the kit or when it was built. Once you're done with a batch, have someone spot count 15% of the batch. If any errors are found, then the entire batch must be reviewed.

The bill of materials for a device often includes capacitors and resistors, but for kits, you'll need to create an assembly BOM that includes things like plastic bags and packaging materials as well. Just like keeping enough 0.1-uF capacitors and 10K resistors on hand, you'll need to keep tabs on your kitting materials as well. Also remember that if you are shipping a USB cable with a circuit board, this has an aspect of kitting, too, and these items will need to be kitted together as well.

Design for Manufacturability

In Chapter 5, you read about how to prototype your circuit and create the initial bill of materials (BOM). At SparkFun, the engineers creating new products are tightly coupled with the production team responsible for mass-producing the design. When SparkFun took a first look and agreed to collaborate on the MaKey MaKey project, there were some early obvious design improvements that needed to be made to complete the manufacturing of the board design. A number of SparkFun's basic, core design for manufacturability (DFM) standards needed to be applied to the original design of the MaKey MaKey. This section describes the process that SparkFun used to help bring that idea to fruition. The process is roughly the same for contract manufacturers, although each will have its own preferences at each step.

The first step is to scrub the design and BOM. Depending on the decisions already made by the design engineer, this is where the design is likely to experience small changes as the manufacturer's DFM rules are applied to ensure the design is built efficiently and consistently every time. This includes swapping out parts that fit a list of standard, in-stock, readily available parts that are often lower cost than those specified on the original BOM. There are also dozens of other design tradeoffs to consider (see Appendix D for the full list):

- Performance of the part versus requirements of the design.
- Can we swap **plated through hole** (PTH) parts for **surface-mount device** (SMD) parts for ease of manufacturing?
- Consider size, cost, availability, **minimum order quantity** (MOQ), among other factors.
- .New parts: do you have a vendor for the new parts? Setting up vendors and getting stock can take time. Are there long lead times? Are there shortages? MOQs? Is **end of life** (EOL) a concern?

Next, the footprints of parts on the printed circuit board are modified to better fit the manufacturing process. A common change is reducing the **cream layer** on the center pad of an integrated circuit (IC) component to reduce the amount of solder that may short to surrounding pads. (The cream layer is the metal layer between glue layers to which parts are soldered.) Other examples of DFM-dictated changes include adding pin 1 indicators and polarity indicators.

The shape of the PCB is considered and sometimes modified if possible. Reducing the size of the PCB can greatly reduce the cost of the board and the overall BOM. Milling internal slots or cutouts can add to the expense of the PCB, as that is an extra process that the PCB fabricator will have to go through to provide those cutouts.

The layout of the traces is then redrawn to reduce the number of vias, length of traces, and overall complexity of the circuit. Parts of the schematic are exchanged to maintain the functionality of the circuit while lowering the cross-routing of traces.

Thickness of the board is an important consideration. A thinner board can be cheaper to ship in large quantities and easier to pack into an enclosure. A thicker board, however, will provide greater rigidity. Board thickness will affect how the board is handled through the manufacturing process (stenciling, pick and place, reflow) as well as testing and inspection. Radio frequency (RF) performance is also drastically affected by board thickness, so these tradeoffs need to be considered and discussed with the circuit designer to make sure a manufacturing decision doesn't negatively affect the end product.

Next, the silkscreen on the board is reviewed to confirm that it can be printed clearly and repeatedly by any PCB fabricator. Labels are added and updated to make board connections as easy as possible to understand. A common example is adding "on/off" indicators to switches, LED meanings, and any important instructions for use of the board, such as "5V DC only!"

Smaller PCB designs are often multiplied into a larger panel. This process, called **panelization,** requires someone close to the manufacturing process to think through how the board will be handled during the manufacturing process. The most common pitfall is having connectors on the edge of a board that will interfere with components on the neighboring copy of the board. Bigger panels are not always better. You may want a smaller panel if you are stenciling the PCBs by hand. If you are placing components by hand, the solder paste on a large PCB may begin to dry out before you are able to get all the parts placed.

Although those are the most important DFM considerations to make, other details to consider include the following:

- Consider adding fiducials for ease of repeatable manufacturing and **automated optical inspection** (AOI). Fiducials are tiny metal dots found on the edge of the board and sometimes the panel.

- Consider adding side bars to aid in handling the board in panel form with **mouse bites.** Mouse bites are small perforations used to hold the side bars to the boards and can be easily snapped off in postproduction.

- Consider the user experience versus the cost of manufacturing. For example, different LED colors are better for user experience, but using all red LEDs is cheaper in terms of cost and placement than sourcing multiple LED colors.

- Stenciling solder paste by hand requires a smaller panel versus an automated stenciling machine capable of larger panels.

- PTH connectors have more mechanical anchoring for robustness, but the difficulty and cost of manufacturing will increase due to the extra soldering step.

- Consider the PCB color. Green is cheap. White PCBs turn yellow during reflow if the manufacturer is not careful.

- Consider assembled PCB cleaning. Most mass-produced electronics require cleaning to remove a chemical residue that can break down solder connections over time. However, not all parts can withstand a wash cycle. Does your design contain parts that cannot be washed?

- Consider how the end device will be tested. Where are the test points? Is programming required? Do you have to take it outside to get a GPS lock? How fast is the test procedure?

- Is this a kit—that is, will the user put the parts together? Does it require multiple pieces, such as a board + USB cable + screws?

- Does it have printed materials that need to go in the box?

- Are you shipping to the European Union? Do all the components need to meet RoHS standards? Do all the components need to be child friendly?

- Is this design double sided? That doubles the manufacturing cost. This is a tradeoff that is often made to reduce PCB size.

- Can the reflow oven handle and not damage the parts on the double-reflow side?

- Consider the PCB panel's overall width. Will it fit in the pick-and-place machine? Will it fit on the conveyor belt of the reflow oven?

- Can the part footprints be optically inspected easily during the AOI step? Can the AOI machine recognize 0603 versus 0402 component footprints?

Once all of these details are figured out, a new production prototype PCB (usually just a single copy, not yet a full panel) is created and sent off to a PCB fabricator. This production prototype is then given to an engineer for verification that it still works as designed. Such prototypes may also be tested out on beta users. Changes are subsequently made as necessary.

If no changes are needed, the BOM is evaluated one last time by both the designer and the manufacturer. An estimated retail price is determined by taking the total BOM cost plus the estimated manufacturing labor of the design (excluding any overhead costs for now) and multiplying by 4. That rough retail price is then used to determine whether the product still makes sense in the market. Is it competitive with similar products, given its feature set? This moment of truth for the designer leads to a decision being made between proceeding, going back for another round of prototypes, or abandoning the project altogether. Assuming the decision is made to move forward, it is now time to panelize the design, apply the necessary DFM alterations, and move forward with production.

Equipment Selection and Implementation

Regardless of whether you have a single model of your product, several slightly varying models of the same product, or a wide range of different products you'll be building to share with the world, there is a chance that you will try to accomplish some, or maybe all, of the assembly process with the help of specialized equipment and tooling. You may not necessarily opt for a fully automated assembly line, and that's okay. The scale of production you need will determine how complex and, by association, expensive your equipment and tools will be. Therein lies the key to any and all decisions being made on how to equip your assembly shop or production facility with the necessary machinery.

These days, a wide range of equipment options are available to match just about any level of volume and complexity. You need to prepare yourself and your assembly operations team for the anticipated workload. If you are simply making a few prototypes or a small batch of electronics for a proof of concept, scores of manual assembly methods can be employed with small, relatively inexpensive tools and minimal equipment requirements. The word "equipment" is used loosely here; it includes items such as skillets, toaster ovens, Crock-Pots, hot-air guns, low-cost soldering irons, cheap CPU towers purchased through eBay, and self-designed test fixtures that you build yourself (using many of the same parts that you've sourced to build your product, whenever possible).

If you desire to climb one or two notches up the ladder above the most basic, entry-level assembly tools, there is a good chance you're ready to add a pick-and-place machine and a reflow oven to your equipment lineup. SparkFun hit this level after having spent a little more than four years doing its own small electronics assembly with low-cost tools, a few skilled assembly technicians, and a whole lot of patience. When more precise and efficient equipment was needed, SparkFun was already far exceeding the limits that are reached with this more primitive setup. Even though not a single person in the Spark-Fun group was even remotely familiar with how to run this type of advanced, complex machinery, the members collectively believed that it could be learned with enough effort and patience and that the time it would take to develop these skills would pay dividends in the long run.

Equipment

Initially, a secondhand reflow oven—later named Gramps—was purchased from a small business that happened to be shutting down its operations (SparkFun shared an office building with this company). A great workhorse of a pick-and-place machine, the Manncorp MC383, was also purchased; it was affectionately known around SparkFun as Optimus Prime (Figure 12.2). The purchases of both Gramps and Optimus Prime were mostly blind decisions. Little research was done before the purchase decisions were made, mostly because very little information was readily available and easily accessible at the time. Admittedly, Manncorp was one of the top results returned in a Google search for "pick-and-place machine," and it was easy to see how any pick-and-place machine would be an immediate upgrade over SparkFun's existing manually intensive process for assembling circuit boards.

With more experience and knowledge came the realization that there are even better PCB assembly machines out there. Nevertheless, these first two industrial machines represented low-risk, high-reward investments. The only real risks were the possibility that they would ultimately be revealed as lemons, needing repair after repair to remain functional, but they have been keeping up with demand for years now. With these lower-cost alternatives to the top-of-the-line equipment that was available at that time, SparkFun gained machines that were great at teaching the finer nuances of machine operation that are realized only when you actually get your hands on the technology. As the demand for SparkFun-built circuit boards grew, so did the experience levels of the production team. When the time came to invest in additional equipment that would scale up SparkFun's production capacity, the subsequent equipment purchases were made with clearer ideas of what would be needed to help in meeting that growing demand.

By the time that the MaKey MaKey collaboration came along, SparkFun's equipment lineup was set up nicely for managing almost all demands placed on its assembly operations. Every machine in use had been selected and introduced based on current needs and the best possible forecast of its future needs. In early 2012, those operations regularly

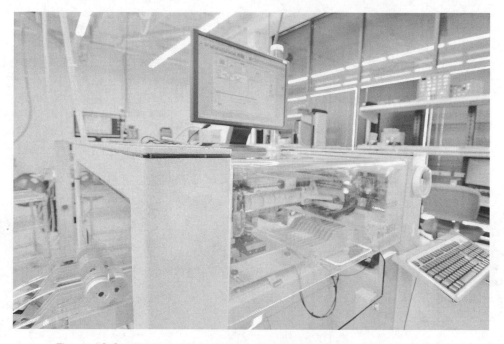

Figure 12.2   Pick-and-place machine affectionately known as Optimus Prime.
(Source: Image CC-BY 2.0 SparkFun/Juan Pena)

involved two shifts that ran two pick-and-place machines and one reflow oven. A single shift was required to operate the **printed circuit assembly** (PCA) batch washer and the automated optical inspection (AOI) machine. The same primary shift assembly staff was also responsible for programming and testing the circuit boards and used custom-designed and -built test fixtures for doing so. (Circuit board testing is discussed in greater detail later.) SparkFun's production floor, circa 2012, is pictured in Figure 12.3.

This equipment setup had, for the most part, been pieced together over the span of five years with not one of the equipment purchases being made under any amount of duress, with the expectation of having it up and running by a specific day. However, it still took us a long time to get up and running. Modern assembly equipment is far from meeting the definition of "plug and play." That all changed when the MaKey MaKey Kickstarter "blew up." It was realized that the anticipated demand from assembling so many MaKey MaKey circuit boards would far exceed SparkFun's existing manufacturing resources. A decision would have to be made to determine how best to increase production capacity. The choice was a relatively simple one: find ways to better utilize and maximize the existing resources *or* add more resources to better match the upcoming demand. SparkFun had already been running a fairly lean operation, so the only truly feasible option was to add new resources.

Figure 12.3   SparkFun's production floor, circa 2012.
(Source: Image CC-BY 2.0 SparkFun/Juan Pena)

We made a choice between two possibilities: adding a third shift to operate the **assembly machinery** *or* adding new equipment resources that could enable a higher volume of circuit board assembly with the same available production personnel hours. This question is one that does not have a truly right or wrong answer. The best answer for you will depend heavily on your own demand forecasts, organizational culture, and facility limitations, plus other considerations. For SparkFun, the decision came down to both the long-term forecasted demand and the cultural implications of adding a third shift to its production operations. Increasing the throughput by upgrading and/or adding new equipment to the SparkFun lineup was given high priority, with a goal of having new equipment selected and installed prior to the start of the initial MaKey MaKey production run.

The two greatest areas for improvement in SparkFun's production capacity were in circuit board assembly speed and the application of solder paste to bare circuit boards. Initially, the priority was placed on finding a new pick-and-place machine, as it had the most potential to deliver the greatest return in terms of building more boards more quickly. Fortunately, SparkFun had been exploring new pick-and-place machines for several months and knew which machine would do the best at meeting SparkFun's growing demand. Shortly after the start of the Kickstarter campaign, the decision was made to purchase a brand-new MYDATA MY100LXe pick-and-place machine (like our other machines, this one was given a new name—Marvin Starscream). This choice was made after considering many different manufacturers and models of machines. There seemed to be as many possibilities to choose from as there are when shopping for a new car.

The right model for the job became obvious after we gave serious consideration to what SparkFun's typical production process flows looked like. SparkFun's high-mix, low-to-medium-volume board production meant that many new production run setups happened every day—far more than are experienced by other PCB assemblers who manufactures thousands or millions of one specific design at a time. The right machine had to be designed in such a way as to make changeovers from one production run to the next as efficiently as possible, resulting in very little downtime for that machine. If a machine could be found that performed well in this area while also delivering a greater **components placed per hour** (CPH) output, then it would immediately be added to SparkFun's short list. Ultimately, it was determined that the MYDATA MY100 model provided the greatest machine downtime capability and CPH rating that could be achieved for the amount that SparkFun was investing in this equipment.

Setting up the infrastructure for a new piece of equipment is a fairly straightforward operation. Space for the new machine must be made, and any required services for the machine must be installed. In many cases, the machine may require compressed air and nonstandard electrical power (three-phase, 240 V instead of single-phase, 110 V). Depending on the source of the new machine, the manufacturer may provide basic training in its use, enough to get you up and running. With time and experience, you will establish your own best practices to achieve operational efficiencies with that particular machine. This new equipment introduction process has played out consistently at SparkFun with each new machine that has been added over the years.

Today, the SparkFun semi-automated assembly machinery lineup includes the following equipment:

- **1 LeadSMT LD-P808AL Stencil Printer:** capable of stenciling 1 large PCB panel every 2 minutes

- **2 Manncorp MC38x Pick-and-Place Machines:** each rated with the capacity to place up to 4000 CPH

- **1 MYDATA MY100LXe Pick-and-Place Machine:** rated at a capacity of 16,000 CPH

- **1 Vitronics Isotherm 500s Reflow Oven:** with an average cycle time of 5 minutes (the time it takes a single board or panel of PCBs to fully reflow and cool)

- **1 Manncorp SMT460C Reflow Oven:** the redundant backup oven for SparkFun, also with an average 5-minute cycle time

- **1 A.C.E. Technologies KISS-102 Selective Soldering Machine:** a more efficient method of soldering PTH components than manually hand-soldering each one with a soldering iron

- **1 YaLan YLPC-1A Hot Bar Soldering Machine:** a high-quality, repeatable, and efficient way to solder displays with flexible PCB connectors to a base PCB design

- **1 Aqueous Technologies Trident CL PCA Batch Washer:** with an average wash cycle time of 30 minutes per batch of boards being cleaned
- **1 Nordson Yestech BX-12 Automated Optical Inspection (AOI) Machine:** an efficient method of inspecting preassembled boards for a variety of defects
- **1 SharpSX Packaging Machine:** capable of packaging up to 35 assembled boards per minute

As SparkFun's manufacturing demands change, there will continue to be new machines that are looked at and considered. Moreover, every future machine purchasing decision will be run through a gauntlet of questions and calculations to ensure that the machine will deliver the expected performance results and provide an adequate return on the investment.

Supply Chain/Purchasing

Knowing which parts and how many of them you will need—information that is often overlooked in the early stages of product development—is most critical to ensuring success in getting your idea to market. Not only is a firm BOM list crucial, but knowing where you will be buying those parts from is of equal importance, if not more so.

Establishing your own supply network is a great deal easier these days thanks to international online marketplaces like Alibaba.com, and many others like it. However, even Alibaba does not fully encompass all of the options out there for sourcing the parts and materials needed to manufacture your design. As anyone attempting to set up a **supply chain** quickly learns that nothing can replace pure persistence and perseverance in the hunt for component sources. However, that effort to dig deeper and deeper into the range of possibilities is sure to eventually deliver competitive benefits when the suppliers with the best **quality-price matrix** are discovered. Put simply: who can deliver the highest-quality parts, on time, at the best price?

Diversification in your supply chain will benefit you greatly. Inevitably, one of your vendors, at one point or another, will *not* have the quantity of some component you need, when you need it. Do not overestimate the value in having a secondary supplier already vetted and in your back pocket should you need to have that component in your hands at a moment's notice. You will likely pay more per piece for those parts, although only you can determine the lost opportunity cost incurred by not getting your hands on those parts.

SparkFun has typically sourced its proprietary, non-substitute parts from distributors such as Future Electronics, Digikey, Mouser, and Arrow, all of which have North American sales offices and warehouses. Microcontrollers from Atmel, Texas Instruments, or Microchip fall in this category, as do most of the passive components used in SparkFun's designs like capacitors, resistors, buzzers, and sensors. The parts hunting experts at SparkFun have enjoyed considerable success in finding international (and lower-cost) sources for such components as LEDs, displays, batteries, and connectors. The tradeoff in buying from these lower-cost suppliers is that SparkFun often has to keep a larger amount on its inventory shelves because the lead times from those suppliers often greatly exceeds those of the domestic suppliers.

Before the MaKey MaKey Kickstarter campaign went live, SparkFun had already begun ordering additional inventory so that it would have the greatest chance for success in building up the anticipated 300–400 boards and kits by the August deadline. However, by the time the Kickstarter campaign was only 72 hours old, it was already clear that SparkFun would be tasked with building far more than 300–400 circuit boards and kits. This realization quickly triggered a revision of the forecasted demand so that component suppliers could be contacted as soon as possible to increase the requested quantities of the components that would be required to build an amount that was certain to be at least 30 times greater than what was originally planned.

The focus was first put on parts that were being sourced from any international supplier; use of such suppliers, as noted earlier, almost always comes with a longer lead time. It was also important to begin communicating this new demand to SparkFun's domestic suppliers, which normally have no problem meeting requests for several hundred pieces of any component but will usually need additional time to meet requests for several thousand units, especially for the more expensive, active components like the ATmega32U4 microcontroller that was being used in the design of the MaKey MaKey boards and kits. Fortunately, the communication with SparkFun's suppliers began early enough that all of the quantities needed were able to be sourced and delivered soon enough so that SparkFun could complete the full production run in time to ship out the products to the Kickstarter backers by the August deadline.

Unfortunately, supply chains are never perfect and are likely to fail from time to time. Several years ago, SparkFun stumbled into an interesting experience when it was learned that the manufacturer of the ATmega328, Atmel, had announced a coming supply shortage of that popular microcontroller. The shortage was expected to affect SparkFun's ability to build many popular designs in the coming months and was forecast to last for several months. After doing some quick calculations, it became clear how much revenue would likely be foregone if there were no way to build the ATmega328-equipped circuit boards during that time. The quick math exercise revealed that great effort needed to be put into finding a source of the microcontroller that could supplant the normal supplier until Atmel was able to refuel its supply network. Thus the search began for a new supplier of the ubiquitous ATmega328, one that didn't yet exist on the SparkFun supply chain radar.

A seller on Alibaba was found that claimed it had 3000 of this specific microcontroller available to ship out and could have them delivered to the SparkFun dock door within 1 week. It was determined that buying from this unknown source would be a pretty large gamble but worth that risk relative to the amount of lost revenue that was anticipated if no source for this part could be found. Not surprisingly, SparkFun ended up with 3000 excellent-*looking* ATmega328 microcontrollers but 0 units that were capable of doing anything at all when soldered onto a circuit board and powered up. Perhaps even less surprising, the supplier proved impossible to track down and communicate with after the funds to purchase the parts had been wired to its account. You can read about the full adventure on SparkFun's website: www.sparkfun.com/news/350.

Expect to hit plenty of roadblocks along the way to setting up your own supply chain, but know that the end result can be worth the effort required to overcome those road-blocks, in terms of overall cost savings in your products.

Resource Planning and Scheduling

Production inventory planning and production run scheduling is always a challenging and imprecise process, no matter how large and sophisticated your operation. A seemingly infinite number of variables can affect your scheduling, albeit different operations in very different ways. If a company has only one product that needs to be built, stocked, and supported, the way it goes about planning the logistics for that single model will be vastly different from the systems of another company that manufactures a larger mix of products. For example, a production run of iPhones built at the Foxconn factory will look far different from the day-to-day feel of the SparkFun production floor, where hundreds of unique designs are manufactured, but in far smaller volumes.

To be successful in setting up your own manufacturing process, the more you know about what your demand is or will be for your product(s), the better you will be able to scale your resources to most effectively meet that demand. From that estimation, it is possible to set up your assembly operations and equip each step of the process with the re-sources needed to give you the overall production capacity that you will need. It will also be important to determine how long each step of the process will take, given the tools available at each step. This information will help you identify where the bottlenecks in your production system are expected to occur. Bottlenecks are inevitable and can be used to your advantage to improve the timing of your production scheduling.

Most likely, you will already have your production "line" set up before you know how well it is sized relative to your demand. That is okay. The production process is always in a state of flux—specifically, in a constant state of improvement. Many lessons will be learned as you build more. Your operation will naturally find efficiency gains as new ideas are con-sidered for how to improve the bottlenecks in the system.

When preparing for the production run of the MaKey MaKey boards and kits—the largest single production run in SparkFun's history—it was recognized early on that SparkFun's production capacity was not great enough to be able to take on the addi-tional 13,000-plus MaKey MaKey kits while also keeping the rest of the more than 450 in-house built circuit boards and kits in stock. To meet the goal of shipping out all MaKey MaKey kits by the August deadline, a primary decision would have to be made, though a relatively simple one: find a way to increase production capacity or strategically decide to disregard a segment of SparkFun's standard catalog offerings so that more focus could be given to the MaKey MaKey boards and kits. This decision painfully brought to light how difficult it can be to add more capacity when needed. Ultimately, it was decided to cut back on fulfilling the demand for a number of the lower-volume and lower-priority designs until the MaKey MaKey units had been shipped to every supporter of the MaKey MaKey Kickstarter campaign.

The silver lining came in the aftermath of the MaKey MaKey experience. SparkFun discovered new ways of increasing its capacity for building more boards and kits and learned how to quickly scale up its capacity if, and when, a situation ever calls for this in the future.

Regardless of what state your production process is in, it is inevitable that, at some point, production runs of your product(s) will need to be scheduled and started. Mostly, this is a very logical and intuitive step in getting your products built. However, there are a number of nuanced variables to keep in mind when determining when to build, in which order to build, and which quantities to build.

When setting up your own manufacturing operations, you will likely end up working with a **manufacturing resource planning** (MRP) software package that should offer a scheduling tool. Many years ago SparkFun wrote its own MRP software (Figure 12.4), which has provided the opportunity to modify that toolset as demands and priorities have changed.

Regardless of which system is used, it is important for that system to consider each bottleneck in the manufacturing process. Each step along the way has its own capacity, and the demands made on that resource may not match the demands made on other resources in the chain. Other details to consider that will help you effectively schedule production of your product(s) include the following:

- **Takt time:** the time it takes to produce a completed unit from start to finish (often referred to as "the drumbeat" of the assembly line)
- **Component inventory levels:** production quickly comes to a halt if unknown stock shortages are discovered
- **Desired production completion dates:** used to help determine priority within the schedule
- **Anticipated yields, based on a design's historical results:** important to know when deciding how many units to schedule

Production planning and scheduling is very much a science, one that has far-reaching impacts on your operation's culture and the efficiency with which you are able to manufacture your products. Many factors must be considered when determining how to set up your assembly process. Your production schedule will be the tool that is deployed to help manage that process and must be responsive to and account for all of the variables in that process.

Testing and Quality Control

You've now designed and made a thing. And you're proud of that thing, right? You want your users and customers to be as happy with that thing as you are. But by the time you've completed your first production run, if not well before then, you will probably have already identified weaknesses in your assembly process that will make you question

status	priority	batch	build	Step	part	Name burn detail	Time to Due (9 days)	Time to 0 (days)	qty	model
	1	53966 Scheduled	37369	*Pulling Parts*		MicroView USB Programmer New Unposted Product C-List	–3.4		120	DEV–12893 SUB–12065
in_process	3	54538 Started	37565	Manual Assembly		RedBoard-Programmed with Ard.. Live A-List	–1.4	10.93	132	DEV–12757 SUB–11962
in_process	4	54284 Started	37112	Manual Assembly		MP3 Trigger Live A-List		0.00	20	WIG–11029
in_process	5	54278 Started	37490	Manual Assembly		LilyPad Development Board-As... Short Timer A-List		0.00	20	SUB–11108
ready	11	54708 Started	37645	Ice		Breakout Board for AD5330 Para... Live C-List		0.00	60	BOB–12082

Figure 12.4 SparkFun's production schedule managed within "Sparkle," our self-built MRP system. (Source: Image CC-BY 2.0 Matt Bolton)

whether those assembled products are truly up to your and your future customers' standards.

Never to be overlooked is the importance of confirming that what you've built does what it is supposed to after it has been put together, while also finding methods for testing product functionality that do so as simply and as efficiently as possible. Testing can be a time-consuming process, but is an absolute must. It becomes more important the less refined your assembly processes are. Although it is quite difficult to be absolutely perfect (as defined by a single defective product never getting into a customer's hands), your product's reputation depends on making every reasonable effort possible to minimize the number of undesirable experiences that your customers have with your product. If you find a manufacturing run has gone awry, see Chapter 13, Troubleshooting from Your Design to Your Manufacturer.

In the early days of SparkFun's manufacturing operations, the assembly processes employed were far from perfect. As a result, a great deal of emphasis was placed on fully testing the built circuit boards to identify and correct all of the boards that experienced flaws during the assembly process. To some degree, performing a more detailed test for each board was the easiest method of ensuring high-quality, fully functioning boards for the customers. The other option was perfecting every step in the assembly process, but that path would have required a much larger investment in equipment, tools, and training that could not yet be afforded on SparkFun's bootstrapped budget. As a result of that decision, the 100% test methodology taught the SparkFun Productioneers a great deal about the ins and outs of each board design and resulted in their collective ability to troubleshoot and repair nearly every initially defective board they touched. These days, the SparkFun board-building experts achieve, on average, a 99.5% final yield on all boards, meaning that they have to scrap only 1 out of every 200 boards that are built.

To reach this level of quality, a great amount of focus and effort was put into developing test procedures that were thorough, efficient, and intuitive. To effectively identify assembly defects and program its circuit boards, the SparkFun test developers approached the problem by designing a unique test fixture for each separate board (Figure 12.5), with most fixtures borrowing on the "bed of nails" method already common in the electronics assembly industry. The difference, however, was that the SparkFun testbeds utilized lower-cost components and the same circuit board material already being used in the boards being built. The early test apparatuses were nowhere near as robust and useful as the ones regularly being designed and introduced today. But much attention was given to constantly searching for new techniques and then revising SparkFun's older testing hardware, especially for those board designs that were being built in larger volumes. For example, the electromechanical buttons put to use on these test fixtures began to break because of the number of times they were being pressed during testing. In recognition of this problem, it was decided that all future testbeds should replace physical buttons with a capacitive touch pad solution.

In early 2012, the test developers were already beginning to experiment with designing and building SparkFun's own devices that could test and program multiple boards in

Figure 12.5   Test fixture.
(Source: Image CC-BY 2.0 SparkFun/Chris Rojas)

a single instance. These devices are commonly known in the electronics assembly industry as **ganged programmers.** When the MaKey MaKey collaboration began to take shape, that design was immediately identified as one that would benefit greatly from a ganged programmer (Figure 12.6), given the greater volumes that were expected to hit Spark-Fun's production operations. Therefore, the test procedure for the MaKey MaKey boards and kits was designed from the outset to be capable of programming and testing multiple boards in a single pass. This differed from past designs where a single unit testing device was typically used when a new product was initially introduced to the SparkFun digital storefront. But, again, the number of MaKey MaKey units that were expected to be manufactured during the initial production run far outstripped the volume of any other new design ever produced by SparkFun.

The development of SparkFun's own customized ganged programmers has been a process characterized by great trial and error. Nevertheless, the cliché about necessity being the mother of invention has proved true, time and again, in terms of SparkFun's continuous efforts to build high-quality boards as quickly as possible. To learn more about this progressive journey of testing efficiency improvements, check out the tutorial written by SparkFun's Testing Guru, Pete Lewis: learn.sparkfun.com/tutorials/constant-innovation-in-quality-control.

In the end, it all comes down to making the best decisions for your product and the many customers out there who will want to buy that product. Most of these decisions can be made by asking the right questions, which will most likely lead to obvious answers in determining how thorough your testing must be to deliver the quality level that your product must meet.

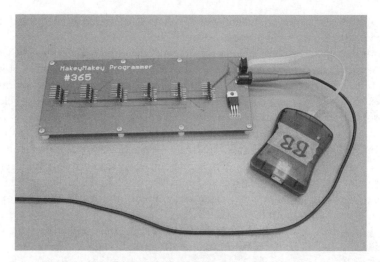

Figure 12.6   Ganged programmer.
(Source: Image CC-BY 2.0 Matt Bolton)

Future of Open Source, Small-Scale Manufacturing

The electronics manufacturing industry has, over the last several decades, produced a wide range of automated and semi-automated manufacturing solutions that make it possible to manufacture and assemble high-quality electronics at a similarly wide range of production volumes. These constant improvements in equipment and tooling are, in no small way, one of the primary reasons that SparkFun has been able to grow its own circuit board assembly operations, which are at least as cost-effective as outsourcing those operations overseas. However, the world of more generalized industrial automation has not yet produced the same range of options to assist in efficiently introducing other assembly operations, including both packaging and inventory movement. Yes, there are some amazing automated systems out there, but they have all been designed to meet the needs of assemblers with exceedingly high-volume operations. Yet even the most modern automated systems still require a great deal of customization so that they are capable of handling an organization's specific product(s).

In addition to assembling hundreds of uniquely different circuit board designs, Spark-Fun puts together several hundred distinctive kits to make its electronics available in an inviting and approachable way. These are an attractive option for anyone looking to tinker with electronics for the first time, including children and educators who want to teach electronics to students. In terms of manufactured kits, probably the most famous kit-building company in the world is LEGO. LEGO has certainly solved the automation challenge in assembling its highly popular kits as efficiently as possible, without sacrificing quality. In this case, however, the company's volumes clearly justify the capital investment required for the necessary automation equipment.

If your required assembly volumes are orders of magnitude lower than LEGO's, and if your volumes are spread among dozens or even hundreds of vastly different kits with many uniquely shaped components, the automated assembly equipment options that currently exist are severely limited. Thus there is a great opportunity for the development of less-sophisticated automated or semi-automated solutions that can sufficiently handle lower volumes of inventory handling and assembly work, at a far lower cost than the existing automated systems being built today by the likes of FANUC, Omron, and Honeywell. For DIY manufacturing to continue to succeed in opening doors for entrepreneurs to get their product into the marketplace more quickly and at a lower price, regardless of the size of the market those products serve, automated solutions for low-volume assembly must become more readily available.

The good news is that more economical industrial automation systems are already being developed. For example, Rethink Robotics has put a great deal of energy and effort into its Baxter design, which can be introduced to your operations at a base cost of $22,000. Relatively speaking, that is a very attractive price point. More realistically, the amount of customization required to equip the Baxter unit to handle your unique components will send that starting price a good bit higher before any amount of utility can be realized from this system.

It is clear that the industrial automation industry is in great need of, and ripe with opportunity for, open source solutions to be developed and shared with the world. A Boulder, Colorado, company called Modular Robotics has been contributing an open source testing platform called FARKUS that has led the way in open source automated PCB testing. Other groups are working on creating open source PCB mills, pick-and-place machines, and reflow ovens. The parts, materials, and infrastructure for supporting an open source model of automated assembly machinery implementation are already in existence. With the right incentives, more open source automated assembly solutions will likely emerge and would be expected to realize similar successes to those seen in the general open source hardware movement of the last decade.

Because the products that most manufacturers, of any size, will be assembling are one-of-a-kind items, the amount of customization that will be required to introduce automated assembly solutions to any manufacturing operation will need to be as unique as each product being built. Therefore an open source automated assembly machinery design will find the most success, in terms of market penetration, when that design is accompanied by very clear documentation and a strong support community whose members assist one another by sharing and teaching others how to build up customized versions of the system that can deliver useful and efficient results for each user's unique application. This model has already proved wildly successful for Arduino, and it could produce similar results if replicated for industrial automation applications.

Anecdote: Open Source Factory Automation
Eric Schweikardt

We make robot construction kits like Cubelets and MOSS, and we make them in our own little factory in Boulder, Colorado. People think that this is completely crazy, but it's not. We don't manufacture our robots here because we're particularly patriotic or because we want to set an example of altruism: we do it because it makes better sense for us from a business (and particularly a financial) perspective.

Oddly, the decision to manufacture our products ourselves began on a flight home from China, where we had visited five contract manufacturers to talk about making our products for us. I was filled with unease on that flight home; contract manufacturing just seemed wrong for our little robots. As I reflected on the trip, I realized that there were huge differences between the first- and second-tier factories that we visited. At the low-end factories, there were people everywhere: three people running each injection molding machine to press buttons, inspect parts, and so on. In contrast, at the high-end factories, there was no one on the assembly floor; there was only the rhythmic buzz, click, and whir of gantries and robot arms doing all the work automatically. Wait a minute: if the best manufacturers had robotized their entire operations due to Chinese labor getting so expensive in the last few years, perhaps throwing our lot in with an automated manufacturer would be short-sighted. Anyway, our company makes robot construction kits—so if anyone is set up to robotize and automate a factory, it's us!

Typically, when you automate a factory, you'll pick up a few million-dollar KUKA or ABB robot arms or a Baxter robot that makes smiley faces at you. These approaches entail a huge financial investment, and they're massive overkill for the work that we do. Our commercial products are tiny, simple robots, and many of the assembly tasks involved in their construction are tiny, simple tasks. We built some more tiny, simple robots to automate repetitive tasks and save time and money on our factory floor called FARKUS. FARKUS is the open source Factory Automation Robotics Kit for US (Figure 12.7)! That's "us" like in *you and me and all of us,* not like in *United States,* by the way.

FARKUS is more than an assembly robot; it's an ecosystem of simple robots that work together. In the same way that our commercial products are made out of lots of tiny robots, the power of FARKUS lies in the modularity and interconnection between various modules that can be reconfigured quickly to support different assembly processes and production lines.

At a basic level, a factory performs a bunch of operations to a bunch of products. The Modular Robotics factory, for instance, uses operations like soldering, ultrasonic welding, programming, testing, and printing to make products like Cubelets and MOSS. FARKUS consists of several parts: *movers,* to move products through the factory; a collection of *modules* that perform operations to the products; a *control* system to manage the ecosystem; and *nests* to cradle the products as they make their way through a production line.

(continues)

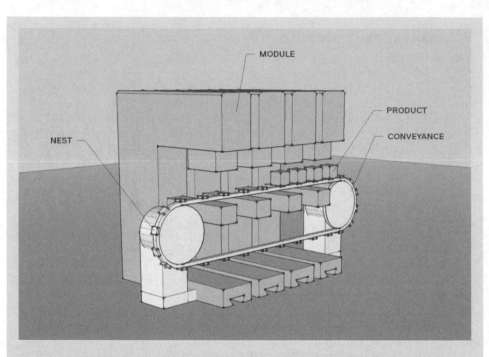

Figure 12.7   FARKUS conveyance with four attached modules.
(Source: Image CC-BY-SA Modular Robotics)

We've designed and built two movers so far. The conveyance is something like a conveyor belt: it uses a stepper motor, a Geneva mechanism, and a chain drive to move products along a linear path through a series of modules. The carousel looks more like an old slide projector and moves a carousel of a few hundred products (we're using it for small printed circuit boards) around so that each of them can be programmed/tested/operated on by a module. Other great movers for future design will be a vibratory bowl feeder and a mechanism to separate passed and failed products from the end of a conveyance.

Modules are easily swappable on a conveyance or a carousel so that FARKUS systems can be quickly customized. On a typical conveyance—say, a Cubelets Flashlight Tester—we'll have four modules. The first has a mechanical arm that tests all five faces of the Cubelet for mechanical defects, such as short circuits or lack of connectivity. The second module uses an Arduino microcontroller to program the Cubelet's firmware. The third module has another mechanical arm to simulate five connected Cubelets and make sure the data transfer is correct. The fourth arm has a photocell to test that the actual flashlight LED on the Cubelet is illuminating correctly at various states. As a Cubelet makes its way through the series of modules, the control module keeps track of its progress and state. There's also room on the conveyance for a fifth module that will put Cubelets that pass the tests in one box and those that fail in another container. We've built modules to

Figure 12.8   A FARKUS module that tests digital communication on six
faces at once about to descend onto a Cubelet during final testing.
(Source: Image CC-BY-SA Modular Robotics)

test and program circuit boards to test for short circuits and connectivity on Cubelets, to
ultrasonically weld plastic bits, to test digital communication (Figure 12.8), and to functionally test robot drive mechanisms.

Another thing you'll notice at a traditional robotized factory is a set of little white boxes
called programmable logic controllers (PLCs). PLCs control the robot arms and conveyor belts.
They are simple and reliable, but they cost approximately $2000 and they consist only of a
circuit board and a few relays. We use $20 Arduino microcontrollers instead. I'm not suggest-
ing that PLCs are always a bad idea. In some factories, giant robot arms swing steel beams
around and could kill someone if an electrical glitch occurs. Other factories can lose millions
of dollars per hour if the production line stops running, so the reliability of a PLC is critical.
In our little factory, though, simple, safe, tiny robots with large red STOP buttons can do the
work. The agility that this brings us means that when faced with an outage, we can easily reconfigure the robot ecosystem or begin building material buffers in other parts of the factory.

A custom Python application called FARKUS Desk controls everything. Desk currently runs
on a Raspberry Pi and uses straightforward serial data transfer over USB to communicate
with the modules (each contains an Arduino microcontroller, movers, and individual products). Desk conducts the orchestra: it controls the operations at each point in the system,
and sets and keeps track of the state of each part. We're currently using a touchscreen

(continues)

display to interact with each FARKUS Desk, but it would be nice to have everything connected to a server so that factory status could be monitored and tracked from anywhere.

The last major component of FARKUS is a set of nests: electromechanical connectors that attach to the products themselves as they make their way down the production line. Both Cubelets and MOSS have simple, self-aligning magnetic connectors, so building their corresponding nests entails just a quick 3D print of a connector and a PCB to break out the electrical connections. Many products won't need electrical connections—if your FARKUS system manufactures T-shirts or laser-etches Jesus faces into toast, you won't need serial data to and from the toast or T-shirt. Nests for circuit boards are usually laser-cut plastic sandwiches inspired by the SparkFun manual pogobed design and fitted with header pins to interface with a carousel. We also have nests that are milled from steel so that MOSS faces can be ultrasonic-welded into their plastic frames. Depending on what you're making, designing appropriate nests for a product can range in complexity from straightforward to extremely complicated, and this sort of necessary customization is one of the main reasons we decided to open source FARKUS.

I'm not filled with open source dogma; I don't think that everything should be open source. FARKUS is open source even though our consumer products are closed source. Our consumer products are designed to be used, not to be taken apart and rebuilt. Hacking into Cubelets and circumventing the battery protection circuitry, for instance, could cause the product to subsequently catch fire in a nine-year-old child's hands. But open source is perfect for FARKUS for a couple of reasons. Automating a factory requires a significant amount of customization. Although FARKUS can provide common features like conveyor modules, material-handling modules, indexing, testing, and sorting modules, an actual implementation will need custom tools, jigs, and nests that handle the actual product being manufactured perfectly. Factories are usually run by capable engineers who can modify and hack assemblies safely and at their own risk. We also decided that we didn't want to get into the factory automation business.

FARKUS could have become an in-house, proprietary system, but we're thrilled to think about a future in which all products aren't made halfway around the world. FARKUS is still an experiment, and we're publishing the results of each build: both time saved and return on investment. We're amped on local manufacturing. I heartily encourage you to build a conveyance and a couple modules, share them, and manufacture a few thousand widgets right in your garage.

Details, CAD, code, schematics, videos, and more information can be found at this address: www.modrobotics.com/farkus.

Summary

In the end, the steps followed in manufacturing an open source product are not really any different from the steps required to assemble a closed source product. Surrounding the open source movement, however, is a DIY ethos that encourages those pushing the bounds of open source hardware progression to own as much of the development of that hardware as possible. Manufacturing your own products is an extremely rewarding experience, albeit one that comes with a unique set of challenges that are both separate and yet intrinsically tied to the challenges of designing those same products. Those challenges can be overcome with greater ease as the community of open source manufacturers continues to share the lessons learned and best practices that have been developed along the way. With the reassurance that you're not alone in this challenge, you can go forth and make . . . in extremely large volumes!

13

Troubleshooting from Your Design to Your Manufacturer

Kipp Bradford

"Things were going badly; there was something wrong in one of the circuits of the long glass-enclosed computer. Finally, someone located the trouble spot and, using an ordinary tweezers, removed the problem, a two-inch moth. From then on, when anything went wrong with a computer, we said it had bugs in it."

—Grace Hopper

Debugging the manufacturing process starts with understanding the manufacturing process. Many of the most common manufacturing problems are easily avoidable, with a little knowledge of what it means to manufacture a product. If you have ever backed a project on a crowd-funding site that involves manufacturing, then you are all too familiar with an email that sounds something like this:

Dear supporter, thank you for your support. Due to unforeseen circumstances, our ship date will not be what we promised. It will probably take us several extra months, if we are lucky, to figure out why we cannot get our product manufactured. We hope to resolve these issues and actually deliver a product to you. Eventually.

You might think to yourself, "What are the designers doing wrong? Will my product ever get delivered? Why didn't they see this coming?" After you support your second or third or fourth crowd-funded project, the weekly update emails announcing another delay or production problem become background noise in your inbox. If and when the projects do ship, your expectations have been set so low that you forget what the project was all about in the first place.

The actual emails that you receive will probably go into much greater detail about where the product is in the manufacturing process and which specific problems are currently being debugged at the current phase of production. Many of these emails refer to critical details being out of spec, such as the product's finish not being correct or parts not mating properly. It might seem as if these are engineering or technical problems, and they are—but the cause of all these problems comes down to one simple and nontechnical issue: communication. Herein lie some of the benefits of manufacturing an open source project. Communication is generally easier with transparency and openness. If all of your designs are readily available for evaluation and review, it's easier for a prospective manufacturer to understand what you are trying to make and why.

Before you think about manufacturing a product, it's important to understand that, like you, manufacturers are running a business. Like any business, manufacturing involves a lot of decision making and tradeoffs. Manufacturers generally seek to offer you a competitive price that gives them the best profit. That's how they make money and stay in business. This should sound totally obvious, but hidden in that reality is a warning: beware the manufacturers that offer impossibly low prices. They are either taking shortcuts that will cause you problems, or they are not operating a sustainable business and will probably go out of business before your product sees the light of day.

Figuring out how to run a successful manufacturing business is not the focus here. Figuring out how to successfully get your product manufactured is the point of this chapter. In a perfect world, you would sit with the manufacturing manager of the factory you've selected and hash through every step of the production process as decisions are made regarding your product. You would review each decision to ensure that your design isn't compromised. You would be able to instantly consider the best options when the manufacturing team hits the inevitable problems as your parts are prepared for production and then fabricated. In the real world, however, you send some files off to a factory that you've evaluated and hope for the best. What could really go wrong, after all? We live in an age where automation is king and designs, whether electrical or mechanical, are represented by ones and zeroes that can be turned into physical objects, which are perfect copies of one another.

Avoiding the most common mistakes should be easy in this day and age, yet even experienced teams will miss things. Even though every project is different, following the best practices will help you avoid common problems. For example, making sure your design can be manufactured using widely available materials and techniques is a great place to start, but your selection of a manufacturer may also play a big role in your success. Knowing how to communicate with that manufacturer to hand off materials is important, as is working with the manufacturer to optimize your design for manufacture and assembly. Before any parts are made in volume, pilot production and quality testing are also critical. This chapter gets you started with these topics and then shows some examples of errors.

Manufacturable Designs

The first step in manufacturing a product is to design a product that can be manufactured. Chapter 12, Accelerate from Making to Manufacturing, covered design for manufacture (DFM), but that's not what we are talking about here. DFM is primarily a process of optimization to reduce the time, cost, and complexity of a product while maintaining or improving quality and function. It concerns primarily how the product will be manufactured. Before you get to that stage, you should be concerned with "what" you are manufacturing. Is your product something that can be manufactured in the first place? Are its parts readily available? Can the manufacturer correctly read the files you've sent? Do you require precision thin-wall machined plastic or complicated multipart injection molds that are hard to make? Are your traces too small or too close to the edge of your PCB? These are important questions to answer in the design phase, as you read about in Chapter 5, The Design Process: How to Get from Nothing to Something, but are rarely considered until it's too late.

Can You Source It?

Many open source designs start off as a hand-assembled single prototype made with very specialized components or parts from SparkFun or Adafruit. In production, finding off-the-shelf components available from multiple distributors is a better path to success than using parts from a single supplier that may or may not want to work with you.

Consider the example of the Wireless Sensor Mote shown in Figure 13.1 that I designed and manufactured for Google in 2013. I had inherited the initial open source design from colleges at the Data Sensing Lab. With only about four weeks available to spin

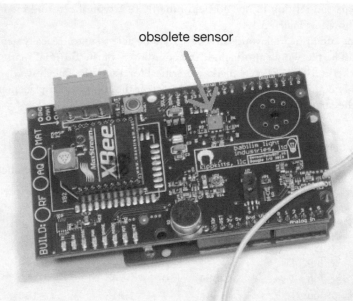

Figure 13.1   The Data Sensing Lab's Sensor Mote. The sensor indicated by the arrow almost stopped production.
(Source: Image by Kipp Bradford)

a new design and all the software already written, there could be no changes to the bill of materials.

Unfortunately, the design used a sensor that became obsolete, with only a limited supply being available, after we manufactured our bare circuit boards. Our production was delayed by several days as I scoured distributor websites around the globe searching for available parts. I managed to find just enough components to complete our production run and get the product to Google on time. Things could have been much worse. Had I not found enough parts, we would have had to throw out thousands of dollars of circuit boards and the entire project would have been killed by the missed deadline, probably resulting in a lawsuit.

File Types for Effective Communication

Once you've made sure your design uses widely available parts, you need to confirm that you can generate files for your design in a format that's compatible with your potential manufacturers. This is really part of the process of selecting a manufacturer, so we'll discuss it more later. If your manufacturer is also assembling parts on the PCB, it will generally need a file that contains centroid data. I cannot stress how important this file is. The **centroid** file information gives the location of each component to be placed on the circuit board. This file is commonly a .CSV spreadsheet file that specifies the X,Y coordinates of each part in relation to one corner of the PCB. A typical centroid file includes the coordinates shown in Table 13.1.

Any decent circuit board layout software should be able to automatically generate the centroid data. The file should also include the coordinates of the **fiducial** marks that you included on the PCB. The fiducial marks are critical for assembly. They give the automated assembly equipment a reference point to orient the robotic part placement device in regard to the circuit board (Figure 13.2).

Table 13.1 **A Centroid File**

RefDes	Layer	LocationX	LocationY	Rotation
A1	Top	0.07	1.99	0
A2	Top	1.35	0.325	0
A3	Top	3.5	1.775	0
ACT	Top	1.225	0.125	180
ASSOC	Top	0.975	0.125	180
C1	Top	1.884	1.745	180
C2	Top	1.884	1.213	180

The fiducial mark locations are indicated with A1, A2, and A3.
Measurements are in inches. Comma delimited.
Only surface-mount components are included.

Source: Centroid Data for PC Board: "SensorMoteSMT_V1.1.brd" as of: 4/19/13 3:45 P.M.

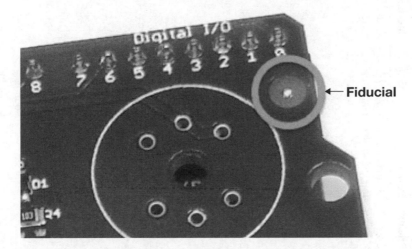

Figure 13.2   Typical fiducial marks for PCB assembly.
(Source: Image by Kipp Bradford)

In addition to this basic list of files, the circuit board assembly contractor will want a complete bill of materials (BOM), as is laid out in Chapter 14, Taxonomy of Hardware Documentation. To avoid troubleshooting, your BOM should have complete details, as shown in Table 13.2.

It is not unusual for a manufacturer to make substitutions for parts specified in the BOM. Sometimes this is done because the manufacturer can get substitute parts at a lower cost than what you've priced out, or sometimes the manufacturer might not have access to large enough quantities of the components you used in your prototype. This is where a highly detailed BOM becomes very important. The more detail you add to the BOM, the more likely the manufacturer will be to find a suitable replacement part.

The file requirements for the mechanical parts of your products are similar to the electronics parts, but there are a few key differences. One interesting difference that while PCB manufacturers expect Gerber files, you will not be asked to provide the mechanical equivalent, "G-Code," to a machine shop. In the mechanical world, several file formats are commonly used that allow for easy exchange of design files—namely, *DXF, IGES, STEP,* and *STL.* DXF is a file format created by Autodesk for use with its software. Most non-Autodesk software typically include import/export capability for DXF files. This is a common way to send two-dimensional objects data that might be fabricated by a laser cutter, water-jet cutter, or router. IGES is an open file format created by the U.S. Air Force to simplify the exchange of information between design and manufacturing.[1]

---

1. http://en.wikipedia.org/wiki/IGES

Table 13.2 **BOM for Production**[a]

Inventory ID	Qty	Manuf P/N	Device	Parts	Distributor P/N	Unit Pricing	Total Pricing	Extras	Lead Size	Hole Checking
DT-1	1	EVQ-PAC04M	6-mm Light Touch Switch 100 GF	RESET	P8006S-ND	0.27	0.27	6-mm Light Touch Switch 100 GF	Hole diameter 1 mm, +0.1, −0	Actual 1.02 mm
DT-2, DT-3	5	SR203-TP	Diode Schottkey 2-A 30-V DO41	D1, D2, D3, D4, D5	SR203-TPCT-ND	0.43	2.15	Diode Schottkey 2-A 30-V DO41	Lead diameter 0.7–0.9 mm	Actual 0.81 mm
DT-4	6	SLR-342VR3F	LED 3.1 mm 650-nm Red Diffused	LED1, LED3, LED4, LED5, LED6, LED7	511-1250-ND	0.41	2.46	LED 3.1-mm 650-nm Red Diffused	Hole diameter 1 mm, pad diameter 2 mm	Actual 0.81 mm
DT-5	1	TLW-102-06-G-S	JP1Q	JP1	SAM1100-02-ND	1.1	1.1	JP1Q	Lead diameter 0.64 mm square, 0.025 inch square	Actual 0.91 mm
DT-6	1	TSW-103-23-T-S	CONN HEADER 3POS 0.100" SNGL TIN	JP3	SAM1075-03-ND	0.43	0.43	PINHD-1×3	Lead diameter 0.64 mm square, 0.025 inch square	Actual 0.91 mm

DT-7	2	TSW-106-06-G-S	PINHD-1X6	J2, POWER	TSW-106-06-G-S-ND	0.83	1.66	PINHD-1×6	Lead diameter 0.64 mm square, 0.025 inch square	Actual 1.02 mm
DT-8	2	TSW-150-07-T-S	1×50 PIN MALE HEADER	J1, J3	SAM1035-50-ND	2.04	4.08	PINHD-1×8	Lead diameter 0.64 mm square, 0.025 inch square	Actual 1.02 mm
DT-9	1	TSW-150-08-T-D	2×50 PIN MALE HEADER	JP2	SAM1048-50-ND	4.19	4.19	PINHD-2×10HAND	Lead diameter 0.64 mm square, 0.025 inch square	Actual 1.02 mm
DT-10	1	ED100/4DS	Terminal Block 5 mm Vertical 4pos	X2	ED2233-ND	0.94	0.94	W237-4	Lead diameter 1 mm. Data sheet secured.	Actual 1.19 mm; suggested is 1.3 mm—small difference.
DT-11	2	OSTTC060162	Terminal Block 5 mm Vertical 6pos	X3, X5	ED2604-ND	0.77	1.54	W237-6	Lead diameter 1 mm, hole size 1.3 mm	Actual 1.19 mm

[a] Component part number and source are usually included.

STEP (ISO 10303) is a file standard developed by the International Standards Organization that also aims, like IGES, to be a vendor-neutral exchange format for sharing 2D or 3D design information across different design tools, or between design tools and manufacturing software.[2] As low-cost 3D printers have become widely available, the STL file format has become a preferred format for sharing 3D model data with manufacturers. Originally created by 3D Systems for use with its 3D printers,[3] STL is a simple format that most mechanical CAD software can read and write. Occasionally, a manufacturer will ask for a PDF file or, more commonly, physical drawings of the part. I've had several sheet metal manufacturers request my CAD drawings on paper. It may seem odd, but a decent number of sheet metal fabricators continue to run completely manual equipment. A properly drawn paper part sketch might be perfectly adequate if you want to make a simple part or if you are working with less technologically advanced manufacturers where your digital files will not be very helpful regardless of which file formats you can generate.

It is becoming more common to find manufacturers asking for high-level design files versus these common data exchange file formats. 3D CAD software packages such as Solidworks, Pro-E, Autodesk, and others support direct import of their competitors' file formats, and many factories have reached a level of automation where they prefer the proprietary design file as the source. This is where things get interesting for open source hardware creators. Unlike when manufacturing and assembling a circuit board, where everything is printed on or placed on a flat sheet of fiberglass, mechanical components have tremendous variation in geometry, materials, tool paths, setup, and other factors. All of these issues leave a lot of room for error as the manufacturer interprets your design in relation to the available equipment and machine operator skills.

Make Makable Parts

Not everything that you can cook up in your CAD software can be fabricated. Prototypes that you have made out of ABS on a 3D printer may be impossible to machine or cast out of metal. For example, sharp internal corners and square holes can be 3D printed but not easily machined. Thin-walled plastic parts are also very difficult to fabricate. A high-quality surface finish or tight precision maintained over a large part dimension may be very difficult to achieve at a reasonable cost. Ultimately, the difference between what is easy to manufacture versus what is expensive and time consuming will depend on the capabilities of the manufacturer you select. The key to making your parts makable is to begin working with a manufacturer at an early stage, and to get its feedback on the ease of fabrication of the product you are designing. Don't wait until your project is far downstream in the development process to make sure your parts can be fabricated. Mistakes made in the later stages of design work are much more costly and much harder

---

2. http://en.wikipedia.org/wiki/STEP_(ISO_10303)
3. http://en.wikipedia.org/wiki/STL_(file_format)

to fix than the same mistakes noticed early on. Clearly, then, it's best to think about manufacturability of your design while you are designing it. That means you need to find a manufacturer!

Selecting Manufacturers

Chapter 12, Accelerate from Making to Manufacturing, delves deeply into selecting and handing off designs to manufacturers, but the following sections will go over this process from a troubleshooting perspective. Finding a good manufacturer is no easy task, but it's the starting point to getting your product made properly. There are an enormous number of companies around the globe that would be happy to take your money, but they may not be able to make the product that you want.

Every search begins with defining the category of product that you are manufacturing. Is it a wearable computer, a robot, a wireless sensor system? Is it purely mechanical, like a valve or waterproof battery box? As you narrow down the category, it will be easier to define the kind of capabilities best suited to producing your product. Then reach out to other designers, particularly those in the open source hardware community. You may get lucky and come across someone who has already been down the same path that you are about to travel and can help you. Even if that's not the case, other contributors or supporters of your open source project can help you narrow down the list of manufacturers. Also, many folks in the open hardware world are happy to share insights and direct newcomers to known good manufacturers. It certainly helps grow the relationship between a manufacturer and a designer if the designer brings in new business. For the newcomer, it's valuable to have the referral to the manufacturer as well as someone on the outside with experience dealing with that particular manufacturer.

If your search for references comes up dry, you may have to do things the hard way, by visiting a website such as thomasnet.com (the old Thomas Register), alibaba.com, or MadeInChina.com. You might also consider hiring an agent to find factories for you. Make sure the agent has local offices near you and in the location of your factory. You'll be spending a lot of time working with the agent throughout your production process, and most likely spending a lot of money on the agent as well.

As you compile a list of possible manufacturers, the best way to assess their ability to deliver the product that you want is to visit the manufacturer's office in person, tour its facilities, and see samples of what the company has made. If you can't visit the factories, then getting samples of parts made by each factory is critical. After you've gotten hold of samples, the factory background check begins.

Evaluating a prospective manufacturer involves answering the questions:

- Does it make things that are similar to what you intend to manufacture?
- Who are the manufacturer's other customers (that it can tell you about)?
- Does the manufacturer have experience working with the materials that you'd like your product to be made from?

- Do the samples have a similar number of parts and level of complexity compared to your product?
- Is the surface finish quality what you are looking for?
- Do the parts have the same level of precision and fit that you desire?
- Which CAD file formats does the factory use?
- Does the factory employ engineers who will work with you to see your product through to production?
- Is the factory responsive to your requests?

This is not an exhaustive list, but it's enough to get you started and keep you out of trouble later on! Appendix D provides a more complete manufacturing checklist.

If you do have the opportunity to visit the factory, another important consideration is the quality of the factory itself, and the workers inside it. In addition to not wanting to support sweatshops and dangerous work conditions, a clean, well-run factory with well-treated workers is a good sign that you will also be treated with respect as the customer. Unfortunately, it can be hard to assess the quality of the factory without making a site visit.

After you've done your evaluation and background check of several manufacturers, the fun begins. It's time to make some stuff.

The Manufacturing Handoff

Once you have a final list of prospective manufacturers, you need to get price quotes with lead time information included. This will involve sending all of your design files, documentation, data sheets, and any prototypes to the prospective manufacturers. The more detailed the documentation, the better. See Chapter 14 for details of the documentation process. In general, you'll need to send all of your CAD files in the format agreed upon between you and the manufacturer. You will get more predictable results if you do the file conversion into a format that the factory can use, rather than relying on the factory to convert files for you. This gives you the opportunity to verify that the converted file contains the correct information. If you are sending mechanical CAD files, you need to make sure every part is properly dimensioned and tolerances are included. It's easy to create CAD parts that fit perfectly together in the virtual world, but once they become tangible objects in the real world, proper tolerances can mean the difference between a perfect fit and a ruined product. If you don't know how to establish tolerances for a part, work with your prospective manufacturers to understand what is possible. Sometimes they can help you set tolerances within the range that they can achieve in production. Your drawings need to include materials selection and material finishes, lest the manufacturer select materials and finishes for you. Your files should also include part numbers, quantities, part function, revision information, and assembly information. Make sure this information is also cross-referenced in your bill of materials.

Here is a sample RFQ.

MyCo, LLC
REQUEST FOR QUOTATION (RFQ) FOR
MANUFACTURING OF COOLING SYSTEMS
DATE: August 20, 2013

We intend to offer a firm-fixed price contract for the manufacture and delivery of cooling systems.

Interested vendors should submit a quote and lead times for the services as described in this RFQ. Supplier Unit Quotes shall be a Firm Fixed-Price, and inclusive of any administrative or overhead costs.

Quote Quantity A	Quote Quantity B	Quote Quantity C
1 unit	10 units	500 units

A. Specifications
   1. The manufactured systems will have the following usage:
      a. Providing 5000 W of cooling for process fluid
      b. Minimum process fluid temperature of 0°C
      c. Maximum process fluid temperature of 50°C
      d. Ambient temperature of 35°C
      e. Flow rate of 5 L/min
      f. Process fluid volume of 50 liters

B. Statement of Work
   1. Assembly, integration, charging, and testing of micro chiller core
      a. Assembly consists of the following parts:
         i. Compressor
         ii. Evaporator
         iii. Condensor
      b. Integration: The following materials provided by vendor will be used to complete the Assembly
         i. Copper tubing
         ii. Capillary tube
         iii. Brazing supplies
      c. Charging: Assembly will be brazed and charged with R744.
         i. Sealed process tubes will be used.
   2. Refer to included image, CAD files, assembly files, and BOM.

Unless you have a lot of experience in designing products for manufacture, you will probably have a number of conversations with the prospective manufacturers to clarify your needs. They will most likely have suggestions for making your product easier to manufacture. This is a good opportunity to further differentiate the capabilities of the various factories that you are considering. Whether you choose a factory based on price, capability, or any number of other factors that have been discussed here, your main goal is to minimize the risk of production problems at a reasonable price, and to get your parts after a predictable length of time. At this point, you should have a good feeling about the best choice of manufacturer. If not, don't worry. Pick the factory that has the best combination of evaluation results and cost, and start working with it.

Stay away from the outliers in your evaluation. As with most things, prices that are too good to be true probably are. Either the factory will make poor-quality parts for you or it misquoted the price and will demand more money once it has your business. I had a battery manufacturer offer me prices that were more than 50% lower than the prices offered by all the other vendors I received quotes from. As an experiment, I requested samples from the company. Six months and countless emails after I sent money to the manufacturer, it sent the wrong parts and disappeared.

Keep in mind that even very good factories will make honest mistakes. What the factory does to correct each mistake is a good indicator of whether it will make a good long-term manufacturing partner. If the factory is exceedingly slow, is unresponsive to your corrections, demands payments to correct errors, or just points the blame at you (even if it was your error), then it might be time to move on to a manufacturer with better customer service and better problem-solving skills.

If things don't go as planned, that's not great, but it's survivable. You have now made a list of potential factories, and have a process to find more if necessary.

Prior to beginning a volume production run of any product, it's a good idea to work with the factory to optimize your product for its production capabilities. Not only does this step reduce the cost of the product, but it will increase the chances that your product can be made successfully at the volumes you desire with the lead times that you've agreed upon.

DFMA

Just about anything can be manufactured, given enough time and money. The goal of design for manufacture and assembly (DFMA) is to minimize the amount of time and money required, while maintaining quality, fit, form, and function. My colleague Peter Dewhurst[4] co-founded a company called Boothroyd Dewhurst Inc. and received the National Medal of Technology for his work on DFMA tools. He created the following elegant description of DFMA:

> *During the early stages of design, control of part count is paramount to meeting cost targets . . .*
>
> *This analysis allows you to determine the theoretical minimum number of parts that must be in the design for the product while maintaining 100% functionality. When you identify*

---

4. I was a co-founder of a company called Dewhurst Solution, Inc., with Peter Dewhurst.

and eliminate unnecessary parts, you eliminate unnecessary manufacturing and assembly costs, along with "downstream" costs associated with warranty and service, engineering change orders, and utilization of factory floor space. Suppliers are a rich source of feedback during product simplification, particularly if one of your options is to combine multiple parts into one part with multiple features. As a design matures, DFA tools help avoid part proliferation and ensure that costs do not creep back into the product.[5]

You've already learned enough about design for manufacture from Chapter 12. You can take a course on DFMA at many universities to go further, but it probably won't be especially useful unless you are also intimately familiar with your factory's capabilities and processes. The factory should have experience with optimizing your design for production in its facility. Your job is to make sure that none of the design intent is lost in that optimization process, as that's where many errors occur. The best way to do so is by getting samples of your product made.

What Could Really Go Wrong?

I'm always impressed by the more unusual stories I hear from friends about their first encounter with manufacturing, like the team behind Pen Type-A having to unpack, disassemble, and hand-wash machining oil out of each one of their pens before shipping them to customers.[6] It's critical to identify and eliminate as many problems as possible before initiating full-scale production. This is typically done through iteration—first making numerous prototypes until they are perfect, and then manufacturing samples via a small pilot production run of the product.

Making samples effectively means undertaking a small-volume production run with the final production design and manufacturing process. This is where the majority of debugging takes place. It is also where you will need to begin paying the factory. Fortunately, by starting small, you can minimize the amount of money you could potentially lose. In six years of sending money to factories I've never visited, I've lost money several times. But the total damage has been less than $2000 because I made a small sample production run. Other friends have lost tens of thousands of dollars, but have managed to avoid bigger problems. I had a wire transfer flat-out disappear, and my tiny local bank couldn't trace it. I switched to an international bank after that. I have received products that were out of spec, that were of poor quality, or, like the fans in Figure 13.3, that were completely smashed and broken when I received them.

Twice, I've had manufacturers send me parts that were not what I designed and ordered, and once I had to chase a battery vendor for four months to have it fill the order that I had paid for in full. Sending wire transfers to factories sight unseen is always a risky endeavor. If you don't have the stomach for this risk, you are better off working with local factories. Even if you do work with offshore factories, it's a good idea to send your money

5. http://www.dfma.com/software/index.html
6. https://www.kickstarter.com/projects/cwandt/pen-type-a-a-minimal-pen/posts?page=4

Figure 13.3   Samples shipped from a distributor.
All were damaged in transit.
(Source: Image by Kipp Bradford)

through a bank that has extensive international wire transfer capabilities. Large multi-national banks typically have a wire fraud department that can perform a full trace on a transfer and help you recover lost funds.

Ideally, if you've done your homework, at this point you will have identified a good factory that is trustworthy, has integrity, and has given you a reasonable quote. You should have done a design review of all your files and some optimization to work with this factory's engineers. You will have sent the first payment and the factory will have received it. Now it will begin to make a small production run of your parts, and will send you samples. Don't celebrate just yet. You will spend a lot of time sending samples back to the factory with notes about what it didn't quite get correct. Sometimes, the factory will mis-interpret your instructions. I have a batch of 100 complex circuit boards that are missing the silkscreen text because the manufacturer did not generate the silkscreen from the cor-rect board layer (Figure 13.4). Unfortunately, the error wasn't caught until after the boards were manufactured, and the boards were rendered useless. It's much better when the error is caught in the production sample.

Figure 13.5 shows the foam insulation used in a cooling system. There is a slight offset to the right of the holes in the bad sample that was the result of a manufacturing measure-ment error. This caused the insulation to not fit the enclosure for which it was designed. Fortunately, the error was corrected before volume production commenced. The manu-facturer was able to make the correction based on the photographs, and sent the corrected sample for validation. It took only two tries to get it right.

Figure 13.4   The board on the right lost information
from its prototype on the left.
(Source: Image by Kipp Bradford)

Figure 13.5   Insulation samples that were critical for
detecting a manufacturing flaw.
(Source: Image by Kipp Bradford)

The factory will also make decisions that its engineers think are unimportant as they design the production tooling to minimize their own costs. If you don't specify and communicate every last detail, you may find what you consider small flaws in your parts that resulted from manufacturing optimizations or manufacturing decisions made by the factory without you being in the loop. Here are a few examples from Kickstarter projects I've backed:

- "The good news is that we received the first plastic samples coming out of our injection factory. However, these samples had a lot of cosmetic problems and the quality was well below the standard we would want to have . . ."

- "We are going back and forth with our vendor to dial the tolerance in. It looks like they should be able to meet us halfway on our tolerance request . . ."

- "It seems the particular aluminum alloy the metal fabricator is using cannot take colored anodization, which made us go to baked enamel. And the enamel is proving difficult too, partially because of the smallness of the part . . ."

As each of these problems emerged, the project designers were able to find a solution. Problems like these caused by a lack of communication between the designer and the manufacturer are easily caught through each round of samples. The more details you include in your parts specification, the better the manufacturer will be able to meet your needs. Your ultimate goal is to come to agreement with the manufacturer on your specification, with the understanding that any changes that deviate from that spec are to be previewed by you, the designer, first.

The best way to establish this process is through a requirements document that you create with the manufacturer. A typical requirements document is clear and unambiguous, and is complete as possible. The importance of each requirement should be established by the designer. A common way to do that is to label each requirement with the words "MUST," "SHOULD," or "MAY" as a simple method of indicating where tradeoffs can be made versus where the design intent is critical. Examples of requirements documents can be easily found online, and some manufacturers can give you a template to start with.

Upon the completion of each iteration, the samples are checked against the requirements and specifications. Any flaws that are found should be clearly documented and sent back to the manufacturer for correction. Updating the requirements document allows you to capture both the production error and the corrective measure required for the next iteration. If your current manufacturer can't resolve the issue, at least you now have a more exacting set of instructions that you can hand off to another manufacturer to continue production with minimal interruption.

Quality Control

When the manufacturer finally sends you samples that look and work the way that you want, it's time to ramp up production. It feels really bad to get a batch of products with some noticeable defect. It feels much worse to have unhappy customers sending a product back because some problem slipped into the manufacturing process. For small production runs, it's a good idea for you to test each and every product before boxing the products and shipping them to customers. In many cases, testing must be done at the factory to your specifications. Typically the manufacturer will design the testing jig with your input to meet the necessary testing requirements. Testing can be a boring, repetitive job that requires constant focus and attention. It's easy for fatigue to creep in and for a tester to miss an error. That being the case, it's good to design testing systems that keep the operator entertained and occupied. An example of an interesting testing system design is one that works as a game and plays fun sounds when all the tests are carried out and confirmed.

It's a good idea to take samples from each batch of your product to retest and confirm that the factory quality control process is effective. If you can catch problems before your product goes out to customers, your product will be much more likely to succeed.

Creative Fixes

Sometimes, as with the Pen Type-A, things go wrong but the product is still salvageable. This is where you might have to roll up your sleeves and perform a bit of manual labor and maybe some heroics to ship a satisfactory product to your customers. There is a great and underutilized term for this kind of manual repair in the electronics world. "Suck-muck" appropriately describes the hand-modifications made to a circuit board after production to get it working properly.

When the entire silkscreen is missing from a circuit board with many components, there isn't much you can do other than use the boards for coasters. If the board is missing only a positive or ground indicator, it might be easily repairable (though it might take a lot of time). Tod Kurt and Mike Kuniavsky had exactly this experience when they accidentally left the indicators off the circuit board they manufactured for their BlinkM product. To fix this problem, they used permanent markers to apply a red dot indicating power and a black dot indicating ground on the front of their board (Figure 13.6). They fixed the error in the next production run, but the cost of a couple Sharpies and several hours was all it took to rescue the initial production run of boards.

A more direct example of suck-muck is the early version of the SparkFun 9DOF (9 Degrees of Freedom) board. The board design was sent off to production with a gap between the ground connections in the design. Throwing boards away is never an appealing option, so SparkFun engineers came up with a simple fix that let them avoid the extra costs and time required to manufacture a new batch of boards. They were able to solder a jumper wire between two ground connections to complete the circuit (Figure 13.7). Manually soldering this jumper wire required the time of a paid technician, but it was still less expensive than scrapping the entire production run, and it enabled SparkFun to avoid a 6-week delay of the product launch.

Figure 13.6   An early ThingM BlinkM. Note the two
hand-drawn dots below "PWR."
(Source: Image CC-BY-SA ThingM Corp/Tod E. Kurt)

Figure 13.7   Note the wire soldered onto the board connecting the two
different ground segments together.
(Source: Image CC-BY-SA SparkFun Electronics)

Anecdote: Hackable Hardware and Its Discontents
Amanda Williams and Bruno Nadeau

The following advice on designing hackable hardware was written just a few weeks after we returned from China, where we were supervising the first manufacturing run of our first product ever. We set out to make a smart and expressive lamp that people can customize and reprogram easily. Clyde (yes, we gave it a person name) comes with autodetectable sensor modules that allow people to change his behavior without programming. His firmware and hardware are also open source and Arduino compatible, so anyone from a newbie to an expert can find interesting ways to modify our creation. Not many companies make consumer electronics that are truly modular, accessible, and hackable at the hardware level. And there's a reason for that: it's not easy. Here are some challenges we ran into:

- Modular hardware is more expensive to manufacture. If we made all the decisions for our users and built everything into one self-contained board, we would have had much lower manufacturing costs. We also ended up paying more for components because we needed to add connectors so people can add or remove different sensor modules. We decided to make a modular product with higher costs anyway, because over the course of the product's lifetime, it will give us flexibility and it will be less wasteful to replace or upgrade one part, rather than the whole product.

- It's much harder to test modular hardware. For every PCB you manufacture, you need to make a test jig, as well as another set of PCBs and software to run tests on your production PCBs. Our testing process involved four times more work because we chose to make four separate reconfigurable modules.

- Testing a module on its own won't always cover errors that could happen when the module is in place and interacting with other components. For example, it won't determine that the module generates too much electromagnetic interference (which depends a lot on the spatial layout of components and traces) once the assembly is put together.

- The connector was tested separately. Problems that might come up after assembly, however, include the interaction between the parts, noise, and other issues related to the components as an aggregate.

- We had to make hard decisions about whether to put complexity in hardware or software. This isn't an issue with modularity per se, but it is an issue with hackability. It's not enough for a hackable product simply to work—it has to explain to its owners *how* it works. Thus we had to make both our hardware and our software accessible and understandable to our users. For example, we have an IR emitter–receiver pair that detects deformation in a silicone film that our users can poke to turn our lamp on and off. The hardware is dead simple, and that's great! It's easy for people to see how it works, and it's easy to connect something else if you want; it's just an analog sensor. But the tradeoff is that to get our product working in different lighting conditions, we had to put some fancy calibration in the software that makes it harder to understand exactly how the silicone "eye" works algorithmically. We made some

(*continues*)

choices about which parts of our product would be easier to hack, but the complexity had to go somewhere.

- More room to hack means more room for users to make mistakes, and that has major implications for customer support. We understood, in the abstract at least, that a sense of accomplishment in hacking really comes about only when you've successfully done something that you *could have* screwed up. Now that we've shipped our products, we truly understand this point: *people will screw things up.* (And that's great! That's how we learn!) And they will ask us for help often (as they should). We have to be ready to help with the depth and breadth of troubleshooting that individual customers need.

- It is useful to document and post each customer's troubleshooting advice as a resource for everyone else. Anyone hoping to release a hackable product to more than a handful of experts should recognize how absolutely crucial good customer support and community management will be to the end user's experience—and how much work it is to provide.

None of this is intended to discourage people from building modular, hackable hardware. In the end, design is about working within and around constraints. We chose to accept the constraints of creating a hackable product, and it turned out to be a really interesting design problem. Now we're sharing some of the challenges we encountered so more people can anticipate what they'll be—because even with the difficulties, we still think it's worth doing!

Summary

Some years ago, NASA did a nice study called "Error Cost Escalation through the Project Life Cycle."[7] That title may sound like a managerial torture technique, but it is a really eye-opening look at how much it costs to fix your mistakes the closer you get to shipping your product. NASA discovered that errors caught in the final stage of a project can cost more than 1500 times more to fix than errors caught before design begins. Giving an extra few hours of thought to your product specification could save you tens or hundreds of thousands of dollars later in the project. The bottom line is, catch your errors early and often.

Of course, if you've never manufactured something before, this can be quite challenging. This chapter has covered a number of the common-sense approaches to debugging the manufacturing process. Like any debugging, it's made easier when you start with a good design that uses readily available components and conforms to the capabilities of the manufacturer that you've selected. You are also less likely to encounter errors when you carefully select your manufacturing partner and establish good communication with it. It's important to draw on the manufacturer's expertise to identify and correct any design

---

7. http://ntrs.nasa.gov/archive/nasa/casi.ntrs.nasa.gov/20100036670.pdf

features that could turn into manufacturing nightmares later on. Remember, you chose that particular manufacturer because you believed in its capability to manufacture your product. Manufacturers spend all day figuring out how to manufacture what their customers want with minimal errors or problems. They are familiar with their tools and the tool limitations. Ignore their advice at your own peril! Even so, mistakes will happen. Many of those can be identified and corrected with a pilot production run and through good quality control.

The worst-case scenario, and one that is often encountered by the leaders of crowd-funded projects who've never manufactured a product before (and plenty who have!), is that a problem pops up as components are coming off the factory floor in volume. Even at this point, there is still a chance you can salvage your project. Get creative. The solution will probably cost you a lot in terms of time and money, but it's certainly going to be less costly than starting over from scratch.

Nathan Seidle, founder of SparkFun, once reminded me that what might be perfect for the obsessive engineer inside all of us usually doesn't make the best business sense. You can iterate and prototype until you run out of money or your market opportunity passes you by as new technology and new products are introduced. I certainly have designed more than one product where this has been the case. Nathan said, "Even the best-designed projects have issues. If your run of 1000 items doesn't meet 100% of the requirements or specifications that you originally intended, consider selling the device with a limited feature set. As long as your users are not surprised by a missing feature or incorrect label, they will generally be understanding."

Despite your best efforts and intentions, errors will slip through the cracks. Minor errors may be survivable. Educate yourself about manufacturing and manufacturers. Incorporate that knowledge into your product design and process. This will lead to fewer errors in the first place, and you will be well on your way to a successful product launch.

14

Taxonomy of Hardware Documentation

Addie Wagenknecht

"The future is here, it's just not evenly distributed yet."

—William Gibson

This chapter explains how to properly document your open source hardware product and projects. It discusses setting up your documentation, structuring the community, starting the project, and avoiding some common pitfalls of open source hardware documentation.

Successful open hardware projects depend on successful documentation. Without easy-to-understand documentation, a project cannot be reproduced. Without reproduction, a project cannot grow or easily be forked. The Open Source Hardware Definition requires open documentation so that anyone may reproduce your hardware. In this chapter, we discuss important aspects to consider when documenting an open hardware project.

One of the first questions to consider when developing an open hardware project is, Who do you want to build it? It's important to consider the community in terms of practices, skill levels, languages, and geographical locations. For example, do you want this project to be developed only in North America? Europe? Asia? Africa? Just at your school's fabrication lab? It is also important to think about how users can access and find the documentation of your open hardware project. Is it a website? A git repo? Is it search-able by a search engine? Documentation is used as an entry point to discover a project and determine whether it's feasible. In addition, it is important to consider writing your documentation in a way that is consistent across the project and clear enough for any user to contribute to. Doing so enhances the project's repeatability and growth, which often translates into a larger community of developers in the long run. The goal of an improved documentation taxonomy is that it enables anyone, at all levels of expertise, to study, re-produce, and improve open source hardware projects.

The power of open source is that it allows community members to build and progress freely based on others' work, making advancements happen faster that might not oth-erwise be economically feasible. Good documentation, in turn, is the key to progress in this community of exchange. The goal of open hardware documentation is to facilitate a framework in which collaboration can encourage contributions, making extensions of the project possible. The easier it is to parse instructions, the easier it is to contribute new developments toward maintaining a successful long-term project and the community around it.

An example of source files, README.txt, assembly instructions, and images for the Blinky Buildings kit associated with this book can be found at http://bit.ly /blinkybuildings.

README.txt

The README.txt, or in some cases the product homepage, introduces the hardware through documentation. Beginning developers of open hardware projects often rely on documentation the most heavily. The landing page of your project, whether it consists of a website or a text file, is the place you want to provide an overview identifying the following items:

- The project
- Licenses
- Attribution
- Expected time to build it
- Cost
- Expertise level

I like to think of the landing page as a quick summary of what people can expect and attempt to answer questions before they ask them. The introduction, or README text, not only gives an overview of the project, but also carefully leads developers into the project's build structure. It's important that these instructions are summarized as clearly as possible. I like to also note the last time the documentation was updated, as a reference for people who are unfamiliar with the project or who are unsure how up-to-date the information is. This item can be as simple as a small notation at the bottom of the webpage.

The README.txt should also include licenses and attribution information, which can sometimes go hand in hand. For example, SparkFun's README.txt (Figure 14.1) for the

---

License Information

The hardware is released under Creative Commons Share-alike 3.0.

Hardware authors: Original Arduino Mini design by Team Arduino

Pro Mini design by Nathan Seidle @ SparkFun Electronics

Revision work by Pete Lewis @ SparkFun Electronics

Distributed as-is; no warranty is given.

Figure 14.1   README licensing text example from SparkFun, with a
licensed use of the Arduino trademark.
(Source: Screenshot is from github.com/sparkfun/Arduino_Pro_Mini_328
/blob/master/README.md)

Arduino Pro Mini includes a CC–SA license, attribution to the original Arduino Team, attribution for the Pro Mini, and attribution for revisions made to the board. This file is also a good place to record any warranty information, although you may also want to include warranty information on the product packaging.

Product Webpage

As an entry point, the webpage is a good place to redirect users to other services or resources around the project that remain more active—for example, a Twitter account or a way to contact the community. Community contact typically includes forums, an active community support list, or versioning on a site such as GitHub for a codebase. The Best Practices state:

> *Provide links to the source (original design files) for your hardware on the product itself, its packaging, or its documentation.*

Labeling on the product pages also helps to make your intentions clear. For example, you could label the product as open source hardware and use the open source hardware logo (Figure 14.2) on the product page as well as your hardware, rather than making users hunt for the design files and licensing clauses to ensure the designs and hardware are open. The open source hardware logo was created to give users a visual cue that documents can be found on the source and the hardware follows the Open Source Hardware Definition. The Best Practices remind you to use the logo clearly to convey which parts are open:

> *Use the open-source hardware logo on your hardware. Do so in a way that makes it clear which parts of the hardware the logo applies to (i.e., which parts are open-source).*

Figure 14.2   Open Source Hardware logo.
(License: CC-SA. Source: Image CC-BY-SA Macklin Chaffee)

Arduino Pro Mini 328 - 3.3V/8MHz

DEV-11114 RoHS✔ ⌂ 🄳   ▌f 🄿 ◁ SHARE

🄯 images are CC BY-NC-SA 3.0

Description: It's blue! It's thin! It's the Arduino Pro Mini! SparkFun's minimal design approach to Arduino. This is a 3.3V Arduino running the 8MHz bootloader. Arduino Pro Mini does not come with connectors populated so that you can solder in any connector or wire with any orientation you need. We recommend first time Arduino users start with the Uno R3. It's a great board that will get you up and running quickly. The Arduino Pro series is meant for users that understand the limitations of system voltage (3.3V), lack of connectors, and USB off board.

We really wanted to minimize the cost of an Arduino. In order to accomplish this we used all SMD components, made it two layer, etc. This board connects directly to the FTDI Basic Breakout board and supports auto-reset. The Arduino Pro Mini also works with the FTDI cable but the FTDI cable does not bring out the DTR pin so the auto-reset feature will not work. There is a voltage regulator on board so it can accept voltage up to 12VDC. If you're supplying unregulated power to the board, be sure to connect to the "RAW" pin on not VCC.

The latest and greatest version of this board breaks out the ADC6 and ADC7 pins as well as adds footprints for optional I2C pull-up resistors! We also took the opportunity to slap it with the OSHW logo.

Can't decide which Arduino is right for you? Arduino buying guide!

Note: A portion of this sale is given back to Arduino LLC to help fund continued development of new tools and new IDE features.

Dimensions: 0.7x1.3" (18x33mm)

Features:

- ATmega328 running at 8MHz with external resonator (0.5% tolerance)
- Low-voltage board needs no interfacing circuitry to popular 3.3V devices and modules (GPS, accelerometers, sensors, etc)
- 0.8mm Thin PCB
- USB connection off board
- Weighs less than 2 grams!
- Supports auto-reset
- 3.3V regulator
- Max 150mA output
- Over current protected
- DC input 3.3V up to 12V
- On board Power and Status LEDs
- Analog Pins: 8
- Digital I/Os: 14

Documents:

- Schematic
- Eagle Files
- Getting Started Tutorial
- GitHub

Replaces:DEV-09220

Figure 14.3   SparkFun product page as an example.
(Source: Screenshot is from www.sparkfun.com/products/11114)

At the time this book was written, SparkFun had the most comprehensive product pages to document its open source hardware (Figure 14.3). Icons at the top near the product title graphically describe a number of things, including Restriction of Hazardous Substances (RoHS) compliance, Fritzing libraries, 3D modeling designs, open source hardware, and so on. A description, notes (including whether a royalty is given back to original designers), dimensions, a feature set, the source files, and source code are listed under documents, and versions of the product follow. At the time this book was written, SparkFun was also the only website that had an "Open Hardware" category that allowed consumers to see at a glance which products are open source and choose to shop that way.

Hardware Source Files

Open hardware source files are commonly referred to as design files and contain the source materials to build your product. For electronics, open hardware source files are commonly schematics and board files. The Open Source Hardware Definition states this about documentation:

> *The hardware must be released with documentation including design files, and must allow modification and distribution of the design files. Where documentation is not furnished with the physical product, there must be a well-publicized means of obtaining this documentation for no more than a reasonable reproduction cost, preferably downloading via the Internet without charge. The documentation must include design files in the preferred format for making changes, for example the native file format of a CAD program. Deliberately obfuscated design files are not allowed. Intermediate forms analogous to compiled computer code—such as printer-ready copper artwork from a CAD program—are not allowed as substitutes. The license may require that the design files are provided in fully-documented, open format(s).*

From this piece of the definition, we know that to consider our project open source, we must release design files allowing modification and distribution of the design files (or hardware source files). This means design files cannot be copyrighted, and must be released under an open source license and preferably released on the Internet because the cost of reproducing and sharing those files when done so electronically is free. It is also worth considering which file types are most commonly used. If you use an unusual or obsolete format, that choice can affect the user's experience. Consider also using version control and commonly accepted units of measurement.

For example, an error often made in design files that depend on measurements is to not specify the unit of measure used in the design. For example, many designers use millimeters, but others use inches or centimeters. Including a "key" for measurements and other important information somewhere within the file listing can help users exchange information, thereby ensuring more continuity between users. All too often, and especially with .svg files, a user will move a file between systems, only to find that one system's default is in inches while the other system defaults to centimeters. What this can mean when fabricating is that you might end up with the same piece in two different sizes: one printed 10 centimeters in length and another printed 10 inches in length!

Source files must be licensed openly so that people may copy and disseminate how to create the open source hardware, since the hardware is derived from the source. The licensing structure for source files relies on copyright because source files are generally written or drawn. The source files must have an open copyright alternative or copyleft applied. Popular licenses for source files are CC-BY, CC-BY-SA (noncommercial [NC] is not appropriate on source files), GNU, Apache, and BSD, to name a few. Not only is this a legal standard for open sourcing your hardware, but a license also clarifies the intent of the creator.

At this time, there is no real "industry standard" for licensing open hardware, which makes matters even more complicated. You will want to look at the various types of licenses available, and try to find one that covers what is important to you, in your specific project. As with a lot of things, one size doesn't fit all when it comes to licensing. If you are feeling a bit overwhelmed, look at how some of your favorite open hardware projects license their work (or don't). At the very least, the existence of multiple licensing structures has started a dialogue within the open source hardware community about why or how people or communities choose to license their projects. This subject is comprehensively covered in Chapter 3, Licensing Open Source Hardware. One practice that is not a licensing standard, but rather simply states your intention of following the Open Source Hardware Definition, is to use the open source hardware logo (Figure 14.2) on the hardware itself, along with the relevant source files, webpage, and other documentation.

Chapter 10, Physical Materials, provides many examples of the various types of hardware and the source files that may go along with them. In addition, the Best Practices[1] outline what constitutes original design files and give several examples of original design files and auxiliary design files. Examples of original design files include the following:

- 2D drawings or computer-aided design (CAD) files, such as those used to describe two-dimensional laser-cut, vinyl-cut, or water-jet-cut parts, in their original format. Example formats: native 2D design files saved by Corel Draw (.cdr), Inkscape (.svg), Adobe Illustrator (.ai), and AutoCAD.

- 3D designs that can be 3D printed, forged, injection molded, extruded, machined, and otherwise fabricated. Example formats: native files saved by SolidWorks (.sldprt, .sldasm) and Rhino.

- Circuit board CAD files such as capture files (schematics) and printed-circuit board (layout) design files. Example formats: native files saved by Eagle, Altium, KiCad, and gEDA.

---

1. http://www.oshwa.org/sharing-best-practices/

- Component libraries (e.g., symbol, footprint, fastener) necessary for native modification of CAD files.

- Additional technical drawings in their original design formats, if required for fabrication of the device.

- Additional artwork that may be used on the device and is included as part of the OSHW release, such as an emblem or a cosmetic overlay in the original design format.

Making the Pieces Visible: Bill of Materials

Your bill of materials (BOM) is a part of your documentation. See Chapter 5, The Design Process: How to Get from Nothing to Something, and Chapter 13, Troubleshooting from Your Design to Your Manufacturer, for more information on how to build a BOM. For open source hardware, there are some important aspects to consider that will shape not only the community but also the future of your project:

- Consider suppliers that ship internationally or to multiple countries if you want a project that is globally repeatable.

- Pick suppliers that are dependable, have stock, and maintain an updated website with inventory.

- Data sheets, which come from the supplier, should be part of your documentation.

- If your project includes parts that are 3D printed or laser cut, remember to include those files and the correct licenses attached to them.

- If parts for your project can be pulled off preexisting products, include that information in your documentation.

The Lasersaur Project was developed because we wanted a laser cutter but could not afford the $60,000 to $100,000 cost to buy a commercially made system. We also wanted the system to be globally repeatable, so that anyone who wanted a laser cutter could have a commercial-grade system available for 5% to 10% of the price. To do that, we had to develop a BOM for more than 1000 parts that could be sourced worldwide (Figure 14.4). This BOM can be sorted by subsystem (for example, if you just wanted to build the frame) and by supplier (so you can order easily and quickly all the parts based on where to get them, not where they go). Figure 14.4 shows how the BOM page looks on the Lasersaur website.

As you can see in Figure 14.4, the Lasersaur BOM is divided by North American and European suppliers. It is also clearly marked by version, maintaining a list of older system BOMs for reference. This is helpful for previous systems still in use, enabling their owners to source or repair parts of the system. In addition, once you select a BOM, you can view it by supplier or by subsystem, again making ordering and building a lot less painful than if everything was listed without a source organization.

Please note the parts can be sorted (1) by subsystem and (2) by supplier. As you might have guessed (1) is best suited for ordering all the parts and (2) is good to understand the CAD model and the various subassemblies.

Also see the revisions/roadmap page for upcoming upgrades.

Current BOMs:

- BOM for North America v14.03-rc1
- BOM for Europe v14.03-rc1

Upgrade from v13.04 to v14.03 BOM:

- Upgrade BOM for North America v14.03
- Upgrade BOM for Europe v14.03

Older BOMs for reference:

- BOM for North America v14.01
- BOM for Europe v14.01
- BOM for North America v13.04
- BOM for Europe v13.04
- BOM for North America v12.08
- BOM for Europe v12.08
- BOM for North America v12.02
- BOM for Europe v12.02
- BOM for North America v11.08
- BOM for Europe v11.08

Figure 14.4   Lasersaur BOM page.
(Source: http://www.lasersaur.com/manual/bom)

Tutorials

Videos and photographs should be used as a part of your documentation and for tutorials. Good visual documentation can make a project visible and repeatable, which in turn can make it more popular. As documented in the Best Practices, images or videos are an excellent way to share information:

Photos help people understand what your project is and how to put it together. It's good to publish photographs from multiple viewpoints and at various stages of assembly. If you don't have photos, posting 3D renderings of your design is a good alternative. Either way, it's good to provide captions or text that explain what's shown in each image and why's it's useful.

Photos are useful for several areas of documentation, not only tutorials, but assembly guides, Hello World instructions, hook up guides, troubleshooting, etc.

Lulzbot offers an excellent example of universally understandable, easy-to-understand instructions. These instructions are almost not language dependent and can be understood visually. They include large detailed images that are clearly shot, with step-by-step instructions and often examples are included to help would-be makers (Figure 14.5).

Lulzbot created its own open source software documentation tool called the OHAI-kit (www.ohai-kit.alephobjects.com/). In Figure 14.5, note how the documentation lists every tool needed for the project as step 1.

Another example of a step-by-step instruction platform used for a plethora of projects is Instructables (www.instructables.com). Not everything on Instructables is open source hardware, but it is a good resource on which to look for open source designs and tutorials. Similar to the Lulzbot instructions, most Instructables begin with the tools and supplies you will need to complete the project and then provide detailed images to show the user how to build the project.

Some open source hardware has accompanying video tutorials. Becky Stern of Adafruit has uploaded a great series of wearable electronics tutorials to YouTube; some of these tutorials are discussed by Becky in Chapter 9, Wearables. This method of developing visual-based documentation doesn't rely on your drawing skills. Tutorials may also take the form of books, such as *Getting Started with Arduino* by Massimo Banzi. Tutorials differ from source files in that there is no requirement on how to share them. Tutorials, videos, and instruction books can be copyrighted or shared openly. Because tutorials do not cover how to rebuild the hardware, they are not considered source files; thus more flexibility is allowed in how they are shared from a licensing standpoint.

Hello World

I like the "lunch break rule" when it comes to starting out on a new platform or project. I want a tutorial that gets me excited and up and running in less than 30–60 minutes. When you think about how quickly 30 minutes can pass, you have to think easy. Processing, for example, is a programming language that was introduced in 2001 for beginners with little or no understanding of how to program. In keeping with this ethos, it has excellent comprehensive beginner tutorials (as well as a great development environment and online community). Arduino reflects the hardware equivalent—that is, the drive to offer a comprehensive user-developed "getting started" tutorial base. Not only is the Arduino documentation available on its own website, but other community-developed tutorials and documentation can be found almost anywhere on the Internet because Arduino is so widely used as a platform. Thanks to all of this support, Arduino is extremely well documented. Having others document your project is a benefit of open source hardware.

So back to the "lunch break rule": this should be your "hello world" introduction as to why your project is awesome. If your project can give potential developers the warm and fuzzies quickly, they will walk away excited about all the possibilities that spending a

Figure 14.5 OHAI-kit documentation.

(Source: Screenshot from ohai-kit.alephobjects.com/project/extruder_calibration/)

longer period with your project might open up. As on a first date with a romantic interest, you want to walk away excited about the future together.

Generally speaking, in the long run you want to have a wide range of tutorials available so that people can get a sense of what is possible within realistic means. They often serve as a starting point for inspiration and new contributions. Know your audience—that is, decide who will most likely be reading your tutorials. Did you make your tutorials for the general hacker community, or are they more specific to one particular audience, such as users of academic research lab equipment. Make sure you are defining terms and keep assumptions to a minimum about what your audience might already know.

A great source for project leads is often the community: see what they have made and if they are willing to write up a guide and share it online for future members. If you are just starting from scratch, make what interests you; chances are, it will interest others, too.

FAQs

Frequently asked questions (FAQ) are often as important as the introduction to the project. A good FAQ will cover the basics, from how to contact the primary developers, to the level of skill required to start the project, the amount of time one can expect to spend on it, costs, and tools, to more detailed information such as how people can contribute (in terms of development or other forms of capital). It might also cover logistics such as shipping, contacting founders, testing, or finding answers to more questions (e.g., Twitter handle, community forms or list, email contacts of the leading developers). The FAQ section can also include things about your project you initially forgot in the original documentation, like "gotchas." Gotchas are "oopsies" that can be considered quick fixes the user can make. Another option is to provide your users with some simple troubleshooting tips to make the product work better (or at all). For complete troubleshooting advice, refer to Chapter 13.

Creating Community

A strong community depends on strong content. Community building can take as long as building your project, often even longer. If you are lucky, your community will develop along with your project. Power users become sort of community managers, answering questions before the primary developers even read them. Typically, you will want to introduce a group of "power users" as early as your idea is born. It is not uncommon that these power users at some point join the primary development team.

One of the best pieces of advice I received when starting to develop open source hardware projects in the late 1990s was that I should cultivate a group of people who could shape the community in a direction that encouraged contributions, growth, questions, and answers. The catch? I needed to find them, and I needed to invite them. I had to find people who I could ask to participate, give feedback, and contribute before there was much tangible work to do. In addition, they had to be somewhat knowledgeable about the project in some aspect (e.g., code, hardware, troubleshooting, teaching). I tried to find people who came from a broad range of backgrounds, each of whom I could count on for some period of time to contribute to the community in his or her own ways. A programmer, a hardware hacker, an artist, a handful of old professors, and peers from previous classes were all possible options.

These power users, members of the community who are highly knowledgeable and responsive, represent the backbone of your community. They will often help shape the community in how it approaches and how it builds the tools used, shape the project direction as a whole, and raise awareness of the project to others whom you might not reach without them. In addition, their attitudes can affect everything, so it's important that you find people who are generally positive and helpful. I also like to consider geographical location. If you can have people developing your project across a vast geographical area, more people in those areas are also likely to start to build the project in a public way.

In some ways, your community may be more valuable than your actual project. Valuable communities build valuable content, product support, and ideas. The community is the glue that holds the hardware documentation together. It's what separates your project from others. It draws in developers to the community and convinces them that the best way to express their ideas is by contributing to the content of the community, to the project. The community gives people a reason to know the project, to engage with it, and to introduce it to their friends.

So what sort of content can they contribute?

With the Lasersaur project, we found ourselves in an interesting position. We used Kickstarter to obtain the initial funding for the project, but more importantly we had a community of more than 300 developers supporting the project before we even had a working prototype. The campaign brought in physicists working with laser beam dynamics, NASA engineers, and people who knew a lot more than we ever did about a lot of what we were developing. Their feedback and advice helped shape the project in invaluable ways that capital could not.

Valuable content could be a simple blog post that someone writes about the project. It could be a video, tutorial, or article. By creating valuable content that resonates with people and that they want to share and engage with, you earn links to your site, answer frequently asked questions, and gain social media attention. By doing community building right, you create an entire experience. It then becomes both an advocate for community building and a perpetuating step in continued community building. Community building even helps in sharing documentation standardization! Make sure to check out Appendix E, Mach 30's Documentation Ground Rules, for a checklist of rules when documenting.

Summary

One of the major problems with many open hardware projects is that the documentation and bill of materials are developed over time and, with many users, organically. This means the project lacks any real organization or reasoning to its structure. What happens when the primary developer is ready to walk away? Contributors and founders often leave, and other people come; some are replaced, but others never are. The documentation is what keeps the project alive and the community thriving. In a way, the documentation is a good place where past or current contributors can share with future ones. Think of the project documentation as a kind of asynchronous communication channel.

Resources

Here are a few good resources for tutorials, the open source hardware logo repository, and guides for documentation:

Good tutorial examples and platforms:

Aleph Objects (www.ohai–kit.alephobjects.com)

SparkFun (www.learn.sparkfun.com/tutorials)

Adafruit (www.learn.adafruit.com)

Instructables (www.instructables.com)

Ifixit (www.ifixit.com)

Open source hardware logos:

Logo repository (www.oshwa.org/open–source–hardware–logo)

Guides for documenting:

What to Write by Jacob Kaplan-Moss (www.jacobian.org/writing/what-to-write)

How to Make an Awesome Guide by Ifixit (www.ifixit.com/Info/Writing_Guides)

15

Business

Lars Zimmermann

> "The business model of open source hardware? You won't believe
> how boring it is. We sell products for more than they cost."
>
> —Chris Anderson; in his OH Summit talk 2012, "Microeconomics
> for Makers: Business Models for the New Industrial Revolution"

This chapter guides you through a variety of business models fit for open source hardware and open design. We start with some remarks about the obvious natural business model that comes with hardware and the importance of the brand. The chapter then presents and explains the Open Source Hardware Business Model Matrix, a tool that aims to help people ask the right questions and research answers while figuring out their business model for open source hardware. Company quotes embedded within this chapter were collected by Alicia Gibb in an open source hardware business survey.

"You can't make money being open" is a common criticism of open source development, although history shows many opportunities work better and more effectively when explored through an open approach. Several businesses were studied for this chapter that debunk the myth that you can't make money by being open source. Open source is often an ideal strategy for developing a more innovative, financially successful, and sustainable business, where money can be made not in spite of being open, but *because* you are open. Of course, this isn't a case of just changing a license and carrying on with business as usual. Open strategies require certain adjustments to a company's business model—sometimes minor alterations, but sometimes transformative change.

A Natural Business Model

The main answer to the business model question for open source hardware could not be simpler: you sell products. Hardware is any physical object—atoms, things, minerals that take work to extract from the Earth. In software, there is little difference between one copy of an MP3, a JPEG, or an ODT file and 1 million copies of it. In contrast, there is a huge difference between one and 1 million copies of a piece of hardware. Every new copy is a new physical object requiring materials, time, work, and energy for production and distribution. It is not hard to understand why you should pay for a physical object. An economics rule is that scarcer things can sell for more: having 1 million copies doesn't create scarcity, but having a few handmade boards you are willing to part with does!

The core of an open source hardware business is the same as for any other hardware business: you produce and sell physical objects at a greater price than the cost of parts and labor. Traditional business strategies are the same as open hardware business strategies: marketing, pricing, efficiency, quality, and distribution. All of the open source hardware companies interviewed for this chapter reported that their problems are overwhelmingly business problems, not open source problems. With openness, you can do some of these things a little different. There are possible collaborative advantages to gain from having open design files, money to be made by innovating faster, and efficiencies to be achieved by persuading a greater number of participants to work on your project. You can download design files very easily but you cannot (yet) download physical objects or a community around a project. Physical objects still need to be produced from design files with skilled people, infrastructure, and care.

The Brand

Here is where the brand comes in. Assume your hardware is open sourced and out into the world for others to reproduce. It makes a difference who produces the products you buy! Brands in open source hardware are as important as they are for businesses with closed source, or patented, hardware. Open source hardware businesses protect their brands just like any other business—that is, with a trademark. Brands are about trust and protecting the consumer rather than intellectual property. The reputation for trust and quality a brand carries with it is something that cannot be copied or downloaded, but must be earned over time. People prefer to deal with people whom they trust. For example, many clones of the Arduino microcontroller are available in the market, but many people prefer to buy the original. They recognize the original by the Arduino brand.

> "Under an OSHW license, we release a design so that anyone can make an exact copy of the machine and sell it, so long as they respect our trademarks. However, we've had cases where (sometimes awesome) derivatives were made, but kept our name and/or our product name on it. Or worse, cases where complete derivatives were made where nothing *except* our trademark was kept onboard. As a business based around OSHW, we don't want to play the "bad guys" telling off these people, but derivatives like this are very bad for us and the rest of the OSHW community." (Evil Mad Scientist Laboratories)

A brand is a communication asset, and open source is all about communication. If you share design files and emit resources of great quality, you will gain attention and build up your brand. Deliver good quality and engage in reliable and valuable connections with others, and many people will prefer to buy from you and collaborate with you.

> "Find some way to make your offering unique. Sometimes it feels that this industry is a race to the bottom; many manufacturers are essentially making different versions of the same thing—the massive success of Chinese companies on eBay and their free shipping is one

example. In this day and age OSHW companies have got to concentrate on the "value add"—why should people purchase products from you over someone else?" (Parallax, profitable, revenue of $9 million in 2013)

"Trademarks create a brand, the brand is how you produce value. Trademarks are not covered by Open Source licenses so they remain your property. It is a rather easy process to file a trademark. Generally speaking, they are inexpensive compared to patents registration, and you can file one for about $300 in the US, 800Euro in Europe." (Lasersaur, profitable)

"Basically, what we have is the brand," says Tom Igoe, an associate professor at the Interactive Telecommunications Program at New York University, who joined Arduino in 2005. "And brand matters." (quoted in Wired *magazine 16.11, October 20, 2008, "Build It, Share It Profit" by Clive Thompson on the first three years of Arduino)*

The Open Source Hardware and Open Design Business Model Matrix

The Open Source Hardware and Open Design Business Model Matrix was developed by the Open It Agency, an open source business development and communication agency based in Berlin, Germany. The matrix is a collection of open source benefits and advantages and possible income sources. The tool helps users map out complex and fitting business models and strategies for an individual case. It is appropriate for all sorts of physical products, not just for electronic hardware. Some items in the matrix reflect theoretical, yet promising notions for the future; others have been tried and tested by successful open source hardware businesses. The field of open source hardware is very young and has a long way to go, so the matrix is intended to remain flexible. There are more things to find that will be developed by you and others in the future, but the matrix should suffice to get you started.

Should Your Product Be Open?

The matrix (Figure 15.1) is part of a toolkit that is made to answer the question, "Should your business be open?" The top two rows of the matrix should help you decide if your business should be open. Open sourcing products is not for every business, but it does offer many advantages to developers.

Another model includes a partially open product, in which both open and closed source parts are combined to create the whole product. Having a combination is fine as long as the company clearly states which parts are open source and which are closed source.

No matter which course you decide to follow, these are questions your company should decide first, because it is nearly impossible to pull your product back into a proprietary model once it has been put in the community as open source. Any individual or company producing open source hardware should be prepared to have its hardware

		Less Costs for R&D *Open innovation, faster bug fixes*	Better Products *interactive, longlasting, more features, freedom, sustainability, connectivity*	Less Legal Fees *Less legal expenses, less time to market*
Why? Advantages & Possibilities to Win with Open Source →				
Collaboration & Synergies *Material Cycles, open standards, product-as-a-platform, in-house communication*	**Ethical Bonus for the Brand** *Transparency through community, sustainability, education*	**Less Costs For** *support, ads, PR, etc.*	**Better Employees**	
			Donations, grants, sponsoring, public research	Funding & crowdfunding
Your Channels *Advertisement, product-partnerships, rent, fees*	**Education & Training** *Workshops, certificates, consulting, events*	**SUPPORT** *Install, operate, maintain, upgrade, repair*	**On Request** *Individual development, customization, adaptation*	**Closed Parts** *Open core, closed add-ons, new version closed, some parts closed, etc.*
Foundation/ Consortium Model *Members fees*	**Selling the Service** *(e.g., prints, energy, waste-disposal, food-growing, data) using OSHW*	**Produce & Sell Products** *Quality, warranted, shipped*	← **How to Make Money €/ Where Does the Money Come From?**	

Figure 15.1   Open Source Hardware and Open Design
Business Model Matrix vs. 0.6.
(Source: CC-BY Lars Zimmermann)

copied, changed in unintended ways, used in various fields, and sold for profit as the open source hardware definition allows.

The matrix is divided in two parts, as shown in Figure 15.1. The top part addresses advantages and possibilities you can benefit from after making your hardware open source. The bottom part considers possible money income sources. Most business models or cases will be a combination of several squares of the matrix. In this section, you will find some information on every square, although the matrix will undoubtedly continue to grow as more benefits are discovered in open innovation. You are encouraged to add your experiences and findings to the matrix: it is also open source! Use the matrix as a set of questions to inspire your own queries and research. The visual element will help you to organize your thoughts, knowledge, and ideas. You can download a picture of the matrix for comparison while reading here: http://bloglz. de/business-models-for-open-source-hardware-open-design/

Advantages and Possibilities to Win with Open Source Hardware

The upper part of the matrix lists advantages and possibilities to gain from being open. The advantages mentioned here are somewhat unique to open source hardware. Here you will find your possible reasons for being open. If you want to leverage these benefits, you should choose to open source your hardware. Ask yourself, "Can I design my business model and strategy around this?"

Lower R&D Costs

"You can clone us but you can't innovate as quickly as our community can. And that is better than patents." (3D Robotics)

Reducing the cost of research and development through open innovation is one of the most important advantages for many open source businesses. If your design files are open, people have the chance to study them and play with them. If there is a channel for community interaction, users can submit feedback, ask interesting questions, suggest bug fixes, contribute ideas and so on. This communication can help you avoid mistakes and dead ends. Sometimes surprising things and perspectives can emerge. In an open community, you have access to the expertise and skills of people you might never be able to hire because you could not pay them what they are worth or because they have no interest in working for you full time, are retired, work for someone else, or live in another place.

"The most helpful aspect of open source hardware at Aleph Objects, Inc. is the ease and speed with which we research and develop our products to get them into the hands of our customers around the world. This applies beyond initial product release, including our ability to rapidly iterate and incorporate feedback from our community to make products better over time." (Aleph Objects [Lulzbot], very close to being profitable, revenue of $1.7 million in 2013)

With the right context, the right product, and a strong community you can innovate very quickly. People might clone your hardware but they cannot clone your community and the pace of innovation you achieve with them. In some fields, having a faster pace of innovation and being ahead of others is the most important competitive advantage.

There are a lot of different examples of open innovation, and a lot of literature about this development pathway. How do you design your platform and product in a way to trigger rich derivatives with open innovation? Which channels are you using or providing for it (e.g., forums, workshops, labs)? Do you incentivize contributions, or present tasks and challenges? Different products need different solutions. If everything is designed with transparency and respects the rights of open source hardware, however, it is very likely that your open innovation processes will produce faster, cheaper and better outcomes.

"If people are going to hack your products anyway, then you may as well get ahead of the game. It's better than suing the people who love your product most. Make your products modular, reconfigurable, and editable. Set the context for open innovation and collaboration; provide venues. Build user-friendly toolkits. Supply the raw materials that collaborators need to add value to your product and make it easy to remix and share." (Ahmad Sufian Bayram [author], promoting the state of collaborative economy in the Arab world)

"We shared our schematics and firmware to our products because when SparkFun started, we didn't have tech support staff, we didn't have a phone number, we didn't even have a 'we.' Open source hardware means you can learn as a group and support each other." (SparkFun Electronics, profitable, revenue of $30 million in 2013)

For most people, it is very important to provide a channel or place where your open innovation can happen. But open innovation does not necessarily mean that the innovation appears in the channels you provide for the process. For example, a forum might be set up with the intention of an innovation platform, but it can appear someplace else on the web. People might also create new use-cases you never thought of before. Sometimes entire new markets are created—just look at the example of OpenKnit growing out of RepRap in Chapter 10. Keep an eye out for such developments and learn from them. You are invited to explore these markets as well. Enable the process. One of the reasons Tesla Motors opened its patents in 2014 was to provide the possibility for others to work on spreading electromobility and innovating to bring it to places where Tesla would not be able to go as quickly. The benefit to Tesla is a larger electromobility market.

Better Products

There are a lot of reasons why open products can be better than closed ones. There is the chance that the pressure to become open will grow in some markets. This subsection highlights some reasons why an open product can be a better choice for the customer.

An open product can provide more possibilities to interact with it—that is, more ways to use it or adapt it. An open product is easier to hack. MacGyverize the world! This aspect of the product can be very interesting for customers. Make your product easy to hack and rearrange. This will also allow third parties to develop more features, invent and provide add-ons, or create new use-cases and connect the product to other items through the internet of things. The value for the consumer of the product rises with this extension of the product's capabilities. You provide freedom for people to control their technology and shape their lives as they wish instead of being controlled by their technology.

"What is the most helpful aspect of open source hardware at your company? *Increased customer knowledge. By giving users access to design files, they can better understand and use our products. In the case of open sourcing the Propeller microcontroller, we expect it to allow customers to get closer to the architecture and truly understand its inner workings.*" *(Parallax)*

Openness can make it easier to repair things or reuse or repurpose individual parts. This makes products a longer-lasting and better investment for the consumer. For many companies, open source solutions are the better choice to buy for their infrastructure because open source gives them independence from certain producers, suppliers, or support-contractors and freedom to develop their business as they wish. All of these considerations lead to a more efficient use of resources.

Product as a Platform

The product as a platform approach is something very interesting for open source hardware developers. An open source product is much more likely to become a platform than a closed one, two great examples of this being the 3D printing industry and the Arduino microcontroller with its many derivatives. Open design files give people many more possibilities to interact with your product. Such interactions are especially likely to occur when others can find interesting ways to make a living with your product by developing and providing add-ons or services, or by adapting your product to local circumstances. In this fashion, your product will grow as a platform. For example, many professionals are using Arduino products for consulting or professional prototyping. The more stakeholders there are, the more powerful and useful the product can become, and the more stable the platform will be. For this reason, having your product copied by others is not necessarily a bad thing. Just design your business model to accommodate this possibility. You can see here why a noncommercial license is not open source. Not giving others the possibility to make a living out of your product would reduce the number of stakeholders and limit the potential growth of your platform. Of course, not every product is fit for the "product as a platform" approach.

Lower Legal Fees and Quicker Time to Market

Closing things is expensive. Patents, lawyers, lawsuits, secrecy agreements, and safety measures like prohibitively expensive insurance, to name a few, take a lot of time and money. In the United States, the patent application fee is $17,000 plus legal fees and engineering fees. Usually patents cost a company upward of $50,000. But the real cost of a patent comes from fighting the battle if someone infringes on that patient; resolving such a dispute can take millions or billions of dollars depending on how big your wallet is. Going open source could mean lower legal fees. Big companies often spend more money on the legal side than they devote to research and development. Being open source can save you a lot of money, which you can then invest in other things. Of the companies interviewed for this chapter, five reported that they bootstrapped. For those five bootstrapped companies, the annual legal fees combined was $110,000, which includes a frivolous trademark battle from an outside company for having a similar (but different) name. Most companies noted that the money spent on legal fees was earmarked for obtaining trademarks.

"How much money do you spend each year on legal fees? *'Approximately $5000 a year, but the bulk of this is for contract review and is not tied to IP [intellectual property]. Our IP legal fees are nominally $0.'"* (SparkFun Electronics)

"Publish early, publish often" is a common mantra of the open source software community. Publishing early and often establishes prior art, which is a legal hook that open source hardware depends on. When a physical object has prior art, it means another company should not be able to patent it.

"Have you had any products that have failed due to openness? *'Never. Our products are rapidly developed and gaining traction in the market precisely because they are open, not in spite of it.'"* (Aleph Objects)

As of 2014, no open source hardware company had reported to us that they failed due to failure to protect its IP. In other words, the fact that it has open source IP has not been why a company shut down. Companies shut down because of other business problems that occur in closed source businesses as well, such as marketing, pricing, or hiring failures.

Collaboration and Synergies

Open source is about collaboration—about new decentralized collaboration patterns that are possible with the Internet. Published plans can reduce the collaboration costs for some things, synergies can be found more easily through transparency, and some things become possible that weren't before. There are obvious ways that outside collaboration has helped each and every open source hardware company. Look at how RepRap has grown, or how many products at SparkFun are labeled "This project is in collaboration with . . ." and lists a collaborator.

However, one of the most promising synergies that comes with open source hardware development as a result of its transparency is the possibility to collaborate, develop, and organize complete recycling of a product or material. This is sometimes called closed material cycles, regenerative design, Cradle to Cradle design, or zero-waste economy. There are not yet examples in the world of successful closed material cycles that are using the term "open source" to describe how they work. Instead, most of these projects use the term "transparency" to express the fact that open communication made it possible to develop and maintain closed loops and save resources.

Open source often means using or allowing use of open standards (for more on standardization, see Chapter 4). In fact, open sourcing a technology is a common approach to establish it as an open standard. Standards are helpful for collaboration between different companies and work focusing on shared and complex goals (e.g., an ecological zero-waste or circular economy). Open source is also about transparency and adds a whole new layer on top that makes global material cycles even more likely. This is a very strong and interesting potential on a worldwide scope for open source hardware, yet almost an entirely unexplored potential for the future of open source hardware and open design. We will likely see more of this trend in the future. Having transparency to the outside world also means that you have transparency within your company. This can make in-house communication and collaboration much easier. Ensuring that all information is accessible to all people prevents hierarchy and secrecy problems from hindering collaboration.

Most of these considerations have a connection to sustainability. Openness can make it easier and possible to organize an ecological economy with closed material cycles. Open innovation processes might be essential for the future development and spreading of ecological or sustainable products. Sustainability is perceived as valuable; in fact, many customers are asking for such products or companies that support sustainability. Being on the road to sustainability provides many businesses with more opportunities to do better business—for example, to meet governmental regulations or recycling standards.

Ethical Bonus for the Brand

It is not difficult to understand that producing open source hardware might deliver an ecological bonus. However, this aspect of open source development has nothing to do with intellectual property, but rather is a side effect of open source transparency. Open source hardware and open design are still very young and unknown to many people, so there are some good prospects for growth. The more popular narratives today—"Open source is for free" and "Open source means do it yourself"—will clearly be outgrown. "Open source means lower quality/usability" will lose ground, too. Whatever the successful new narratives will be—perhaps "Open source is for sustainability," "Open source is for freedom," or "Open is a smart choice"—chances are high that they will have positive spins. "I think open source could be the next organic or fair trade," the journalist Christoph Gurk said in a conversation with me. Almost everything you can say about open source is valued by people and considered a good thing. The bigger and better the movement grows, the more attractive the brand strategy will be with open source hardware.

Strongly tied to open source development are inputs from the community view. Open source products address and include people as intelligent, creative, caring and responsible co-creators of the world. They educate and enable people rather than looking at them as mindless consumers. Open source provides a lot of new and unique strategies for achieving a sustainable world and economy.

To get serious on another level for a second, closed things are progressively suspected to be unsustainable and work against the consumer. Open source is about giving you the freedom to understand and control your technology at a fundamental level. Closed devices may not give you the option to repair them. Closed devices may collect information about you and send it to anyone for whatever reason. They might also receive orders from someone else with the goal of manipulating you with wrong information. If they are closed, you will never have the chance to determine whether they are or are not doing this. Such a statement might sound like a conspiracy theory today, but the more complex and networked our world becomes (think about the internet of things), the more serious these issues will be. Having the design files of things open for inspection will be key for sustaining our personal freedom and democracy. The more time that goes by, the larger the number of people who understand this point and will be guided by it—especially while making purchasing decisions.

> *"[A]nd because everything we do today involves the Internet and everything we do tomorrow will require the Internet, that means that copyright policy becomes the organizing principle for everything we do in the world. And that's silly!*
>
> *"There is no way to fight oppression without free devices and free networks." (Cory Doctorow [author], in his talk "It's Not a Fax Machine Connect to a Waffle Iron" at re:publica Berlin 2013)*

Lower Costs for Support and Marketing

If you have an active community and a place where community members can discuss things and exchange knowledge online, their interaction can make a lot of support work obsolete. People can share questions and help each other in forums and other venues. Nevertheless, support does not necessarily have to come only from the online community. If your product is open, it is easier for third parties to offer support, compete in the marketplace, and make support faster, more accessible and cheaper for the consumers, thereby increasing the value of your product.

> *"What is the most helpful aspect of open source hardware at your company? 'Free PR from those same engineers who tell lots of others about my products. Free PR from people who make my products from my well documented online plans.'" (Cornfield Electronics, profitable, revenue of $178,500 in 2013)*

An active community with volunteers and stakeholders means a customer base interested in the success of your product. They will do some marketing for free. They will talk about your product, share it online and offline, and get something viral going. People are searching the web for good resources. Putting your design files online can attract even more attention than purchasing ads could.

> *"Being open is the most effective form of marketing, so publish early and often." (Open Source Ecology, nonprofit, revenue of $300,000 from grants in 2013)*

Publishing early and often is a development approach that can help reduce marketing costs and allow you to spend less time on marketing in general. Having open design files and an open development process means that people will already know about your product before it hits the market. If they love it and are active contributors, they will also spread the word and will be happy to help its success.

> *"What is the most helpful aspect of open source hardware at your company? 'Reduced transaction cost in business. I don't have money for marketing or business development, so I just hang it all out there and let the informed buyer choose.'" (Andrew (Bunnie) Huang [Sutajio Ko-Usagi], profitable in 2013)*

"If you build it, they will come" is a saying that does not automatically hold true with open source hardware. It takes a tremendous amount of work to create a community that will help support your products. Community building requires cultivation, encouragement, and appreciation of those members who do outstanding work. There are numerous examples of open source companies that have created positive communities that in turn have helped grow their brands. Notably, Lasersaur, RepRap, Open Source Ecology, and DIYdrones have all been intentional in fostering very positive communities whose support has led to explosive growth of these companies.

> *"This is always the first thing I hear when I talked to people about open source: 'If I open source my schematics, code, designs, I can't sell a product and make money!'*
>
> *"First, your project is not really about the nuts and bolts. The value of any project, open or otherwise, is much more about the service, community, and support that come with it. Great real-life examples are companies like Adafruit and SparkFun. Their products are entirely open source and transparent, and people buy from them because their support, community, and documentation are top-notch. People can still clone their products, but it's unlikely that people would buy others because they do not come with the same support, quality, and compatibility guarantees." (Lasersaur)*

Better Employees

Some companies are using forms of openness to attract and recruit highly motivated and qualified employees. Most people are good at what they do professionally because they learned a lot from others. Learning happens while sharing knowledge. Being allowed to share and interact with others enables people to improve their knowledge base. Having your name appear next to great resources makes you visible in your community, and allows you to burnish your reputation and grow your cultural capital. Public design files allow people to find a product online, study it, learn something about it and the company behind it, and take an interest in their fate.

Remarks on Dual Licensing and Closed Parts

While licensing is discussed in depth in Chapter 3, this section briefly considers what **dual licensing** means as a business model. Dual licensing is a mixture of both open and closed hardware models. Having a combination of some open source hardware and some patented parts on the same project is considered dual licensing. Having some source files that are open source and covered by a Creative Commons (CC) license and some that are closed and covered by a noncommercial (NC) license is considered dual licensing. This strategy can provide certain advantages, as it enables you to publish some of your design files without making them open source. It means that you add licenses to the design files or hardware that forbid certain uses, such as commercial use, production of derivatives, or military use. With an NC license, the design files are public and open to be studied by everyone and to be worked with by hobbyists and academics; if people want to make commercial use of the design, however, they must obtain a license from the project originator.

This is not open source hardware: the Open Source Hardware Definition states that an open source license cannot discriminate against fields of endeavor or specific business uses. Thus, if you apply an NC clause to your work, you cannot call your hardware open source.

Perhaps most importantly, NC clauses produce a legal minefield because it is not entirely clear where commercial use starts. If I help a friend produce an NC-licensed device and beer is exchanged, are we violating the license? In the field of education, it is unclear whether educators can freely use and make copies of files that are under NC license if they teach at a for-profit university. Given the many gray areas associated with NC and dual licensing, why should someone choose your NC-covered hardware over fully open source hardware that gives the user ultimate freedom and a future full of yet unknown possibilities?

Publishing your design files without making them fully open source can help you realize some of the advantages mentioned earlier: with open design files your hardware could be used for education; it might be easier to hack, repair, and recycle; it can help people understand their technology and sustain their freedom; you would be transparent; and you could even get some bug fixes or improvements submitted. Nevertheless, this strategy quickly encounters some limitations.

The world is complex and cases are infinite. There may be instances where dual licensing is the right thing to do and would allow for some important things to happen (such as sustaining freedom or allowing recycling). Especially when you are thinking about venture capital, it is very likely that you will be asked to close some of your things. Maybe dual licensing in some cases might be a good first step toward open sourcing something fully. Study carefully what you lose and what you win with closing some parts.

Numerous combinations of closed and open parts are possible. You could close the newest version and open up the older ones. You could create an open core with closed add-ons—for example, a printer that is open, but uses cartridges that are closed. You could open source the inner functionality of your hardware but protect your three-dimensional brand or shape; in other words, you could ensure that the inner workings of a mechanical puppet are open, but its outside appearance is protected. You could open source the design files of your products but keep the organizational structure of your production-chain or your backend software closed. Is it really possible or necessary to open source your packaging? Find your own individual combination.

> *"Pick the flavor that is right for your business. There isn't a 'one size fits all' business model or license. I recommend a balanced approach between open and protected, especially if you want external funding." (LittleBits, partly VC funded)*

If you are closing things, you probably won't be able to take advantage of open source hardware for the closed parts. Taking away the ability of others to study, adapt, co-develop, and make commercial use of your hardware reduces the number of roles and motivations you offer to people. Your chances of growing your product into a strong platform (see the earlier discussion of the "product as a platform" approach) will probably decrease as well.

Of course, every case is different. Perhaps having something closed is the smartest and best option for your business and for the community around it.

Where Does the Money Come From?

Where will you find the money needed to start your business? There are a lot of possible income sources for a company. None of them are specific or unique to open source hardware, but working in the open source world can suggest unique ways to combine the advantages and possibilities that come with open source development and turn them into cash. Think about which assets you have or need to make an income. Usually monetizing a venture is connected to growing its assets. Build up your assets in the right way so you are likely to create a profitable business.

Produce and Sell Products

Hardware comes with a natural business model, regardless of whether those products are open source or closed source: you sell physical objects. It might be easy to argue about who the owner of an MP3 file is, but buying and selling a physical chair is a very straightforward process. This is the classic business proposition: I have this thing for sale for $19.95. You may be able to raise the sheep to create the wool yourself, or hammer the fork into the correct shape, or solder the resistors together, but is it really worth your time? Can you produce the thing with the same quality or with the tools you currently own? It doesn't matter if your product is open or closed: people are willing to spend money so they can save time and focus on larger projects. If you design an open source product that people need, they will pay real money for it. People are always searching for reliable, warrantied and high-quality products and are willing to pay for them.

> *"The secret to open source is innovation. If your company cannot innovate quickly, it will lose to the competition. This is the essence of a capitalistic marketplace. Behind every open source company, you will find people innovating quickly and freely. Open source entrepreneurs make money quite simply because they are innovating faster. Surprising to many people outside the open source community, these companies are making more money than their closed source competitors." (SparkFun Electronics)*

Make your open source product easy to purchase, keep it in stock, and describe it clearly. Focus on business basics, and customers will choose to shop with you simply because you run a good business; open source will be the surprise filling in your pastry that they didn't know they would enjoy.

How much should you sell a product for? In his keynote speeches and his book *Makers,*[1] Chris Anderson of 3D Robotics talks about the 2.6 multiplier used at 3D Robotics. According to Anderson, he learned this concept from others: set the price for your product by taking its production costs and multiplying them by 2.6, and you will be

---

1. http://www.makers-revolution.com/#about-makers

able to sustain your business by selling the product. This markup also incorporates a margin for all people in the distribution chain; they are part of the community as well.

Don't give up if your business is not the cheapest source in the marketplace. Many factors cross a customer's mind when deciding which company to purchase from. Price is important, but so are quality, availability, sustainability, support, and ease of use (just to name a few!).

Foundation/Consortium Model

The foundation model is something we know from the open source software world. With this approach, the administration of the product is handled by a (nonprofit) foundation. Members of this foundation are different companies, public institutions, and private persons who have an interest in using the product and the advantages that come from its being open source. Different models for foundations exist, but in most cases each member pays fees for the common infrastructure and contributes to the development process. Companies hire and pay developers to work full time on the project. Foundations may also generate standards, and charge members to use the standard. Finally, some foundations are nonprofit organizations that receive grant funding for their projects, such as Open Source Ecology.

The consortium model is a lot like the foundation model, except that the consortium can be a for-profit entity. There may be fewer members; indeed, the consortium may potentially serve only large companies. To use this approach, you need to have the right product and a lot of potential stakeholders. You also need a good development model, a governance model, a suitable license and IP model, and a maintenance and support model. If you are thinking about pursuing a consortium model, a good starting point for research could be open source software foundations such as the Eclipse Foundation and the Document Foundation.

Selling the Service Using OSHW

Making money from open source hardware does not necessarily mean selling the hardware itself. You can also sell what you are producing with that hardware. For example, you might sell 3D prints rather than your open source printer. You might sell energy, rather than the open source power plant you use to create it. You might sell transportation, rather than the technology you use to provide that service. You might sell a data service, rather than the hardware you use to collect the data. You might repair open source garbage disposals as your revenue stream, rather than manufacturing or selling those products.

If your infrastructure and your machines are open source, you can make the advantages of open source work for you to create a better and cheaper service with them. Marcin Jakubowski, for example, started Open Source Ecology because his tractor broke and he needed a new one for his farming operation but could not afford to buy one.

It is likely that we will have more discussions in the future about open source hardware for public service infrastructure. Think of the democratic value the community and society will attach to it. It should become more difficult to justify why our police cars, power plants, street lightning, and water treatment plants are not open source if there are open source solutions available to meet these needs.

> *"This is precisely how the Arduino team works. It makes little off the sale of each board—only a few dollars of the $35 price, which gets rolled into the next production cycle. But the serious income comes from clients who want to build devices based on the board and who hire the founders as consultants.*
>
> *"What's more, the growing Arduino community performs free labor for the consultants. Clients of Banzi's design firm often want him to create Arduino-powered products. For example, one client wanted to control LED arrays. Poking around online, Banzi found that someone in France had already published Arduino code that did the job. Banzi took the code and was done." (*Wired *magazine 16.11, October 20, 2008, "Build It, Share It, Profit" by Clive Thompson on the first three years of Arduino)*

Hardware on Request

If your products are not made for an assembly line, you might be able to make your money from individual development, customizations, or adaptations addressing individual needs, cases, or scenarios. An example is the installation of a sophisticated irrigation system. Make things special for individual customers, such as "aspirin tailored to your DNA" (Kevin Kelly[2]), an example of a truly enabling product. Can you imagine selling unique prototypes like art or making the first copies worth more than later ones? This model produces hardware on request, although it might also seem close to "selling the service." Using or creating open source hardware for individual solutions allows you to make the advantages of open source work for your product or service and your customer. Imagine a marketing campaign based on this capability: customers buy your expertise for the product created.

Support

There are two ways to make money from support. First, the business model may focus on selling support to install, repair, or be on call for hardware. This support model has been successful in the open source software business world; a notable example is RedHat. For some software, you need professional help to install it and run it. Some open source hardware might potentially use the same model; that is, you need professionals to operate, maintain, upgrade, or sometimes repair the hardware. "The copy of code, being mere bits, is free—and becomes valuable to you only through the support and guidance" (Kevin Kelly[3]). Consider offering a support or service deal. If you're a small start-up, the fact that you're a co-developer of the hardware might make it easier for clients to trust you owing to your expertise.

---

2. http://kk.org/thetechnium/2008/01/better-than-fre/
3. http://kk.org/thetechnium/2008/01/better-than-fre/

Education and Training

Selling education and training is also a possibility derived from the open source software world. You can download design files everywhere, but hand-holding or trained skills may be more difficult to obtain. Some people will be happy to book a workshop to learn how to make something or hack on your product. Perhaps you can sell physical copies of books. Working with open source hardware, providing it, or developing it can make you a visible and proven expert in a field. You can monetize that expertise by holding workshops or consulting. SparkFun's education department bought an RV and drove it around the United States while teaching workshops to teachers. A school would pay for SparkFun to make a stop in its town to train its teachers. If special training is needed to operate or maintain the hardware, you can offer courses and tests or a certificate program to become a proven administrator for the hardware. If you are the main developer of the hardware, it might be easier for *you* to be the trusted institution.

All sorts of events focusing on or celebrating open source hardware are an excellent place to gain leverage, such as hackathons. Physical objects to touch, test, or play with also attract attention. You can sell tickets for such events, and then display your hardware there. Open things are often easier to celebrate because all layers are visible to celebrate. Which sounds like more fun: a hackathon exploring an Arduino-driven washing machine, or a trade fair with closed source washing machines to look at and hear numbers about?

Your Channels

In open source hardware ventures and any other businesses, things get exchanged. Products and parts are sold; building plans and knowledge are communicated, viewed, shared, and downloaded. These exchanges need channels. Webpages and webshops, forums, stores, workshops, and other venues focused on communication are all examples for channels. Channels offer special ways to generate revenues for those people running them. Do you have your own successful and trusted webshop? Use it to sell not only your own products but also the products of others and gain a profit margin. There are several ways to monetize the customers you already have. Can you find some elegant possibilities for advertisement?

Product partnerships could be another possibility. If you build your hardware with supplies from certain companies or shops, get them on board and cross-advertise your products. Ask for a discount on their hardware or ask for a public relations (PR) fee when mentioning their product in your tutorials and design files. If your webpage is a trusted place for certain information, use it to sell workshops or certificates. Can you rent out your hackerspace or some of your machines—offer a full library of things to play with, test, or experiment with, while collecting fees from visitors.

Channels are important for everything else mentioned in this chapter as well. When you create your business, ask yourself: Which things get exchanged and which channels are needed for this industry? Which of these channels do you want to create and maintain yourself? Which channels could be used by others, and how could they pay for it? Channels are assets you can make money from.

Funding and Crowd Funding

Funding and crowd funding are options that you can pursue to get some early money into your pockets. Most of the open source hardware businesses are bootstrapped, but some are backed by venture capital funding. When businesses obtain VC funding, they are often asked to close some designs down. VC funding, however, is not as big or important as people tend to think. As Diane Mulcahy pointed out in her *Harvard Business Review* piece "Six Myths about Venture Capitalists,"[4] fewer than 1% of U.S. companies have raised capital from VCs and the VC industry is shrinking.

> *"If you can, bootstrap it. If you own 100%, then every dollar you earn is a dollar you can keep. Once you get VCs involved, you're diluted out; also, your gains are illiquid until a so-called "liquidity event" when you get VCs involved—it can take years before you see a dime, if anything. The VC wants to shoot the moon, and will encourage you to squander every dime building the company up to be huge, even if you don't want that. Remember, the VC is paid out of management fees and performance of a composite fund, but you're paid out of just one horse in the race. However, if you own 100%, you can take a dividend or a payment out of your company anytime you think is appropriate." (Bunnie [Sutajio Ko-Usagi])*

An alternative to VC funding is crowd funding. Crowd funding is very popular with open source hardware projects. Most crowd-funding platforms require a working prototype, so such campaigns are often used for gaining attention and growing a community for an existing or advancing product. Crowd funding leverages viral videos of campaigns. It is also used to test the water and collect feedback for the product, in the form of open innovation, or to collect pre-orders and collect some money before getting in touch with producers. Click through literature about crowd funding before you jump into these waters, as crowd-funding sites have different stipulations.

Anecdote: Crowd Funding
Marcus Schappi

The process of crowd funding a project can lead to better OSHW projects, and vice versa. The necessity of having to pitch your project to would-be backers forces you to distill the project down to its most crucial elements. The platform provided by crowd funding means that there are many like-minded individuals checking out your project. In our latest Kickstarter project, we made the schematics to the MicroView immediately available for download. Soon after, one of our backers identified an issue with the circuit and provided a fix that we were able to incorporate into the shipping product. As they say, starting is easy and finishing is hard. Having backers is a great motivator, as they'll be sure to tell you off if you don't post regular updates, and really let you know about it if you don't ship!

---

4. http://hbr.org/2013/05/six-myths-about-venture-capitalists/ar/1

Sponsoring, Grants, Donations, Public Research

In keeping with the rationale for the "ethical bonus" of open source hardware, it may be possible to fund some kinds of initiatives through donations or grants. There is often a public interest or promise to "make the world a better place" that is considered worthy of funding. Large companies may sponsor such efforts by partnering with smaller open source hardware projects. Jobs in public research could be dedicated to developing open source hardware. The more that the advantages and values of open source hardware for our communities are realized, the better democracy and the environment will become, and the harder it will be to justify enormous public research funds being devoted to closed source innovations. The more we work on developing examples that show and explain how open source is good for the public, the easier it will be to support open source hardware projects with public funding, grants, and donations in the future. For more information about the benefits of open source hardware projects in research, refer to Chapter 16.

Anecdote: Open Source Hardware in Public Art
Brandon Stafford

The realm of electronics, like the Arduino and its ecosystem, has dominated the open source hardware efforts of the last decade. Despite the success of the Arduino, most electronic hardware is still proprietary. Large hardware companies are reluctant to open source their designs because they see the blueprints for their designs as a source of advantage over their competition. If their competitors knew exactly how to fabricate their designs, they could replicate everything, without having to pay any engineers to come up with the designs. Additionally, virtually the entire electronics industry is funded by private investment. Occasionally, we see public investments like Small Business Innovation Research (SBIR) grants in the United States, but they are rare. We could summarize the situation in the electronics world as follows: "private money pays for originals; payback comes from replication."

In the world of art, the situation is reversed, and in public art, even more so. The summary for public art is this: "public money pays for the original; the original is the payback." Open sourcing public art can add an even greater payback, as future artists can build on the work of their predecessors.

Today, reproducing art is no longer a serious challenge. Paintings can be forged well enough that ordinary people are fooled, and any kid with a computer can duplicate music or movies. If the only thing that makes a Monet a Monet is that the guy holding the paintbrush was named Monet, then the argument of whether the methods of creation need to be secret is over. The greatest forger can paint all day long, and she'll never make a Monet. Like Marcel Duchamp submitting a urinal to a gallery in 1917, the art lies in the act of creating the art, not the physical object itself.

Public art, where an artist is paid to create art that is installed in a public setting, like a park or city plaza, has the same characteristic: the identity of the artist makes the art.

The funding for public art usually comes from public sources, such as municipal governments or neighborhood advocacy groups, or occasionally private philanthropists for the benefit of the public. Public art tends to be site specific and unique; we don't want replicas of Anish Kapoor's giant shiny bean ("Cloud Gate") in Chicago duplicated in every city around the world. Leo Villareal's LED installation on the Bay Bridge in San Francisco needs the bridge to hold it up; it wouldn't work in Phoenix, Arizona, where there is no water, never mind bridges.

Some public art is already being open sourced. For the last few years, I have worked as part of New American Public Art, a group of five artists in Boston and Philadelphia, that open sources all the art we create. We've found that open sourcing public art is harder than it seems. Open sourcing our code and electronics designs is easy, but most of our art has large mechanical elements that are largely undocumented. As we're building, we make a few pencil sketches, but they're often inaccurate by the time the design is finished, due to design changes made along the way. As we start to use more digital fabrication tools, such as 3D printers, CNC routers, and laser cutters, we're finding that open sourcing our mechanical designs is easier, but we often can't afford to spend the time to detail assembly and finishing procedures. Of course, that's where the open source hardware community can come in!

Summary

When you are selecting a model for an open source hardware business, you have a variety of options to choose from. Concentrate on making the advantages of open source hardware work for you, and combine them with means to generate income. Figure out the best mix and strategy for your individual case. Keep an eye on other projects, and learn about the business models followed by other open source hardware companies. Open source hardware and open design are still in their early stages, so there is a lot of room for improvement and a lot of things worth trying.

Many of the points made in this chapter are easily said, but not easy to do. Building a hardware business—open or not—is hard. All of the open source hardware companies interviewed for this chapter reported that their problems were overwhelmingly business problems, not open source problems. While making your hardware open source will give you some possible advantages, it will also add some challenges to your workload. Creating and providing useful information, maintaining up-to-date design files, and managing a community take a lot of time and skill. Nevertheless, this is where the collaborative advantages of the open source world come into play. Currently, a lot of the tools used to collaborate on complex hardware projects are lacking or are not as effective as software collaboration tools, but you can help make those better. The more people start working on open source hardware, the more development will gain speed and get more powerful, modular, and distributed. The better the tools, the better the open source hardware, the easier it will be to build a business on top of it, and the more important it will become for our economy.

16

Building Open Source Hardware in Academia

Joshua M. Pearce

"It's mine but you can have some
With you I'd like to share it
'Cause if I share it with you
You'll have some too"

—Raffi, "The Sharing Song"[1]

Open source hardware (OSHW) is a powerful tool for academics to improve their performance in research, teaching, and service. This chapter discusses the world of academia for the non-academic and then details methods for professors to improve their performance with the use of open source hardware. First, examples and preliminary studies on the use of open source hardware in research show the benefits of (1) substantial pre-peer review in the development of background material and experimental design, which leads to (2) improved experimental design and laboratory hardware design (often with radically reduced economic costs, superior performance, and customization). Such improvements foster (3) increased visibility, citations, and improved public relations, which then lead to (4) increased funding opportunities and enhanced student recruitment as well as (5) improved student research-related training and research education. Second, examples and preliminary studies focusing on the use of open source hardware in the classroom as part of service learning are described that indicate students are more motivated, work harder, learn more and are left with lasting benefits from their experience. Finally, developing and publishing open source hardware either as part of a research program or in the classroom is shown to be an effective method of performing outreach on both grants and tenure applications.

---

1. Excerpt from "The Sharing Song" written and performed by Raffi, courtesy of Homeland Publishing.

Life in the Ivory Tower: An Overview

To understand how open source hardware is a true paradigm shift and an enormous benefit to those who work in the ivory tower of academia, it is important to understand some of the basics of academic life. The majority of professors have ascribed to an unwritten pact: we accept less monetary compensation for our work than we would receive from employment in the business world in exchange for *academic freedom*. Academic freedom is meant to enable professors to teach, research, and share their ideas (particularly those that are inconvenient to political groups, the powerful, and state authorities) without being targeted for repression, job termination, or imprisonment.[2] This freedom is guaranteed through *tenure* for the professor; this status provides senior academics with contractual rights not to have their positions terminated without just cause essentially for life, or at least until retirement. In today's economy, very few positions have such job security, and the tenure process at most institutions is a hard-won prize—one that is normally bestowed only after five to seven years of hard labor as a tenure-track assistant professor.[3] The value of tenure for academics can hardly be understated. Thus, for the first five years or more after landing their first academic position, all of their efforts are focused on ensuring success in the tenure process.[4]

For many people outside of the academic world, the life of the professor appears to involve only the part that they remember from college: teaching in the classroom. Although nearly all professors teach, the vast majority of their time is actually spent elsewhere and what they actually do in the classroom accounts for only a small part of the evaluation of their performance. There are also different kinds of professors, depending on the type of university or college they work for. In general, if the school is a household name (e.g., Notre Dame, MIT, Stanford, Penn State), the university is a research school. At these schools, the professors spend the vast majority of their time writing grants to do research, supervising graduate students to do the research, writing papers and grant reports, and to

---

2. In practice, academic freedom is curtailed by many mechanisms, but it does ensure that at least some of professors' time is spent any way they like (e.g., researching the answers to questions that are the most important to ask or teaching lectures on what they think is the most important topic for a class).

3. After receiving their PhDs, many academics serve in multiple low-paid, zero-job-security post doc positions to gain enough experience so that they will be offered a tenure-track position. The life of the post doc and assistant professor at many institutions is a lot like indentured servitude, where the would-be-tenured professors must work for a number of years doing the worst of the academic labor (e.g., large mandatory service classes made up of uninterested students from other majors) and essentially earning a living stipend. Interestingly, indentured servitude in the American colonies lasted for about the same amount of time and paid about the same amount (e.g., enough to cover room, board, clothing, and training).

4. Academics lose their jobs if they are denied tenure and in general will find it much more difficult to land another tenure-track position. Even though he or she might spend five to eight (or more) years in graduate school, up to two years or longer as a post doc fellow, and seven years as an assistant professor, losing tenure means that the academic might well be unemployable in his or her specialty.

a lesser extent teaching. They may teach one or two classes a year. At smaller, teaching-centered schools, these roles are reversed. At these schools, professors teach three, four, or even more classes per semester. Research at this type of school normally revolves around teaching methods, learning effectiveness, and pedagogy theory. Although many professors at teaching schools still do non-teaching-focused research, it is generally a smaller program than that engaged in by their colleagues at research institutes.

Regardless of the type of school, a professor is evaluated in three areas: research, teaching, and service/outreach. The research aspect is the easiest to quantify and carries the majority of weight at all larger schools, as well as at many of the teaching schools. Professors are evaluated based on their external grant income; graduate-level (PhD and master's) degrees awarded; publications in peer-reviewed journals; impact factors or prestige of the publications[5]; citations—that is, the number of times their papers are referenced by others; and presentations and invited presentations at professional conferences, among other areas. The quality of teaching is usually evaluated by student surveys conducted after the course ends, peer observation, and new or novel pedagogies developed. Finally, to a much lesser extent in terms of their overall score, professors are evaluated on their service or outreach through committee involvement; service to the community, whether professional (e.g., peer reviewing of articles) or the broader community (e.g., giving lectures on their specialties to youth groups); and good publicity, such as having the university favorably mentioned in media.

Most academics, who as researchers and teachers dedicate their lives to information sharing, are already familiar with the ethic behind the open source hardware culture. There is a well-established gift culture in the tenure process, as professors are judged not by what they hoard, but rather based on how much information is shared (and how valuable that information is). Thus open source hardware is an extremely good fit for the academic, as open source hardware can assist build a professor's tenure package in all three areas of research, teaching, and service, and can continue to bolster the academic's career after he or she receives tenure. The remainder of this chapter provides details and examples about how open source hardware is being used in academia and explains why professors should be integrating it into their labs and classrooms for their own benefit, the benefit of their students, and the benefit of literally everyone through the accelerated development of their disciplines.

Benefits of OSHW for the Academic

The benefits of open source hardware in academia include improved research and teaching for the professional development of the professor.

OSHW in Research

The original and ongoing purpose of universities was to spread knowledge, yet—in an ironic twist—information sharing from research faculty members is now often restricted.

---

5. A method to quantify how often the articles within a journal are recently cited or referenced.

At many institutions, there is considerable pressure on professors to lock down intellectual property (IP) into the anti-commons by patenting and or commercializing research to prevent its use without the university making a profit (Lieberwitz, 2005). Although the legitimacy of IP (even as a concept) is highly contested within academia (Boldrin and Levine, 2008), the well-documented influence of corporate thought on universities has propagated an *intellectual monopoly* view of research even in what was once the free academic literature (Chan and Fisher, 2008). This can make it difficult to replicate experiments and may even potentially "threaten the foundation of scientific discourse" (Gelman, 2012). Current practices of (1) holding back key information until patent applications are filed, (2) using closed standards, (3) maintaining a lack of universal open access to the literature, and (4) treating course information (e.g., syllabi, homework problems, lectures, learning aids) as proprietary information all hurt academic communication and directly hamper innovation, education, and progress. This last point is perhaps best driven home by Nobel Prize winner Eric Maskin and his co-author James Bessen (2009), who found that when discoveries are "sequential" (such that each successive invention builds in an essential way on its predecessors), *patent protection discourages innovation.*

Although this is common knowledge in academia, academics must walk the line carefully before tenure even though their natural tendencies and the history of academia are much more in line with the *hacker ethic* that underpins the development of free open source software (FOSS) (Levy, 1984) and now open source hardware. The combination of the hacker ethic with the general principles of sharing, openness, decentralization, free access, and world improvement creates an ethic that professors in general would support. This philosophy is enabled by the gift culture of open source, in which recognition of an individual is determined by the amount of knowledge given away (Bergquist and Ljungberg, 2001)—a perspective identical to that found in the academic culture. In a gift economy, the richer you are, the more you give; the more valuable the gift, the more respect you gain. This is the real currency: respect. For academics, their contributions are acknowledged through the formal process of peer review to gain respect in the literature and by giving presentations at professional conferences. The more we give away and the more valuable it is scientifically, the better off are our careers.

Open source hardware provides academics with the opportunity to share and gain five key benefits:

- Substantial pre-peer review in the development of background material and experimental design, which leads to . . .
- Improved experimental design and laboratory hardware design (often with radically reduced economic costs) and hardware with superior performance and customization.
- Increased visibility, citations and improved public relations, which lead to . . .
- Increased funding opportunities and enhanced student recruitment and . . .
- Improved student research-related training and research education.

We discuss each of these benefits in turn in the following subsections.

Pre-Peer Review in the Development of Background Material and Experimental Design

Experiments conducted in my labs represented a first attempt to apply the lesson learned from the natural experiment of software patents analysis conducted by Bessen and Maskin to research. Overall, these experiments involving open source research were successful, and there was an observable increase in the quality and quantity of both research and applications (Pearce, 2012a).

First, there were several advantages we saw as academics when we used an open wiki (e.g., Wikipedia). A *wiki* is a webpage that is easily edited; such editing has a relatively shallow learning curve.[6] Multiple members of the research teams are able to edit pages (e.g., a methodology description) at the same time, asynchronously or from different locations. These advantages of version control and collaboration hold true for closed wikis as well, but an open wiki enables others from outside the research group to assist your research— that is, to participate in the open source way in the same way that teams of open source software developers collaborate. For example, our group is routinely helped by external collaborators, which saves us time and directly improves our work. Other examples of assistance from wiki users not affiliated directly with research groups include giving helpful comments on the discussion tab of group pages; fixing grammar/spelling errors and typographical errors; making improvements to algorithms and electronic tools; correcting mistakes or improving our 3D printable designs; and listing our work on other sites, placing it in categories within the wiki, and hyperlinking either to or within work that a group has done, which adds to the value and accessibility of the work (Pearce, 2012a).

In all of these cases, sharing research as it is done facilitates others in improving it free of charge. Most importantly, outsiders often submit improvements to methods and experimental apparatus designs. This improves research quantitatively, as discussed next.

Improved Experimental Design and OSHW Design

The standard protocols in open source hardware sharing can be applied directly to research equipment for experimental design (Pearce, 2012b; 2014). One of the most successful enabling open source hardware projects for the academic world is the Arduino electronic prototyping platform,[7] which can be used in both the lab and the classroom. The $20–$60 Arduino is a powerful, yet easy-to-learn microcontroller that can be used to run a burgeoning list of scientific apparatuses directly, including the open source Polar Bear Environmental Chamber, Arduino Geiger (radiation detector), pHduino (pH meter), Xoscillo (oscilloscope), and OpenPCR (DNA analysis) (Pearce, 2014). However, one of the Arduino's most impressive technological evolution-enabling applications deals with open source 3D printing.

Although the number of variants of open source 3D printers is proliferating rapidly, the vast majority build off of the RepRap platform, so named because it is a self-replicating rapid prototyping machine (Jones et al., 2011). Currently, the RepRap, which

---

6. A college student can master the basics of wiki markup in less than 30 minutes.
7. www.arduino.cc/

uses fused-filament fabrication of complex 3D objects, can fabricate approximately half of its own parts and can be made for less than $1000. A low-cost version developed in my lab can be built for less than $500 and assembled in a weekend. For more on building your own 3D printer, see Chapter 8. This ability to inexpensively and freely self-replicate has resulted in an explosion of both RepRap users and design improvements. RepRaps are used to print many kinds of objects, but their transformative power finds its greatest promise in significantly reducing experimental research costs. As many scientists with access to RepRaps have found, it is less expensive to design and print research tools, and a number of simple designs have begun to flourish in Thingiverse, which is a free and open repository for digital designs for real physical objects. For a curated list of 3D printable hardware for science tools, see www.appropedia.org/Open-source_Lab.

Open source 3D printable hardware includes single-component prints such as parametric cuvette/vial racks, as well as an entirely new class of reactionware and microfluidics for customizing chemical reactions (Dragone et al., 2013; Kitson et al., 2012; Symes et al., 2012). Combination devices have also been developed in which a 3D-printed object is coupled with or integrated into an existing hardware tool such as the portable cell lysis device for DNA; this 3D-printable adapter which converts a Craftsman automatic hammer into a bead grinder for use with DNA extraction (Pearce, 2014). Similarly, the DremelFuge chuck is a 3D-printable rotor for centrifuging standard micro-centrifuge tubes and miniprep columns powered by a common Dremel drill. Thus, for an investment of $50 in a drill and a few pennies' worth of printed plastic, one can have the functionality of commercial centrifuge systems, which cost hundreds and sometimes thousands of dollars. Similar savings can be found in a wide range of other scientific equipment classes (Pearce, 2014), such as optics (Zhang et al., 2013), biology (Wijnen et al., 2014), and chemistry (Anzalone et al., 2013).

The most aggressive savings can come from coupling open source Arduino controls to 3D-printed objects to make completely open source automated scientific hardware. For example, the less than $200 Arduino-controlled open source orbital shaker fits inside a standard 37°C/5% CO_2 cell incubator and replaces commercial versions whose prices start at more than $1000 (a factor of 5× savings). As the scientific tools grow in complexity, the cost differences between the open source and closed source versions become even more substantial. Our lab has developed a customizable automated filter wheel for less than $50 that replaces a $2500 commercial version (a factor of 50× savings) (Pearce, 2012b). The filter wheel changer[8] uses an open source Arduino microcontroller to turn the wheel and put different optical filters in the path of light for our solar photovoltaic experiments. All of the source code to make and use it is open source, including the design files, which are scripted in OpenSCAD,[9] itself an open source software tool. This example

8. Open-source filter wheel changer: www.thingiverse.com/thing:26553
9. OpenSCAD: www.openscad.org/

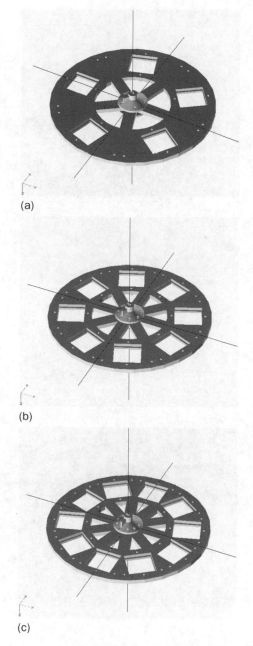

(a)

(b)

(c)

Figure 16.1   Parametric open source automated filter wheel. OpenSCAD rendering of a wheel
with (a) 5 filters, (b) 8 filters, and (c) 10 filters. (continues)
(Source: Images [parts a through h] CC-BY-SA Joshua Pearce)

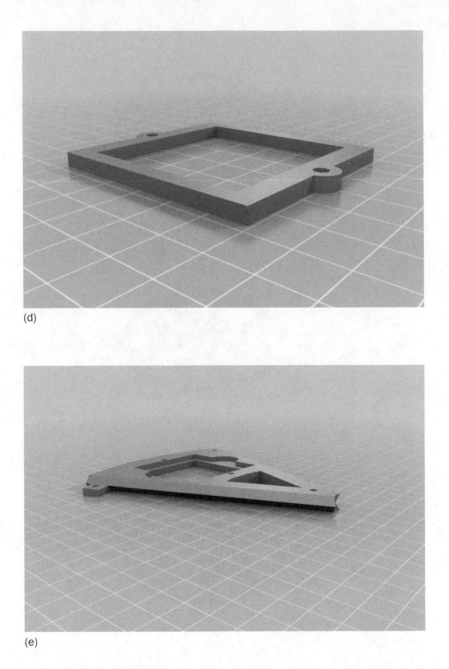

(d)

(e)

Figure 16.1 (continued) The number of filters can be changed by altering a single variable. After the design is customized, STL files are generated for the (d) filter bracket, (e) filter wheel segment.

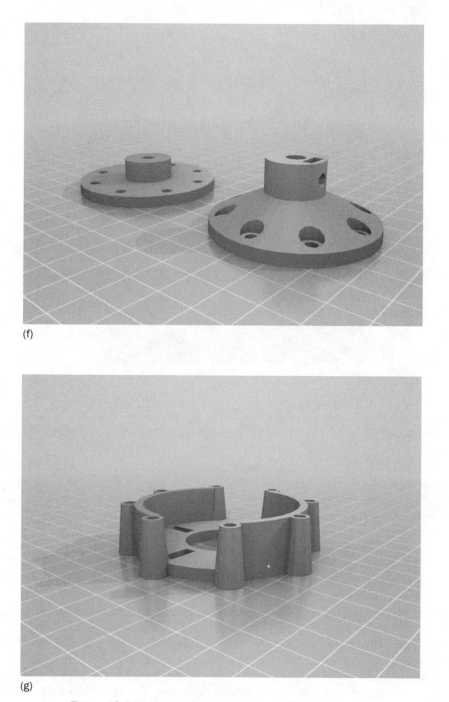

(f)

(g)

Figure 16.1 (f) motor hub, and (g) motor mount. (continues)

(h)

Figure 16.1 (continued) Finally, the designs are printed and
(h) assembled with standard metric-size nuts and bolts.

demonstrates the power of open source hardware particularly effectively, as it was written carefully in OpenSCAD to be parametric (Figure 16.1), so that other scientists can easily adjust the number or size of filters for their specific applications. The electronics, firmware, and software are also open source, so the need to pay for high-cost equipment for this purpose is now completely eliminated for all scientists.

Many research groups are also sharing the designs for their hardware. As additional research groups begin to freely share the designs of their own laboratory hardware, not only can everyone in the greater scientific community enjoy those same discounts on equipment, but following the FOSS approach, the equipment will also continue to evolve to become even better in the open source scientific design community. In addition, research costs will be decreased even when scientists choose a commercial version of a tool because of the price pressure from the open source community. The academic world is on the verge of a new era where low-cost scientific equipment puts increasingly sophisticated tools into the hands of not just academics at the top universities, but also their peers at every university and even the public (Pearce, 2012, 2014).

Sharing of the designs can also be expanded to encompass methods, protocols, and experimental designs. The first advantage to doing so is intrinsic. When it is stressed to students that these experimental designs will be web searchable for all of time, graduate students tend to be more careful about their experimental designs because they are being shared as a quasi-publication. More importantly, by sharing, professors can gain external support. On a routine basis, academics, industry members, and government scientists and engineers from all over the world will be able to improve shared equipment and experimental designs. For example, in our work, outsiders have recommended new software or ways to use existing software; improved programs, device drivers, and firmware to meet our needs; and on the hardware side provided component 3D designs, improved electronics, improved mechanical designs, or advice on assembly of experimental setups. In some cases, external supporters helped us correct errors and oversights in our write-ups before we started non-optimized experiments, which saved us enormous quantities of resources (time and money) by avoiding the need to repeat poorly optimized experiments. These benefits all came from massive peer review and our willingness to actively share. For example, many of our examples of using open source hardware and software have been viewed more than 10,000 times. Following on Eric Raymond's idea, this is a lot of eyeballs looking for potential mistakes and better ways of running experiments (Raymond, 1999).

Academics can also directly benefit by building on the open source hardware that has already been created. For example, for work related to the lowest-cost method of using solar energy to provide clean and safe drinking water in the developing world (Denkenberger and Pearce, 2006), my group needed a highly effective, extremely low-cost heat exchanger. We developed one using a thin, polymer-based expanded microchannel design (Denkenberger et al., 2012), but making the prototypes commercially would have been prohibitively expensive. Instead, we developed a polymer-laser welding system to make them that was derived from an open-source 3D-printable laser cutter[10] and Arduino controls (Pearce, 2014). Our experience was that the time for development was a tiny fraction of what we would have needed to develop the tool without the support of the open source hardware community. Today, we literally save several thousand dollars every day that we make multiple prototype heat exchangers.

Increased Visibility, Citations, and Public Relations

Sharing following the open source paradigm can improve academics' visibility not just within their specialty and among their peers, but also with the general public. This improved visibility of research can often attract media attention, which increases positive public relations for the university. At many schools, this "good ink" (publicity) is highly valued because it assists with recruitment, alumni donations, and an overall sense of pride that brings high morale through the association with a particular institution.

---

10. www.thingiverse.com/thing:11653

Citations (which occur when another academic references your work) are a prized figure of merit for an academic over which the individual has very limited control. Open source hardware, however, provides an easy path for others to replicate and build on past work for all academics working in experimental research. If other research groups can quickly and cheaply build copies of the experimental apparatuses, it increases the impact of a specific research group's work in their discipline—and it can also assist in increasing citations.

Increased Funding Opportunities and Student Recruitment

For the most part, being a professor is wonderful, but like all jobs, it has its distasteful parts. Other than grading, the least appealing part of being a professor is the constant hunt for funding. The increased exposure from sharing open source hardware can lesson this burden by directly resulting in funding. One of the projects our group has been working on for several years is investigating the effects of snow on solar photovoltaic performance. We published our research plans, experimental schematics, protocols, and software on an open wiki (appropedia.org, the largest sustainability-based wiki), which led to our project page being ranked number 1 in Google searches related to snow and photovoltaic technology. This exposure resulted in a successful open source partnership being formed among 20 organizations, including more than a dozen companies, all of which directly contributed funding, equipment, and in-kind support to produce a world-class research testbed called the Open Solar Outdoors Test Field (OSOTF) (Pearce, Babasola, and Andrews, 2012). The entire OSOTF was developed on open source hardware principles. In addition to the design and layout being open, all data and analysis when completed are made freely available to the entire photovoltaic technical community and to the general public. Data including real-time photos of the OSOTF (Figure 16.2) are available in 5-minute increments on a live basis.[11]

The OSOTF partners were willing to overcome the challenges of doing open source research because they saw value in having free access to critical research data that would be useful for product improvement, more reliable predictions of performance for funding, and reductions in solar electric system losses. It is clear from the number of collaborators that contacted the group that many of the partners would never have known about the project without the open source hardware research approach. In addition, the coverage assisted in attracting high-quality *domestic* graduate student researchers.[12]

---

11. www.appropedia.org/OSOTF
12. Domestic graduate students in the science and engineering fields are becoming an endangered species.

Virtuous Cycle

If more academics used an open source hardware approach, the benefits would scale and everyone would benefit even more than they do now. In a vibrant and well-populated open source research community, developing research hardware in every discipline would become a community affair and not the primary work of a single group, as it is most commonly accomplished now. In many fields, custom equipment designs, methods, and software are kept private to an institution or research group. If these elements were provided openly in some form of website, via a wiki protocol or "instructable," the benefits for all in the particular field would be greatly enhanced.

The results of using and contributing to research-related open source hardware in our group has shown that scientific research can be accelerated and the results disseminated faster than when following the closed paradigm of the past (Pearce, 2012). The pragmatic, purely self-serving benefits for most academic research groups to adopt open source hardware are clear. Academics will save money, get more money, get better students, rack up more citations, have a higher probability of obtaining tenure at any institution, and have a larger impact on their fields and the greater society.

(a)

Figure 16.2   (a) A digital photograph of the Open Solar Outdoors
Test Field, which is a project used to measure solar photovoltaic system
performance. (continues)
(Source: Images [a and b] CC-BY-SA Rob Andrews)

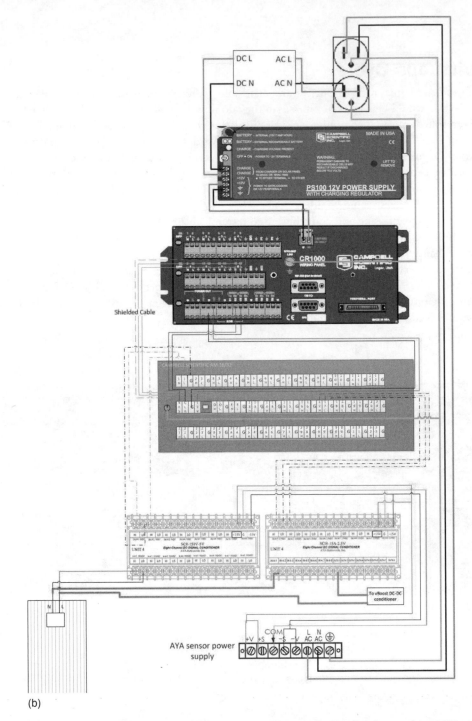

(b)

Figure 16.2 (continued) (b) A wiring diagram showing a single circuit (of more than 100) of the data acquisition system for measuring solar photovoltaic module output, which represents some of the "source" associated with the open source hardware project.

Anecdote: A Cautionary Tale for Education
John English

Considering the similar histories of open source software and open source hardware, the following anecdote is a cautionary tale of having closed source software in education for the open source hardware world to learn from. Software is a fundamental part of modern creativity. From writing music to writing code for microcontrollers, a broad set of software is typically involved at some point in the process. Learning to effectively use software tools requires study and practice, in the same way that one would expect for traditional skills such as calculus or fluency in foreign languages. It's often difficult for people to find the time to develop new software. Students in primary school and college have a special opportunity to learn new software skills, and in many cases the software to which they're exposed will determine what they use later on in life.

This concept of software incumbency is a major element in marketing strategies for software companies. Products such as Labview and Matlab are given to educational organizations at significantly reduced cost or no cost at all. Companies are motivated to distribute their products to students as early as possible, so as to build familiarity and engrain habits. This strategy can be seen in many other markets, ranging from cars to cigarettes. When students graduate and move into their professional careers, they are much more likely to purchase an expensive software package if they have spent time in school using it. Likewise, teachers who have developed curriculum based on commercial software packages may have a hard time moving away from those packages. If a professor has been teaching with Matlab for many years, for example, it can be a daunting task to migrate to alternative platforms.

While comfort and familiarity with any tool is a good thing, there are some significant downsides to this trend of education using low- or no-cost licenses of very expensive software tools. Beyond the obvious issue of high costs (often measured in the thousands or tens of thousands of dollars for a single license), closed source software does not allow students to explore the inner workings of the tools they are using. A student who is using Labview might wish to find out exactly *how* a facial-recognition function differentiates her face from her sister's, and perhaps even modify it to behave differently. A student who is using Matlab might wish to explore the intricacies of its compiler. With either of these tools, there are impassible barriers to satisfying this curiosity, enforced by closed source binaries and user licenses. If these students had been exposed to open source software instead, they would be free to explore the full stack of the tool they're using. They might even go on to share code changes, contributing to the distributed development of their software tools.

Education in its purest form has no barriers to inquiry and no restrictions on exploration of ideas. Open source values align splendidly with education, providing students with the opportunity to dive into any layer of tools that they find compelling. Closed source software in education implicitly tells students that there should be limits to their curiosity—that they should not look behind the curtain, but should instead be satisfied with what has been given to them. While this strategy may be effective at selling software licenses, it promotes a mentality of consumption over creation that is detrimental to students' education

(*continues*)

and personal development. Open source hardware is in a wonderfully formative stage. Because open source hardware is easier to use and reaches a younger audience, it has the opportunity to become a stakeholder in education and push closed source platforms out before they infiltrate our education system to an even greater extent.

OSHW Teaching and Service

Developing and sharing open source hardware designs can be viewed as a form of service—service you do for the entire world and for those to come in the future who build from your work. When this service is brought into the context of the classroom, it is best discussed as *service learning*, which is a teaching method that combines community service with academic instruction as it focuses on critical reflective thinking and civic responsibility (Campus Compact, 2000). One of the unique aspects of service learning is that it benefits both the provider and the recipient of the service and requires that the service and the learning occur in tandem (Furco, 1996). Service learning began as a somewhat fringe educational endeavor, particularly in engineering. However, now that the evidence shows service learning outcomes are positive for students, faculty, educational institutions, and involved community partners, it has grown into a formidable trend (Bielefeldt and Pearce, 2012; Bringle and Hatcher, 1996; Cohen and Kinsey, 1994; Driscoll et al. 1996; Giles and Eyler, 1994; Kellogg Commission, 1999; Panici and Lasky, 2002; Pearce, 2007a, 2009; Pearce et al., 2008; Pearce, 2009). There is now an entire journal (*The International Journal for Service Learning in Engineering*) devoted to the topic.

Engineering service learning can take part in any community, but some of the most exciting programs happen overseas. Programs such as the Kefalonia Program in Sustainable Community Development (Zaferatos, 2007) should be viewed as the ideal because not only do they offer students rich learning opportunities, but they also directly partner with developing communities and take students overseas to implement service learning projects. Although they are successful and useful, these programs lack the potential of universal replication. It is simply cost prohibitive to have students constantly traveling in large numbers for a single course in developing appropriate technologies for those most in need of those technologies in the developing world. This is where open source hardware teaching pedagogy becomes extremely powerful. It provides a form of *virtual service learning* because it enables students to work on service learning projects at their home institutions and then scale their solutions to the technical problems over the entire world.

By using service learning in place of more conventional classroom based projects, students are more motivated, work harder, learn more, and are left with lasting benefits from their experience (Cohen and Kinsey, 1994; Giles and Eyler, 1994; Pearce 2001, 2009; Pearce and Russill, 2003, 2005). In particular, I have observed that when students are focused on open source appropriate technology projects for sustainable development, they are highly engaged and motivated (Pearce, 2007a; 2007b; 2009). Similar to the open source hardware research just described, Appropedia.org can be used as a platform for service learning with open source hardware.

Virtual Service Learning Developing OSHW

It should be clear to any academic with teaching experience in engineering that open source hardware design can be brought into the curriculum for their classes. For example, electrical engineering professors can assign projects based on the open source Arduino microcontroller and have their students post new designs online. Similarly, mechanical engineering and design professors could, for example, have their students post their CAD/CAM designs in 3D design repositories with open licenses. All of the normally closed projects, whether back of the book or industry sponsored, can be ported into the open source realm. Doing so actually provides more flexibility, so that students can benefit from the increased motivation associated with service learning and professors are better able to tailor the class projects to the curriculum.

This combination works great for engineering professors, but what if the professor is teaching less applied work, such as in the sciences? This use of OSHW in the classroom can also be accomplished with relatively minor adjustments to the class.

As a professor teaching physics, I had great success using open source hardware projects in the classroom, which would be classified as *open source appropriate technology* (OSAT) projects (Pearce, 2007a). Appropriate technologies are defined here as technologies that are based on readily available resources and are easily and economically used by local communities in the developing world. OSAT must meet the boundary conditions set by the environmental, cultural, economic, and educational resource constraints of the local community (Pearce, 2007b; 2012b).

For a physics class, the assignment was for students to fortify the information in Appropedia on an OSAT of their choice that used the type of physics we were discussing. Students identified an OSAT that interested them through research, examples from former students or class content, the department's collection of books and articles, or the Internet. Students having trouble with a specific class topic (e.g., heat transfer) were asked to consider targeting a technology that used this area of physics to help them review it (e.g., home insulation with straw bale construction). Next, students coordinated their projects on the class category page, which allowed for collaboration while eliminating duplication. Then, they researched the technical specifications of their chosen device, paying close attention to its underlying physics so they might understand how to improve its performance. Finally, students wrote an article (or several integrated articles) on their chosen OSAT. These articles generally contained a title, abstract, science principles (often with links to basic definitions in Wikipedia), all of the necessary equations governing the topic, examples, cultural/regional context, required materials/tools/skills, technical specifications and sometimes drawings and schematics, costs, common mistakes, and sources.

This assignment provided students with an opportunity to directly participate in global collaboration to support sustainable development. Alterations of this assignment can be made to fit into almost any curricula, but meld particularly well with design courses. Students can be assigned design, simulation, or experiments to help drive open source hardware forward while learning conventional material and collaborating virtually with nonprofit organizations.

Consider the Kingston Hot Press (KHP) shown in Figure 16.3. The organization Waste for Life develops poverty-reducing solutions to specific ecological problems. Through a large collaboration with researchers, community members, and service learning projects, the KHP has been designed and developed to provide the means of production to smaller cooperatives in communities in Argentina and Lesotho. The KHP allows the user to produce a value-added composite tile out of waste plastic and fiber (most commonly cardboard and paper, as shown in Figure 16.3d). A service learning project was initiated to provide a useful heat transfer model that could improve the design and reduce the cost of the KHP. Rather than simply learning the skills necessary to complete the project in a normal course, the source was published[13] so that others could build on the work and improve the hot press design in the future.

Appropedia pages were being ported to the One Laptop per Child (OLPC) project, which has enjoyed widespread publicity in the major media. The OLPC (Figure 16.4) is a low-cost laptop designed to revolutionize education for the world's children. Specifically, the OLPC initiative hopes to provide educational opportunities for the world's most isolated and poorest children by giving each child a rugged, low-cost, low-power, connected laptop as well as open source software tools and content designed for collaborative, joyful, self-empowered learning.[14]

If the student work was of high enough quality and fit the necessary guidelines, there was a real chance it might be translated and used by millions of children all over the world to improve their lives by building and using open source hardware plans on their laptops. The student authors with the best work were offered credit for furthering their projects in independent study courses. For example, in an undergraduate course in general physics, an open source hardware service learning project on removal of arsenic from groundwater was expanded into full research projects the following semester (Hashmi and Pearce, 2011).

Overall, these projects proved successful at both assisting students to learn course material (Pearce, 2007a) and providing high-quality content in the open source hardware and OSAT movements. Students were motivated to do high-quality work. By tracking the history pages on the wiki, it was possible to see that students spent significantly more time working on their open source hardware projects than they did on their conventional homework projects assigned and tracked in conventional courseware. The conversations

---

13. www.appropedia.org/Kingston_Hot_Press:_Process_Improvements
14. wiki.laptop.org/go/The_OLPC_Wiki

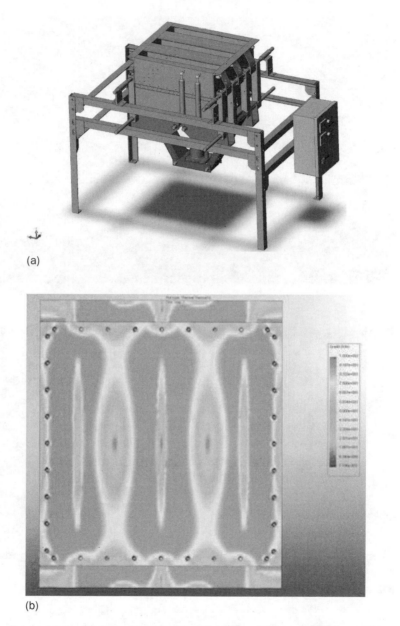

(a)

(b)

Figure 16.3   (a) CAD of the Kingston Hot Press. (b) A heat transfer model
showing the temperature gradient across a component. (continues)
(Source: Images [a through d] CC-BY-SA Nate Preston)

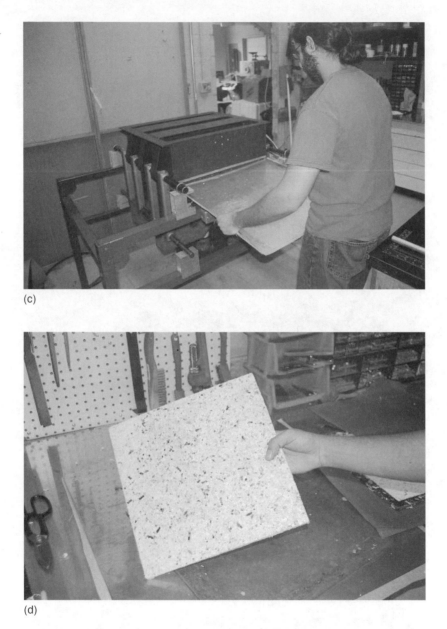

(c)

(d)

Figure 16.3 (continued) (c) The improved press in use. (d) The resultant
waste-plastic composite material.

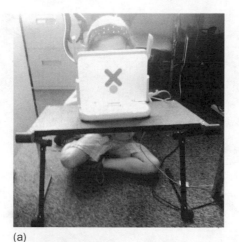

(a)

(b)

(c)

Figure 16.4   (a) The XO Laptop from OLPC in use by a young child on an
open source adjustable laptop stand (www.thingiverse.com/thing:134081)
constructed from (b) OpenBeam, an open source hardware aluminum
extrusion system, standard nuts and bolts, and (c) custom hinges. (continues)
(Source: Images [a through d] CC-BY-SA Joshua Pearce)

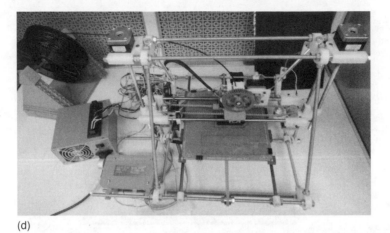

(d)

Figure 16.4 (continued) These items can be fabricated with (d) a low-cost
open source RepRap 3D printer, which is itself fabricated with printed parts,
stock hardware, open source electronics, and recycled materials such as an
old computer supply for power and a cardboard spool holder.

in the discussion board about the project were also all positive and encouraging. Students found the work in Appropedia exciting and interesting. Several noted that the wiki coding was challenging. At the end of the semester, the students made only positive comments about the project in their teacher evaluations, and several students expressed gratitude for being exposed to the assignment. The Appropedia Foundation was also pleased with the students' work because it had filled some of the holes in Appropedia's coverage of energy. Some student projects were even chosen to be highlighted on Appropedia's Welcome page.

Appropedia is now used by many universities as a repository of open source hardware that fits into the sustainable development classification. In addition, many top universities now feature courses dedicated to developing sustainable appropriate technologies (AT) in their engineering or science curricula (Pearce, 2009). With the help of the open source hardware paradigm, these schools can integrate AT research development and diffusion into the university curriculum using virtual service learning.

There are many other ways to integrate open source hardware into the classroom for the benefit of the students. The only requirement to do so in many cases is a minor modification to a standard project to include sharing the designs following an open model. As more of our educational system begins to rely on Internet-based collaboration for student projects, the simplicity of integrating open source hardware into the classroom becomes relatively straightforward in any field.

Summary

Open source hardware improves academic performance in research, teaching, and service. Open source hardware benefits research by providing substantial pre-peer review in the development of background material and experimental design, which leads to improved experimental design and laboratory hardware design (often with radically reduced economic costs) and hardware with superior performance and customization. It also produces increased visibility, citations, and improved public relations, which can result in increased funding opportunities and enhanced student recruitment, as well as improved student research-related training and research education. Using open source hardware in the classroom as part of service learning helps motivate students to work harder and learn more, and leaves them with lasting benefits from their experience. Finally, using, developing, and publishing open source hardware, either as part of a research program or in the classroom, is an effective method of performing outreach on both grants and tenure applications.

References

Anzalone, G. C., Glover, A. G., and Pearce, J. M. 2013. "Open-Source Colorimeter." *Sensors* 13 (4): 5338–5346.

Bergquist, M., and Ljungberg, J. 2001. "The Power of Gifts: Organizing Social Relationships in Open Source Communities." *Information Systems Journal* 11: 305–320.

Bessen, J., and Maskin, E. 2009. "Sequential Innovation, Patents, and Imitation." *RAND Journal of Economics* 40 (4): 611–635.

Bielefeldt, A. R., and Pearce, J. M. 2012. "Service Learning in Engineering." In T. H. Colledge (Ed.), *Convergence: Philosophies and Pedagogies for Developing the Next Generation of Humanitarian Engineers and Social Entrepreneurs.* NCIIA, pp. 24–52.

Boldrin, M., and Levine, D. K. 2008. *Against Intellectual Monopoly.* Cambridge, UK: Cambridge University Press.

Bringle, R. G., and J. A. Hatcher. 1996. "Implementing Service Learning in Higher Education." *Journal of Higher Education* 67: 221–239.

Campus Compact, National Center for Community Colleges. 2000. *Introduction to Service Learning Toolkit.* Providence, RI: Brown University Press.

Chan, A. S., and Fisher, D. 2008. *Exchange University: Corporatization of Academic Culture.* Vancouver, BC: University of British Columbia Press.

Cohen, J., and Kinsey, D. F. 1994. "Doing Good and Scholarship: A Service Learning Study." *Journalism Educator* 48 (4): 4–14.

Denkenberger, D. C., Brandemuehl, M. J., Pearce, J. M., and Zhai, J. 2012. "Expanded Microchannel Heat Exchanger: Design, Fabrication and Preliminary Experimental Test." *Proceedings of the Institution of Mechanical Engineers—Part A: Journal of Power and Energy* 226: 532–544.

Denkenberger, D. C., and Pearce, J. M. 2006. "Compound Parabolic Concentrators for Solar Water Heat Pasteurization: Numerical Simulation." *Proceedings of the 2006 International Conference of Solar Cooking and Food Processing,* p. 108.

Dragone, V., Sans, V., Rosnes, M. H., Kitson, P. J., and Cronin, L. 2013. "3D-Printed Devices for Continuous-Flow Organic Chemistry." *Beilstein Journal of Organic Chemistry* 9 (1): 951–959.

Driscoll, A., Holland, B., Gelmon, S., and Kerrigan, S. 1996. "An Assessment for Service Learning: Comprehensive Case Studies of Impact on Faculty, Students, Community and Institution." *Michigan Journal of Community Service Learning* 3: 66–71.

Gelman, I. J. 2012. "Missing Methods." *The Scientist.* http://the-scientist.com/2012/05/03/opinion-missing-methods/

Giles, D. E., and J. Eyler. 1994. "The Theoretical Roots of Service Learning in John Dewey: Toward a Theory of Service Learning." *Michigan Journal of Community Service* 1 (1): 77–85.

Hashmi, F., and Pearce, J. M. 2011. "Viability of Small-Scale Arsenic-Contaminated Water Purification Technologies for Sustainable Development in Pakistan." *Sustainable Development* 19 (4): 223–234.

Jones, R., Haufe, P., Sells, E., Iravani, P., Olliver, V., Palmer, C., and Bowyer, A. 2011. "RepRap: The Replicating Rapid Prototyper." *Robotica* 29: 177–191.

Kellogg Commission on the Future of State and Land-Grant Universities. 1999. *Returning to Our Roots: The Engaged Institution.* Washington, DC: National Association for Higher Education.

Kitson, P. J., Rosnes, M. H., Sans, V., Dragone, V., and Cronin, L. 2012. "Configurable 3D-Printed Millifluidic and Microfluidic 'Lab on a Chip' Reactionware Devices." *Lab on a Chip* 12 (18): 3267–3271.

Levy S. 1984. *Hackers: Heroes of the Computer Revolution.* New York, NY: Doubleday.

Lieberwitz, R. L. 2005. "Educational Law: The Corporatization of Academic Research: Whose Interests Are Served?" *Akron Law Review* 38 (759): 764–765.

Panici, D., and Lasky, K. 2002. "Service Learning's Foothold in Communication Scholarship." *Journalism & Mass Communication Educator* 57 (2): 113–125.

Pearce, J. 2001. "The Use of Self-Directed Learning to Promote Active Citizenship in Science, Technology, and Society Classes." *Bulletin of Science, Technology, and Society* 21 (4): 312–321.

Pearce, J. M. 2007a. "Teaching Physics Using Appropriate Technology Projects." *The Physics Teacher* 45: 164–167.

Pearce, J. M. 2007b. "Teaching Science by Encouraging Innovation in Appropriate Technologies for Sustainable Development." *Proceedings of the 11th Annual National Collegiate Inventors and Innovators Alliance Conference,* pp. 159–167.

Pearce, J. M. 2009. "Appropedia as a Tool for Service Learning in Sustainable Development." *Journal of Education for Sustainable Development* 3 (1): 47–55.

Pearce, J. M. 2012a. "Open Source Research in Sustainability." *Sustainability: The Journal of Record* 5 (4): 238–243.

Pearce, J. M. 2012b. "The Case for Open Source Appropriate Technology." *Environment, Development and Sustainability* 14: 425–431.

Pearce, J. M. 2014. *The Open-Source Lab.* Amsterdam: Elsevier.

Pearce, J. M., Babasola, A., and Andrews, R. 2012. "Open Solar Photovoltaic Systems Optimization." *Proceedings of the 16th Annual National Collegiate Inventors and Innovators Alliance Conference,* pp. 1–7.

Pearce, J. M., Grafman, L., Colledge, T., and Legg, R. 2008. "Leveraging Information Technology, Social Entrepreneurship and Global Collaboration for Just Sustainable Development." *Proceedings of the 12th Annual National Collegiate Inventors and Innovators Alliance Conference,* pp. 201–210. http://www.nciia.org/conf08/assets/pub/pearce.pdf

Pearce, J. M., and Russill, C. 2003. "Student Inquiries into Neglected Research for a Sustainable Society: Communication and Application." *Bulletin of Science, Technology and Society* 23 (4): 311–320.

Pearce, J. M., and Russill, C. 2005." Interdisciplinary Environmental Education: Communicating and Applying Energy Efficiency for Sustainability." *Applied Environmental Education and Communication* 4 (1): 65–72.

Raymond, E. 1999. "The Cathedral and the Bazaar." *Knowledge Technology and Policy* 12: 23–49.

Symes, M. D., Kitson, P. J., Yan, J., Richmond, C. J., Cooper, G. J., Bowman, R. W., Vilbrandt, T., and Cronin, L. 2012. "Integrated 3D-Printed Reactionware for Chemical Synthesis and Analysis." *Nature Chemistry* 4 (5): 349–354.

Wijnen, B., Hunt, E. J., Anzalone, G. C., and Pearce, J. M. 2014. "Open-Source Syringe Pump Library." *PLoS One* 9(9): e107216.

Zaferatos, N. C. 2007. "Sustainable Planning Education as Intercultural Service Learning: Kefalonia Program in Sustainable Community Development." *Journal of Education for Sustainable Development* 1 (2): 199–208.

Zhang, C., Anzalone, N. C., Faria, R. P., and Pearce, J. M. 2013. "Open-Source 3D-Printable Optics Equipment." *PLoS One* 8 (3): e59840.

Conclusion

Whether you read only parts of this book or the entire thing, I hope you found the communal advice useful. Many of the authors can be found giving talks on YouTube or Vimeo on their subject matter or on topics related to open source hardware. This book sought to cover the theoretical side of open source hardware from historical and economical viewpoints as well as the practices and methods used to create a piece of open source hardware. It prepared you for the holistic experience of open source hardware from designing to manufacturing, and outlined the benefits, standards, and incentives for such efforts. As stated many times throughout this book, the open source hardware movement is young and malleable. Whether you're just joining the discussion or have been part of the community since the beginning, there will be many more decisions to be made, many more changes to endure, and many more projects to build!

Changing Incentives

On the one hand, open source hardware is a young movement gaining popularity in the last decade. On the other hand, open source hardware has been around for as long as people were inventing things, from repair manuals to patterns and recipes. The patent system was designed to document and share the synthesis of your invention, although one might argue the original design and incentives of the patent system no longer correlate with the contemporary patent system. The rise of open source hardware occurred partially in response to the frustrations associated with the current patent system. When patents were first created, they were meant to incentivize inventors. Today's inventors, however, are looking for other incentives than patents, and some find a motivation for sharing their hardware in the knowledge that they'll receive attribution and share-alike licensing.

The patent application process has become a behemoth of litigation, paperwork, and high price points; that is, for many small businesses the price to apply for a patent is too high, and the price to defend a patent is well out of their reach. The paperwork to get a patent and the timeline to wait for one hinders innovation as it is too time consuming and the patent is out of date by the time it gets awarded.

The patent system has also been subjected to criticism on becoming too loose in its definition of "unique." Indeed, it has had to back-pedal on some patents, such as the patent Google obtained for the base functionality of a cellphone. As lawyer Tom Ewing pointed out in an interview on *This American Life*, "It took 121 years for us to get the first 1 million patents. Now it takes more or less six years to get another million patents."[1] This

---

1. www.thisamericanlife.org/radio-archives/episode/496/when-patents-attack-part-two

leaves a question to be answered: "Have humans really become 10 times more innovative since last century or has the patent system changed its standards?" The Industrial Revolution is trumpeted as a time of high innovation, when many of the first million patents were awarded, with the railways and steam engines being the poster children of technology at the time. The Industrial Revolution is often paralleled with the Internet Age, with both seen as eras when inventors focused on shortening time and space. The Internet, which was largely built upon open source software, has had a sister movement of hardware grow over the past decade. Open sourcing hardware is proving to be as lucrative as open sourcing software, and this revolution will likely be as important as the Industrial Revolution. First, however, we must reconcile the incentives that inventors want and the public benefit derived from the inventors' creations.

Maturity of the Open Source Hardware Movement

As was stated in the Introduction, it would be irresponsible to write this book as though every aspect of open source hardware has been figured out. Remember, the definition of open source hardware was created by the community and for the community. Communities, along with technologies, change over time. The definition upholds "the spirit of" open source hardware as a consideration for labeling your hardware as open source. This sentiment leaves the definition somewhat open ended because the community cannot see into the future and know what upholding the definition of open source hardware will look like in 20 years.

Much of the gray area within open source hardware is due to the fact that openness does not yet extend to all layers of hardware. For example, it is not expected that an open source hardware company will mine the copper to ensure openness on that layer. The layer of opening raw materials may be considered in the future, or potentially never. Something that seems easier for this particular community to alter the openness of are the closed source programs that we use to build hardware. Eagle is one of the most popular programs for electronic layout, but is closed source. There are open source alternatives, such as KiCad and Fritzing. This leaves the community with the question of whether open source software design tools need to have open source code, or whether Eagle should be used because it is the most popular and therefore most accessible option, with an existing community of users who already know how to use Eagle. Making a decision as a community either to use only open source software in our tools or to put pressure on Eagle to create an open version of its software may be something that slows growth in the movement.

Integral pieces of hardware, such as the chip, are also often closed. However, I'm excited to say that while this book was being written, Parallax announced its open source silicon.[2] This development is an exciting step forward for open source hardware and a milestone in the growth of the movement.

---

2. www.parallax.com/microcontrollers/propeller-1-open-source

Another way the movement will continue to mature is by gaining more traction in various fields. The open source hardware movement started in electronics but has quickly encompassed several other fields in industry. This trend continues to grow each year and covers more standards and further thinking through the necessary source files. User generations also affect societal norms on transparency and openness, which may cause more companies to open up in the future. Younger generations tend to have a different comfort level with openness and transparency than older generations do. Businesses built by members of younger generations could look much different from businesses built today.

Looking to the Future

There are several ways in which open source hardware can move forward. The following ideas to make the open source hardware movement stronger have come from the community:

- **Laundry label for hardware.** The laundry label concept was brought to OSHWA's mailing list by Tom Igoe and Catarina Mota. The laundry label concept is a labeling system that would provide specific attributions for each piece of hardware. Such labels would be similar to those found in clothing that instructs you how to care for it. The laundry label concept is different from the open source hardware logo. The logo simply states that the hardware follows the Open Source Hardware Definition. The laundry label might contain information such as how to recycle the parts of the hardware, which pieces and design files are open and which are closed, which software includes libraries of the parts, and which parts need to be verified again by a standards entity, such as the FCC, after alteration. For resellers, the label might contain the amenities associated with a product, such as whether it has a 3D design file to accompany it. An example of this practice is pointed out in the Best Practices section of Chapter 2.

- **Open source hardware repository.** Creating and managing a repository is no small task, but it has been requested by many that the Open Source Hardware Association create one. The community understandably prefers that the repository be held by a nonprofit organization that would not benefit from closing the repository's intellectual property. It may take a while for the community to determine what the core functions and features of a repository would be, but it is certainly worth starting the conversation.

- **Further protections.** Unfortunately for open source hardware, the patent system, in the United States at least, has gotten out of hand. Prior art is what allows open source hardware to be recognized and stay open rather than patented. Many open source hardware creators recognize that the U.S. Patent and Trademark Office (USPTO) is not doing a comprehensive job of finding prior art when awarding patents. Dealing with a change on this level will take an enormous effort and may end up with open source hardware inventors facing layers of unwanted bureaucracy and piles of paperwork. However, one benefit of an open source hardware repository would be that the USPTO could check it against patent applications for prior art.

- **Use of the open source hardware logo.** The Open Source Hardware Association recognizes that it is the institution best situated to complete the previously mentioned tasks, and many people are asking OSHWA to do just that. Although implementation of the prior tasks may take a while and the community may change directions, the best way that OSHWA will be able to tackle any of these items is to ensure that there is a way to easily identify which projects are open source without digging for source files. Using the open source hardware logo (find links to the files in Chapter 14 or on www.oshwa.org) on your work will make it easy for the laundry label or repository committee to identify it as open source. One can imagine a future where the USPTO has a poster of the open source hardware logo to compare with logos on source files and thereby identify open source hardware, invalidating similar patents. It's a starry-eyed future—but most of my futures are.

In the 1980s, few thought open source software was a legitimate business model. Even 10 years ago, it was not as big of an industry as it is today. Open source hardware is still immature, but is currently at least a $100 million industry, if not more. What will it be in 10 years if we follow a growth pattern like the one demonstrated by the open source software movement? Will open source hardware be running the Internet? Open source hardware has so many opportunities to grow in different directions. It can lead education in how people use, personalize, and fix their hardware, ranging from electronics to tractors. Open source hardware can make people more educated buyers and more impactful users. It can facilitate the conversation between users and companies. It can make companies more competitive, which benefits the consumer. Open source hardware can help in disaster relief situations and initiatives paid for by the public, where knowledge about making the world a better place should belong to the people rather than to a business. Open source hardware saves time for inventors by allowing them to build off the knowledge of others and produce new things faster than ever before.

Groups working together in the open source community will quickly surpass closed groups through innovation and utilizing one another's shared work. It's not about reinventing the wheel; it's about cross-pollinating ideas, building upon, and hacking that wheel to get to solutions that could not have been created otherwise. Society has been open sourcing hardware for thousands of years—it's how we learn! It is only recent legal structures that have made intellectual property a priority over sharing. I hope you consider joining us in enjoying the benefits of open source hardware!

A

Open Source
Hardware Checklist

This checklist is made up from key points of the Open Source Hardware Definition and Best Practices. It is meant to serve as a quick reference guide to ensure that your project is properly labeled as open source hardware.[1]

- ❑ Does your hardware comply with the Open Source Hardware Definition (http://www.oshwa.org/definition/)?
- ❑ Have you allowed anyone to study, modify, distribute, make, and sell the hardware?
- ❑ If you used a Creative Commons license for your source files (documentation), did you chose options compatible with the definition? Noncommercial and no derivatives licenses are not open source.
- ❑ Did you put the OSHW logo on your hardware so people can easily identify it as open source hardware? (Strongly recommended)
- ❑ Do all company logos on the hardware belong to you? Do not infringe on trademarks!
- ❑ Are your source files in an easily attainable format?
- ❑ Are the source files publicly available online?
- ❑ Are your source files easy to find—for example, are they linked to and from the product page?
- ❑ Have you documented your project in such a way that people will be able to copy it?
- ❑ Is your documentation free of charge?
- ❑ Have you included images in your documentation? (Strongly recommended)
- ❑ Are you emotionally prepared to allow your project to be copied?
- ❑ If not all parts/versions are open, have you clearly specified which portions of the design are being released as open source hardware and which are not?

If you answered yes to all of these questions, your project is considered open source hardware!

---

1. This checklist created CC-BY-SA OSHWA and is part of the *OSHW Quick Reference Guide*.

OSHW Musts and Mays

For your project to be truly open source, you must do the following:[2]

- ❏ Allow anyone to study, modify, distribute, make, and sell the hardware.
- ❏ Provide publicly accessible design files and documentation (the source).
- ❏ Clearly specify which portion of the design, if not all of it, is being released under the license.
- ❏ Do not imply that derivatives are manufactured, sold, covered under warranty, or otherwise sanctioned by the original designer.
- ❏ Do not use trademarks of other companies without permission.
- ❏ Do not release the hardware with a noncommercial or no derivatives license.

The following steps are optional:

- ❏ Require attribution be given.
- ❏ Use the open source hardware logo to signify the hardware follows the Open Source Hardware Definition.
- ❏ Require derived works to carry a different name or version number from the original design.
- ❏ Hardware may be copied directly or have derivatives created from it.
- ❏ Require a viral license.

---

2. This checklist was created CC–BY–SA OSHWA and is part of the *OSHW Quick Reference Guide*.

Open Source Hardware Security Do's and Don'ts

Josh Datko

So you are building open source hardware that will change the world? Ideally, it will be used by thousands—if not millions—of users, and everyone will have one—if not two—of your devices! You might not think that your device needs to be secure, but if people depend on it and make decisions based on the data the device presents, then it needs to be secure and reliable. Adding security to your OSHW project after it's deployed is too late; you need to think about this issue before your hardware ships.

The following tips are geared toward embedded OSHW devices that run firmware, whether in a FPGA, a microcontroller, or a CPU. More complete resources are listed in this appendix. Here are some basic do's and don'ts that can help make your device more secure and reliable:

- **Don't** store a hard-coded password or key in your firmware. First of all, your firmware is open source, right? Even if it's not, this step provides almost no extra security because your firmware can be disassembled and it's trivial to find fixed strings.

- **Don't** roll your own crypto algorithm. It easy to convince yourself that your crypto is unbreakable. The thinking goes like this: "I'm the smartest person I know and I can't break this, so nobody can." This kind of assumption almost never turns out well. Instead, you should use an academically reviewed algorithm from a well-maintained crypto library. There are also dedicated hardware integrated circuits (ICs) that will implement these algorithms and provide a random number generator for you.

- **Don't** hide the plaintext key on your system. This is slightly better than a hard-coded password, but not by much. If the first step is to load a key from an EEPROM over I2C, then all it takes is a logic analyzer to watch that traffic and discover the key. Read *Hacking the Xbox* (listed in the Resources section) to see why this approach doesn't work.

- **Do** consider denial of service attacks. Reliability and security engineering share similar features. Consider cases like what happens when your device receives too many messages. Does it need redundant power supplies? If it's part of a distributed system, how many inputs (or votes) should be needed before your device makes a decision? (Hint: One is usually not enough.)

- **Don't** ship a binary blob! You are already shipping open source hardware, so why restrict the software? A binary blob doesn't make your product any more secure. This fallacy essentially relies on "security through obscurity." If your device is popular, it will be reverse engineered.

- **Do** have a secure and reliable firmware updating mechanism. You might hope that your device will be used in 5 years, but how will users update the firmware? Inevitably, a vulnerability will be found, and users will need to update the device. Also, can your device be updated without using the Internet? Can users update it even if your company no longer exists? (Hint: The answer should be yes.) Consider generating an asymmetric key pair and signing your firmware updates so that users and devices can trust the updates.

- **Do** let users have control of the device. The users bought your product; they should be able to run their own software on this device. Plus, the users want to be able to perform any maintenance themselves if there is a problem or a critical vulnerability they want to fix. Even if you are signing your firmware, provide an option for the users to upload their own. As Jim Gettys says, "Friends don't let friends run factory firmware."

- **Do** add integrity checking mechanisms to your communication protocols, even between ICs. A glitch on one wire can make a difference between a high and a low. What happens if the data is used with the one wrong bit? At a minimum, consider adding a cyclic redundancy check (CRC) to each message, to ensure that the intended message is the delivered message. Consider what happens when a fault is detected.

- **Do** consider who else can access the data on the device. Adding a logger to your device is great, but don't make it easy for other parties to access the data if the user wants to keep it private. You have a responsibility to protect users' data.

- **Do** use a static code analysis tool on your firmware. C is a popular language for embedded development, but it's very easy to make a programming mistake that results in an exploitable loophole. There are free (for open source projects) static analysis tools, such as Coverity Scan, that will scan your code and catch your mistakes.

Happy hacking!

Resources

Computer Related Risks, by Peter G. Neumann (Addison-Wesley, 1994). This book catalogs a plethora of engineering failures and provides answers to the question, "What can go wrong?" It is as relevant today as it was when first published.

Hacking the Xbox, by Bunnie Huang. Available for free at No Starch Press (www.nostarch .com/xbox.htm). This should be your first stop on hardware reverse engineering. In addition to being a great all-around book, it clearly shows how even big companies, like Microsoft, make devastating security mistakes.

(In)Security in Home Embedded Devices, by Jim Gettys (http://cyber.law.harvard.edu /events/luncheon/2014/06/gettys). An hour-video, presented at the Berkman Center for Internet & Society at Harvard University, on the social and policy issues with regard to home devices.

"The Internet of Things Is Wildly Insecure—and Often Unpatchable," by Bruce Schneier (https://www.schneier.com/essays/archives/2014/01/the_internet_of_thin .html). While it focuses on routers, this article succinctly captures why the embedded world needs to care about security.

C

Design Process Checklist

The content for this appendix has been taken from Chapter 5, The Design Process, and reflects the license of that chapter.

Concept Refinement

Answer the following questions before you begin designing your project into a product:

- ❏ Is there a market for what I want to make?
- ❏ How big is that market?
- ❏ Who are my target users?
- ❏ What do my target users want?
- ❏ What do my users need this product to do?
- ❏ Which features do I need to add to make this usable?
- ❏ Which of my features are critical and which ones are optional?
- ❏ How much can I charge for this and still make a profit?
- ❏ How many of these will I make?
- ❏ What is my deadline? Will someone else scoop me to market?
- ❏ Do I want this to be a kit?
- ❏ (If assembled) Will I make this myself, or will I contract that step to a manufacturer?
- ❏ Does this product require any regulatory certifications (e.g., child safety, FCC, FDA, CE)?

Managing Iteration

Have you maintained an archive of the following items to facilitate iteration?

- ❏ A copy of your parts library, schematic, and layout files
- ❏ A copy of your BOM

❑ A copy of your build package (Gerbers, drill files)

❑ Purchasing records for parts and PCBs

❑ Test notes (on both test procedures and your test data)

❑ A bug tracker for new issues (and old)

Preparing to Manufacture

Do you have the following items ready for manufacture?

❑ Gerbers

❑ NC drill file

❑ Assembly drawings

❑ Pick-and-place coordinates (or kit assembly instructions)

❑ Bill of materials, where the following information is identified for each part:

   a. Part ID

   b. Reference designators

   c. Part type

   d. Package footprint

   e. Part value

   f. Part tolerance (if important)

   g. Part critical specification (if any)

   h. Manufacturer part number

   i. Vender part number

   j. Alternate part sources (1, 2, 3, 4)

❑ Test instructions

D

Design for Manufacture Checklists

The content for this appendix has been taken from Chapter 12, Accelerate from Making to Manufacturing, and Chapter 13, Troubleshooting from Your Design to Your Manufacturer.

Finding the Right Contract Manufacturer

❑ Does the contract manufacturer (CM) make things that are similar to what you intend to manufacture?

❑ Who are the CM's other customers (that it can tell you about)?

❑ Does the CM have experience working with the materials that you'd like your product to be made from?

❑ Do the CM's samples have a similar number of parts and level of complexity compared to your product?

❑ Can the CM provide a fully turnkey solution, including the procurement of all parts? What is the difference in total unit cost between the turnkey solution and the "assembly only" cost?

❑ What is the CM's average turnaround time once an order becomes official? If you are working with an international contractor, has it verified that the quoted turnaround time includes shipping?

❑ What are the CM's minimum order quantity requirements? Does that requirement differ depending on who is supplying the parts for the production run?

❑ Is the CM capable of sourcing bare printed circuit boards (PCBs) in any color desired?

❑ Is the surface finish quality what you are looking for?

❑ Do the parts have the same level of precision and fit that you desire?

❑ Does the CM have a non-disclosure agreement (NDA) and/or a documented policy on intellectual property to govern the partnership and give you the protections you desire for your open source hardware?

❑ Does the potential CM have any current or former customers that can be independently contacted for their opinions on working with that particular CM?

❑ Will the CM accept orders without requiring that its own design for manufacturability (DFM) engineering be applied to the design, especially if that engineering service comes at an additional cost?

❑ Can the CM support your materials and process requirements (i.e., solder and flux type, Restriction of Hazardous Substances [RoHS] or conflict-free compliance, 100% testing of each solder joint)?

❑ Is the CM accepting of both infrequent and unpredictable orders with potentially varied unit quantities in each order?

❑ Which CAD file formats does the factory use?

❑ Is the factory responsive to your requests?

SparkFun's Core Design for Manufacturability Standards

❑ Scrub the design and bill of materials (BOM). There are dozens of design tradeoffs to consider:

- Performance of the part versus requirements of the design.
- Can you swap plated through hole (PTH) parts for surface-mount device (SMD) parts for ease of manufacturing?
- Consider size, cost, availability, minimum order quantity (MOQ), and other factors.
- Do you have a vendor for the new parts? (It can take weeks or months to set up new vendors.)
- Are there long lead times?
- Are there shortages?
- What is the minimum order quantity?
- Do you have a plan for end-of-life (EOL) components?
- Can the footprints of parts on the printed circuit board be modified to better fit the manufacturing process?

❑ PCB board

- Does a pin 1 indicator need to be added?
- Do polarity indicators need to be added?
- Does the cream layer need to be reduced?
- Can you reduce the size of the PCB?
- Is the board thickness appropriate?

❑ Layout of the traces that need to be redrawn to:

- Reduce the number of vias.

- Reduce the length of traces.

- Reduce the complexity of the circuit.

❑ Silkscreen

- Review it to make sure it will print clearly.

- Add labels.

- Add important instructions.

❑ PCB panelization

- Are there connectors on the edge of a board that will interfere with components on the neighboring copy of the board?

SparkFun's Ancillary Design for Manufacturability Standards

❑ Add fiducials for ease of repeatable manufacturing and automated optical inspection (AOI). Fiducials are tiny metal dots on the edge of the board and sometimes the panel.

❑ Add side bars to aid in handling while in panel form with mouse bites. Mouse bites are small perforations used to hold the side bars to the boards and can be easily snapped off in postproduction.

❑ Consider the user experience versus the cost of manufacturing. For example, different LED colors are better for the user experience, but using all red LEDs is cheaper in terms of cost and placement than sourcing multiple LED colors.

❑ Stenciling solder paste by hand requires a smaller panel versus an automated stenciling machine capable of handling larger panels.

❑ PTH connectors have more mechanical anchoring for robustness, but they increase the complexity and cost of manufacturing due to the extra soldering step needed.

❑ Consider the PCB color. Green is cheap. White PCBs turn yellow during reflow if the manufacturer is not careful.

❑ Consider assembled PCB cleaning. Most mass-produced electronics require cleaning to remove a chemical residue that can break down solder connections over time. However, not all parts can withstand a wash cycle. Does your design contain parts that cannot be washed?

❑ Consider how the end device will be tested. Where are the test points? Is programming required? Do you have to take it outside to get a GPS lock? How fast is the test procedure?

❏ Is this a kit—that is, will the user put the parts together? Does it require multiple pieces, such as a board + USB cable + screws?

❏ Do printed materials need to go in the box?

❏ Are you shipping to the European Union? Do all the components need to be RoHS compliant? Do all the components need to be child friendly?

❏ Is this design double-sided? That doubles the manufacturing cost, but is a tradeoff that is often made to reduce PCB size.

❏ Can the reflow oven handle and not damage the parts on the double-reflow side?

❏ Consider the PCB panel's overall width. Will it fit in the pick-and-place machine? Will it fit on the conveyor belt of the reflow oven?

❏ Can the part footprints be optically inspected easily during the automated optical inspection (AOI) step? Can the AOI machine recognize 0603 versus 0402 component footprints?

Troubleshooting

❏ Is your product something that can be manufactured in the first place?

❏ Are your parts readily available?

❏ Did you convert your files into formats the factory can use? (Do not rely on the factory to perform this conversion for you.)

❏ Can the manufacturer correctly read the files you've sent?

❏ Do you require precision thin-wall machined plastic or complicated multipart injection molds that are hard to make?

❏ Are your traces too small or too close to the edge of the PCB?

❏ Did you include a centroid file for assembly? Remember: It is your responsibility to ensure the manufacturer has the correct combination of files to make your product.

❏ Did you make your parts makeable to begin working with by working with a manufacturer at an early stage to get its feedback on the ease of fabrication of the product you are designing?

❏ Have you reached out to other designers, particularly those in the open source hardware community? You might get lucky and come across someone who has already been down the same path and can help you.

❏ Did you send your parts with proper dimensions?

❏ Did you include tolerances?

❏ Did you include materials selections and material finishes?

❏ Did your BOM include parts numbers, quantities, part function, revision information, and assembly information?

❑ Did you get samples made of your product before approving a whole manufacturing run?

❑ Did you create a requirements document for the manufacturer, labeling each requirement with the words "MUST," "SHOULD," or "MAY"?

❑ Did you specify and communicate every last detail?

❑ For small production runs, have you tested each and every product before boxing the units and shipping them to customers?

❑ For larger production runs, have you tested samples from each batch of your product to confirm that the factory quality control process is effective?

Mach 30's Documentation Ground Rules

J. Simmons

We've all been there. After a long day of working in the shop/lab/makerspace/garage, we have made amazing progress on our project, but now as open source hardware developers we have to go back and document what we did. Fellow developers are waiting on the documentation to continue their own work. Fans are waiting so they can follow along at home. And, the very definition of open source hardware means we aren't really done until we have written sufficient documentation so that someone else can recreate our work.

What a chore! What a pain!

Mach 30's documentation ground rules help ease this pain by building documentation into the process. Lessons from projects like the Shepard Test Stand and Ground Sphere ground station have taught us it is much easier to capture documentation as we go along than to come back and do it later.

1. Every project needs a home (for its documentation).

   Start project documentation as soon as you have the idea for a project. Capture its purpose, your general design concept, the budget, and other details right from the beginning. At Mach 30, we have an understandable preference to use Open Design Engine for hosting our projects. Open Design Engine is a one-stop project-hosting portal that is free for open source hardware projects. Its users can add wikis, forums, source code repositories, and more with just a couple of clicks, making Open Design Engine a strong choice for projects of all types and sizes. Of course, there are several other sites to choose from, and in a pinch, even setting up a folder in Google Drive will suffice to get things started. Our experience has shown that it is much easier to expand existing documentation than to port it from one location/format to another. In your project development, you should find what works for you and start even small projects in your preferred solution. That way, projects that grow beyond your expectations are already in fertile soil and don't need to be transplanted.

2. Document before you act.

As soon as you make any decisions about a project, write them down. If you have an idea about which embedded processor board you want to use in your next project, start your preliminary design document and your bill of materials. If you're getting ready to go shopping for parts (online or offline), create a draft BOM and do your shopping based on its contents. Even if there are items for which you have only a partial description (e.g., you know you need a magnet, but maybe not which one), put them on the BOM and leave the part number blank. Then keep the BOM handy while you are shopping and fill in the blanks as you make your purchases. It is much easier to add to and modify existing documentation as you work through the design and testing of a project than it is to create all of the documentation at the end from memory or random notes.

3. Document as you act.

So you saw and followed Rule 2. Good. But you aren't done: you must also document as you act. Take pictures of each and every step as you build and test prototypes. For this process-oriented documentation, a cellphone camera is perfectly fine. Capturing some detail about every step and doing so easily is far more important than capturing specific steps in excruciating detail. And photos aren't the only thing you need to capture. Take notes (public notes are best, but handwritten or even— gasp—private notes are acceptable as long as you make sure to record them publicly shortly thereafter). The Shepard team uses Open Design Engine's News module to record development logs. These development logs are essential to keeping the team and the public informed about the progress and changes in Shepard projects. Such development logs also provide a reference from which more formal documentation can be written and allow anyone following the bleeding edge of the project to replicate your work.

For those developers who think only the final documentation counts, consider this. Presenting a project as a fait accompli blunts two of the major advantages of open source methods: contributions from volunteers and the educational benefits of open source methods. Without up-to-date documentation, potential contributors cannot follow along and offer up their own ideas or make other contributions, because they have no way to know about the design or the work that needs doing. Similarly, the opportunity to explore the full history of a project makes it possible to learn lessons from the project team about what does and does not work (in terms of design and process).

4. Document after you act.

This is the one documentation ground rule everyone knows. In fact, they usually assume it is the only one, making it a huge chore to satisfy. If you follow Rules 2 and 3, however, documenting after you act becomes more about formatting and editing. In addition, creating final documentation from draft documentation is something that can be done by a group of people (unlike documenting exactly what you spent all afternoon doing), giving your entire project team and community a way to help out with the documentation.

5. If there aren't minutes, the meeting didn't happen.

This is one of Mach 30's general ground rules. If there is a meeting between two or more project team members (with or without third parties), it is essential that those members present take minutes of the meeting. Recordings and transcriptions do not count; they are too long and too difficult to search through when you need to find the relevant parts of a meeting. Someone needs to record the essential elements of the discussion(s), making sure to capture individuals' opinions/ideas, agreed-upon action items, and the final outcome of any decisions made in the meeting.

Without this documentation, people who did not attend the meeting cannot get caught up, and those who did attend the meeting won't have a clear record to refer back to when they can't remember what happened at the meeting. The exception to this rule is work sessions. When people get together to produce a specific product (be it physical or documentation), there is little to no need for minutes. The product (and its accompanying documentation—you did follow the advice to "document as you act," didn't you?) serves as the record of the work session.

6. Show me.

To borrow a phrase from Missouri, don't just assert something works the way you say it should, show me! Make a demo video. Take pictures of the project working. Document your test plan and results. Take screenshots of companion desktop applications or websites with the results showing. Then post this documentation on the forums or in a project wiki or development log or wherever.

Blinky Buildings Source Files

Blinky Buildings is a simple kit to teach people how to make derivatives of open source hardware. You are welcome to create a derivative of this kit as long as it abides by the Open Source Hardware Definition. All source files for the Blinky Buildings kit are online at http://bit.ly/blinkybuildings. This appendix contains the README file and source files suitable for a print version of this book.

README

This README file consists of the following headings: About this Kit, Material and Tools, Attribution, and Licensing. README files do not always contain the exact same information, but if you're building open source hardware, you can use this README file as a guide.

About This Kit

This kit blinks 20 LEDs from an ATtiny85. The code was written in Arduino and uses a technique called charlieplexing to drive multiple LEDs using just 5 pins of the ATtiny.

This kit assumes you know how to solder. If not, there are plenty of online tutorials on soldering. The kit is fairly quick to put together, taking roughly 10 minutes, and the chip has been programmed for you!

Materials and Tools

Here are the parts you need to get started:

20 LEDs (with a maximum current of 20 mA)

5 resistors (for 3.2 V forward-voltage LEDs, I used 680 ohm resistors)

1 ATtiny85

1 battery holder

1 3 V battery

1 switch

Here are the tools you'll need to get started:

Soldering iron

Solder

Wire clippers

More information and documentation, including an assembly guide, lives at http://bit.ly/blinkybuildings.

Attribution

The code for this project was downloaded from http://code.google.com/p/avr-hardware-random-number-generation/. The code was written by Geoff Steele. Alicia Gibb altered the code by commenting out the fade functions so the building blinks LEDs on and off rather than fade LEDs on and off.

The original Fritzing design by Davy Uittenbogerd of charlieplexing 20 LEDs was downloaded from http://fritzing.org/projects/charlieplex-snowfallshooting-star-20-leds. Alicia Gibb altered this schematic into a Blinky Building form factor.

The original code and the hardware source files are both under a CC-BY-SA Creative Commons license.

Code: CC-BY-SA: Geoff Steele.

Fritzing layout: CC-BY-SA: Davy Uittenbogerd.

Blinky Building schematic and board file: CC-BY-SA: Alicia Gibb.

Licensing

Blinky Buildings is an open source hardware product and follows the Open Source Hardware Definition: www.oshwa.org/definition.

The license on the source files for Blinky Buildings is CC-BY-SA.

Distributed as is; no warranty given. Not suitable for people who might eat electronics.

Source Files

For the ease of reading, the main source files (schematic, board file, and code) are included here as images. (See Figure F.1 and Figure F.2.) All source files for the Blinky Buildings kit, including the schematic, board file, 3D-printed enclosures, and 1:1 conversion, are online at http://bit.ly/blinkybuildings.

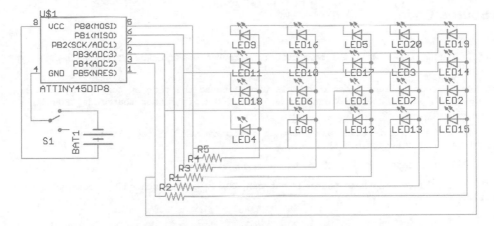

Figure F.1   Blinky Buildings Schematic.
(Source: CC-BY-SA Alicia Gibb)

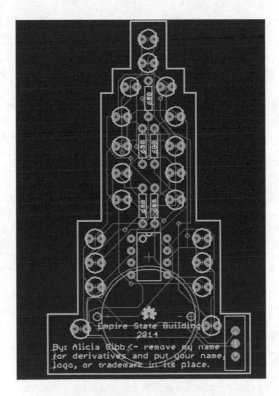

Figure F.2   Blinky Buildings board layout.
(Source: CC-BY-SA Alicia Gibb)

Source Code

```
#include <Entropy.h>
```

/* Original code downloaded from https://github.com/strykeroz/ATTiny85-20-LED-snowflakes

Original code by Geoff Steele. Alicia Gibb altered the code by commenting out the fade functions so the building blinks LEDs on and off rather than fade LEDs on and off.

The original code is still all there if others wanted to keep playing with it; just put the duty cycle back in,

which have a fade effect rather than a blink effect.

The delays have also been changed, but can easily be reinstated by looking at the original code.

```
 ___ _ _ _ _ ___
/ __| |__ _ _ _ _| (_) _ _ _ | | ___ _|__ \ / _ \ _ _ _ ___ _
| | | '_ \ / _` | '_| | |/ _ \ '_ \| |/ _ \ \/ / __) | | | / _| '_ \ / _ \ \ /\ / /
| |__| | | | (_| | | | | | | __/ |_) | | | __/> < / __/| |_| \_ \ | | | (_) \ V V /
\___|_| |_|\_,_|_| |_|_|\__| .__/|_|\___/_/\_\____|\__/|___/_| |_|\__/ \_/\_/
|_|
```

Charlieplexing 20 LEDs using 5 ATTiny85 pins with fading by

varying the duty cycle of each LED in the 'tail'.

ATTiny85 connections

Leg Function

1 Reset, no connection

2 D3 GREEN

3 D4 ORANGE

4 GND

5 D0 WHITE

6 D1 BLUE

7 D2 YELLOW

8 +5V

Tested on ATTiny85 running at 8MHz.

*/

//// Each block of 4 LEDs in the array is groupled by a common anode (+, long leg)

```
//// for simplicity of wiring on bread board, using a color code
#define GREEN 0
#define ORANGE 1
#define WHITE 2
#define BLUE 3
#define YELLOW 4

//// Pin definitions {GREEN, ORANGE, WHITE, BLUE, YELLOW}
const int charliePin[5] = {
  3, 4, 0, 1, 2};

//// Charlieplexed LED definitions (current flowing from-to pairs)
const int LED[20][2] = {
  {
    ORANGE, GREEN }
  , //// 0 (GREEN GROUP)
  {
    WHITE, GREEN }
  , //// 1
  {
    BLUE, GREEN }
  , //// 2
  {
    YELLOW, GREEN }
  , //// 3
  {
    GREEN, ORANGE }
  , //// 4 (ORANGE GROUP)
  {
    WHITE, ORANGE }
  , //// 5
  {
    BLUE, ORANGE }
  , //// 6
```

```
      {
        YELLOW, ORANGE }
      , //// 7
      {
        GREEN, WHITE }
      , //// 8 (WHITE GROUP)
      {
        ORANGE, WHITE }
      , //// 9
      {
        BLUE, WHITE }
      , //// 10
      {
        YELLOW, WHITE }
      , //// 11
      {
        GREEN, BLUE }
      , //// 12 (BLUE GROUP)
      {
        ORANGE, BLUE }
      , //// 13
      {
        WHITE, BLUE }
      , //// 14
      {
        YELLOW, BLUE }
      , //// 15
      {
        GREEN, YELLOW }
      , //// 16 (YELLOW GROUP)
      {
        ORANGE, YELLOW }
      , //// 17
```

```
  {
    WHITE, YELLOW }
  , //// 18
  {
    BLUE, YELLOW } //// 19
  };


//// Other
int current = 0; //// LED in array with current focus
int previous = 0; //// Previous LED that was lit


void setup() {
  Entropy.Initialize();
  randomSeed(Entropy.random());
}


void loop() {
  unsigned long loopCount = 0; // Used to determine duty cycle of each LED
  unsigned long timeNow = millis(); //
  unsigned long displayTime = 10 + random(10); // Milliseconds to spend at each
focus LED in descent
  while(millis()- timeNow < (displayTime+current)) { // Animation slows toward
end
    loopCount++;
    //// The "snowflake" gets full duty cycle. When it gets to the end, hold it
at the end until the tail collapses.
    if (current > 19) charlieOFF(19); //This is altered from the original code,
to turn LEDs off once the blink is over
    else charlieON(current);
    //// Each member of tail has reduced duty cycle, and never gets to the final
position
    if(!(loopCount % 3)) if(current-1 >=0 && current-1 < 19)
charlieOFF(current-1);
    if(!(loopCount % 6)) if(current-2 >=0 && current-2 < 19)
charlieOFF(current-2);
    if(!(loopCount % 9)) if(current-3 >=0 && current-3 < 19)
charlieOFF(current-3);
```

```
        if(!(loopCount % 12)) if(current-4 >=0 && current-4 < 19)
charlieOFF(current-4);

    }


    current++;

    if(current==23) { //// start over

        //Alicia commented out the below code to make the LEDs blink on and off
rather than fade out.

        //// Now fade out the snowflake in that final position #19

        for(int dutyCycle = 3; dutyCycle <= 15; dutyCycle += 3) {

          //loopCount = 0;

          //timeNow = millis();

          //while(millis() - timeNow < (displayTime+current*2)) { //// fade out as
slow as animation has achieved by now

          // loopCount++;

          if(!(loopCount % dutyCycle)) charlieON(19);

          else charlieOFF(19);

          // }

        }

        current = 0;

        charlieOFF(19); // Turn off the remaining (possibly) lit LED

        delay(50);

        ////+ random(3000)); // Then rinse, repeat ... after a short pause

    }

}


//// -------------------------------------------------------------------------
//// Turns on LED #thisLED. Turns off all LEDs if the value passed is out of
range.
////

void charlieON(int thisLED) {

    //// Turn off previous (reduces overhead, only switch 2 pins rather than 5)

    digitalWrite(charliePin[LED[previous][1]], LOW); //// Ensure internal pull-ups
aren't engaged on INPUT mode

    pinMode(charliePin[LED[previous][0]], INPUT);

    pinMode(charliePin[LED[previous][1]], INPUT);
```

```
  //// Turn on the one that's in focus
  if(thisLED >= 0 && thisLED <= 19) {
    pinMode(charliePin[LED[thisLED][0]], OUTPUT);
    pinMode(charliePin[LED[thisLED][1]], OUTPUT);
    digitalWrite(charliePin[LED[thisLED][0]], LOW);
    digitalWrite(charliePin[LED[thisLED][1]], HIGH);
  }
  previous = thisLED;
}


//// ---------------------------------------------------------------------------
//// Turns off LED #thisLED.
////
void charlieOFF(int thisLED) {
  digitalWrite(charliePin[LED[thisLED][1]], LOW); //// Ensure internal pull-ups
aren't engaged on INPUT mode
  pinMode(charliePin[LED[thisLED][0]], INPUT);
  pinMode(charliePin[LED[thisLED][1]], INPUT);
}
```

Glossary

This is a glossary of the bold terms within this book. Many terms cover the spectrum of open source hardware, including a wealth of manufacturing terminology. Many definitions of the following terms are contextual to open source hardware.

A

assembly machinery Specialized equipment that assembles items, such as a reflow oven or pick-and-place system.

attribution When using a design with a license containing an attribution clause, you must publish or redistribute the original design or a derivative design, giving credit to the author of the original design.

automated optical inspection (AOI) A machine that optically inspects solder joints and verifies quality.

B

bill of materials (BOM) The list of materials or components that your product is made of.

C

centroid file A file containing information about the location of each component to be placed on the circuit board. The centroid file is commonly a .CSV file that specifies the x, y coordinates of each part in relation to one corner of the PCB.

clone An open source hardware product that has been directly copied and is in line with the Open Source Hardware Definition because it does not infringe on the trademarks of other companies. Also called a copy.

components placed per hour (CPH) The number of components a machine can place on a PCB in 1 hour.

contract manufacturer (CM) The manufacturer with which you contract to build your product.

copy An open source hardware product that has been directly copied and is in line with the Open Source Hardware Definition because it does not infringe on the trademarks of other companies. Also called a clone.

cost–benefit analysis A comparison of the cost, quantity, and speed to obtain a product or component. Also called a quality–price matrix.

counterfeit A piece of open source hardware for which the trademark has been copied onto a clone or derivative piece of hardware, and that does not abide by the Open Source Hardware Definition because the trademark is not owned by the person or company creating the derivative. Proper attribution does not include copying trademarks. Copying trademarks is also illegal.

cream layer The layer that is used to create solder paste stencils.

D

definition The outcome of the product definition phase.

derivative Open source hardware that has been altered or modified but is based on an original design by another person or company.

design for manufacturing (DFM) Modifying the shape, layout, or construction of a product to make it easier and faster to manufacture.

design history file A record of what you built, what you changed, and why you changed something between design iterations.

design input The formal definition you created during the definition phase.

design output Every successive prototype you build (whether it works or not).

design phase The flow going back and forth between generating and testing ideas that naturally occurs while building something.

design review The process of reviewing the function of your design with your peers.

dimension A layer designated as the outer perimeter of a PCB board.

dual licensing A type of licensing in which some source files or parts of your hardware are open source and some are closed source.

E

Eagle PCB power tool A tool that generates an Eagle script (SCR) file from a DXF file.

end of life (EOL) The point at which a component or product is no longer manufactured.

execute script A command in Eagle to execute scripts.

F

fiducial Marks on the PCB board critical for the automated assembly equipment; a reference point to orient the robotic part placement device in regard to the circuit board.

firmware Software that runs on hardware other than general-purpose computing platforms such as personal computers, tablets, or phones. This term is a double entendre referring to the mixing of software running on hardware (i.e., soft + hard = firm).

fork The point at which a developer or set of developers starts developing with a copy of the code.

G

ganged programmer A programming platform created to program many devices at once.

Gerbers Board fabrication files that describe the layout of board layers in a vector format.

H

housed board A PCB board within an enclosure.

I

Import DXF Polygons An Eagle user language program that generates a board outline directly in Eagle given a DXF file.

IPC standards Standards developed by Interconnecting and Packaging Electronic Circuits, the dominant accrediting organization within the electronics manufacturing industry.

K

kit A collection of parts that are assembled by the end user to create a product.

L

layout review The process of reviewing the layout of your design with your peers.

license Permission to do something, usually conditioned on some sort of behavior or action.

M

manufacturer part number A part number generated by the manufacturer, to be included in your bill of materials.

manufacturing The process of making your prototype in mass.

manufacturing resource planning (MRP) A software package that offers a scheduling tool and inventory control.

minimum order quantity (MOQ) The minimum number of parts that a vendor will allow you to order.

mouse bites Small perforations used to hold the side bars to the boards; they can be easily snapped off in post production.

N

noncommercial A designation indicating that any derivatives made from a design cannot be used for commercial advantage or monetary exchange and are not considered open source hardware.

O

open source hardware Hardware whose design is made publicly available so that anyone can study, modify, distribute, make, and sell the design or hardware based on that design. The hardware's source—that is, the design from which it is made—is available in the preferred format for making modifications to it.

P

panelization Smaller PCB designs multiplied into a larger panel.

part library A library of parts generated for PCB layout.

part PCB footprint The footprint of the component on the PCB.

PCB layout The process of converting a schematic into a physical PCB board.

plated through hole (PTH) Components meant to be placed through the PCB board.

printed circuit assembly (PCA) A PCB fully populated with components.

product definition phase The phase of development where you nail down the specific details of your purpose, resources, scope, and critical requirements.

production capacity The number of items a manufacturer can create per amount of time.

purpose A grand (and possibly vague) idea for something you want to build.

Q

quality–price matrix A comparison of the cost, quantity, and speed to obtain a product.

R

release phase The design that meets all of your critical requirements.

S

schematic The plan for how all components will function together.

schematic capture The process during which you focus on reproducing the logical design of your bread-board circuit.

schematic symbol A symbol that designates a certain type of circuit design in a schematic.

scope An understanding of what you practically will (or will not) be able to do.

share alike A type of license in which any future derivatives of the original design must also be filed under the same share alike license. It is commonly used in the open source hardware world.

specifications and requirements Key features of a project including anything from design elements to production requirements, that represents all the information you need to do and to build for your project to be a success.

stand-alone board A PCB board without an enclosure.

supply chain A network of vendors that supply parts.

surface-mount device (SMD) A component meant to be placed on the top and sometimes on the bottom of the PCB board.

T

takt time The time it takes to produce a completed unit from start to finish (often referred to as "the drumbeat" of the assembly line).

testing Checking whether the prototype meets the requirements listed in the product definition. Also called validation and verification.

turnkey solution An approach in which the contract manufacturer handles all the purchasing of inventory for each production run.

U

user manual The guide for how you want your users to use your product.

V

validation and verification Checking whether the prototype meets the requirements listed in the product definition. Also called testing.

vendor part number A part number generated by the vendor, to be included in your bill of materials.

Index

3D CAD software, free and open source, 109. *See also specific packages.*

3D design files, sharing information online, 133–134

3D modeling software, web sources, 109. *See also specific packages.*

3D printable hardware, research benefits in academia, 258

3D printer bureaus, 97

3D printers
  costs, 96–97
  derivatives, 96–97
  as manufacturing tools, 107–108
  open source, sources of, 97–98, 109
  RepRap printer, 95–97, 109
  research and production, 107–108

3D printers, finding designs to print
  attribution, 99
  Beaglebone Black case, 99–100
  with Blender, 100–105
  derivative designs, 100–105
  existing designs, 98–100
  licensing considerations, 99
  noncommercial licenses, 99
  remixing a design, 100–105
  share-alike licenses, 99
  .STL files, 99
  web sources, 98, 109

3D printing
  personal manufacturing, 155
  products from OSHW, 140–142
  software for, 70

3D Robotics, 142, 245

9DOF board, SparkFun Electronics, 213–214

Academic applications for OSHW. *See* OSHW in academia.

Academic freedom, 254

Acknowledgment (credit). *See* Attributions.

Adafruit, 131, 227

Agricultural products. *See* Products from OSHW, industry and agriculture.

Air and space exploration. *See* Products from OSHW, air and space exploration.

Aleph Objects, 141, 237

Anderson, Chris, 7, 142, 245

AOI (automated optical inspection) machine, 176, 179

Appropedia Foundation, 269, 274

Archives, recommended, 61. *See also* Backing up files.

Arduino board derivatives. *See also* Derivatives.
  board outline, determining, 87–89
  board outline, importing, 88–89
  Christmas tree ornament (example), 85
  components, choosing, 86
  footprint, reducing, 87
  housed boards, 84
  manufacturing, 91–93
  microcontroller, choosing, 86
  preparation for, 84, 86–87
  shapes, 83–84
  space-limiting components, identifying, 86
  speedometer board (example), 85
  stand-alone boards, 84

Arduino board derivatives, layout
  clearance for screw caps, 91
  moving from Eagle to CAD, 91
  placing constrained components, 89

Arduino board derivatives, layout (*continued*)
  scale printouts, 91
  spacing for programming headers, 89–91
  testing for fit, 91
Arduino, 66-68, 257
Arduino, case study, 157–160
Arduino orbital shaker, 258
Arduino and Wiring, 46
Arduino trademark, 67–68
Arias, Gerard Rubio, 147–148
Armadillo Aerospace, 29
Art, reproducing, 250–251
Art/Science Bangalore, 148
Artwork. *See* Gerbers.
Asynchronous *vs.* synchronous discussions, 29
Attributions
  accuracy, 68
  Blinky Buildings project,
    301–302
  citing, 68
  definition, 50
  distribution terms, 15–16
  giving, 79–81
  onboard bylines, 80–81
  per OSHW Definition 1.0, 68
  printing 3D designs, 99
Automated optical inspection (AOI) machine, 176,
  179
Automation systems for manufacturing, 190,
  191–194
Automotive industry, products from OSHW, 138
Auxiliary design files, project element, 19

Backing up files, recommended archives, 61
badcafe process, 89
Banzi, Massimo, 7, 227, 247
Barragan, Hernando, 46, 66
Batteries and power, for wearables,
  123–124

Baxter robots, 190, 191–194
Bdeir, Ayah, 7–8
Beaglebone Black case, 99–100
Benjegerdes, Troy, 4
Bessen, James, 256, 257
Best Practices, 17. *See also* OSHW Definition 1.0;
  OSHW Prime Directive.
Better products with an open business model,
  238–239
Bicycles, from OSHW, 138
Bike projects, wearables, 112
Bill of materials (BOM). *See* BOM (bill of materials).
Binary code, 44
BioCurious, 148
Biomedical research machine, from OSHW, 149
Biotechnology, from OSHW, 148–150
Blender program
  cutting shapes, 103–105
  description, 100–102
  designing from scratch, 105–107
  importing a 3D model, 102
  keyboard shortcuts, 102
  moving a 3D model, 102–103
  printing 3D designs, 100–105
  scaling a 3D model, 102–103
  toolbox add-on, 101
  user interface, 101
  web address, 109
Blinky Buildings project
  Board file, sample, 75
  BOM (bill of materials), 73,
    75
  comment block, 71
  Eagle program, 70
  enclosure case, 77–79
  Fritzing project, 70
  giving attribution, 79–81
  KiCad program, 70
  making a derivative of, 79
  onboard byline, 80–81

overview, 69–70

PCB, sample, 69

schematics, sample, 72, 74

suppliers, cost-benefit analysis, 76–77

Blinky Buildings project, design files

attribution, 301–302

as images, 303

licensing, 302

materials and tools, 301–302

overview, 70–73

README, 301

source code, 304–309

About This Kit, 301

Board file, sample, 75

Board thickness, in manufacturing, 175

Boards

Arduino derivatives. *See* Arduino board derivatives.

laying out. *See* Replay construction kit.

layout. *See* Arduino board derivatives, layout.

Bolton, Matt, 57

BOM (bill of materials)

Blinky Buildings project, 73, 75

designing hardware, workflow, 60

project element, 20

sample from the Lasersaur project, 225–226

troubleshooting, 201–203

Books and publications

"Build It, Share It, Profit," 235, 247

Design Control Guidance for Medical Device Manufacturers, 57

"Error Cost Calculation through the Project Life Cycle," 216

Getting Started with Aduino, 227

The International Journal for Service Learning in Engineering, 268

The Long Tail, 7

Makers, 245

"Six Myths about Venture Capitalists," 249

Boothroyd Dewhurst Inc., 208

Bootloaders, 47

Botanicalls, from OSHW, 135, 138

Bowyer, Adrian, 95

Bracelet wearables, 115–116

Brand, in a business model, 234–235

Brownstein, Jason, 77-79

Buechley, Leah, 66, 67, 112-116

Bug Labs, 7

"Build It, Share It, Profit," 235, 247

Business model. *See also* **Open Source Hardware and Open Design Business Model Matrix.**

the brand, 234–235

trademarks, 235

traditional business strategies, 233–234

CAD software. *See* **3D CAD software.**

CC (Creative Commons) licenses

basis for open licenses, 32–33

copyright protection, 37

Centralized hub for sharing information online, 129-130

Centroid file information, 200

CERN OHL (Open Hardware license), in the history of open hardware, 8-9

Chaffee, Macklin, 8

Change management, 57

Channels, in an open business model, 248

Checklists for OSHW

CMs (contract manufacturers), finding, 291–292

concept refinement, 289

designing hardware, 58–59

labeling hardware, 283

managing iteration, 289–290

musts and mays, 284

preparing to manufacture, 290

security do's and don'ts, 285–286

troubleshooting, 294–295

Checklists for OSHW, SparkFun
  ancillary manufacturability standards, 293–294
  core manufacturability standards, 292–293
China, as manufacturing partner, 169–170
Christmas tree ornament (example), 85
Circuit boards. *See* PCBs (printed circuit boards).
Circuit diagram (illustration), for wearables, 122
Citations (academic), 264
Citations (OSHW). *See* Attributions.
Clearance for screw caps, 91
Clones, 66. *See also* Derivatives.
Closed parts, 243–245
CMs (contract manufacturers), 168–170, 291–292
CNC (computer-numeric control) machines, personal manufacturing, 155–156
CNC (computer-numeric control) router, products from OSHW, 139–140
Collaboration
  case study, 158–159
  in an open business model, 240–241
Comment block, 71
Communication between houseplants and people, 135, 138
Community building through documentation, 229
Compilers, 46
Components, choosing, 86
Components, sewable, 118–119
Components placed per hour (CPH), 181
Computer-numeric control (CNC) machines, personal manufacturing, 155–156
Computer-numeric control (CNC) router, products from OSHW, 139–140
Concept refinement, 58–59, 289
Conditional copying, 38
Conductive textiles, 117
Configurations, 45–46
Consortium business model, 246
Constrained components, placing, 89
Consumer electronics, case study, 160–163

Contract manufacturers (CMs), 168–170, 291–292
Cooper, Danese, 9
Copenhagen Suborbitals, 144
Copies, definition, 66. *See also* Derivatives.
Copying conditionally, 38
Copyleft (viral) licenses, 23
Copyright. *See also* Patent; Trademark.
  applied to hardware, 22–23
  automatic protection, 32
  CC (Creative Commons) licenses, 37
  conditional copying, 38
  copyleft (viral) licenses, 23
  definition, 33
  duration of protection, 34
  free-software licenses, 22–23
  for hardware, 36–37
  licensing, 36–37
  on nonfunctional design elements, 37
  obtaining, 34
  open-source licenses, 22–23
  overview, 33–34
  vs. patents, 13, 35
  permissive licenses, 23
  violations, 34
Corona wires, 119–120
Cost of fixing mistakes, 216
Counterfeit, definition, 66. *See also* Derivatives.
CPH (components placed per hour), 181
Cream layer, reducing, 175
Creative Commons (CC) licenses. *See* CC (Creative Commons) licenses.
Credit (acknowledgment). *See* Attributions.
Critical features first, 61–62
Crowd funding, for an open business, 249
CubeSats, 143
Current length, extending in wearables, 120
Cutting shapes with Blender, 103–105

Derivatives. *See also* **Arduino board derivatives; RepRap printer.**

of the Blinky Buildings project, 79

case study, 157–160

change categories, 66

definition, 66

examples of. *See* Blinky Buildings project; LilyPad.

printing 3D designs, 100–105

printing on 3D printers, 100

processes and practices, 24–25

Derived works

as defined by OSHW Definition 1.0, 65–66

distribution terms, 15

***Design Control Guidance for Medical Device Manufacturers,* 57**

Design files

3D, sharing online, 133–134

auxiliary, 19

as documentation, 223–225

for Blinky Buildings, 302–309

hosting, 22

original, 18–19

Design for manufacture and assembly (DFMA), 208–209

Design for manufacturing, rule checking, 60

Design for manufacturing (DFM). *See* **DFM (design for manufacturing).**

Design input, 57

Design output, 57

Design patents, 34

Design phase, 57

Design review, 60

Designing

hackable hardware, 215–216

for manufacturing, 174–177

vs. prototyping, 57

Designing hardware

change management, 57

checklist of questions, 58–59

concept refinement, 58–59

constant iteration, 61

critical features first, 61–62

design input, 57

design output, 57

design phase, 57

designing *vs.* prototyping, 57

determining profitability, 58–59

exit strategy, 61–62

iterative design, 58–59

manufacturing package, 62

manufacturing phase, 57

potential problems, 59

processes and practices, 21–22

product definition, 56

product definition phase, 56

project phases, 56–58

prototyping, potential problems, 59

purpose, 56

recommended archives, 61

release phase, 57

requirements, 56

scope, 56

shipping untested hardware, 62

specifications, 56

testing phase, 57, 62

validation phase. *See* Testing.

verification phase. *See* Testing.

waterfall method, 58

Designing hardware

artwork. *See* Gerbers.

BOM (bill of materials), 60

design for manufacturing, 60

design review, 60

Gerbers (board fabrication files), 60

layout phase, 60

Designing hardware (*continued*)

layout review, 60

manufacturer part numbers, 60

part PCB footprints, 60

parts library, 60

PCB layout, 60

prints. *See* Gerbers.

schematic capture, 60

schematic symbols, 60

schematics, 60

selecting your parts, 60

vendor part numbers, 60

Dewhurst, Peter, 208

DFM (design for manufacturing)

role in troubleshooting, 198–199

standards, 175–177

DFMA (design for manufacture and assembly), 208-209

Digital fabrication machines, personal manufacturing, 155–156

Disaster relief, products from OSHW, 144–145

Distributing open source hardware, processes and practices, 23

Distribution terms

attributions, 15–16

derived works, 15

documentation, 15

free redistribution, 15

licenses, 16

necessary software, 15

non-discrimination, 16

restrictions, 16

scope, 15

technology neutrality, 16

DIYBio, 148

DIYdrones, 142-143

DMF (digital microfluidic) system, from OSHW, 150

DNA analysis, from OSHW, 149

Documentation. *See also* **BOM (bill of materials); OSHW Prime Directive on documentation.**

community building, 229

design files, 223–225

distribution terms, 15

Mach 30's rules for, 297–299

OHAI-kit, 227, 228

per Open Source Hardware Definition, 223

product webpage, 221–223

for products from OSHW, 132–133

README.txt, 220–221

requirements documents, 212

visuals, 226–227

for wearables, 120–123

Documentation, tutorials

FAQs (frequently asked questions), 229

Hello World project, 227, 229

lunch break rule, 227, 229

overview, 226–227

testing and quality control, 188

Donations, funding an open business, 250

Dougherty, Dale, 7

Drones, products from OSHW, 142–143

Dropbot, 150

Dry cleaning wearables, 125

Dual licensing, open business model, 243–245

Eagle PCB Power Tools, 88

Eagle program

acceptable file formats, 17

getting, 70

Import DXF Polygons, 88

importing DXF files, 88–89

Eagle program, board layout

clearance for screw caps, 91

moving from Eagle to CAD, 91

placing constrained components, 89

scale printouts, 91

spacing for programming headers, 89–91

testing for fit, 91

Eden, Sahana, 144

Education and training, selling, 248. *See also* Teaching and service.

Education modular toolkits, from OSHW, 145, 147

EL (electroluminescent) wire, 119–120

Electric skillet reflow technique, 170–171

Electroluminescent glow, 119–120

Electronics, personal manufacturing, 156–157

Email *vs.* forums, 28

Empire State Building as PCB. *See* Blinky Buildings project.

Employees, in an open business model, 243

Enclosures
    Beaglebone Black case, 99–100
    case for a PCB, 77–79
    case study, 162–163
    from natural materials, 162

English, John, 267–268

Environmental preservation, from OSHW, 144–145

EOL (end of life) concerns, 175

Equipment. *See* Manufacturing, equipment.

"Error Cost Calculation through the Project Life Cycle," 216

Ethical bonuses, of an open business model, 241–242

Ewing, Tom, 279

Exit strategy, 61–62

Eyebeam workshop, in the history of open hardware, 7

Fabrication services, 157

Fabtotum 3D printer, 140–141

FAQs (frequently asked questions), 229

FARKUS assembly robot, 190, 191–194

Fashion, from OSHW, 147

Fiducial marks on PCBs, 200–201

Filabot 3D printer, 140–141

Filament extruder, 140–141

File formats, acceptable, 17

File types for effective communication, 200–204

Files, recommended for projects
    auxiliary design files, 19
    BOM (bill of materials), 20
    firmware, 20
    instructions and explanations, 21
    original design files, 18–19
    overview/introduction, 18
    photos, 20
    software, 20

Firmware. *See also* Software, firming up.
    definition, 44–45
    vs. firming up software, 44–45
    project files, 20
    softening, 47

Floor tiles from waste products, 270

FLORA line, 67, 118–119

Footprint, reducing, 87

Forks
    vs. configurations, 45–46
    firming up software, 45–46
    vs. plugins, 45–46
    standardizing software, 45–46

Forums *vs.* email, 28

Foundation business model, 246

Four Freedoms of open hardware, 6

FreeCAD program, 106, 109

Freeman, David, 4

Free-software licenses, 23

Frequently asked questions (FAQs), 229

Fried, Limor, 7

Fritzing project, 70

Fry, Ben, 66

Fundamental research, and ITAR (International Traffic in Arms Regulation), 50–51

Funding an open business
    crowd funding, 249
    donations, 250

Funding an open business (*continued*)
grants, 250
sources of money, 245–250
venture capital funding, 249
Funding OSHW in academia, 264

Ganged programmers, 188–189
Gear logo. *See* OSHW logo.
GenSpace, 148
Gerbers (board fabrication files), 60
Getting Started with Aduino, 227
Gibb, Alicia
Blinky Buildings project, 73
chair of the OHS (Open Hardware Summit), 8
at Eyebeam 2010, 7
founding of OSHWA, 9–10
Gilmer, Ken, 7
GitHub repository, 71, 134
Global Village Construction Set, 135
GPL licenses, 32–33
Gracey, Ken, 7
Grants, funding an open business, 250
Ground Sphere CubeSat Ground Station, 142
Guidelines. *See* Checklists.

Hacker ethic, 256
HacKIDemia, 145
Han, Momi, 169–170
Hardware
customizing. *See* Hardware, making more flexible.
open source, *vs.* open source software, 14
source files. *See* Design files.
standardizing. *See* Standardization, hardware.
Hardware, making more flexible
hardware interfaces, 49

mechanical hardware, 47–48
modularity as a design principle, 49
physical communication, 48
reimplementing the wheel, 49
standard electronic components, 47–48
Hardware interfaces
making hardware more flexible, 49
standardizing hardware, 49
Hardware layers of products from OSHW, 132–133
Hardware on request, 247
Heat exchanger, low-cost, 263
Hello World project, 227, 229
Hill, Benjamin Mako, 7
History of open hardware
CERN OHL (Open Hardware license), 8–9
Eyebeam workshop, 7
Four Freedoms of open hardware, 6
Linux Fund, 5
littleBits, 7
NYC Resistor, 9
OHANDA (Open Hardware Design Alliance), 6–8
OHF (Open Hardware Foundation), 5
OHS (Open Hardware Summit), 7–8
OHSpec (Open Hardware Specification Project), 4
OKEYs, 6
Open Design Circuits website, 4
Open Graphics Project, 5
Open Hardware Certification Program, 4
open hardware forked from open source hardware, 9
Open Hardware Repository, 8–9
"open hardware" trademarked, 4–5
openhardware.org, home to OSHW, 9
openhardware.org trademarked, 4–5
OSHW Definition 1.0 released, 8
OSHW (open source hardware), 9
OSHWA (Open Source Hardware Association) created, 9–10

oshwa.org created, 9

SPI (Software in the Public Interest), 4–5

TAPR OHL (Open Hardware license), 6

TAPR (Tucson Amateur Packet Radio Corporation), 6

Traversal Technology, 5

unique product IDs, 6

Homebrew Computer Club, 3

Home-made rockets, products from OSHW, 144

Hosting design files, processes and practices, 22

Housed boards, 84

Houseplants

communication with people, 135

monitoring, 135, 138

Huang, Andrew 7

Hydroponics, 134–135

Igoe, Tom, 7, 235

Importing a 3D model, with Blender, 102

Indiegogo, 140

Industrial machines, from OSHW, 134–135

Industry and agriculture, products from OSHW. See Products from OSHW, industry and agriculture.

Infringement on trademarks, 35–36

Inkscape editor, 89

Innovate with China, 169–170

Instructables, 134

Instructions and explanations, project element, 21

Intellectual monopoly, 256

Intellectual property, 33–36, 256. See also specific types.

The International Journal for Service Learning in Engineering, 268

Inventory planning, 184–185

ITAR (International Traffic in Arms Regulation), 50–51

Iteration in the design process, 61

Iteration management, checklist, 289–290

Iterative design, 58–59

Kefalonia Program in Sustainable Community Development, 268

Kelly, Kevin, 247

Keyboard shortcuts, Blender program, 102

Kharkhana, 148

KHP (Kingston Hot Press), 270–272

KiCad program, 70

Kickstarter campaigns, 172–174

Kickstarter categories, 17

Kitting, 174

Knitting machine, from OSHW, 147–148

Kuniavsky, Mike, 213

Kuniholm, Jonathan, 7–8

Kurt, Tod, 213

Labeling hardware, checklist, 283

Labitat, 148

Lamberts, Reinoud, 4

Laser cutting, 139

Lasersaur (laser cutter)

BOM (bill of materials), 225–226

community building, 230

description, 139

Laundry labels for OSHW, 281

Layout, boards. See Arduino board derivatives, layout; Replay construction kit.

Layout phase, hardware design workflow, 60

Layout review, hardware design workflow, 60

Legal fees, in an open business model, 239–240

Lewis, Pete, 188

Libraries, 46

Licenses

CC (Creative Commons), 32–33

copyleft (viral), 23

definition, 31

distribution terms, 16

free-software, 22–23

GPL, 32–33

industry standards for, 224

Licenses (*continued*)
noncommercial, and open source, 23
open, 23, 32–33
permissive, 23

Licensing
Blinky Buildings project, 302
copyright, 36–37
designs, processes and practices, 22–23
OSHW products, 32–33
overview, 31–32
patents, 37–38
printing 3D designs, 99
share-alike provision, 33
trademarks, 38–39, 67–68

LifePatch, 148

LilyPad, 66–68, 112–116, 118

Linux Fund, in the history of open hardware, 5

LittleBits, 7, 145, 147

Logo. *See* OSHW logo.

The Long Tail, 7

Lulzbot
OHAI-kit documentation tool, 227, 228
TAZ 3D printer, 140–141

Lunch break rule, 227, 229

Mach 30
guidelines, 27–29
project, 142
rules for documentation, 297–299

Machine-readable code, 44

MadeInChina.com, 205

Makers, 245

Makey Makey kit, 172–173, 188

Managing iteration, checklist, 289–290

Mann, Steve, 112

Manufacturability standards, SparkFun, 292–294

Manufacturer part numbers, hardware design workflow, 60

Manufacturers
CMs (contract manufacturers), 168–170
selecting, 168–170, 205–206

Manufacturing. *See also* Business model; Personal manufacturing.
AOI (automated optical inspection), 176
Arduino board derivatives, 91–93
automation systems, 190, 191–194
board thickness, 175
choosing a partner, 168–170
cream layer, reducing, 175
debugging. *See* Troubleshooting.
designing for, 174–177
DFM (design for manufacturing) standards, 175–177
electric skillet reflow technique, 170–171
EOL (end of life) concerns, 175
examples. *See* SparkFun Electronics.
factors to consider, 175
FARKUS assembly robot, 190, 191–194
five critical points, 172
floor tiles from waste products, 270, 272–273
future of, 189–190
innovate with China, 169–170
inventory planning, 184–185
kitting, 174
MOQ (minimum order quantity), 175
mouse bites, 176
MRP (manufacturing resource planning), 185
open source hardware products. *See* Personal manufacturing; Products from OSHW; Projects.
panelization, 176
PLCs (programmable logic controllers), 193
preparation checklist, 290
quality control, 185, 187–189
redrawing trace layouts, 175
resource planning, 184–185
scheduling, 184–185
scientific hardware, 258–263

shaping the PCB, 175

SMD components, 170–171

solder, reducing, 175

startup money. *See* Funding.

supply chain/purchasing, 182–184

swapping parts, 175

takt time, 185

testing, 185, 187–189

turnkey solutions, 169

Manufacturing, equipment

AOI (automated optical inspection) machine, 179

CPH (components placed per hour), 181

PCA (printed circuit assembly) batch washer, 179

pick-and-place machine, 178–179

selecting and implementing, 177–182

at SparkFun, 178–182

Manufacturing, testing and quality control

final yield (example), 187

ganged programmers, 188–189

testbeds, 187–188

tutorial for, 188

Manufacturing handoff, 206–209

Manufacturing package, 62

Manufacturing phase, 57

Manufacturing resource planning (MRP), 185

Mapping, products from OSHW, 144–145

Marketing costs with an open business model, 242–243

Martino, Gianluca, 7

Maskin, Eric, 256, 257

McNamara, Patrick, 5

Mechanical engineering products. *See* Products from OSHW, mechanical engineering and manufacturing.

Mechanical hardware, 47–48

Mellis, David A., 7–8, 14, 16–17

Microcontrollers

choosing, 86

development boards, case study, 157–160

sewable, 118–119

Miller, Timothy, 5

Milling and cutting, personal manufacturing, 155–156

MIT Media Lab, case study, 160–163

Modeling software. *See* 3D modeling software.

Modular Robotics, 190

Modularity as a design principle, 49

Money. *See* Funding.

MOQ (minimum order quantity), 175

Mota, Catarina, 3, 8, 9

Mouse bites, 176

Moving a 3D model, with Blender, 102–103

MRP (manufacturing resource planning), 185

Mulcahy, Diane, 249

Murphey, Stephen, 143–144

Nadeau, Bruno, 215

Nanoracks, 143–144

Nguyen, Thinh, 7

Noncommercial licenses

and open source, 23

printing 3D designs, 99

processes and practices, 23

Non-discrimination, distribution terms, 16

Nonfunctional design elements, copyright, 37

Nortd Labs, 139

NYC Resistor, in the history of open hardware, 9

Obfuscating design files, 24

OHAI-kit, documentation tool, 227, 228

OHANDA (Open Hardware Design Alliance)

in the history of open hardware, 6–8

OHF (Open Hardware Foundation), in the history of open hardware, 5

OHS (Open Hardware Summit), in the history of open hardware, 7–8

OHSpec (Open Hardware Specification Project), in the history of open hardware, 4

OKEYs, definition, 6

OLPC (One Laptop Per Child), 270, 273–274

Onboard bylines, 80–81

Online resources. See Sharing information, online.

Open business. See also Open Source Hardware and Open Design Business Model Matrix.

    advantages of, 237–245

    deciding on, 235, 237

Open Design Circuits website, 4

Open Graphics Project, in the history of open hardware, 5

Open hardware, forked from open source hardware, 9

Open Hardware Certification Program, in the history of open hardware, 4

Open Hardware Design Alliance (OHANDA). See OHANDA (Open Hardware Design Alliance).

Open Hardware Foundation (OHF), in the history of open hardware, 5

Open Hardware license (CERN OHL), in the history of open hardware, 8–9

Open Hardware license (TAPR OHL), in the history of open hardware, 6

Open Hardware Repository, in the history of open hardware, 8–9

Open Hardware Specification Project (OHSpec), in the history of open hardware, 4

Open Hardware Summit (OHS), in the history of open hardware, 7–8

"Open hardware" trademarked, 4–5

Open licenses, 32–33

Open Solar Outdoors Test Field (OSOTF), 264–266

Open source, claiming products as, 17

Open source appropriate technology (OSAT), 269

Open source community mark. See OSHW logo.

Open Source Ecology, 17, 134

Open source hardware. See OSHW (open source hardware).

Open Source Hardware and Open Design Business Model Matrix

    advantages of an open business, 237–245

    better employees, 243

    better products, 238–239

    channels, 248

    closed parts, 243–245

    collaboration and synergies, 240–241

    consortium model, 246

    crowd funding, 249

    deciding on an open business, 235, 237

    donations, 250

    dual licensing, 243–245

    education and training, selling, 248

    ethical bonuses, 241–242

    foundation model, 246

    grants, 250

    hardware on request, 247

    illustration, 236

    legal fees, 239–240

    producing and selling products, 245–246

    product as platform, 239

    product partnerships, 248

    in public art, 250–251

    public research, 250

    quicker time to market, 239–240

    R&D costs, 237–238

    service, selling, 246–247

    sources of money, 245–250

    sponsoring, 250

    support, selling, 247

    support and marketing costs, 242–243

    venture capital funding, 249

Open Source Hardware Association (OSHWA). See OSHWA (Open Source Hardware Association).

Open Source Hardware Definition, on documentation, 223

Open source hardware (OSHW). See OSHW (open source hardware).

Open Space Initiative, 143–144

openhardware.org

home to OSHW, 9

trademarked, 4–5

OpenKnit, 147–148

OpenPCR, 149

OpenRelief platform, 144

OpenSCAD program, 70

Open-source licenses, 23

Original design files, project element, 18–19

OSAT (open source appropriate technology), 269

OSHW Definition 1.0, 14-16 *See also* **Best Practices; OSHW Prime Directive.**

distribution terms, 15–16

purpose of, 13

released, 8

OSHW in academia. *See also* **Teaching and service with OSHW.**

academic freedom, 254

citations, 264

funding opportunities, 264

life of a professor, 254–255

open source hardware combined with closed source software, 267–268

overview, 254–255

public relations, 264

student recruitment, 264

tenure, 254

tenure-track positions, 254

visibility, 263–264

OSHW in academia, research benefits

3D printable hardware, 258

Arduino electronic prototyping platform, 257

Arduino orbital shaker, 258

background material, pre-peer review, 257

experimental design, 257–263

hacker ethic, 256

intellectual monopoly, 256

intellectual property, 256

key benefits, 256

low-cost heat exchanger, 263

manufacturing scientific hardware, 258–263

OSOTF (Open Solar Outdoors Test Field), 264–266

pre-peer review, 257

RepRap platform, 257–258

research, 255–263

solar-powered water purifier, 263

testing photovoltaic equipment, 264–266

wikis, 257

OSHW logo

Golden Orb design, 8

trademarking, 9

use of, 14, 282

OSHW (open source hardware)

benefits for designers and customers, 130

best practices, 16

changing incentives, 279–280

combined with closed source software, 267–268

creating products from. *See* Products from OSHW.

definition, 14

developing. *See* Projects.

forked from open hardware, 9

future of, 281–282

guidelines. *See* Checklists for OSHW.

hardware *vs.* software, 14

in the history of open hardware, 9

laundry labels for, 281

maturity of the movement, 280–281

in public art, 250–251

repository for, 281

statement of principles, 14, 26

OSHW (open source hardware), distribution terms

attributions, 15–16, 68, 79

derived works, 15, 79

documentation, 15

free redistribution, 15

licenses, 16

OSHW (open source hardware), distribution terms
(*continued*)

necessary software, 15

non-discrimination, 16

restrictions, 16

scope, 15

technology neutrality, 16

OSHW Prime Directive on documentation. *See also*
**Best Practices; Documentation; OSHW Definition
1.0.**

definition, 26

forums *vs.* email, 28

guidelines, 26–27

Mach 30 guidelines, 27–29

social media, 28–29

statement of principles, 26

synchronous *vs.* asynchronous discussions,
29

testing, 29

OSHWA (Open Source Hardware Association)

creation of, 9–10

in the history of open hardware, 9–10

incorporation, 10

purposes of, 10

website, 3

oshwa.org, created, 9

Oskay, Windell, 7–9, 14

OSOTF (Open Solar Outdoors Test Field), 264–266

OSVehicle, 138

Overview/introduction, project element, 18

Owen, Ivan, 141

Panelization, 176

Part PCB footprints, hardware design workflow, 60

Partnerships

with China, 169–170

in manufacturing, 168–170,
205–206

in an open business model, 248

Parts for hardware design, selecting, 60

Parts library, hardware design workflow, 60

Patents. *See also* **Copyright; Trademark.**

vs. copyright, 13, 35

definition, 34

design, 34

duration of protection, 35

future of, 281

licensing, 37–38

obtaining, 34–35, 37

for open source hardware, 37–38

overview, 34–35

utility, 34

PCA (printed circuit assembly) batch washer, 179

PCBs (printed circuit boards)

fiducial marks, 200–201

personal manufacturing, 156–157

in shape of Empire State Building. *See*
Blinky Buildings project.

shaping, 175

PCBs (printed circuit boards), layout

hardware design workflow, 60

software for, 70

Pearce, Joshua, 133

Peppler, Kylie, 115

Perens, Bruce, 4, 9, 14

Permissive licenses, 23

Personal manufacturing. *See also* **Business model;
Manufacturing.**

future of, 165–166

general principles, 163–164

startup money. *See* Funding.

Personal manufacturing, case studies

Arduino electronics platform, 157–160

collaboration, 158–159

consumer electronics, 160–163

derivatives, 157–160

microcontroller development boards,
157–160

MIT Media Lab, 160–163

Personal manufacturing, processes
  3D printing, 155
  access to fabrication, 157
  CNC (computer-numeric control) machines, 155–156
  digital fabrication machines, 155–156
  electronics, 156–157
  fabrication services, 157
  milling and cutting, 155–156
  PCBs (printed circuit boards), etching, 156–157
  precision and tolerances, 155–156

Phones as wearables, 112

Photos, project element, 20

Photovoltaic equipment, testing, 264–266

Physical communication, 48

Pick-and-place machine, 178–179

PLCs (programmable logic controllers), 193

Plugins, 45–46

Polis, Jared, 9

Pollution-sensing gown, 115

Principles of open source, 14, 26

Printed circuit assembly (PCA) batch washer, 179

Printed circuit boards (PCBs). See PCBs (printed circuit boards).

Printers, 3D. See 3D printers.

Prints, 60

Processing language, 227

Processors, 46

Product as platform, 239

Product definition phase, 56

Product webpages, 221–223

Products, producing and selling in an open business model, 245–246

Products from OSHW
  automotive industry, 138
  bicycles, 138
  biomedical research machine, 149
  biotechnology, 148–150
  criteria for being labeled open source, 130–131
  disaster relief, 144–145
  DMF (digital microfluidic) system, 150
  DNA analysis, 149
  Dropbot, 150
  education modular toolkits, 145, 147
  environmental preservation, 144–145
  fashion, 147
  HacKIDemia, 145
  hardware layers, 132–133
  knitting machine, 147–148
  LittleBits, 145, 147
  mapping, 144–145
  OpenKnit, 147–148
  OpenPCR, 149
  OpenRelief platform, 144
  prototyping electronic projects, 145, 147
  Public Lab, 144–145
  radiation monitoring, 145
  required documentation, 132–133
  Safecast, 145, 146
  Tabby (vehicle), 138
  vehicles, 138
  Velocar (bicycle), 138

Products from OSHW, air and space exploration
  Copenhagen Suborbitals, 144
  CubeSats, 143
  DIYdrones, 142–143
  drones, 142–143
  Ground Sphere CubeSat Ground Station, 142
  home-made rockets, 144
  Mach 30 project, 142
  Nanoracks, 143–144
  Open Space Initiative, 143–144
  satellite design, 143
  Shepard Test Stand, 142
  shuttle service to the International Space Station, 143–144

Products from OSHW, industry and agriculture

agricultural machines, 134

Botanicalls, 135, 138

communication between houseplants and people, 135, 138

Global Village Construction Set, 135

household plant monitoring, 135, 138

hydroponics, 134–135

industrial machines, 134–135

Open Source Ecology, 134

tractor hydraulics, 134–137

urban farming, 134–135

Windowfarms, 134–135

Products from OSHW, mechanical engineering and manufacturing

3D printing, 140–142

CNC (computer-numeric control) router, 139–140

Fabtotum 3D printer, 140–141

Filabot 3D printer, 140–141

filament extruder, 140–141

laser cutting, 139

Lasersaur (laser cutter), 139

Lulzbot TAZ 3D printer, 140–141

Robohand project, 141–142

robotic hand, 141–142

Professors, life in academia, 254–255

Profitability, determining, 58–59

Programmable logic controllers (PLCs), 193

Programming environments, 46

Programming headers, spacing for, 89–91

Programming tools, 47

Project phases, 56–58

Projects, elements of

auxiliary design files, 19

BOM (bill of materials), 20

firmware, 20

instructions and explanations, 21

original design files, 18–19

overview/introduction, 18

photos, 20

software, 20

Projects, processes and practices

building derivatives, 25

designing hardware, 21–22

distributing open source hardware, 23

hosting design files, 22

licensing designs, 22–23

noncommercial licenses, 23

obfuscating design files, 24

respecting trademarks, 25

Projects, recommended files

auxiliary design files, 19

BOM (bill of materials), 20, 225-226

firmware, 20

instructions and explanations, 21, 220-221, 226-229

original design files, 18–19, 223-225

overview/introduction, 18, 220

photos, 20

software, 20

Protecting your works

creative or artistic. *See* Copyright.

goods in the market. *See* Trademarks.

useful articles. *See* Patents.

Prototyping

with 3D printers. *See* RepRap printer.

vs. designing, 57

potential problems, 59

Prototyping electronic projects, products from OSHW, 145, 147

Public art, reproducing, 250–251

Public domain, and ITAR (International Traffic in Arms Regulation), 50–51

Public Lab, 144–145

Public relations, in academia, 263–264

Public research in an open business model, 250

Purchasing, 182–184

Purpose of a new product, determining, 56

Quality control. *See* Testing and quality control.

Radiation monitoring, products from OSHW, 145

Raymond, Eric, 263

R&D costs, in an open business model, 237–238

README.txt
  Blinky Buildings project, 301
  overview, 220–221
  SparkFun Electronics, 220

Reas, Casey, 66

Redistribution, distribution terms, 15

Redrawing trace layouts, 175

Registering trademarks, 39

Reimplementing the wheel, 49

Release phase, 57

Remixing a design. *See* Derivatives.

Renardias, Vincent, 5

Replay construction kit
  definition, 84
  determining board outline, 88
  illustration, 86
  offloading components, 86
  sample board layout, 93
  size reduction, 87
  web address, 109

Replicating Rapid Prototyper. *See* RepRap printer.

RepRap platform, research benefits in academia, 257–258

RepRap printer, 95–97, 109

Requirements documents, 212

Requirements for product design, 56

Research applications for OSHW. *See* OSHW in academia, research benefits.

Resource planning, 184–185

Restrictions, distribution terms, 16

Rethink Robotics, 190

RFQ (request for quotation) sample, 207

Roberts, Dustyn, 8

Robohand project, 141–142

Robotics
  3D Robotics, 142
  Baxter robots, 190, 191–194
  controlling, 193–194
  FARKUS assembly robot, 190, 191–194
  Modular Robotics, 190
  PLCs (programmable logic controllers), 193
  Rethink Robotics, 190
  Robohand project, 141–142
  robotic hand, 141–142
  watercoloring art bot, 173–174

Rosenbaum, Eric, 172

Safecast, 145, 146

Satellite design, products from OSHW, 143

Scale printouts, 91

Scaling a 3D model, with Blender, 102–103

Schappi, Marcus, 249

Scheduling, manufacturing, 184–185

Schematic capture, hardware design workflow, 60

Schematics
  samples, 72, 74
  symbols, hardware design workflow, 60

Schweikardt, Eric, 191

Scientific hardware, manufacturing, 258–263

Scissors, tools for making wearables (illustration), 122

Scope, distribution terms, 15

Scope of product design, 56

Screw caps, clearance for, 91

Seaman, Graham, 4

Security do's and don'ts, 285–286

Seeed Studio, 169–170

Seidle, Nathan
    best practices, 16–17
    founding of OSHWA, 9
    on good *vs.* perfect, 217
    manufacturing circuit boards, 170
    on the open source hardware logo, 8
    at the Opening Hardware workshop, 7
Seltzer, Wendy, 9
Semmelhack, Peter, 7
Serrano, Javier, 8–9
Service learning, 268–269. *See also* Teaching and service with OSHW.
Services, selling in an open business model, 246–247
Sewable microcontrollers and components, 118–119
Shapeoko, 139–140
Shapes, Arduino board derivatives, 83–84
Shapesmith program, 106, 109
Share-alike licenses
    force of, 33
    printing 3D designs, 99
Sharing information, online
    3D design files, 133–134
    3D modeling software, 109. *See also specific packages.*
    3D printers, 97–98, 109
    centralized hub, 129–130
    GitHub, 134
    Instructables, 134
    social media, 28–29
    Thingiverse, 133–134
Shepard, Mark, 115
Shepard Test Stand, 142
Shipping untested hardware, 62
Shuttle service to the International Space Station, 143–144
Silver, Jay, 172
Simmons, J., 25–29, 297-299
"Six Myths about Venture Capitalists," 249
Sketchup Make program, 106, 109

SketchUp program, 70
SMD components, manufacturing, 170–171
Smith, Zach, 7
Social media, documenting open source projects, 28–29
Software
    binary code, 44
    customizing. *See* Software, firming up.
    machine-readable code, 44
    project files, 20
    standardizing. *See* Standardization, software.
Software, firming up. *See also* Firmware.
    bootloaders, 47
    compilers, 46
    configurations, 45–46
    forks, 45–46
    libraries, 46
    plugins, 45–46
    processors, 46
    programming environments, 46
    programming tools, 47
    software interfaces, 45
Software interfaces
    firming up software, 45
    standardizing software, 45
Solar-powered water purifier, 263
Solder, reducing, 175
Source files. *See* Design files.
Sourcing materials, 199–200
Space exploration. *See* Products from OSHW, air and space exploration.
Space-limiting components, identifying, 86
Spacing for programming headers, 89–91
SparkFun Electronics
    9DOF board, 213–214
    ancillary manufacturability standards, 293–294
    core manufacturability standards, 292–293
    growth in manufacturing, 170–172

identifying open source hardware, 24

manufacturing equipment, 178–182

manufacturing process, 172–173

product webpage, 221–223

production floor (illustration), 180

quality price matrix, 182

README.txt, 220

resource planning and scheduling, 184–185, 186

selling education and training, 248

supply chain failure, 183

supply chain/purchasing, 182–184

SparkFun Electronics, testing and quality control

final yield, 187

ganged programmers, 188–189

history of, 185, 187

testbeds, 187–188

tutorial for, 188

Specifications for new products, 56

Speedometer board (example), 85

SPI, in the history of open hardware, 4–5

Sponsoring an open business model, 250

Stafford, Brandon, 250–251

Stand-alone boards, 84

Standard electronic components, 47–48

Standardization, hardware

hardware interfaces, 49

mechanical hardware, 47–48

modularity as a design principle, 49

physical communication, 48

reimplementing the wheel, 49

standard electronic components, 47–48

Standardization, software

bootloaders, 47

compilers, 46

configurations, 45–46

forks, 45–46

libraries, 46

plugins, 45–46

processors, 46

programming environments, 46

programming tools, 47

software interfaces, 45

Standards. See Best Practices; OSHW Definition 1.0; OSHW Prime Directive.

Startup money. See Funding.

Statement of principles, 14, 26

Steele, Geoff, 71, 302, 304

STEP (ISO 10303) file standard, 204

Stern, Becky, 7, 227

.STL files, 99

Student recruitment, in academia, 264

Suck-muck, 213–214

Suppliers, cost-benefit analysis, 76–77

Supply chain, 182–184

Support

costs with an open business model, 242–243

selling, 247

Synchronous vs. asynchronous discussions, 29

Synergies, in an open business model, 240–241

Tabby (vehicle), 138

Takt time, 185

TAPR OHL (Open Hardware license), in the history of open hardware, 6

TAPR (Tucson Amateur Packet Radio Corporation), in the history of open hardware, 6

Teaching and service with OSHW

Appropedia Foundation, 269, 274

floor tiles from waste products, 270, 272

Kefalonia Program in Sustainable Community Development, 268

KHP (Kingston Hot Press), 270–272

OLPC (One Laptop Per Child), 270, 273–274

OSAT (open source appropriate technology), 269

service learning, 268–269

Teaching and service with OSHW (*continued*)
  virtual service learning, 269–274
  Waste for Life, 270
Technology neutrality, distribution terms, 16
techp.org, 5
Tenure, in academia, 254
Tenure-track positions, in academia, 254
Testbeds, 187–188
Testing and quality control
  board layout fit, 91
  documentation, 29
  final yield (example), 187
  ganged programmers, 188–189
  in the manufacturing process, 185,
    187–189
  photovoltaic equipment, 264–266
  on products from suppliers, 212–213
  shipping untested hardware, 62
  at SparkFun Electronics, 185, 187–189
  testbeds, 187–188
  tutorial for, 188
Testing phase, definition, 57
Thingiverse, 133–134
Thomas Register, 205
thomasnet.com, 205
Thompson, Clive, 235, 247
3D modeling software, web sources, 109. *See also specific packages.*
3D printable hardware, research benefits in academia, 258
3D printer bureaus, 97
3D printers
  costs, 96–97
  derivatives, 96–97
  as manufacturing tools, 107–108
  open source, sources of, 97–98, 109
  RepRap printer, 95–97, 109
  research and production, 107–108
3D printers, finding designs to print
  attribution, 99

  Beaglebone Black case, 99–100
  with Blender, 100–105
  derivative designs, 100–105
  existing designs, 98–100
  licensing considerations, 99
  noncommercial licenses, 99
  remixing a design, 100–105
  share-alike licenses, 99
  .STL files, 99
  web sources, 98, 109
3D printing
  personal manufacturing, 155
  products from OSHW, 140–142
  software for, 70
3D Robotics, 142, 245
Time to market in an open business model, 239–240
Tinkercad program, 106, 109
Todd, Sylvia, 173
Torrone, Phillip, 7, 9
Trace layouts, redrawing, 175
Tractor hydraulics, from OSHW, 134–137
Trademarks. *See also* **Copyright; Patent.**
  Arduino, 67–68
  in a business model, 235
  definition, 35
  infringement, 35–36
  licensing, 38–39, 67–68
  obtaining, 36
  overview, 35–36
  registering, 39
  respecting in derivatives, 25, 67–68
Training and education, selling, 248
Traversal Technology, in the history of open hardware, 5
Troubleshooting
  BOM (bill of materials), 201–203
  centroid file information, 200
  checklist, 294–295
  cost of fixing mistakes, 216

creative fixes, 213–214

designing hackable hardware, 215–216

DFMA (design for manufacture and assembly), 208–209

examples of problems, 209–212

fiducial marks on PCBs, 200–201

file types for effective communication, 200–204

making makable parts, 204–205

manufacturing handoff, 206–209

requirements documents, 212

RFQ (request for quotation) sample, 207

role of DFM (design for manufacturing), 198–199

selecting a manufacturer, 205–206

sourcing materials, 199–200

STEP (ISO 10303) file standard, 204

suck-muck, 213–214

Tucson Amateur Packet Radio Corporation (TAPR), in the history of open hardware, 6

Tutorials. *See* Documentation, tutorials.

Uittenbogerd, Davy, 71–73, 302

under(a)aware, 115–116

Unique product IDs. *See* OKEYs.

Urban farming, from OSHW, 134–135

USBs, in hardware designs, 48

Utility patents, 34

Validation phase. *See* Testing.

van As, Richard, 141

Vehicles, manufactured from OSHW, 138

Velocar (bicycle), 138

Vendor part numbers, hardware design workflow, 60

Venture capital funding for an open business, 249

Verification phase. *See* Testing.

Violations of copyright, 34

Viral (copyleft) licenses, 23

Virtual service learning, 269–274

Visuals in documentation, 226–227

Washing wearable electronics, 124–126

Waste for Life, 270

Water purifier, solar-powered, 263

Watercoloring art bot, 173–174

Waterfall method, 58

Wearables

batteries and power, 123–124

bike projects, 112

bracelet, 115–116

circuit diagram (illustration), 122

conductive textiles, 117

corona wires, 119–120

documentation, 120–123

dry cleaning, 125

EL (electroluminescent) wire, 119–120

electroluminescent glow, 119–120

extending current length, 120

FLORA line, 118–119

future of, 126–127

history of, 111–112

LilyPad line, 112–116, 118

managing expectations, 125–126

modifying existing items, 123

phones, 112

pollution-sensing gown, 115

scissors (illustration), 122

sewable microcontrollers and components, 118–119

under(a)aware, 115–116

washing electronics, 124–126

zigzag stitching, 120–121

Web resources. *See* Sharing information, online.

Weinberg, Michael, 68

Wikis, 257

Wilbanks, John, 7

Williams, Amanda, 215

Williamson, Aaron, 9

Windowfarms, 134–135

Wireless Sensor Mote, 199–200

Wiring language, 46

Workflow. *See* Designing hardware, project phases; Designing hardware, workflow.

www.makexyz.com, 97–98

Zigzag stitching, 120–121

Other Books
YOU MIGHT LIKE!

ISBN: 9780789752055

ISBN: 9780672337123

ISBN: 9780133887921

SAVE 35%

Use discount code **MAKER**

Visit **informIT.com**
to learn more!

ALWAYS LEARNING

PEARSON

Blinky Building Kit Available for Purchase!

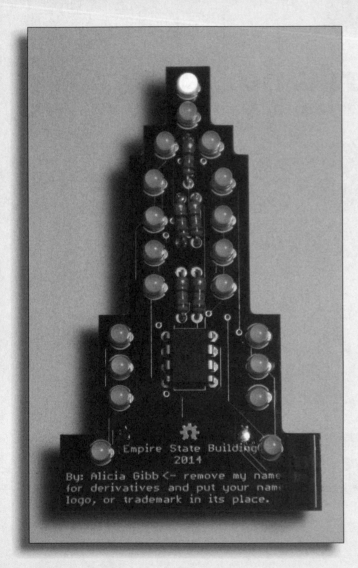

The Blinky Buildings kit can be purchased to accompany this book. Walk through Chapter 6 and see how open source hardware works by making your own derivative of this kit.

Make your board another building in your city or a landmark that is near and dear to your heart.

Make the building roll away on wheels or create a glow in the dark version by 3D printing an enclosure.

Use it as a nightlight, flashy model train landscapes, or just impress your friends!

This kit can be purchased at bit.ly/blinkybuildings or at SparkFun.com